FROM THE MOST TRUSTED NAME IN TRAVEL

# Frommer's
# EASYGUIDE
## TO
# WASHINGTON, D.C.
## 2017

**Quick to Read   Easy to Carry   For Expert Advice
In All Price Ranges**

By Elise Hartman Ford

## FROMMER'S STAR RATINGS SYSTEM

Every hotel, restaurant, and attraction listed in this guide has been ranked for quality and value. Here's what the stars mean:

★ Recommended
★★ Highly Recommended
★★★ A must! Don't miss!

## AN IMPORTANT NOTE

The world is a dynamic place. Hotels change ownership, restaurants hike their prices, museums alter their opening hours, and buses and trains change their routings. And all of this can occur in the several months after our authors have visited, inspected, and written about these hotels, restaurants, museums, and transportation services. Though we have made valiant efforts to keep all our information fresh and up-to-date, some few changes can inevitably occur in the periods before a revised edition of this guidebook is published. So please bear with us if a tiny number of the details in this book have changed. Please also note that we have no responsibility or liability for any inaccuracy or errors or omissions, or for inconvenience, loss, damage, or expenses suffered by anyone as a result of assertions in this guide.

Jefferson Memorial.

# CONTENTS

Washington Monument.

# A LOOK AT WASHINGTON, D.C.

For many visitors, a trip to Washington, D.C., isn't just a vacation. It's a pilgrimage of sorts. Schoolchildren are bused in by the thousands and swarm the Mall in organized platoons, determined teachers feeding them facts about its importance. Veterans pay homage at memorials to fallen comrades. And ordinary citizens arrive in droves to be part of the most powerful city in the world, at least for a short time. Where else, after all, are decisions made that affect not only the lives of every American citizen, but also the lives of people across the planet? The city was designed, from its very inception, to be a worthy place for pilgrimage, with its monuments, broad avenues, and traffic circles (symbolic of the rays of the sun). But over the years, Washington has become even more multi-faceted than the original planners could have envisioned. It's a highly cosmopolitan, multiracial, and wonderfully diverse city, thanks to its embassies (and their resident staff), large immigrant populations, and proud African-American community. What follows is just a sampling of the impressive sights you'll see and adventures you'll have in this engrossing capital.

Many visitors make the Smithsonian Castle (p. 155) on the National Mall their first stop, so they can pick up info about special events and exhibitions at other Smithsonian museums.

## THE MALL

The National Mall stretches from the Lincoln Memorial (p. 137) in the west to the U.S. Capitol (p. 115) in the east, the Washington Monument (p. 157) near its center.

Artist Daniel Chester French's statue of Abraham Lincoln towers 19 feet inside the Lincoln Memorial.

President Thomas Jefferson's Memorial (p. 136) is set in a rotunda like the one he designed for the University of Virginia.

v

FDR's beloved dog Fala is included in the Franklin Delano Roosevelt Memorial (p. 132).

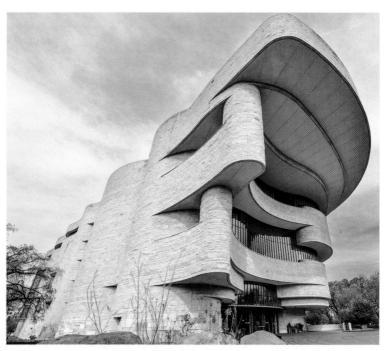

The curvilinear National Museum of the American Indian (p. 150) was created by a team of celebrated Native-American architects and is meant to invoke forms found in nature.

A National Parks ranger leads a guided tour of the Vietnam Veterans Memorial (p. 156).

The Albert Einstein statue outside the National Academy of Sciences (p. 184).

Contemporary art, like this untitled sculpture by Ron Mueck, is the focus of the Hirshhorn Museum and Sculpture Garden (p. 135).

The Apollo 11 command module at the National Air and Space Museum (p. 139).

The famed Hope Diamond on display at the National Museum of Natural History (p. 151).

The Star Spangled Banner exhibit at the National Museum of American History (p. 149).

The trendy Adams Morgan neighborhood is home to many festivals.

Lively nightlife in Adams Morgan (p. 46).

Statue of Irish patriot Robert Emmet near the Irish Embassy.

A "panda-cam" watches the National Zoo's (p. 186) most beloved residents 24/7.

The Islamic Center on Embassy Row on Massachusetts Avenue.

The Dupont Circle fountain is one of 18 Civil War memorials in the city.

Homes along the C&O Canal in Georgetown.

Embassies often open to the public for special events. This is the dining room of the Embassy of Indonesia.

Chef Luigi Diotaiuti hosts cooking classes at his Dupont Circle restaurant, Al Tiramisu (p. 105).

An evening stroll along Georgetown's waterfront.

Beautiful tree-lined streets in Georgetown's Historic District (p. 263).

Healy Hall on the main campus of Georgetown University.

# OTHER D.C.

Washington, D.C., has the largest Ethiopian community outside of Ethiopia itself, making it a top place to try this often-fiery cuisine.

In 1912, Japan donated 3,020 ornamental cherry trees to Washington, D.C. Their blooms inspire the iconic yearly Cherry Blossom Festival (p. 24).

Many visitors are surprised by how small the White House (p. 165) looks in person.

White House staff work in the handsome Eisenhower Executive Office Building (p. 260).

At the Newseum (p. 177), you can see the broadcast antennae that once topped the World Trade Center.

The infamous Watergate complex.

The African American Civil War Memorial (p. 185).

# NORTHERN VIRGINIA

Alexandria's waterfront draws crowds with its al fresco restaurants, street performers, and Potomac River views.

Outdoor dining in Old Town Alexandria (p. 240).

Over 1 million people visit George Washington's home, Mount Vernon, yearly (p. 235).

American flags along King Street in Old Town Alexandria.

The Tomb of the Unknown Soldier at Arlington National Cemetery (p. 192).

A fully functioning distillery and gristmill (pictured here) are among the working exhibits at Mount Vernon.

# THE BEST OF WASHINGTON, D.C.

The sun has come up, dappling the surface of the Potomac. It warms the front plaza of the Supreme Court building, where visitors stand in line awaiting their chance to attend an oral argument. Sunlight splays across the National Mall and pours through the south-facing windows of the Oval Office, where the president works away at the problems of the day. Commuters of all sorts, from diplomats to nonprofit wonks to corporate execs to shopkeepers, spill from cars and buses and Metro stations onto sunlit downtown streets armed with briefcases, coffee cups, smartphones, and newspapers. They rub elbows from sunup to sundown, in the halls of Congress, in Penn Quarter restaurants, in Georgetown shops, in bars along 14th Street. The city bustles. Bustle with it. It's a beautiful day.

Each day dawns anew in this "city of magnificent intentions," as Charles Dickens once called it. Maybe this will be the day that Republican and Democratic lawmakers hammer out a deal on combating climate change or that the new president welcomes world leaders to the White House for a Middle East summit. Or maybe today's the day that you fulfill your own intentions, sublime or otherwise, of setting eyes on the original Declaration of Independence perhaps, or tasting something called a "half-smoke," or listening to a jazz concert in the same place where Duke Ellington once performed. Things happen here that can happen nowhere else on earth. You're in America's capital, and this city and this day belong to you. Best get crackin'!

# THE most unforgettable WASHINGTON, D.C., EXPERIENCES

o **Watching the Supreme Court in Action:** Behind the stately marble facade of the Supreme Court building, the nation's nine (or eight, if the late Antonin Scalia's replacement has not yet been confirmed) black-gowned justices reveal their intellectual brilliance and individual personalities as they listen to and question both sides of an argument. Will the famously silent Justice Thomas talk today? Will Justice Kennedy, considered the "swing vote" on the Court, reveal which way he's likely to swing? Who will volley the wittiest remark into the discourse? Only one way to find out: Wait in line for entry and a coveted seat inside the courtroom. See p. 127.

o **Viewing Washington Landmarks by Moonlight:** There is nothing as spectacular as the Lincoln Memorial illuminated at night, unless it's the sight of the White House, the Capitol, or the Washington Monument lit up after dark. Go by Old Town Trolley, by bike via a Bike and Roll excursion, or by boat aboard a Potomac Riverboat Company cruise; all three operations offer narrated day and nighttime tours. See p. 298.

o **Visiting Your Senator or House Representative:** If you're a U.S. citizen, take advantage of your constituent status and stop by your senator's and/or

The Lincoln Memorial and the Reflecting Pool.

Anti-war protesters heading toward the U.S. Capitol.

representative's office on Capitol Hill to offer your two cents on current issues. Pick up passes to the Capitol's Senate and House chambers and attend a session to observe your elected politicians at work. Make sure you've reserved Capitol tour passes online and tour the Capitol. See p. 115.

o **Bicycling Past the Potomac River and Around the Tidal Basin:** Rent a bike and cycle the paved bike/pedestrian path that extends 11 miles from the Lincoln Memorial, alongside the Potomac River, and through Rock Creek Park to the Maryland border. Or head the other direction, following the combination of street, sidewalk, and pathway that encircles the Tidal Basin and leads to the 3.5-mile roadway looping East Potomac Park. On view as you go are Washington's landmarks. For a really epic ride, follow the pathway past the Lincoln Memorial, cross the Arlington Memorial Bridge to the trail on the other side, and pedal the 19 miles to Mount Vernon. See p. 200.

o **Participating in a Protest:** What causes do you believe in? I mean this sincerely. Find out if there's a gathering on the National Mall, a protest at an embassy, or some other public event that reflects your point of view, and join in! This is the capital of the United States, the world's most successful democracy, imperfect though it may be. Countless such protests take place here annually. It can be thrilling and inspiring, or really just plain fun, to meet up with other citizens of the world and make your presence known.

# THE best FAMILY EXPERIENCES

○ **Hanging Out at the National Zoo:** Make faces at the cute giant pandas; listen to the mighty lion's roar; laugh at the playful monkeys; watch an elephant exercise; ride the solar-powered carousel. The National Zoo is essentially one big (163 acres!), family-friendly park, offering the chance to observe some 1,800 animals at play (or snoozing or eating). See p. 186.

○ **Ice Skating at the National Gallery:** The pool in the National Gallery of Art Sculpture Garden turns into an ice-skating rink in winter. Rent some skates and twirl around on the ice, admiring sculptures as you go. Treat yourself to hot chocolate and sandwiches at the Pavilion Café in the garden. See p. 204.

○ **Paddling Your Way Around the Tidal Basin:** Rent a paddle boat for four people and skim the surface of the Tidal Basin for an hour. You'll still be sightseeing as you pedal away, in full view of the Washington Monument on the Mall, the Jefferson and Martin Luther King, Jr. memorials bordering the Basin, and, should you be here during cherry blossom season, the blooming cherry trees encircling the Tidal Basin. See p. 203.

○ **Riding a Roller Coaster or Piloting a Jet:** Two Smithsonian museums offer amusement-park-like rides in their simulator machines. At the National Air and Space Museum, children can choose to simulate a ride inside either a jet aircraft, a vintage airplane, or a space shuttle zooming to the International Space Station; or simulate the experience of piloting a combat plane. At the National Museum of American History, your simulated adventures feel real in futuristic, high-speed racecar and roller coaster machines. *Note:* Height requirements and fees apply. See p. 139 and 149.

# THE best FOOD

○ **Best for a Splurge:** I've got two suggestions for you, as different as night and day. Dupont Circle's **Komi** (p. 105) is a sparely appointed town-house dining room with just 12 tables. The genius chef, Johnny Monis, sends out 12 or so little gastronomic masterpieces that often hint of the sea, such as the round of carrot topped with sea urchin; the cost is $150 per person. Georgetown's waterfront **Fiola Mare** (p. 109) is as splashy as Komi is serene and offers a stunning view of the Potomac. Like its sister Fiola in the Penn Quarter, its fare is sophisticated Italian, the decor and clientele head-turning.

○ **Best for Romance:** Is there anything more romantic than a good little French restaurant? The capital has a number of them, including upper Georgetown's **Bistrot Lepic,** where on Monday and Wednesday evenings, you can dine on *truite de meuniere* (pan-seared rainbow trout) in the wine bar and listen to live jazz. But if a trendy, sexy scene and exotic tastes appeal, consider the Penn Quarter's softly lit **Rasika** (p. 98), with hot Indian food to spice up the night.

Ben's Chili Bowl.

- **Best for Families:** Beyond the usual burger (**Five Guys,** p. 100) and pizza (**Pizzeria Paradiso,** p. 106) places, why not introduce your kids to international cuisine at the **Lebanese Taverna** (p. 114) or **Jaleo** (Spanish tapas; p. 96)?

- **Best for Regional Cuisine: Hank's Oyster Bar** (p. 106) is the place to go for superb Eastern Shore delicacies such as crab cakes and soft-shell crabs. (Hank's also serves up seafood specialties from New England and New Orleans.) While Washington doesn't have its own cuisine per se, its central location within the Mid-Atlantic/Chesapeake Bay region gives it license to lay claim to these local favorite foods. And locals say nobody does 'em better than Hank's.

- **Best All-Around for Fun and Food:** Unstoppable José Andrés is behind the always-crowded **Oyamel** (p. 98), where everyone's slurping foam-topped margaritas and savoring small plates of authentic Mexican food. A few blocks away, **Central Michel Richard** (p. 93) makes everybody happy with its convivial atmosphere and chef Richard's take on French bistro and American classics, from mussels in white wine to fried chicken.

- **Best for a "Taste of Washington" Experience:** Eat lunch at the **Monocle** (p. 89) and you're bound to see a Supreme Court justice, congressman, or senator dining here, too. For some down-home fare, sit at the counter at **Ben's Chili Bowl** (p. 103) and chat with the owners and your neighbor over a chili dog or a plate of blueberry pancakes. The place is an institution, and you can stop by anytime—it's open for breakfast, lunch, and dinner.

1

The Best Things to Do for Free in Washington, D.C. | THE BEST OF WASHINGTON, D.C.

- **Best for Vegetarians: Amsterdam Falafelshop** (p. 104) draws lovers of its mashed chickpea falafels and 21 possible toppings, plus the twice-cooked Dutch-style fried potatoes. **Zaytinya** (p. 98) offers a most diverse selection of sweet and savory veggie tapas, including a Brussels sprouts dish that vegetarians and carnivores alike go crazy for. *FYI:* Zaytinya is also recommended for all-around food and fun; bring a crowd to share the mezze.

# THE best THINGS TO DO FOR FREE IN WASHINGTON, D.C.

- **Peruse the Constitution:** Only in Washington and only at the National Archives will you be able to read the original documents that grounded this nation in liberty. Here you'll find the Declaration of Independence, the Constitution of the United States, and the Bill of Rights—all on display behind glass. See p. 141.
- **People-Watch at Dupont Circle:** This traffic circle is also a park—an all-weather hangout for mondo-bizarre biker-couriers, chess players, street musicians, and lovers. Sit on a bench and watch scenes of Washington life unfold around you—or join in the fun: The Circle is also the setting for outdoor yoga classes, World Cup screenings, and an annual snowball fight. See p. 180.
- **Attend a Millennium Stage Performance at the Kennedy Center:** Every evening at 6pm in its Grand Foyer, the Kennedy Center presents a free 1-hour concert performed by local, up-and-coming, national, or international musicians. And though the Kennedy Center doesn't advertise it, you might be interested to know that the Grand Foyer's bars near Millennium Stage host food and drink happy hours between 5 and 6pm nightly. So before the performance, purchase a cocktail and head through the glass doors to the terrace, where you can enjoy your drink and a view of the Potomac River. See p. 220.
- **Groove to the Sounds of Live Jazz in the Sculpture Garden:** On summery Friday evenings at the National Gallery of Art Sculpture Garden you can dip your toes in the fountain pool and chill out to live jazz from 5 to 8pm. The jazz is free; the tapas, wine, and beer served in the Pavilion Café are not. See p. 143.
- **Pick a Museum, (Just About) Any Museum:** Because this is the U.S. capital, many of the museums are federal institutions, meaning admission is free. The National Gallery of Art, the U.S. Botanic Garden, and the Smithsonian's 18 Washington museums, from the National Air and Space Museum to the just-opened National Museum of African American History and Culture, are among many excellent choices. See chapter 6.
- **Attend an Event on the Mall:** Think of the National Mall as the nation's public square, where something is always going on—as many as 3,500 events annually, according to the National Park Service. There's the Kite

Festival during cherry blossom season in the spring; the splendid Independence Day celebration every Fourth of July; special events reserved by individuals and random organizations who have obtained a permit, from weddings to speeches to yearly jamborees of, for instance, the National Astronomy Festival; and walking tours, biking, Frisbee throwing, and assorted impromptu sports happening year-round. See p. 23 for a calendar of annual events.

# THE best NEIGHBORHOODS FOR GETTING LOST

o **Georgetown:** The truth is, you *want* to get lost in Georgetown, because it's the neighborhood's side streets that hold the history and centuries-old houses of this one-time Colonial tobacco port. Don't worry—Georgetown is so compact that you're never far from its main thoroughfares, M Street and Wisconsin Avenue. For a back-streets tour of Georgetown, see p. 263.

o **Old Town Alexandria:** Just a short distance from the District (by Metro, car, boat, or bike) is George Washington's Virginia hometown. On and off the beaten track are quaint cobblestone streets, charming boutiques and antiques stores, 18th-century houses and other historic attractions, and fine restaurants. See p. 240.

o **Dupont Circle:** Explore Dupont Circle's lovely side streets extending off Connecticut and Massachusetts avenues. You'll discover picturesque 19th-century town houses serving as homes to small art galleries, historic museums, and actual residences. Stroll Embassy Row (northward on Massachusetts Ave.) to view Beaux Arts mansions, many built by wealthy magnates during the Gilded Age. See p. 180.

o **Foggy Bottom:** Take the White House walking tour (p. 255) if you like, then continue west to mingle with George Washington University's students on its urban campus, staff of the State Department, and international employees of the World Bank and the International Monetary Fund, all of which are headquartered here. Old Foggy Bottom holds 19th-century town houses; historic sites, like the building at 2017 I St. NW, where James Monroe briefly lived; and old churches, like St. Mary's Episcopal, at 728 23rd St. NW, designed by James Renwick (see the Renwick Gallery, p. 164).

# THE best WAYS TO SEE WASHINGTON, D.C., LIKE A LOCAL

o **Shop at Eastern Market:** Capitol Hill is home to more than government buildings; it's a community of old town houses, antiques shops, and the venerable Eastern Market. Here, locals shop and barter every Saturday and Sunday for fresh produce, baked goods, and flea-market bargains as they've done for well over a century. A must: the blueberry pancakes at the Market Lunch counter. See p. 121.

o **Pub and Club It in D.C.'s Hot Spots:** Join Washington's footloose and fancy-free any night of the week (but especially Thurs–Sat) along 14th Street, in Adams Morgan, and in the Penn Quarter.

o **Go for a Jog on the National Mall:** Lace up your running shoes and race down the Mall at your own pace, admiring famous sites as you go. Your fellow runners will be buff military staff from the Pentagon, speed-walking members of Congress, and downtown workers doing their best to stave off the telltale pencil pusher's paunch. It's about 2 miles from the foot of the Capitol to the Lincoln Memorial. See p. 145.

o **Attend a Hometown Game:** Take yourself out to a Washington Nationals baseball game at Nationals Park, drive to FedEx Field to root for Washington's NFL team along with its rabid fans, catch a Washington Wizards or Mystics basketball game at the downtown Verizon Center, or hop the Metro to RFK Stadium for a D.C. United soccer match. To experience the true soul of the city, attend a Washington Capitals ice hockey match at the Verizon Center. Wear red. See p. 233.

o **Sit at an Outdoor Cafe and Watch the Washington World Go By:** Locals watching locals. What better way to keep tabs on each other? The capital is full of seats offering front-row views of D.C. on parade. Here's a bunch: **Fiola Mare** (not a cafe, but its terrace tables can't be beat for watching Georgetown's waterfront scene; p. 109), **Le Bon Café** (p. 93), **Montmartre** (p. 90), **Paul** (p. 108), **Central** (p. 93), **Zaytinya** (p. 98), **Le Diplomate** (p. 101), and **Martin's Tavern** (p. 111).

Attending a home game at Nationals Park.

# THE best PLACES TO STAY

o **Best Historic Hotel:** The **Willard InterContinental** celebrated its 110th anniversary in 2016 as the "new" 12-story Willard, replacing the original, smaller "City Hotel" that existed here between 1816 and 1906. Whether known as the City or the Willard, the hotel has hosted nearly every U.S. president since Franklin Pierce in 1853. President Ulysses S. Grant liked to unwind with a cigar and brandy in the Willard lobby after a hard day in the Oval Office; literary luminaries such as Mark Twain and Charles Dickens used to hang out in the Round Robin bar. See p. 63.

o **Best for Romance:** Its discreet service, intimate size, and exquisitely decorated guest rooms, and the fact that you need never leave the hotel for pampering or dining, makes **The Jefferson** (p. 71) perfect for a romantic rendezvous. A pianist plays romantic classic melodies Tuesday through Saturday in the cozy-comfortable bar, **Quill,** with a menu that features drinks with names like "Swept Away." The hotel's small spa offers massages. There's fine dining in restaurant Plume and cozy spots for reading in the Book Room, where a fire crackles on the hearth.

o **Best When You Have Business on Capitol Hill: The George,** a Kimpton Hotel (p. 57), lies a short walk from the Capitol and offers free Wi-Fi and an excellent in-house power-dining spot, **Bistro Bis,** among other business-friendly amenities.

o **Best Bang for Your Buck:** Its great Georgetown location, spacious studio and one-bedroom suites with kitchens, free Wi-Fi, and reasonable rates recommend **Georgetown Suites** (p. 80) as one of the best values in town.

o **Best Views:** The **Hay-Adams** (p. 65) has such a great, unobstructed view of the White House that the Secret Service comes over regularly to do security sweeps of the place. Ask for a room on the H Street side of the hotel, on floors six through eight.

o **Best for Families:** The **Omni Shoreham Hotel** (p. 81) is adjacent to Rock Creek Park, within walking distance of the National Zoo and Metro, and has a large outdoor pool and kiddie pool. Nearby kid-friendly eateries include fast-food choices like McDonald's and local favorites like **Lebanese Taverna** (p. 114). Children receive a backpack upon check-in, and the concierge can provide board games and books (at no charge; just remember to return them). Parents appreciate receiving the first aid/safety kit with outlet covers, nightlights, and a list of emergency numbers.

# THE best OFFBEAT EXPERIENCES

o **Bring a Drum to Meridian Hill Park and Join the Drum Circle:** Sunday afternoons, when the weather is right, Meridian Hill Park (see p. 198), about 1 mile directly north of the White House on 16th Street NW, is the setting for an all-comers-welcome African drum circle. The tradition is 50 years old and dates from the tumultuous days of the 1960s, when activists sought a way to celebrate black liberation but also mourn the death of African-American leader Malcolm X. One drummer started, others gradually joined in, and over time the sonorous Sunday drum circle turned into a steady gig that continues to this day. Participants and spectators are a diverse crowd, reflecting the population of the city. The park is stunning, designed to resemble an Italian garden, complete with statuary, a cascading fountain, and landscaped grounds.

o **Dare to Dine at a Drag Brunch:** Sassy drag queens dressed to the hilt sashay around the room, lip-synching to the DJ's tunes and entertaining all who've turned up for the all-you-can-eat $25.95 buffet at **Perry's Drag Brunch,** 1811 Columbia Rd. NW (www.perrysadamsmorgan.com; ✆ **202/ 234-6218**), held every Sunday from 10am to 3pm. The brunch is a Washington institution: Everyone comes to this Adams Morgan hot spot at some point, so expect to see partiers burning the candle at both ends and straight-laced types likely heading to the office after the show.

o **Explore Washington from an Unconventional Angle:** Yes, it's a graveyard, but Georgetown's Oak Hill Cemetery is also a beautiful wooded and landscaped garden with a grand view of the city from its hillside perch. Here lie monuments and resting places for some of Washington's most illustrious residents, from the city's early days as well as recent years. See p. 269.

o **Play Street Hockey in Front of the White House:** Pennsylvania Avenue in front of the White House is closed to traffic, which makes it a perfect place for street hockey fanatics to show up Saturdays and Sundays at 10am and sometimes Wednesdays at 6:30pm for pickup games. All you need are Rollerblades and a stick, although gloves and shin pads are also recommended. Check out the website, www.whitehousehockey.com, for more info.

# WASHINGTON, D.C., IN CONTEXT

E verybody knows at least a little something about Washington, D.C. It's the nation's capital, after all; what goes on here on a daily basis is top-of-the-news stuff. Images of the Capitol, the Washington Monument, the Potomac River, the National Mall, the White House, and Pennsylvania Avenue immediately spring to mind at the mere mention of this city's name.

There are so many other images I'd like to introduce to you: cherry blossoms, Black Broadway, the Phillips Collection, Nationals Park, Eleanor Holmes Norton, Embassy Row, Eastern Market, and Rock Creek Park, to name just a few; a fraction of the rich history and diverse cultural experiences this city has to offer.

That's what this book is about. This chapter, specifically, aims to provide you with a context for understanding Washington, D.C.'s story and personality beyond the headlines, as well as practical information that will be useful to you while planning your trip and upon your arrival.

## WASHINGTON, D.C., TODAY

Washington, D.C., is both the capital of the United States and a city unto itself; therein lie its charms, but also a host of complications. Control of the city is the main issue. The District is a free-standing jurisdiction, but because it is a city with a federal rather than a state overseer, it has never been entitled to the same governmental powers as the states. Congress supervises the District's budget and legislation. Originally, Congress granted the city the authority to elect its own governance, but it rescinded that right when the District overspent its budget in its attempts to improve its services and appearance after the Civil War. The White House then appointed three commissioners, who ran D.C.'s affairs for nearly 100 years.

In 1972 the city regained the right to elect its own mayor and city council, but Congress still retains control of the budget and the courts, and can veto municipal legislation. District residents can vote in presidential primaries and elections and can elect a delegate to Congress who introduces legislation and votes in committees, but this delegate cannot vote on the House floor. This unique situation, in which residents of the District pay federal income taxes but don't have a vote in Congress, is a matter of great local concern. D.C. residents publicly protest the situation by displaying license plates bearing the inscription TAXATION WITHOUT REPRESENTATION.

Another wrinkle in this uncommon relationship is the fact that Washington's economy relies heavily upon the presence of the federal government, which accounts for about 26% of all D.C. jobs (according to a 2016 trend report issued by D.C.'s Office of the Chief Financial Officer), making it the city's single largest employer, and upon the tourism business that Washington, as the capital, attracts. The city struggles toward political independence, although it recognizes the economic benefits of its position as the seat of the nation's capital.

Will any of this affect you as you tour the city this year? Yes.

You will find Washington, D.C., to be a remarkably vibrant city. The economic hard times that afflicted other parts of the country in recent years have been muted here.

Income remains higher than the national average, 35% of the population is between the ages of 18 and 34, residents are better educated than elsewhere, and the people are remarkably diverse: 49% African American, 12% Hispanic, 14% foreign-born, and 16.5% speaking a language other than English at home. The presence of embassies and the diplomatic community intensifies the international flavor.

In other words, Washington, D.C., is thriving. Restaurants and bars dominate most neighborhoods. In fact, eating out is a way of life here, whether simply for the pleasure of it or for business—the city's movers and shakers meet over breakfast, lunch, and dinner. Washington's restaurant scene offers an immense variety of international cuisines, from Ethiopian to Peruvian, as well as soul food and regional specialties like Chesapeake Bay crabs served in soft-shell, hard-shell, soup, or cake form.

Theaters, music venues, hotels, brand-name stores, and homegrown boutiques abound. Because of the abundance of jobs thanks to tourism and the presence of the federal government, many Washingtonians can afford to go to the theater, attend cultural events, shop, and dine out. But whatever it is, play, concert, or restaurant meal, it had better be good. As well-traveled, well-educated, and, let's face it, pretty demanding types, capital dwellers have high standards and big appetites. They expect the best, and they get it.

But it wasn't always this way. About 20 years ago, Washington wasn't so attractive. Tourists came to visit federal buildings like the Capitol, the White House, and the city's memorials but stayed away from the dingy downtown and other off-the-Mall neighborhoods. The city had the potential for being so much more, and certain people—heroes, in my book—helped inspire action and brought about change themselves: Delegate Eleanor Holmes Norton, who fought steadfastly for states' rights and economic revival for the District; former Mayor Anthony Williams, who rescued the District's budget when his predecessor, the notoriously mismanaging Mayor Marion Barry, brought the city to the brink of financial ruin; and the community-minded developers Abe and Irene Pollin, who used their own funds to finance the $200-million MCI sports center, now called the Verizon Center, in the heart of town (today the wildly successful arena anchors the utterly transformed Penn Quarter neighborhood, now one of the liveliest city centers in the country).

The city's resident population has grown for the 10th straight year and now stands at approximately 672,000, a size not seen in 40 years. (At its peak, during and immediately following World War II, more than 800,000 people called D.C. home.) The growth spurt is especially significant given that the District's population reached a relative low point in 1998, when the U.S. Census counted 565,000 D.C. residents. Revitalization continues to take root throughout the city—from the Capital Riverfront neighborhood in southeast D.C., where a grand baseball stadium, Nationals Park, opened in March 2008, attracting hotel, restaurant, and housing development; to the Columbia Heights enclave in upper northwest D.C., now a mélange of Latino culture, loft condominiums, and ethnic eateries; to the Southwest Waterfront, where urban planners and developers are capitalizing on the community's Potomac River frontage and creating a welcoming neighborhood of parks, residential apartments, walkways, new lodging, and eateries. The city's evergreens—the memorials and monuments, the historic neighborhoods, and the Smithsonian museums—remain unflaggingly popular.

But D.C. has its share of problems, starting with its Metrorail transportation system, which is in the midst of a much-needed overhaul. (See "Getting Around," in chapter 11, for details.) Other problems relate to the city's gentrification efforts, such as the displacement of residents from homes they can no longer afford in revitalized but increasingly expensive neighborhoods. Mayor Muriel Bowser, elected in November 2014, has her work cut out for her in a municipality that struggles to provide health care, good schools, safe neighborhoods, adequate housing, and basic social services to all citizens.

Diverse in demographics, residents are alike in loving their city, despite the issues it faces. Visitors seem to share this love, as statistics bear out: D.C. welcomes 20.2 million visitors a year, 1.9 million of whom are international tourists.

# THE MAKING OF WASHINGTON, D.C.

As with many cities, Washington, D.C.'s past is written in its landscape. Behold the lustrous Potomac River, whose discovery by Captain John Smith in 1608 led to European settlement of this area. Take note of the city's layout: the 160-foot-wide avenues radiating from squares and circles, the sweeping vistas, the abundant parkland, all very much as Pierre Charles L'Enfant intended when he envisioned the "Federal District" in 1791. Look around and you will see the Washington Monument, the U.S. Capitol, the Lincoln Memorial, the White House, and other landmarks, their very prominence in the flat, central cityscape attesting to their significance in the formation of the nation's capital.

2

WASHINGTON, D.C., IN CONTEXT | The Making of Washington, D.C.

But Washington's history is very much a tale of two cities. Beyond the National Mall, the memorials, and the federal government buildings lies "D.C.," the municipality. Righteous politicians and others speak critically of "Washington"—shorthand, we understand, for all that is wrong with government. They should be more precise. With that snide dismissal, critics dismiss, as well, the particular locale in which the capital resides. It is a place of vibrant neighborhoods and vivid personalities, a vaunted arts-and-culture scene, international diversity, rich African-American heritage (see "An African-American History Tour of Washington, D.C.," in chapter 3), uniquely Washingtonian attractions and people—the very citizens who built the capital in the first place and have kept it running ever since.

## Early Days

The settlers who arrived in 1608 weren't the region's first inhabitants, of course. Captain John Smith may have been the first European to discover this waterfront property of lush greenery and woodlands, but the Nacotchtank and Piscataway tribes were way ahead of him. As Smith and company settled the area, they disrupted the American Indians' way of life and introduced European diseases. The Native Americans gradually were driven away.

By 1751, Irish and Scottish immigrants had founded "George Town," named for the king of England and soon established as an important tobacco-shipping port. African Americans lived and worked here, as well. Several houses from its early days still exist in modern-day Georgetown: The Old Stone House (on M St. NW), a woodworker's home built around the 1760s, is now operated by the National Park Service and open to the public, and a few magnificent ship merchants' mansions still stand on N and Prospect streets, though these are privately owned and not open to the public. (Their properties once directly overlooked the Potomac River, but no longer: The Potomac River has receded quite a bit, as you'll see.) For a walking tour of Georgetown, see p. 263.

## Birth of the Capital

After colonists in George Town and elsewhere in America rebelled against British rule, defeating the British in the American Revolution (1775–83), Congress, in quick succession, unanimously elected General George Washington as the first president of the United States, ratified a U.S. Constitution, and proposed that a city be designed and built to house the seat of government for the new nation and to function fully in commercial and cultural capacities. Much squabbling ensued. The North wanted the capital; the South wanted the capital. President Washington huddled with his Secretary of State, Thomas Jefferson, and devised a solution that Congress approved in 1790: The nation's capital would be "a site not exceeding 10 miles square" located on the Potomac. The South was happy, for this area was nominally in their region; Northern states were appeased by the stipulation that the South pay off the North's Revolutionary War debt, and by the city's location on the North–South border. Washington, District of Columbia, made her debut.

2

WASHINGTON, D.C., IN CONTEXT — The Making of Washington, D.C.

The Old Stone House, a woodworker's house built in the 1760s in Georgetown.

The only problem was that she was not exactly presentable. The brave new country's capital proved to be a tract of undeveloped wilderness, where pigs, goats, and cows roamed free, and habitable houses were few and far between. Thankfully, the city was granted the masterful 1791 plan of the gifted but temperamental French-born engineer, Pierre Charles L'Enfant. Slaves, free blacks, and immigrants from Ireland, Scotland, and other countries worked to fulfill L'Enfant's remarkable vision, erecting first the White House (the city's oldest federal structure), then the Capitol and other buildings. (Read *The Great Decision: Jefferson, Adams, Marshall and the Battle for the Supreme Court,* by Cliff Sloan and David McKean [PublicAffairs Books], for excellent descriptions of the early days of the capital, its institutions, and the strong personalities that helped forge them.) Gradually, the nation's capital began to take shape, though too slowly perhaps for some. The writer Anthony Trollope, visiting in 1860, declared Washington "as melancholy and miserable a town as the mind of man can conceive."

## The Civil War & Reconstruction

During the Civil War, the capital became an armed camp and headquarters for the Union Army, overflowing with thousands of followers. Parks became campgrounds; churches, schools, and federal buildings, including the Capitol and the Patent Office (now the National Portrait Gallery), became hospitals; and forts ringed the town. The population grew from 60,000 to 200,000, as soldiers, former slaves, merchants, and laborers converged on the scene. The streets were filled with the wounded, nursed by the likes of Walt Whitman,

WASHINGTON, D.C., IN CONTEXT | The Making of Washington, D.C.

2

one of many making the rounds to aid ailing soldiers. In spite of everything, President Lincoln insisted that work on the Capitol continue. "If people see the Capitol going on, it is a sign we intend the Union shall go on," he said.

Lincoln himself kept on, sustained perhaps by his visits to St. John's Church, across Lafayette Square from the White House. Lincoln attended evening services when he could, arriving alone after other churchgoers had entered and slipping out before the service was over. And then on the night of April 14, 1865, just as the days of war were dwindling down and Lincoln's vision for unity was being realized, the president was fatally shot at Ford's Theatre (p. 170) while attending a play.

In the wake of the Civil War and President Lincoln's assassination, Congress took stock of the capital and saw a town worn out by years of war—awash with people but still lacking the most fundamental facilities. Indeed, the city was a mess. There was talk of moving the capital city elsewhere, perhaps to St. Louis or some other more centrally located city. A rescue of sorts arrived in the person of public works leader Alexander "Boss" Shepherd, who initiated a "comprehensive plan of improvement" that at last incorporated the infrastructure so necessary to a functioning metropolis, including a streetcar system that allowed the District's overflowing population to move beyond city limits. Shepherd also established parks, constructed streets and bridges, and installed water and sewer systems and gas lighting, gradually nudging the nation's capital closer to showplace design. Notable accomplishments included the completion of the Washington Monument in 1884 (after 36 years) and the opening of the first Smithsonian museum in 1881.

A photo from 1861, showing the U.S. Capitol under construction. Lincoln was inaugurated that year.

# Washington Blossoms

With the streets paved and illuminated, the water running, streetcars and rail transportation operating, and other practical matters well in place, Washington, D.C., was ready to address its appearance. In 1900, as if on cue, a senator from Michigan, James McMillan, persuaded his colleagues to appoint an advisory committee to develop designs for a more beautiful and graceful city. This retired railroad mogul was determined to use his architectural and engineering knowledge to complete the job that L'Enfant had started a century earlier. With his own money, McMillan sent a committee that included landscapist Frederick Law Olmsted (designer of New York's Central Park), sculptor Augustus Saint-Gaudens, and noted architects Daniel Burnham and Charles McKim to Europe for 7 weeks to study the landscaping and architecture of that continent's great capitals.

"Make no little plans," Burnham counseled fellow members. "They have no magic to stir men's blood, and probably themselves will not be realized. Make big plans, aim high in hope and work, remembering that a noble and logical diagram once recorded will never die, but long after we are gone will be a living thing, asserting itself with ever growing insistency."

The committee implemented a beautification program that continued well into the 20th century. Other projects added further enhancements: A presidential Commission of Fine Arts, established in 1910, positioned monuments and fountains throughout the city; FDR's Works Progress Administration erected public buildings embellished by artists. The legacy of these programs is on view today, in the cherry trees along the Tidal Basin, the Lincoln Memorial at the west end of the Mall, the Arlington Memorial Bridge, the Library of Congress, Union Station, East Potomac Park, Lafayette Square, and many other sights, each situated in its perfect spot in the city.

The American capital was coming into its own on the world stage, as well, emerging from the Great Depression, two world wars, and technological advancements in air and automobile travel as a strong, respected global power. More and more countries established embassies here, and the city's international population increased exponentially.

## Black Broadway Sets the Stage

As the capital city blossomed, so did African-American culture. The many blacks who had arrived in the city as slaves to help build the Capitol, the White House, and other fundamental structures of America's capital stayed on, later joined by those who came to fight during the Civil War, or to begin new lives after the war. (See p. 185 for a description of the African American Civil War Memorial and Museum, which commemorates the lives of the 209,145 black Civil War soldiers.)

From 1900 to 1960, Washington, D.C., became known as a hub of black culture, education, and identity, centered on a stretch of U Street NW, called "Black Broadway," where Cab Calloway, Duke Ellington, and Pearl Bailey often performed in speakeasies and theaters. Many of these stars performed at the Howard Theatre (p. 229), which was the first full-size theater devoted to black audiences and entertainers when it opened in 1910. Nearby Howard University, created in 1867, distinguished itself as the nation's most comprehensive center for higher education for blacks. (The reincarnated "U&14th Street Corridors," or "New U," is now a diverse neighborhood of blacks, whites, Asians, and Latinos, and a major restaurant and nightlife destination.)

## The Civil Rights Era Ushers In a New Age

By the late 1950s, African Americans made up more than half of Washington's total population of 805,000, and their numbers continued to grow, reaching a peak of 70% in 1970, before beginning a steady decline that would last throughout the rest of the 20th century. One hundred years or so after the passage of the 13th Amendment to the Constitution (abolishing slavery) and the 15th Amendment to the Constitution (outlawing the denial of voting rights based on race or color), African Americans generally remained unequal members of society. Despite the best efforts and contributions of individuals—from abolitionist Frederick Douglass (p. 190), a major force in the human rights movement in the 19th century, to educator and civil rights leader Mary McLeod Bethune (p. 185), who served as an advisor to President Franklin Delano Roosevelt in the 1930s—the country, and this city, had a long way to go in terms of equal rights. (Consider reading works by Edward P. Jones, the Pulitzer Prize–winning author whose short-story collections, *Lost in the City* and *All Aunt Hagar's Children,* will take you beyond D.C.'s political and tourist attractions into the neighborhoods and everyday lives of African Americans during the mid–20th century.)

The tipping point may have come in 1954, when Thurgood Marshall (appointed the country's first black Supreme Court justice in 1967) argued and won the Supreme Court case *Brown v. Board of Education of Topeka,* which denied the legality of segregation in America. This decision, amid a groundswell of frustration and anger over racial discrimination, helped spark the civil rights movement of the 1960s. On August 28, 1963, black and white Washingtonians were among the 250,000 who marched on Washington for jobs and freedom and listened to an impassioned Rev. Dr. Martin Luther King, Jr. deliver his stirring "I Have a Dream" speech on the steps of the Lincoln Memorial, where 41 years earlier, during the memorial's dedication ceremony, black officials were required to sit separately from the white attendees.

Martin Luther King, Jr., speaking at the March on Washington for Jobs and Freedom.

WASHINGTON, D.C., IN CONTEXT — The Making of Washington, D.C.

2

President Kennedy lying in state in the Capitol Rotunda.

2

WASHINGTON, D.C., IN CONTEXT | The Making of Washington, D.C.

The assassination of President John F. Kennedy on November 22, 1963, added to a general sense of despair and tumult. On the day before his funeral, hundreds of thousands of mourners stood in line for blocks outside the Capitol all day and night to pay their respects to the president, who lay in state inside the Rotunda of the Capitol.

Then Martin Luther King, Jr. was assassinated on April 4, 1968, and all hell broke loose. The corner of 14th and U streets served as the flashpoint for the riots that followed. Ben's Chili Bowl (p. 103) was ground zero and remained open throughout the riots to provide food and shelter to activists, firefighters, and public servants.

As the 20th century progressed, civil rights demonstrations led to Vietnam War protests, which led to revelations about scandals, from President Nixon's Watergate political debacle (Ever seen *All the President's Men?* You have to), to the late D.C. Mayor Marion Barry's drug and corruption problems, to President Bill Clinton's sexual shenanigans. It was an era of speaking out to expose corruption and scandal. A president who authorizes illegal activity? Not acceptable. A mayor with a drug problem? Not acceptable. A president who dallies with a White House intern his daughter's age, then lies about it? Nope, not acceptable.

And still the city flourished. A world-class subway system opened, the Verizon Center sports and concert arena debuted and transformed its aged downtown neighborhood into the immensely popular Penn Quarter, and the city's Kennedy Center, Shakespeare theaters, and other arts-and-culture venues came to worldwide attention, receiving much acclaim.

WASHINGTON, D.C., IN CONTEXT | The Making of Washington, D.C.

2

# LITTLE-KNOWN facts

o **Many people—including Washington, District of Columbia, residents themselves—wonder how the city wound up with such an unwieldy name.** Here's how: President Washington referred to the newly created capital as "the Federal City." City commissioners then chose the names "Washington" to honor the president and "Territory of Columbia" to designate the federal nature of the area. Columbia is the feminine form of Columbus, synonymous in those days with "America" and all she stood for—namely, liberty. The capital was incorporated in 1871, when it officially became known as Washington, District of Columbia.

o **The distance between the base of the Capitol, at one end of the National Mall, and the Lincoln Memorial, at the other, is nearly 2 miles.** The circumference of the White House property, from Pennsylvania Avenue to Constitution Avenue and 15th Street to 17th Street, is about 1½ miles.

o **More than 27% of Washington, D.C., is national parkland, which makes the capital one of the "greenest" cities in the country.** The biggest chunk is the 2,000-acre Rock Creek Park, the National Park Service's oldest natural urban park, founded in 1890.

o **Every country that maintains diplomatic relations with the United States has an embassy in the nation's capital.** Currently, the number of embassies approximates 190, mostly located along Massachusetts Avenue, known as Embassy Row, and other streets in the Dupont Circle neighborhood.

## Twenty-First-Century Times

Having begun the 20th century as a backwater town, Washington finished the century a sophisticated city, profoundly shaken but not paralyzed by the September 11, 2001, terrorist attacks. The first decade of the 21st century was marked by the Afghanistan and Iraq wars and by a precipitous economic decline. Here in Washington, these situations fomented rancorous relations in Congress and between Capitol Hill and the White House, as Democrats and Republicans disagreed over workable solutions. Barack Obama's landmark win as the first African-American president, in 2008, temporarily restored some hope and an "all things are possible" perspective. But not for long. Political differences and personal agendas soon took over, interfering with efficient and effective governance.

Nine years later, the economy is more than markedly improved—it's quite strong. However, Congress remains fractious to the point of being dysfunctional. Extreme elements in both the Republican and Democratic parties continue to impede progress on domestic issues, from immigration to the environment, and in foreign affairs, from ways to fight terrorism to international trade agreements. The 2016 presidential campaign only served to exacerbate a sense of divisiveness, both in politics and in the country at large.

At this writing, in early fall 2016, the election had yet to occur. Let's just say that the outlook is not entirely certain. Peace and prosperity? Compromise and goodwill? One can hope.

Meanwhile, in the District, women rule: Congresswoman Eleanor Holmes Norton is in her 14th term in office, representing residents of the District of Columbia; Mayor Muriel Bowser is proving herself a strong champion for the city, tackling education, housing, transportation, and crime problems; and Police Chief Cathy Lanier ably runs the Metropolitan Washington D.C. Police Department, as she has since January 2007.

History informs one's outlook, but so does the present. Look again at the Potomac River and think of Captain John Smith, but observe the Georgetown University crew teams rowing in unison across the surface of the water and tour boats traveling between Georgetown and Old Town Alexandria. As you traverse the city, admire L'Enfant's inspired design, but also enjoy the sight of office workers, artists and students, and people of every possible ethnic and national background making their way around town. Tour the impressive landmarks and remember their namesakes, but make time for D.C.'s home-grown attractions, whether a meal at a sidewalk cafe in Dupont Circle, jazz along U Street, a walking tour past Capitol Hill's old town houses, or a visit to a church where slaves or those original immigrants once worshiped.

# WHEN TO GO

The city's peak seasons generally coincide with two activities: the sessions of Congress, and springtime—beginning with the appearance of the cherry blossoms.

Specifically, from about the second week in September until Thanksgiving, and again from about mid-January to June (when Congress is "in"), hotels are full of guests whose business takes them to Capitol Hill or to conferences. The presidential inauguration on January 20, 2017, will bring many more visitors to the city than normally one would see at this time of year. If you're planning to attend, you should book your reservations now.

Mid-March through June is traditionally the most frenzied season, when families and school groups descend upon the city to see the cherry blossoms and enjoy Washington's sensational spring. Hotel rooms are at a premium, and airfares tend to be higher. This is also a popular season for protest marches.

If crowds turn you off, consider visiting Washington at the end of August or in early September, when Congress is still "out" and families have returned home to get their children back to school, or between Thanksgiving and mid-January, when Congress leaves again and many people are busy with their own at-home holiday celebrations. Hotel rates are cheapest at this time, too, and many hotels offer attractive packages.

If you're thinking of visiting in July and August, be forewarned: The weather is very hot and humid. Despite the heat, Independence Day (July 4th) in the capital is a spectacular celebration. Summer is also the season for outdoor concerts, festivals, parades, and other events (see chapter 8 for details about performing arts schedules). If you can deal with the weather, this is a good time to visit: Locals often go elsewhere on vacation, so the streets and attractions are somewhat less crowded. In addition, hotels tend to offer their best rates in July and August.

## Weather

Season by season, here's what you can expect of the weather in Washington:

**FALL:** This is my favorite season. The weather is often warm during the day—in fact, if you're here in early fall, it may seem entirely *too* warm. But it cools off, and even gets a bit crisp, at night. By late October, Washington has traded its famous greenery for the brilliant colors of fall foliage.

**WINTER:** People like to say that Washington winters are mild—and sure, if you're from Minnesota, you'll find Washington warmer, no doubt. But D.C. winters can be unpredictable: bitter cold one day, an ice storm the next, followed by a couple of days of sun and higher temperatures. The winter of 2013–2014 was freezing and very snowy, the winter of 2014–2015 abnormally frigid and icy, and the winter of 2015–2016 included a little bit of everything: big snowstorm, lots of heavy rain, fierce winds, and periods of mild temps. Who knows what to expect in 2016–2017? Best advice: You should pack with all possibilities in mind.

**SPRING:** Early spring weather tends to be colder than most people expect. Cherry blossom season, late March to early April, can be iffy—and very often rainy and windy. As April slips into May, the weather usually mellows, and people's moods with it. Late spring is especially lovely, with mild temperatures and intermittent days of sunshine, flowers, and trees colorfully erupting in gardens and parks all over town. Washingtonians sweep outdoors to stroll the National Mall, relax on park benches, or laze away the afternoon at outdoor cafes.

**SUMMER:** Anyone who has ever spent July and August in D.C. will tell you how hot and steamy it can be. Though the buildings are air-conditioned, many of Washington's attractions, like the memorials and organized tours, are outdoors and unshaded, and the heat can quickly get to you. Make sure you stop frequently for drinks (vendors are plentiful), and wear a hat, sunglasses, and sunscreen.

### Average Temperatures & Rainfall in Washington, D.C.

|  | JAN | FEB | MAR | APR | MAY | JUNE | JULY | AUG | SEPT | OCT | NOV | DEC |
|---|---|---|---|---|---|---|---|---|---|---|---|---|
| TEMP (°F) | 43/29 | 47/31 | 56/38 | 67/47 | 75/56 | 84/66 | 89/71 | 81/70 | 80/63 | 68/51 | 58/41 | 47/33 |
| RAINFALL (IN.) | 2.8 | 2.7 | 3.5 | 3.1 | 4.0 | 3.8 | 3.7 | 2.9 | 3.7 | 3.4 | 3.2 | 3.0 |

## Holidays

Banks, government offices, post offices, and many stores, restaurants, and museums are closed on the following legal national holidays: January 1 (New Year's Day), the third Monday in January (Martin Luther King, Jr. Day), the third Monday in February (Presidents' Day), the last Monday in May (Memorial Day), July 4 (Independence Day), the first Monday in September (Labor Day), the second Monday in October (Columbus Day), November 11

(Veterans Day/Armistice Day), the fourth Thursday in November (Thanksgiving Day), and December 25 (Christmas). In addition, federal and D.C. government offices, as well as schools, close on Inauguration Day, January 20, 2017.

# Washington, D.C., Calendar of Events

The capital's signature special event takes place every 4 years, when the winner of the presidential election is sworn in on Inauguration Day; mark your calendars for January 20, 2017. Otherwise, the city's most popular annual events are the National Cherry Blossom Festival in spring, the Fourth of July celebration in summer, and the lighting of the National Christmas Tree in winter. But some sort of special activity occurs almost daily. For the latest schedules, check **www.washington.org, www.culturaltourismdc.org, www.dc.gov,** and **www.washingtonpost.com.**

The phone numbers in the calendar below were accurate at press time, but these numbers change often. If the number you try doesn't get you the details you need, call **Destination D.C.** at ✆ **202/789-7000.**

When you're in town, grab a copy of the *Washington Post* (or read it online), especially the Friday "Weekend" section.

## JANUARY

**Martin Luther King, Jr.'s Birthday.** Events include speeches by prominent leaders and politicians, readings, dance, theater, concerts and choral performances, and prayer vigils at the National Martin Luther King, Jr. Memorial on the national holiday (third Mon in Jan; King's actual birthday is Jan. 15). Call the National Park Service at ✆ **202/426-6841.**

**Presidential Inauguration Day.** This quadrennial political event formally inducts into office the winner of the presidential election. In 2017, the nation inaugurates its 45th president. Events include the swearing-in ceremony on the west front steps of the Capitol, a motorcade down Pennsylvania Avenue to the White House, and balls and celebrations throughout the city. No matter who wins, thousands and thousands of people descend upon the city to party. Inauguration Day is always celebrated on January 20, unless the date falls upon a Sunday, in which case the inauguration moves to Monday. The parade and swearing-in events are free and open to the public. At least 14 official balls and quite a number of unofficial balls cap off Inauguration Day; most of the official balls require tickets and are by invitation only. Details at www.presidential-inauguration.com.

## FEBRUARY

**Black History Month.** Numerous events, museum exhibits, and cultural programs celebrate the contributions of African Americans to American life, including a celebration of abolitionist Frederick Douglass's birthday. For details check the *Washington Post* or the Smithsonian Institution calendar of events at www.si.edu/Events, or call the National Park Service at ✆ **202/426-6841.**

**Chinese New Year Celebration.** A Friendship Archway, topped by 300 painted dragons and lighted at night, marks the entrance to Chinatown at 7th and H streets NW. The celebration begins the day of the Chinese New Year (on the day of the first new moon of the new year, which might fall anywhere from late Jan to mid-Feb) and continues for 14 or so days, with traditional firecrackers, dragon dancers, and colorful street parades. Some area restaurants offer special menus. Late January to early February.

**Abraham Lincoln's Birthday.** Expect great fanfare at Ford's Theatre and its Center for Education and Leadership, an exploration of Lincoln's legacy in the time since his assassination (p. 170). As always, a wreath-laying and reading of the Gettysburg Address will take place at noon at the Lincoln Memorial. Call Ford's Theatre at ✆ **202/426-6924,** or the National Park Service at ✆ **202/426-6841.** February 12.

**George Washington's Birthday/Presidents' Day.** The city celebrates Washington's birthday in two ways: on the actual day, February 22, with a ceremony that takes place at the Washington Monument; and on the federal

23

holiday, the third Monday in February, when schools and federal offices have the day off. Call the National Park Service at ✆ **202/426-6841** for details. The occasion also brings with it great sales at stores citywide. (See chapter 9, "Day Trips from D.C.," for information about the bigger celebrations held at Mount Vernon and in Old Town Alexandria on the third Mon in Feb.)

**D.C. Fashion Week.** This biannual event features designers from around the world. The weeklong extravaganza stages parties, runway shows, and trunk shows at citywide venues, sometimes including an international couture fashion show at an embassy. Most events are open to the public but may require a ticket. Call ✆ **202/600-9274** or visit www.dcfashionweek.org. Mid-February and mid-September.

## MARCH

**Women's History Month.** Count on the Smithsonian to cover the subject to a fare-thee-well. For a schedule of Smithsonian events, call ✆ **202/633-1000** or visit www.si.edu/Events; for other events, check the websites listed in the intro to this section. Also see "A Women's History Tour of Washington, D.C.," in chapter 3.

**St. Patrick's Day Parade.** Now in its 46th year, this big parade on Constitution Avenue NW, from 7th to 17th streets, is complete with floats, bagpipes, marching bands, and the wearin' o' the green. For parade information, visit www.dcstpatsparade.com. The Sunday before March 17.

## APRIL

**National Cherry Blossom Festival.** Strike up the band! This year, 2017, marks the 105th anniversary of the city of Tokyo's gift of cherry trees to the city of Washington. This event is celebrated annually; if all goes well, the festival coincides with the blossoming of the more than 3,750 Japanese cherry trees by the Tidal Basin, on Hains Point, and on the grounds of the Washington Monument. Events take place all over town and include the Blossom Kite Festival on the grounds of the Washington Monument, fireworks, concerts, special art exhibits, park-ranger-guided talks and tours past the trees, and sports competitions. A Japanese Street Festival takes place

on one of the final days of the celebration, and a grand parade caps the festival, complete with floats, marching bands, dancers, celebrity guests, and more. Most events are free; exceptions include the Japanese Street Fair, which costs $8 per ticket in advance, $10 per ticket day of, and grandstand seating at the parade, which starts at $20 per person (otherwise the parade is free). For information call ✆ **877/44BLOOM** (442-5666) or go to www.nationalcherryblossomfestival.org. March 20 to April 16, 2017.

**White House Easter Egg Roll.** A biggie for kids 13 and under, the annual White House Easter Egg Roll continues a practice begun in 1878. Entertainment on the White House South Lawn and the Ellipse traditionally includes appearances by costumed cartoon characters, clowns, musicians (Idina Menzel and Ariana Grande are among those who have performed in the past), egg-decorating exhibitions, puppet and magic shows, an Easter egg hunt, and an egg-rolling contest. To obtain tickets, you must use the online lottery system, www.recreation.gov, up and running about 7 weeks before Easter Monday. For details call ✆ **202/208-1631** or visit www.whitehouse.gov/eastereggroll. Easter Monday between 8am and 5pm.

**African-American Family Day at the National Zoo.** This tradition extends back to 1889, when the zoo opened. The National Zoo, 3001 Connecticut Ave. NW, celebrates African-American families on the day after Easter with music, dance, an Easter egg hunt, and other activities. Free. Call ✆ **202/633-1000** for details. Easter Monday.

**Smithsonian Craft Show.** Held in the National Building Museum, 401 F St. NW, this juried show features one-of-a-kind, limited-edition crafts by more than 120 noted artists from all over the country. There's an entrance fee of $20 (or $17 in advance) per adult each day; it's free for children 12 and under. No strollers. For details call ✆ **888/832-9554** or 202/633-5006, or visit www.smithsoniancraftshow.org. Four days in mid- to late April.

## MAY

**Washington National Cathedral Annual Flower Mart.** Now in its 78th year, the flower mart takes place on cathedral grounds, featuring displays of flowering plants and herbs, decorating demonstrations, ethnic food booths, children's rides and activities (including an antique carousel), costumed characters, puppet shows, and other entertainment. Free admission. For details call ℂ **202/537-2937** or visit www.allhallowsguild.org. First Friday and Saturday in May, rain or shine.

**Memorial Day.** Ceremonies take place at the Tomb of the Unknowns in Arlington National Cemetery (ℂ **877/907-8585**), at the National World War II and Vietnam Veterans memorials (ℂ **202/426-6841**), at the Women in Military Service for America Memorial (ℂ **703/533-1155**), and at the U.S. Navy Memorial (ℂ **202/737-2300**). A National Memorial Day Parade marches down Constitution Avenue from the Capitol to the White House. On the Sunday before Memorial Day, the National Symphony Orchestra performs a free concert at 8pm on the West Lawn of the Capitol to honor the sacrifices of American servicemen and servicewomen (ℂ **202/426-6841**). And one other thing: Hundreds of thousands of bikers from around the country roll into town in an annual event called "Rolling Thunder" to pay tribute to America's war veterans, prisoners of war, and those missing in action (www.rollingthunder1.com). Last Monday in May.

Soldier places flags in Arlington National Cemetery for Memorial Day ceremonies.

## JUNE

**DC Jazz Festival.** The festival, now in its 12th year, presents more than 125 performances in dozens of venues all over the city throughout the month of June. Some performances are free, some are not. www.dcjazzfest.org. Early to late June.

**Smithsonian Folklife Festival.** A major event celebrating both national and international traditions in music, crafts, food, games, concerts, and exhibits, staged between 4th and 7th streets on the National Mall. Each Folklife Festival showcases several cultures or themes; the 2016 festival's major presentation explored the culture of Basque country. All events are free; most take place outdoors. For details call ℂ **202/633-6440,** visit www.festival.si.edu, or check the listings in the *Washington Post.* Ten days in late June and early July, always including July 4.

## JULY

**Independence Day.** There's no better place to be on the Fourth of July than in Washington, D.C. The all-day festivities include a massive National Independence Day Parade down Constitution Avenue, complete with lavish floats, princesses, marching groups, and military bands. A morning program in front of the National Archives includes military demonstrations, period music, and a reading of the Declaration of Independence. In the evening, the National Symphony Orchestra plays on the west steps of the Capitol with guest artists. And big-name entertainment precedes the fabulous fireworks display behind the Washington Monument. For details call the National Park Service at ℂ **202/426-6841,** visit www.july4thparade.com, or visit www.nps.gov/subjects/nationalmall4th/index.htm. July 4.

**Capital Fringe Festival.** This event debuted in 2005 and celebrates experimental theater in the tradition of the original fringe festival, held annually in Edinburgh, Scotland. Nearly 130 separate productions take place at some 20 venues daily for three weeks or more. Local and visiting artists perform in theater, dance, music, and other disciplines. All single tickets are $17, plus a one-time fee of $7 for an admission button; purchase them on www.capitalfringe.org or call

866/811-4111 (tickets) or ☎ 202/737-7230 (info). In June 2016, the festival organizers debuted a 2-day Fringe Music Festival, which is also worth checking out; same website as above. Three weeks in mid- to late July.

## AUGUST

**Shakespeare Theatre Free for All.** This free theater festival presents a different Shakespeare play every year for a 2-week run at the Sidney Harman Hall, across from the Verizon Center, in the Penn Quarter. Tickets are required, but they're free. Call ☎ 202/547-1122 or visit www.shakespearetheatre.org. Evenings and some matinees late August through early September.

## SEPTEMBER

**Labor Day Concert.** The National Symphony Orchestra closes its summer season with a free performance at 8pm on the West Lawn of the Capitol. For details, call the National Park Service at ☎ 202/426-6841. Sunday before Labor Day (rain date: same day and time at Constitution Hall or the Kennedy Center).

**Library of Congress National Book Festival.** The Library of Congress sponsors this festival, now in its 17th year, welcoming nearly 100 established authors and their many fans. Previously held on the National Mall, the festival's popularity and the toll the turnout took on Mall grounds necessitated the festival's relocation in 2014 to the Walter E. Washington Convention Center in downtown D.C., between 7th and 9th sts NW, and N St. and Mt. Vernon Place. The festival takes place over the course of one long day, from 10am to 10pm in late August or early September and includes readings, author signings, panel discussions, and general hoopla surrounding the love of books. For details call ☎ 888/714-4696 or visit www.loc.gov/bookfest. A Saturday in late August/early to mid-September.

## OCTOBER

**Marine Corps Marathon.** A maximum of 30,000 may compete in this 26.2-mile race (the third-largest marathon in the United States). The 2017 running marks its 42nd year. The start line is at a spot located between the Pentagon and Arlington Memorial Cemetery, and the course takes racers through Georgetown, through Rock Creek Park almost to the National Zoo, along the Potomac River, past memorials and museums on the National Mall, and so on, before reaching the finish line at the Marine Corps Memorial (the Iwo Jima statue). For details call ☎ 800/RUN-USMC (786-8762) or go to www.marinemarathon.com. Participants must be 14 or older. Register online for the lottery system that determines entry in the marathon. Last Sunday in October.

## NOVEMBER

**Veterans Day.** The nation's tribute to those who fought in wars to defend the United States, and to those who died doing so, takes place in the capital with a wreath-laying ceremony at 11am at the Tomb of the Unknowns in Arlington National Cemetery, followed by a memorial service in the Amphitheater. The president of the United States or a stand-in officiates, as a military band performs. Wreath-laying ceremonies also take place at other war memorials in the city. Call ☎ 877/907-8585 for details about Arlington Cemetery events and 202/426-6841 for details about war memorial events. November 11.

## DECEMBER

**National Christmas Tree Lighting.** At the northern end of the Ellipse, the president lights the National Christmas Tree to the accompaniment of orchestral and choral music, and big-name performers take the stage. The lighting ceremony inaugurates several weeks of holiday concerts performed mostly by local school and church choruses, afternoons and evenings on the Ellipse. (Brrrr!) For details, visit the website, www.thenationaltree.org. To enter the lottery to try to score tickets, visit the website, www.recreation.gov. You can also call ☎ 877/444-6777. There are 17,000 tickets (3,000 seated, 14,000 standing), which are free but required to attend the tree-lighting ceremony. The lottery opens in mid-October. (No tickets are required to attend the other holiday concerts.) The tree-lighting ceremony takes place at 5pm on the first Thursday in December.

# SUGGESTED ITINERARIES & NEIGHBORHOODS

**3**

Ask 10 Washingtonians for their sightseeing hit lists and you'll get 10 different answers. There's so much to see here, and everyone has his or her own way of seeing it. But I can make some suggestions. This chapter lays out a key itinerary for a 3-day tour of the capital's iconic sites, plus three themed itineraries: one devoted to family activities, another to exploring women's history, and the third sketching out an African-American history tour. Follow them to the letter or adapt them for your own purposes—it's up to you.

If you're the type of traveler who doesn't like surprises, call ahead and make sure all of the attractions on your desired itinerary are open. Be calm and flexible: Lines to enter public buildings are longer than ever, thanks to security clearance procedures and the capital's continuing popularity as a tourist destination. Reserve spots on tours to avoid some of those waits, and book advance reservations at recommended restaurants to make sure you get a table. Most importantly, don't be afraid to ask questions. The U.S. Capitol police officers, the National Park Service rangers on duty at the memorials, and the staff at all the museums know an awful lot; take advantage of their expertise.

Following the itineraries in this chapter is an overview of D.C.'s neighborhoods. Among the most enjoyable activities in D.C. is exploring its neighborhoods on foot, so if you tire of crowded museums and structured itineraries, choose a neighborhood that appeals to you and simply stroll. See chapter 10 for walking tours of a few standout neighborhoods.

## ICONIC WASHINGTON, D.C., IN 1 DAY

If you have limited time in Washington, D.C., and would like to have a full-fun experience of several landmark attractions (rather than a rushed experience of many), then this is the itinerary for you. *Start: Metro on the Blue, Orange, or Silver Line to the Smithsonian stop on the National Mall.*

# Iconic Washington, D.C.

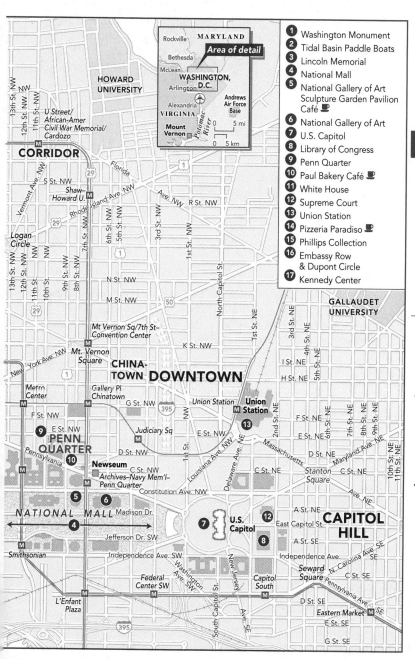

1. Washington Monument
2. Tidal Basin Paddle Boats
3. Lincoln Memorial
4. National Mall
5. National Gallery of Art Sculpture Garden Pavilion Café
6. National Gallery of Art
7. U.S. Capitol
8. Library of Congress
9. Penn Quarter
10. Paul Bakery Café
11. White House
12. Supreme Court
13. Union Station
14. Pizzeria Paradiso
15. Phillips Collection
16. Embassy Row & Dupont Circle
17. Kennedy Center

## 1 Washington Monument ★★★

People often ask: Which is taller, the Washington Monument or the Capitol? The answer is the Washington Monument. Panoramic views stretch for miles (20 miles on a clear day!) from inside the Monument's observation floor. Order free tickets in advance so that you don't waste time standing in line for admission. And if the monument isn't open, then

The view from the Washington Monument.

stand back and consider that this 555-foot, 5⅛ inches-high obelisk, D.C.'s version of a skyscraper, is one of the world's tallest freestanding works of masonry. See p. 157.

Walk up 15th Street and cross Independence Avenue to get to the:

## 2 Tidal Basin Paddle Boats ★

Rent a paddle boat for an hour and skim the surface of the Tidal Basin, sightseeing as you go: Jefferson looks on from his memorial at one end, Martin Luther King presides from the other side of the basin, and the Washington Monument stands tall over all. See p. 203. If the weather isn't permitting or boat season (mid-Mar to mid-Oct) is over, continue on to your next stop.

Return to and cross Independence Avenue and follow it west until you reach the:

## 3 Lincoln Memorial ★★★

There is joy to be had in visiting this temple-like memorial to contemplate the inspiring life and spirit of the nation's 16th president. Citizens of the world surround you, reading aloud the words inscribed on its walls: "Four score and seven years ago our fathers brought forth on this continent a new nation, conceived in liberty, and dedicated to the proposition that all men are created equal . . ." Stand at the top of the memorial's steps and face away from Lincoln to take in the sweeping view, from the Reflecting Pool below you, all the way to the Capitol nearly 2 miles away. In the middle distance is the National Mall, and that's where you're headed next. See p. 137.

Follow the path that parallels the Reflecting Pool, continuing past the National World War II Memorial and the Washington Monument, cross 15th Street, then 14th Street, to reach the:

## 4 National Mall ★★★

Stroll the green promenade or sit upon a bench and watch the Washington world go by: fitness buffs with buzz cuts sprinting back to the Pentagon, office workers playing hooky, and tourists like yourself, enjoying the view. Keep your eyes peeled for your senator or representative trotting past you; a number of congressional members are known to take their daily constitutional along this stretch. See p. 145. Once you've had a chance to catch

Boats on the Tidal Basin.

your breath, it's time to hit the museums. What interests you? Native American culture? Aviation? African art? Avant garde art? The natural world? The Smithsonian museums flanking the Mall cover these and other subjects. If you have time or energy for only one Mall museum, the one I'd recommend isn't a Smithsonian at all. But wait, aren't you starving?

Proceed eastward down the Mall in the direction of the Capitol until you reach 7th Street and the:

5 Pavilion Café at the National Gallery Sculpture Garden 🍽
Order a roasted turkey and bacon sandwich or a Mediterranean salad and maybe some sangria, and if the weather's pleasant, try to snag a seat at one of the outside tables to take in the sights. Be sure to wander through the entire garden to admire all 20 sculptures and a breathtaking mosaic by Chagall, the garden's newest piece. ☎ **202/289-3360.** See p. 144.

Now cross 7th Street to enter the:

6 National Gallery of Art ★★★
Yes, I do believe this to be the capital's best museum, despite the fact that it is not part of the Smithsonian family. The freshly renovated East Building showcases modern and contemporary art, while the West Building's galleries display European paintings and sculptures spanning the 13th to 19th centuries. Don't leave without checking out the gallery's special exhibits, which are always amazing, such as the "Stuart Davis: In Full Swing" show, on view until March 5, 2017. See p. 143. If you're here on a Friday night in summer, return to the Sculpture Garden to enjoy a jazz concert and tasty cafe items. If you're here in winter, return to the Sculpture Garden to go ice skating. And if you're here on a Sunday October through June, attend a classical music concert in the Gallery's Garden Court.

# ICONIC WASHINGTON, D.C., IN 2 DAYS

With a second day added on, you can get to Capitol Hill's capital attractions, tour the Penn Quarter neighborhood, and cap off the day with a presidential flourish. ***Start:*** *Metro on the Blue, Orange, or Silver Line to Capitol South, or on the Red Line to Union Station.*

### 7 The Capitol ★★★

This is Congress's "House," its cornerstone laid in 1793 by President George Washington. The Capitol was completed when the 19-foot, 6-inch *Statue of Freedom* was placed atop the dome in December 1863, at the height of the Civil War—the same year that Abraham Lincoln issued his Emancipation Proclamation. Head inside the Capitol Visitor Center to take the hour-long guided Capitol tour (highly recommended), armed with the timed passes you've ordered in advance online. If you've neglected to order these, you may still be in luck: Go to the "public walk up" line to see if any same-day passes are available. The Visitor Center is itself worth checking out. See p. 115.

Not everyone knows it, but there's a tunnel that runs between the Capitol Visitor Center and the Library of Congress. If you're inside the Capitol Visitor Center, find it and follow it to the:

### 8 Library of Congress ★★

The world's largest library is not only a keeper of books: Rotating exhibits show off other precious objects, such as an "original Rough Draught" of Thomas Jefferson's much marked-up Declaration of Independence and a 1797 manuscript in George Washington's hand, outlining a plan of government for Virginia. See p. 123.

Exit and head south on First Street to hop the Metro at the Capitol South station, catching a Blue, Orange, or Silver Line train to the Metro Center stop, to reach:

### 9 Penn Quarter

This lively neighborhood just off the National Mall is full of restaurants, bars, and assorted sightseeing attractions, all within a short walk of each other. Wander down to Pennsylvania Avenue and up 7th Street, the main arteries, and explore side streets; you're sure to come upon something that strikes your fancy. Some suggestions: Sign up for a **Ford's Theatre**

The dome of the Capitol Building.

(p. 170) "History on Foot" walking tour that brings Civil War Washington to life. Go on a self-guided scavenger hunt or a guided highlights tour at the **Smithsonian American Art Museum** and the **National Portrait Gallery** (p. 179). (Good to know: The American Art Museum and Portrait Gallery each stay open until 7pm nightly, which is later than other museums.) Take a turn at being a TV reporter and otherwise test your journalistic skills at the **Newseum,** which touts itself as "one of the most interactive museums in the world." But first, fortify yourself at one of the Quarter's excellent eateries. Here's one that comes with a view:

10  Paul Bakery Café ☕
Sit at a sidewalk table overlooking the Navy Memorial and Pennsylvania Avenue, or inside the charming French cafe (✆ **202/524-4500**), and treat yourself to a delicious smoked salmon and lemon cream sandwich, or an almond croissant, or a baguette layered with thinly sliced ham and brie, or a chocolate éclair, or . . . all of the above. See p. 108.

Whether you finish your Penn Quarter activities before dinner or aft, hop on the Metro at Gallery Place and take a Red Line train to Metro Center (13th and G St. exit), or walk or cab it, to reach the:

11  White House ★★★
Whether or not you're able to tour the interior of the executive mansion, you can admire its exterior view and consider the facts: Its cornerstone was laid in 1792, making the White House the capital's oldest federal building. It's been the residence of every president but George Washington (although the nation's second president, John Adams, lived here for only 4 months). The British torched the mansion in 1814, so what you see is the house rebuilt in 1817, using the original sandstone walls and interior brickwork. Be sure to walk past the house before 11pm, when the White House dims its exterior lights. ("This is a residence, remember," notes a National Park Service ranger.) See p. 165.

# ICONIC WASHINGTON, D.C., IN 3 DAYS

Last but not least comes the Supreme Court on your third day, and then you're off to a different part of town altogether. *Start: Metro on the Blue, Orange, or Silver Line to the Capitol South stop to reach Capitol Hill.*

12  Supreme Court ★★★
You may be shocked to know that the U.S. Constitution specifies neither an age nor an education level nor even a citizenship requirement for a person to become a Supreme Court justice. No, all that is required is that the president nominates the person and that the Senate confirms the nomination, a simple process often complicated by politicking, such as the refusal in 2016 of Republican senators to consider President Obama's nominee, following the death of Justice Antonin Scalia. Attend a Supreme Court argument, or at the very least, a docent lecture, and be further amazed. See p. 127.

Continue north on First Street (closed to car traffic but not pedestrians), crossing Constitution Avenue and continuing about ½ mile, to reach:

## 13 Union Station ★

Notable for its Beaux Arts architecture, Union Station is also a historic landmark, having hosted inaugural balls and presidential receptions for all sorts of royalty. And it's a shopping mall, let's not forget, so if you want to pick up some corny mementos (Commander in Chief aprons?) from **America!** this would be the place. Washingtonians mostly look on Union Station as a transportation hub, however, because subway, Amtrak, and commuter trains; buses; taxis; and rental car and bike-rental companies all operate here. And that's why you're here, too, to be transported. See p. 128.

Catch Metro's Red Line going in the direction of Shady Grove or Grosvenor and exit at Dupont Circle, on the 19th Street, or south side, of the Circle, to find this favorite pizzeria:

## 14 Pizzeria Paradiso ☕

These pies are a cut above, cooked in an oak-burning oven and topped with your choice of nearly 50 toppings. ✆ **202/223-1245.** See p. 106.

Walk across Massachusetts Avenue to reach the:

## 15 Phillips Collection ★★

Tour this charming museum to view French, American, post-Impressionist, and modernist art, all housed in an 1897 mansion and its modern wings. Always keep an eye out for favorites, such as Renoir's *Luncheon of the Boating Party,* numerous Bonnards, the gallery devoted to Mark Rothko's bold artworks, and on display from time to time, *Night Baseball,* a painting executed by founder Duncan Phillips's wife, Marjorie Phillips.

Return to Massachusetts Avenue and turn either left to reach Dupont Circle and Connecticut Avenue, or right to continue on Massachusetts Avenue, to start your tour of:

## 16 Embassy Row & Dupont Circle

Stop in shops along Connecticut Avenue, and then follow side streets to discover boutiques, little art galleries, and quaint, century-old town houses. If you look carefully, you'll start to notice that some of these buildings are actually embassies or historic homes. The most awesome embassies lie on Massachusetts Avenue, west of Dupont Circle. Flags and plaques clearly identify them. Turn onto S Street NW and look for no. 2340 to see where President Woodrow Wilson lived after he left the White House. The **Woodrow Wilson House** (p. 183) is worth touring if you have time. Few embassies are open to the public; those that are limit their hours. For an in-depth tour of Dupont Circle and Embassy Row, take the self-guided walking tour outlined in chapter 10. See p. 272.

Walk, if you feel up to it, or take a taxi to the:

## 17 Kennedy Center ★★★

Head to the Kennedy Center for the 6pm nightly free concert in the Grand Foyer (part of the center's Millennium Stage program). At concert's end, proceed through the glass doors to the terrace overlooking Rock Creek Parkway and the Potomac River, and enjoy the view. See p. 220.

# WASHINGTON, D.C., FOR FAMILIES

The good thing about the capital, parents, is that history is in plain view. The National Mall, with its green sweep of landmarks from the Capitol to the Lincoln Memorial, offers plenty of opportunities for educational moments. This itinerary leans more toward fun, though as you'll see, there's a lot of learning going on, too. ***Start: The National Museum of American History.***

1 National Museum of American History ★★★

Like all of the Smithsonians, this one has tons of kid-friendly activities and exhibits. If your children are younger than 6, visit Wegmans Wonderplace, full of fun activities and toys related to the museum's collections. Kids 6 and older will appreciate Spark!Lab; the 23-room doll house; "interactive carts" of objects, such as a stereoscope, that children can pick up and experiment with; artifacts on display including Kermit the Frog; sightings of historical figures in your midst (Is that Mary Pickersgill? Yes.); and the simulator rides that make you feel like you're on a roller coaster or driving a race car. See p. 149.

Exit to the National Mall and walk diagonally across it to reach the part of the Mall between the Smithsonian Castle and the Arts and Industries Building, where you'll find the:

2 Carousel

For little and not-so-little children, the carousel is a treat, operating year-round, weather permitting. It's not free, though: $3.50 per child per ride. See p. 200. Good to know: Another carousel awaits at your final destination, the National Zoo, where a solar-powered, custom-designed carousel

Children on the National Mall's carousel.

# Washington, D.C., for Families

**1** National Museum of American History
**2** Carousel
**3** National Museum of the American Indian
**4** Mitsitam ⬛
**5** National Zoo
**6** Lebanese Taverna ⬛

To the National Zoo (see inset)

PENN QUARTER

FEDERAL TRIANGLE

NATIONAL MALL

3rd St. NW

GAO

Gallery Pl-Chinatown

Nat'l Building Museum

Judiciary Sq

4th St. NW

5th St. NW

6th St. NW

G St. NW

E St. NW

C St. NW

D St. NW

National Gallery of Art East

Nat'l Museum of the American Indian

Federal Center SW

1/4 mi
0.25 km

National Gallery of Art West

Madison Dr. NW

Nat'l Air & Space Museum

Dr. SW

L'Enfant Plaza

Verizon Center

Nat'l Portrait Gallery

7th St. NW

8th St. NW

U.S. Navy Memorial

Nat'l Archives

Pennsylvania Ave.

Archives-Navy Mem'l-Penn Quarter

Constitution Ave.

NW

Jefferson

Hirshhorn Museum

7th St. SW

Hancock Park

D St. SW

6th St. SW

Metro Center

F St. NW

9th St. NW

FBI

Dept. of Justice

Arts & Industries Building

Smithsonian Castle

E St. NW

10th St. NW

11th St. NW

Federal Triangle

Smithsonian

Independence Ave. SW

10th St. SW

12th St. NW

Pennsylvania Ave. NW

Freedom Plaza

Pennsylvania Ave. NW

Nat'l Museum of Natural History

Department of Agriculture

14th St. NW

Commerce Dept.

National Museum of African American History and Culture

Nat'l Museum of American History

Constitution Ave. NW

Washington Monument

Sylvan Theater

U.S. Holocaust Museum

Bureau of Engraving and Printing

15th St. NW

White House Visitor Center

NATIONAL ZOO

Beach Dr. NW

1/4 mi
0.25 km

Connecticut Ave. NW

Cathedral Ave. NW

NW

Woodley Rd. NW

Woodley Park-Zoo NW

Adams Morgan

Calvert St.

with 58 animal figures operates daily, for $3 a ride.

Continue down the Mall toward the Capitol until you reach the:

## 3 National Museum of the American Indian ★

Inside the museum's imagiNA-TIONS Activity Center, children can traipse through Amazonian stilt houses, test their balance while learning about kayaks, weave a giant basket, and learn to make beautiful music using traditional instruments.

Follow up that experience with a traditional American Indian meal right inside the museum at:

Storytelling in a tepee in the imagiNATIONS Activity Center at the National Museum of the American Indian.

3

SUGGESTED ITINERARIES | Washington, D.C., for Families

## 4 Mitsitam 🍽

It's easy to learn about Native American culture when learning involves delicious bites of it: fry bread with cinnamon and honey, huckleberry fritters, *totopos*, and more. ℂ **202/633-7039.** See p. 151.

Exit to the Independence Avenue side of the museum, walk to 3rd Street, cross Independence Avenue, and follow 3rd Street to the Federal Center SW Metro station, where you should board either a Blue, Silver, or Orange Line train headed in the direction of Franconia/Springfield. Debark the train at the Metro Center stop, but stay in the station and switch to the Red Line, boarding a train going in the direction of either Shady Grove or Grosvenor. Debark at the Woodley Park–Zoo station and walk up Connecticut Avenue to reach the:

## 5 National Zoo ★★

Certain children's exhibits (the Kids' Farm, the pizza sculpture) lie at the very bottom of this large zoo, situated on a hill. Keep that part in mind as you explore the zoo, since it'll be all uphill—and quite a long hill it is—back to Connecticut Avenue. But you need not go all the way to the bottom of the hill, as pandas, a solar-powered carousel, a fabulous elephant exhibit, and nearly 1,800 other animals that young ones will love to see are on view elsewhere in the zoo. See p. 186.

## 6 Lebanese Taverna ☕

If you're longing for a pick-me-up, head down Connecticut Avenue to this family-friendly establishment. The menu has something for everyone, including gluten-free items, if your child has that allergy. The restaurant stays open straight through from noon until closing. ℂ **202/265-8681.** You might also be happy to know that there's a McDonald's right across the street from the taverna. See p. 114.

# A Women's History Tour of Washington, D.C.

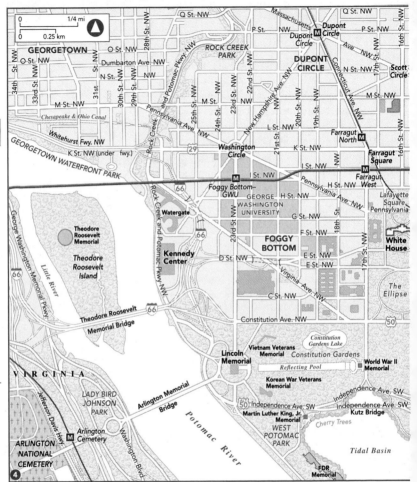

3

SUGGESTED ITINERARIES | A Women's History Tour of Washington, D.C.

# A WOMEN'S HISTORY TOUR OF WASHINGTON, D.C.

"Remember the ladies," Abigail Adams famously advised her husband, John Adams, in 1776, when he was attending the Continental Congress and busy formulating his ideas about the new government. John Adams, who went on to become the second president of the United States in 1797, did his best. But that was a long time ago, and women have long acted as their own advocates. One day, perhaps, Americans might marvel that there was ever a time when a woman couldn't vote, own property, succeed in sports, run a large company, become the president. (This book went to press before the presidential election, alas!) In the

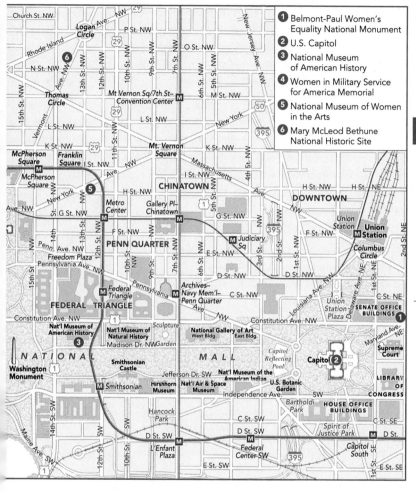

meantime, let us now celebrate the achievements of women in many realms. ***Start:*** *The Belmont-Paul Women's Equality National Monument on Capitol Hill.*

## 1 Belmont-Paul Women's Equality National Monument

On April 14, 2016, President Obama proclaimed the historic Sewall-Belmont House a national monument to women's equality, the first of its kind in the National Park Service. As the headquarters for the National Woman's Party since 1929, the house serves as both a museum honoring the many women who have struggled for women's equality and an

3

SUGGESTED ITINERARIES | A Women's History Tour of Washington, D.C.

education center supporting activities that continue that battle. The monument takes its name from National Woman's Party founder Alice Paul and the party's benefactor, Alva Belmont. See p. 127.

From the house, head up to 1st Street and turn left. Give a nod to the Supreme Court, where three of the nine justices are women, then cross the street to reach the:

## 2 U.S. Capitol ★★★

The 115th Congress (its term begins January 3, 2017) marks the centenary of the election of the first woman to Congress: Rep. Jeannette Rankin of Montana. Look for her statue in the Capitol Visitor Center. In the 100 years since, a total of 313 women have been elected or appointed to Congress. 313? C'mon, people. Let's hope the November 2016 elections increased the numbers of women at every level. (The elections had not taken place when this book went to press.) And for in-depth information about women who have served in Congress, access www.senate.gov, and search for "women in Congress 1917-2015." See p. 115.

Return to Constitution Avenue and either flag a taxi (easy to do in this part of town) or start walking and hop on a DC Circulator National Mall bus, when you reach the bus stop at the National Gallery of Art. Or you can walk the whole way (about 1½ miles) to the:

## 3 National Museum of American History ★★★

The First Ladies exhibit is the most popular one in the museum and gives First Ladies their due as strong and interesting people in their own right. But don't miss Julia Child's Kitchen (within the "Food: Transforming the American Table 1950–2000" exhibit), a tribute to a different kind of icon. And the Star-Spangled Banner? The handiwork of a woman, or rather, several women: Mary Pickersgill and daughter, nieces, and a maid. See p. 149.

You could walk it, but you'll have to navigate a terrifying traffic circle; it will be safer to hop on the Metro at the Smithsonian station on the Mall, directly across from the American History Museum. Board a Blue, Orange, or Silver Line train headed in the direction of Franconia/Springfield and get off at the Arlington Cemetery stop and walk to the:

## 4 Women in Military Service for America Memorial ★

This is the only major national memorial honoring all servicewomen, from the American Revolution onward. Its archives include information about two nurses aboard Commodore Stephen Decatur's ship *United States* during the War of 1812, and the more recent development in 2008 when, for the first time in military history, a woman was promoted to the rank of four-star general in the U.S. Army. See p. 194.

The best thing to do from here is to board the Metro, take the Blue, Orange, or Silver Line headed into D.C., and get off at Metro Center, exiting at 13th and G streets and walking a block north to the:

## 5 National Museum of Women in the Arts ★

From Renaissance paintings to contemporary sculptures to silver pieces created by 18th- and 19th-century Irish and British female silversmiths, this museum is full of masterpieces by women. See p. 177.

*If it's a nice day, consider walking to your last stop, just about half a mile away. Walk to 14th Street and head north, going around Thomas Circle at Massachusetts Avenue to pick up Vermont Avenue on the other side. Proceed about a block to the:*

## 6 Mary McLeod Bethune National Historic Site

Mary McLeod Bethune bought this house not as a residence, but to serve as headquarters for the National Council for Negro Women. So although she did live here from 1943 to 1949, it is the sense of her professional rather than personal life that you absorb from the exhibits. They speak volumes. Look for a black-and-white photo of FDR's cabinet in the 1930s, and there you will see a panel of white men and, in their midst, this black woman. When you consider that Bethune was born poor, the 15th of 17 children of former slaves, you start to truly appreciate her accomplishments. See p. 185.

3

SUGGESTED ITINERARIES | An African-American History Tour of Washington, D.C.

# AN AFRICAN-AMERICAN HISTORY TOUR OF WASHINGTON, D.C.

The story of African Americans in Washington, D.C., actually pre-dates the founding of the capital, for African Americans were here from the get-go. Records show that blacks were living and working in Georgetown, the city's oldest neighborhood, from its 1751 beginnings as a tobacco port. (And worshipping: See p. 271 for information about Georgetown's **Mount Zion United Methodist Church,** which celebrated its 200th year in 2016, making its worshippers the city's oldest black congregation.) The capital's very design was plotted by self-taught mathematician/surveyor Benjamin Banneker, who in 1791 assisted Andrew Ellicott in mapping out Pierre L'Enfant's 10 square mile territorial vision. Slaves built many of the capital's historic buildings, the White House and the U.S. Capitol among them. The population of African Americans in the capital, always significant, now stands at about 50%. This tour aims to shed some light on the local and national history of African Americans, from pre-Revolutionary War times to the present. *Start: Frederick Douglass National Historic Site in Anacostia.*

## 1 Frederick Douglass National Historic Site (Cedar Hill) ★★

Douglass is best known for being an abolitionist, but his story doesn't stop there. After the Civil War, Douglass held a number of government positions, including U.S. Marshal, appointed by President Rutherford Hayes in 1877. His office was in the U.S. Capitol. He was 60. Douglass

# An African-American History Tour of Washington, D.C.

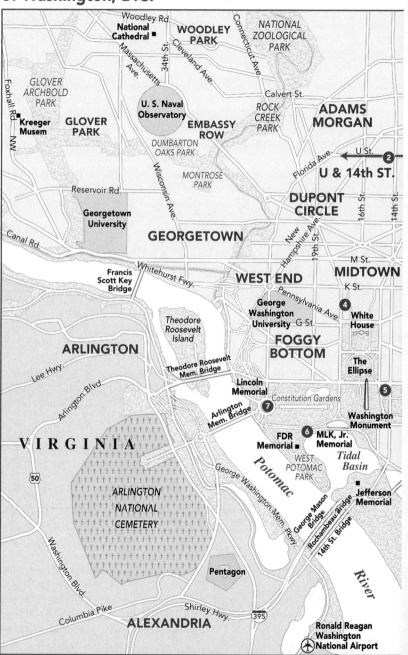

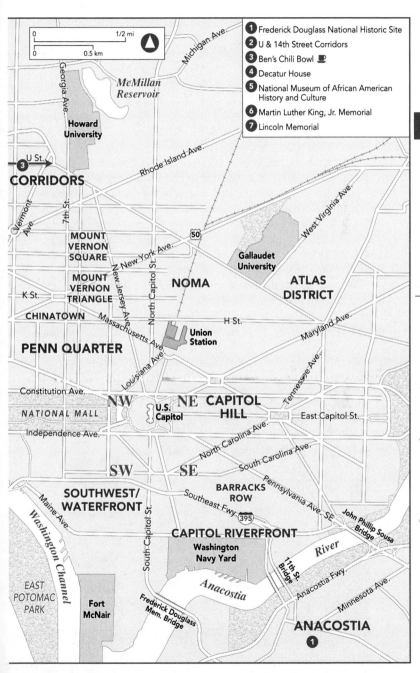

1 Frederick Douglass National Historic Site
2 U & 14th Street Corridors
3 Ben's Chili Bowl ☕
4 Decatur House
5 National Museum of African American History and Culture
6 Martin Luther King, Jr. Memorial
7 Lincoln Memorial

3

SUGGESTED ITINERARIES | An African-American History Tour of Washington, D.C.

walked the 5 miles daily to and fro. So let me ask you something: Do you think the Anacostia site is too far away to visit? You could make the same trek as Douglass, but actually, it's quite easy to get here: Take the Green Line Metro to the Anacostia station, pick up the DC Circulator bus in the direction of Skyland, travel one stop to the corner of W Street SE and Martin Luther King, Jr. Avenue SE, and hop off and walk 2 blocks east to the visitor center at 14th and W streets SE. Easy-peasy. See p. 190.

From the house, simply reverse the steps listed above, picking up the DC Circulator at 14th and W streets SE, this time headed toward Potomac Avenue, hop off at the Anacostia Metro station, and catch the Green Line train to the U Street/African-American Civil War Memorial/Cardozo stop and exit to 13th Street.

## 2 U & 14th Street Corridors

The greater U Street neighborhood these days is a hotspot, the place to go for dining out, hanging out, and nightlife. But for decades, this area was predominantly a cultural and residential stronghold for African Americans, who had started to settle here after the Civil War. In the 1920s, '30s, and '40s, the popularity of jazz venues and their stars, like D.C.'s own Duke Ellington, led fans to dub the area "Black Broadway." And in the 1950s and '60s, the area was a violent hotbed of civil rights activism. Black history references exist among the millennial attractions: the **African American Civil War Memorial and Museum** (p. 185), **Duke Ellington town house residences** at 1805 and 1816 13th St., and historic showcase theaters, such as the **Howard** (p. 229) and the **Lincoln** (p. 224). And one establishment, from the tumultuous days of race riots

Duke Ellington mural on U Street.

and heartbreak following Dr. King's assassination in 1968, has become a legend in its own time: **Ben's Chili Bowl,** 1213 U St. NW, open since 1958, and where you should head now for a break.

3 Ben's Chili Bowl ☕
Famous for its half-smokes and chili fries, Ben's also serves decent vegetarian fare. You'll see a cross-section of the city at Ben's, which is open almost 24/7, 365 days a year. ✆ **202/667-0909.** See p. 103.

From Ben's, walk to the corner of 14th and U streets and board the DC Circulator bus headed south in the direction of McPherson Square. Get off at the last stop, walk 1 block south to H Street, and turn right and follow to 1610 H St. NW.

## 4 Decatur House and Slave Quarters, Lafayette Square ★

When Benjamin Henry Latrobe (one of the architects of the Capitol and the White House) designed the lovely red-brick Federal-style Decatur House for War of 1812 hero, Commodore Stephen Decatur, he made sure to include back stairways and access passages where slaves might toil and traipse without being seen. A tour here takes you through the elegant 1818 main house as well as its "back building" rooms where slaves lived, laundered, and cooked. The guide notes that these slave quarters "are the only ones that exist within view of the White House," which can't help but call up a vision of the White House looming like a plantation mansion over fields being worked and structures being built by enslaved blacks. In fact, slaves constructed the White House, and lived, for the duration, in temporary tiny (10 foot wide by 10 foot long) huts on the muddy land that is now Lafayette Square. See p. 258.

If you don't feel like strolling the mile to your next stop, walk 1 block north to the Farragut West station and board the Blue, Orange, or Silver Line train headed toward Largo. Debark at the Smithsonian stop, exiting onto the National Mall. Cross the Mall to enter the:

## 5 National Museum of African American History and Culture ★★★

The long-awaited National Museum of African American History and Culture opened on September 24, 2016. The enormous museum is stunning in appearance, its three-tiered exterior sheathed in 3,600 bronze-colored cast-aluminum panels, suggestive of 19th-century ironwork created by enslaved craftsmen in New Orleans. And the nine-level museum is staggering in scope, its collections and exhibits designed to illustrate major periods of African-American history, beginning in Africa and continuing through slavery, Reconstruction, the Civil Rights era, and the Harlem Renaissance, and into the 21st century. The collection houses more than 34,000 artifacts, from Harriet Tubman's hymnal to an early-1800s slave cabin from South Carolina. See p. 146.

Exit the museum Mall-side and find the DC Circulator stop at 12th Street and Madison Drive. Take the Circulator bus to the:

## 6 Martin Luther King, Jr. National Memorial ★★

The Martin Luther King, Jr. National Memorial.

In his 39 years, the Rev. Dr. Martin Luther King, Jr. helped found the Southern Christian Leadership Conference, wrote and delivered 2,500 speeches, organized massive protests and drives to register black voters, won the Nobel Peace Prize, and last but certainly not least, led the August 28, 1963, historic March on Washington for Jobs and Freedom that convinced Congress to pass the Civil Rights Act of 1964. Inscribed into the memorial walls are 16 quotes that attempt to define the man, including one that inspired the memorial's design: "Out of the mountain of despair, a stone of hope." Now visit the place where King delivered that line. See p. 139.

Cross Independence Avenue and walk westward along the avenue until you reach a lane leading to the:

## 7 Lincoln Memorial ★★★

Forty-one years before Martin Luther King, Jr. delivered his famous "I Have a Dream" speech from the steps of the Lincoln Memorial, another black man addressed a crowd here. Dr. Robert Russa Moton, the president of Tuskegee Institute, gave the keynote speech at the memorial's dedication, on May 30, 1922. The attendees were mostly white and the seating segregated, but the occasion, nevertheless, was momentous for paying honest tribute to Lincoln's legacy. It's not certain where Dr. Moton stood that day, but Dr. King's step is clearly marked: Ascend to the top of the steps, then count down to the 18th and look for the stone inscribed with the words, "I Have a Dream. Martin Luther King, Jr. The March on Washington for Jobs and Freedom. August 28, 1963." See p. 137.

## The Neighborhoods in Brief

**Adams Morgan** This ever-trendy, multiethnic neighborhood is crammed with boutiques, bars, clubs, and restaurants. Everything is located on either 18th Street NW or Columbia Road NW. Adams Morgan lodging is primarily bed-and-breakfasts. In 2017, however, the neighborhood will get its first hotel, the Line DC. More hotel options lie in the nearby Dupont Circle and Woodley Park neighborhoods (see below). Parking is manageable during the day but difficult at night, especially on weekends (a parking garage on Champlain St., just off 18th St., helps a little). Luckily, you can easily walk to Adams Morgan from the Dupont Circle or Woodley Park Metro stops, or take the bus or a taxi there. (Be alert in Adams Morgan at night and try to stick to the main streets: 18th St. and Columbia Rd.) The weekend begins Thursday nights in the nightlife-centric world of Adams Morgan.

**Anacostia** When people talk about the Washington, D.C., that tourists never see, they're talking about neighborhoods like this; in fact, they're usually talking about Anacostia, specifically. Named for the river that separates it from "mainland" D.C., it's an old part of town, with little commercial development and mostly modest, often low-income housing. Anacostia does have two attractions: the Smithsonian's **Anacostia Community Museum** and the **Frederick Douglass National Historic Site** (see the African-American History Tour, above, and "Museums in Anacostia" box, p. 190).

**Atlas District** The Atlas District, no more than a section of H Street NE to the northeast of Union Station, stretches between 4th and 14th streets, but centers on the 12th to 14th streets segment. Primarily known as a nightlife and live music destination, the neighborhood has its fair share of recommendable casual dining spots, too. A hardscrabble part of town by day, the Atlas District turns into a playground at night, especially Thursday through Saturday, as the city's thirsty scenemakers hit the street. There are no hotels, for now. A much-talked-about streetcar line (see p. 294) finally is operating between the Atlas District and Union Station, which connects with Metrorail.

**Barracks Row** Barracks Row refers mainly to a single stretch of 8th Street SE, south of Pennsylvania Avenue SE, but also to side streets occupied by Marine Corps barracks since 1801 (hence the name). This southeastern subsection of Capitol Hill is known for its lineup of shops, casual bistros, and pubs. Its attractions continue to grow as a result of the 2008 opening of the Nationals baseball team's stadium, Nationals Park, half a mile away. In fact, the ballpark has spawned its own neighborhood, dubbed Capitol Riverfront (see below). The closest hotels are the

**Capitol Hill Hotel** (p. 60), 6 blocks away, at C and 2nd St. SE, close to the Capitol, and those in Capitol Riverfront.

**Capitol Hill** Everyone's heard of "the Hill," the area crowned by the Capitol building. The term, in fact, refers to a large section of town, extending from the western side of the Capitol to the D.C. Armory going east, bounded by H Street to the north and the Southwest Freeway to the south. It contains not only this chief symbol of the nation's capital, but also the **Supreme Court Building,** the **Library of Congress,** the **Folger Shakespeare Library, Union Station,** and **Eastern Market.** Much of it is a quiet residential neighborhood of tree-lined streets, rows of Federal and Victorian town houses, and old churches. Restaurants keep increasing their numbers, with most located along Pennsylvania Avenue SE on the south side of the Capitol and near North Capitol Street NW on the north side of the Capitol—the north side, near Union Station, is where most of the hotels are, too. Keep to the well-lit, well-traveled streets at night, and don't walk alone—crime occurs more frequently in this neighborhood than in some other parts of town.

**Capitol Riverfront** The opening of **Nationals Park** in 2008 has led the way in the development of this overlooked part of town. The revitalized 500-acre neighborhood abuts 1½ miles of the Anacostia River and, besides the ballpark, has a Courtyard by Marriott hotel (p. 61) and a Hampton Inn & Suites (p. 61), with two other hotels due to open by 2017 (see p. 82); several restaurants; and public parks, trails, and docks. More to come.

**Cleveland Park** Cleveland Park, just north of Woodley Park, is a picturesque enclave of winding, tree-shaded streets dotted with charming old houses with wraparound porches. The streets extend off the main artery, Connecticut Avenue. With its own stop on the Red Line Metro system and a respectable number of good restaurants, Cleveland Park is worth visiting when you're near the zoo (just up the street) or seeking a good meal after a bike ride or stroll through nearby Rock Creek Park. Most hotels lie a short walk away in Woodley Park, and farther south in the city.

# Washington, D.C., at a Glance

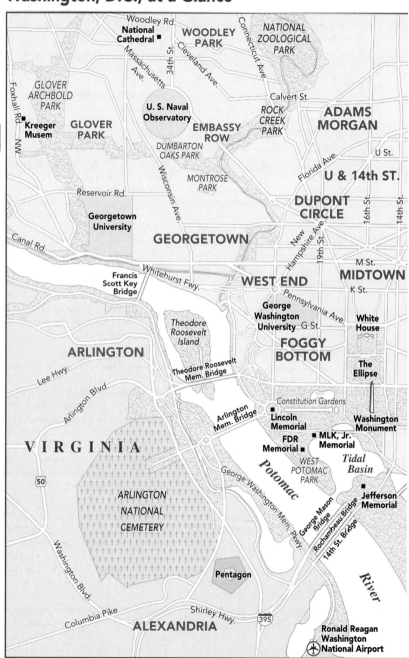

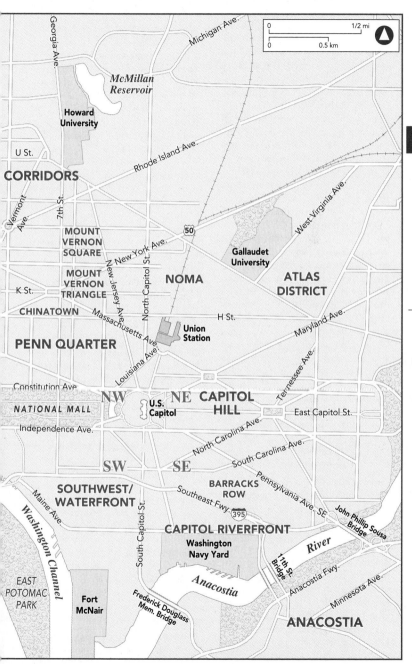

**Downtown** The area bounded roughly by 6th and 21st streets NW to the east and west, and M Street and Pennsylvania Avenue to the north and south, is a mix of the Federal Triangle's government office buildings; K Street, ground zero for the city's countless law and lobbying firms; Connecticut Avenue restaurants and shopping; historic hotels; the city's poshest small hotels; **Chinatown;** the huge Walter E. Washington Convention Center and its companion hotel, the Marriott Marquis (p. 82); and the White House. You'll also find the historic **Penn Quarter,** one of D.C.'s hottest locales, which has continued to flourish since the 1997 opening of the Verizon Center (the venue for Wizards, Mystics, and Georgetown University basketball games; Capitals hockey games; and rock concerts). A number of off-the-Mall museums, such as the mammoth **Newseum** and the **Smithsonian's National Portrait Gallery** and **American Art Museum,** are here. Besides hip restaurants, boutique hotels, and nightclubs, the Penn Quarter claims ultra-trendy **CityCenterDC,** a mini-Manhattan of chic shops such as Dior and Vince, and complementary restaurants such as DBGB and Momofuku. The total downtown area encompasses so many blocks and attractions that I've divided discussions of attractions, restaurants, and hotels in this area into two sections: **"Midtown,"** referring to the area from 15th Street west to 21st Street, and from Pennsylvania Avenue north to M Street; and **"Penn Quarter,"** from 15th Street east to 6th Street, and Pennsylvania Avenue north to New York Avenue.

**Dupont Circle** One of my favorite parts of town, Dupont Circle provides easy fun, day or night. It takes its name from the traffic circle minipark, where Massachusetts, New Hampshire, and Connecticut avenues converge. Washington's famous **Embassy Row** centers on Dupont Circle and refers to the parade of grand embassy mansions lining Massachusetts Avenue and its side streets (see walking tour on p. 272). The streets extending out from the circle are lively, with all-night bookstores, good restaurants, wonderful art galleries and art museums, hip nightspots, and Washingtonians at their loosest. It is also the hub of D.C.'s GLBTQ

community. There are plenty of hotel choices in this neighborhood, and most of them are moderately priced.

**Foggy Bottom/West End** The area west of the White House, south of Dupont Circle, and east of Georgetown encompasses both Foggy Bottom and the West End. Foggy Bottom, located below, or south, of Pennsylvania Avenue, was Washington's early industrial center. Its name comes from the foul fumes emitted in those days by a coal depot and gasworks, but its original name, Funkstown (for owner Jacob Funk), is perhaps even worse. There's nothing foul nor funky about the area today. The West End edges north of Pennsylvania Avenue, booming with the latest big-name restaurants and new office buildings. Together, the overlapping Foggy Bottom and West End neighborhoods present a mix: the **Kennedy Center,** town house residences, George Washington University campus buildings, offices for the World Bank and the International Monetary Fund, State Department headquarters, small- and medium-size hotels, student bars, and several fine eateries, lining either side of Pennsylvania Avenue and its side streets.

**Georgetown** This historic community dates from Colonial times. It was a thriving tobacco port long before the District of Columbia was formed, and one of its attractions, the **Old Stone House,** dates from pre-Revolutionary days. Georgetown action centers on M Street and Wisconsin Avenue NW, where you'll find hundreds of boutiques, chic restaurants, and popular pubs. Expect lots of nightlife here. Luxury hotels, such as the **Capella,** dominate. Fortunately, less pricey options are available as well (see chapter 4). Detour from the main drags to relish the quiet, tree-lined streets of restored Colonial row houses, stroll the beautiful gardens of **Dumbarton Oaks,** and check out the **C&O Canal.** Georgetown is also home to **Georgetown University.** (See chapter 10 for a walking tour of Georgetown.) **Note:** Not surprisingly, the neighborhood gets pretty raucous on weekends.

**Glover Park** Mostly a residential neighborhood, this section of town just above Georgetown and just south of the **Washington National Cathedral** is worth mentioning because of several good restaurants and bars located along its main stretch, Wisconsin Avenue NW. Glover Park sits between the campuses of Georgetown and American universities, so there's a large student presence here.

**Midtown**  This refers roughly to the part of downtown from 15th Street west to 21st Street, and from Pennsylvania Avenue north to M Street. See "Downtown," above.

**Mount Vernon Square**  Located due north of the Penn Quarter and central downtown, east of the U & 14th Street Corridors, and west of Mount Vernon Triangle (see below), this area defines urban renewal, thanks to the opening of the Walter E. Washington Convention Center in 2003, and a convention center hotel, the Marriott Marquis, in 2014. Other development includes a complex known as City Market at O, which holds a Cambria Suites hotel, apartments, markets, and shops.

**Mount Vernon Triangle**  Yet another old neighborhood experiencing renewal, Mount Vernon lies east of the convention center, its boundary streets of New Jersey, Massachusetts, and New York avenues defining a perfectly shaped triangle. Within that triangle, trendy restaurants are starting to multiply. The neighborhood has two hotels, a Hampton Inn and, as of spring 2016, a Homewood Suites.

**The National Mall**  This lovely, tree-lined stretch of open space between Constitution and Independence avenues, extending for nearly 2 miles from the foot of the Capitol to the steps of the Lincoln Memorial, is the hub of tourist attractions. It includes most of the Smithsonian Institution museums and several other notable sites. Tourists as well as natives—joggers, food vendors, kite flyers, and picnickers among them—traipse the 700-acre Mall. Most hotels and restaurants are located beyond the Mall to the north, with a few located south of the Mall, across Independence Avenue. The proper name for the entire parkland area that encompasses the National Mall, as well as the Jefferson, FDR, and Martin Luther King, Jr. memorials and other sites, is actually **National Mall and Memorial Parks,** which is how I refer to it in chapter 6.

**NoMa**  NoMa, as in "North of Massachusetts," is a curious mix of a neighborhood. Located east of downtown D.C. and directly north of Union Station, NoMa's got old residential streets of real character, but also major thoroughfares such as New York Avenue, North Capitol Street, and Florida Avenue slicing through, which makes it not the most walkable of areas. Wide swaths of commuter and Amtrak train tracks form the neighborhood's eastern boundary. Except for the smattering of pleasant side streets, the place has an industrial look about it. And yet, NoMa won't be ignored, and here's why you shouldn't: You're close to Capitol Hill and Union Station; you have access to two Metro stations, bike stations, and a bike path; and the neighborhood has caught the eye of developers, who have built three hotels here in the last few years and more and more restaurants. (The popular Union Market, p. 214, attracts people from all over the city.) If you're here on Capitol Hill business, especially, this might be a good pick.

**Northern Virginia**  Across the Potomac River from the capital lies Northern Virginia and its close-in city/towns of Arlington and Old Town Alexandria. The Arlington Memorial Bridge leads directly from the Lincoln Memorial to Arlington National Cemetery, and beyond to Arlington and Old Town (see chapter 9, "Day Trips from D.C."). Commuters travel back and forth between the District and Virginia all day using the Arlington Memorial Bridge and others, including the Key Bridge, which leads to and from Georgetown; the Theodore Roosevelt Memorial Bridge, whose roadways connect Route 50 and I-66; and the 14th Street Bridge, whose I-395 roadway connects downtown D.C. and Northern Virginia's access to I-95 and points south.

**Penn Quarter**  This refers roughly to the part of downtown from 15th Street east to 6th Street, and Pennsylvania Avenue north to New York Avenue. See "Downtown," above.

**Southwest/Waterfront**  It's happening, people: Investors and developers are at last working to transform the waterfront into an attractive and vital area of the city! You can expect openings of hotels, restaurants, and music venues throughout 2017 and 2018. As the new buildings go up, this stretch of waterfront continues as a working marina, with fishing boats docked the length of the Washington Channel and vendors selling fresh crabs and fish from stalls. This is where locals and restaurateurs come to buy fresh seafood. The neighborhood is also home to the acclaimed **Arena Stage** (p. 219), another excellent reason to visit this out-of-the-way section of town. Southwest does have its own Metro station (Southwest-Waterfront, on the Green Line).

**U & 14th Street Corridors** U Street NW and 14th Street NW form the crux of D.C.'s most diverse neighborhood, where people of varied race, color, nationality, and age mix more comfortably than anywhere else in the city. The area continues to rise from the ashes of long-ago "Black Broadway" nightclubs and theaters, where jazz and blues legends Duke Ellington, Louis Armstrong, and Cab Calloway once performed. Today, clubs such as the renovated Howard Theatre (p. 229) and the smaller Twins Jazz honor that legacy, drawing jazz lovers, while the neighborhood's many bar hangouts fill nightly with the city's young and restless. New restaurants (see chapter 5) and little shops proliferate, including offshoots of successful startups in other neighborhoods. The Penn Quarter may be hot and high energy, but the U & 14th Street Corridors are officially now the hippest part of town. Only one hotel, the Mason & Rook (p. 70), lies within the neighborhood's near reach. *FYI:* My presentation of the U & 14th Street Corridors neighborhood in this book encompasses the greater Shaw neighborhood as well as smaller areas, such as Logan Circle.

**Woodley Park** Home to D.C.'s second-largest hotel (the Washington Marriott Wardman Park, with nearly 1,152 rooms, which now stands behind the new convention hotel, the Marriott Marquis, with 1,175), Woodley Park boasts the **National Zoo,** many good restaurants, and some antiques stores. Washingtonians are used to seeing conventioneers wandering the neighborhood's pretty residential streets with their name tags still on.

# WHERE TO STAY

I f your desire for superb accommodations trumps your concern about expense, you should have no trouble discovering just the hotel for you in Washington, D.C.'s ever-expanding stable of upscale properties. In shorter supply are inexpensive and moderately priced hotels. In fact, the cheapest lodging is found more readily outside the District, in suburban Virginia and Maryland motels and hotels. But do I think you should stay there? No. For a full-blooded experience of the capital, you need to stay overnight and wake up within its urban embrace.

Washington, D.C., has upwards of 130 hotels and scores of bed-and-breakfasts. This chapter describes properties of various types, all of which I have visited. The common denominator is the "distinctly D.C." factor, from the posh **Hay-Adams** (p. 65) showing off its view of the White House; to the **Capitol Hill Hotel** (p. 60), the only hotel truly located on "The Hill"; to the **Embassy Circle Guest House** (p. 72), situated among embassies and elegant residential town houses. Even chain properties I include tend to offer an experience that has as much to do with its "D.C.ness" as with its brand. (Heads up, baseball fans: The **Hampton Inn & Suites Washington DC-Navy Yard,** 1 block from Nationals Park and with a rooftop lounge offering partial views of the action, is *the* place to stay if attending a game!)

**4**

## GETTING THE BEST DEAL

Want the secret for getting the best hotel deal ever in Washington? Easy: Come to Washington when Congress is out, when cherry blossom season is over, or during the blazing hot days of July or August or the icy-cold days of a non-inauguration-year January or February. Not possible? Okay, let's put it this way: Don't try to negotiate a good deal for late March or early April (cherry blossom season); hotel reservationists will laugh at you. I've heard them.

Consider these tips, too:

o **Check out hotels that are located away from big events taking place while you are visiting the capital.** For instance, during cherry blossom season, look at properties in Georgetown, upper Dupont Circle, Woodley Park, or otherwise a few miles from downtown and the National Mall. When the Washington Nationals are playing home games at Nationals Park, consider hotels on the other side of town.

# WHAT YOU'LL really PAY

The prices given in this chapter are based on web searches of both discounter sites and the hotels' own websites; they're the lowest average rates and the highest ones, for both double rooms and suites. At most hotels, you probably won't pay the top rate unless you visit in the spring—especially during cherry blossom season in late March and early April—or during the week of the presidential inauguration, which is coming our way January 20, 2017. These categories are intended as a general guideline only, since rates can rise and fall dramatically.

It's important to note that when the timing's right, it's not impossible to obtain a room at an expensive property for the same rate as a more moderate one. And if you're persistent, or book at the last minute, you could get a steal. Or you could end up paying through the nose if you're visiting during a special event. It's all the luck of the draw, though I do have some tips for savings below.

**Two notes:** Quoted discount rates almost never include the hefty 14.5% hotel sales tax. The word "double" refers to the number of people in the room, not to the size of the bed. Most hotels charge one rate, regardless of whether one or two people occupy the room.

- **Visit on a weekend if you can.** Hotels looking to fill rooms vacated by weekday business travelers lower their rates and might be willing to negotiate even further for weekend arrivals.
- **Ask about special rates or other discounts and whether a room less expensive than the first one quoted is available.** You may qualify for substantial corporate, government, student, military, senior, or other discounts. Mention membership in AAA, AARP, frequent-flier programs, or trade unions, which may entitle you to special deals.
- **Book online.** Because booking online is often the best way to get a discount, I've devoted a box to a discussion of how to get the best deals. See p. 55.
- **Look into group or long-stay discounts.** If you come as part of a large group, you should be able to negotiate a bargain rate because the hotel can then guarantee occupancy in a number of rooms. Likewise, if you're planning a long stay (at least 5 days), you might qualify for a discount. As a general rule, expect 1 night free after a 7-night stay.
- **Consider enrolling in hotel "frequent-stay" programs.** These programs aim to win the loyalty of repeat customers. Frequent guests can accumulate points or credits to earn free hotel nights, and as of 2016, can access special "loyalty rates" on chain hotel rooms, only available to those in the programs who book directly through the chain. Perks are awarded not only by many chain hotels and motels but also by individual inns and B&Bs.
- **Subscribe to e-mail alerts.** Alerts from your favorite hotels or booking sites can keep you informed of special deals.
- **Keep in mind that whether or not you've gotten the best deal possible on your room rate, you can still save money on incidental costs.** D.C. hotels charge unbelievable rates for overnight parking—up to $50 a night at some hotels, plus 18% tax!—so if you can avoid driving, you can save

# TURNING TO THE internet or apps FOR A HOTEL DISCOUNT

It's not impossible to get a good deal by calling a hotel, but you're more likely to snag a discount online and with an app. Here are some strategies:

1. **Browse extreme discounts on sites where you reserve or bid for lodgings without knowing which hotel you'll get.** You'll find these on such sites as Priceline.com and Hotwire.com, and they can be real money-savers, particularly if you're booking within a week of your travel (that's when the hotels get nervous and resort to deep discounts to get beds filled). As these sites mostly feature major chains, it's unlikely that you will be put up in a dump.

2. **Review discounts on the hotel's website.** Sometimes these can be great values, as they'll often include such perks as free breakfast or parking privileges. Before biting, though, be sure to look at the discounter sites below.

3. **Take advantage of aggregator websites, such as Kayak.com (my favorite), that do the work for you.** Kayak, Hipmunk.com, Hotels Combined.com, Momondo.com, and Trivago.com present the discounts available from various online travel agencies such as Hotels.com,

Quikbook.com, and Expedia.com, as well as from the hotels directly, so you have a better chance of finding a discount. **Note:** Sometimes these discounts require advance payment (with draconian cancellation policies), so double-check your travel dates before booking.

**Tingo.com,** founded by TripAdvisor, is another good source. Its model is a bit different than the others. You make a prepaid reservation, but if the price of the room drops between the time you make the booking and the date of arrival, the site refunds the difference in price. It works best for high-end hotels as its prices for budget properties sometimes aren't the lowest on the Internet to begin with.

4. **Try the app HotelTonight.** It works best for day-of bookings, and—WOW!—does it get great prices for procrastinators (up to 70% off in many cases). A possible strategy: Make a reservation at a hotel, then on the day you're arriving try your luck with HotelTonight. Many hotels will allow you to cancel without penalty, even on the date of arrival. HotelTonight also allows bookings up to a week in advance, so check it then, as well.

yourself quite a bit of money. Avoid dialing direct from hotel phones, which usually have exorbitant rates—as do the room's minibar offerings.

*Note:* D.C.'s hotel sales tax is a whopping 14.5%, merchandise sales tax is 5.75%, and food and beverage tax is 10%, all of which can rapidly increase the cost of a room.

## Consider Alternative Accommodations

These alternatives to traditional hotels are another smart way to save:

○ **Hostelling International Washington, DC** (1009 11th St. NW, at K St.; www.hiwashingtondc.org; © **888/464-4872** or 202/737-2333) is well located in the Penn Quarter and nicely equipped, with free Wi-Fi, bike racks, and air-conditioning. Breakfast is complimentary, and the hostel often hosts

## PRICE categories

| | |
|---|---|
| **Expensive** | $300 and up |
| **Moderate** | $200–$300 |
| **Inexpensive** | Under $200 |

complimentary dinners. Guests are welcome to use the full kitchen. Self-serve washers and dryers are available ($1 to wash, $1 to dry). The hostel hosts a free daily walking tour and other activities. In all, there are 250 beds, almost all of which are dorm rooms with shared bathrooms ($29–$49 a night per person). There are 10 private bedrooms, 2 of which have their own bathroom ($89–$119 a night per person). There's a $3 Hostelling International daily membership fee, and the hostel has a staffperson on site 24/7.

o **Check out AirBnB,** a web-based rental operation that matches people looking for a place to stay with locals interested in renting out space in their home, or sometimes the entire apartment or house, often for far less than you might pay at a hotel. As this book went to press, **AirBnB Washington, D.C.** (www. airbnb.com/locations/washington-dc) had upwards of 300 listings scattered among 26 neighborhoods. **Wimdu.com** is a similar service. For rental apartments only (not just rooms in apartments), check out **Vacation Rentals by Owner** (www.vrbo.com), **HomeAway.com,** and **FlipKey.com,** among others; all offer hundreds of furnished apartments for rent in and around the city.

o **Consider house swapping.** Try such organizations as **HomeExchange** (www.homeexchange.com) or **HomeLink International** (www.homelink. org), which offer tens of thousands of would-be swaps worldwide (take into account membership fees when looking at overall costs).

o **Call Washington's tourism bureau, Destination DC** (© 202/789-7000), and ask the tourist rep for the names and numbers of any **new or about-to-open hotels.** If the rep isn't sure, ask her to check with the marketing director. Up-and-coming hotels may have affordable rooms, for the simple reason that few people know about them. See box, "New Hotels Are Popping Up All Over," p. 82, for info on hotels scheduled to open in D.C. in 2017.

o **Consider staying outside the city.** In Northern Virginia, Route 1, also known as the Jefferson Davis Highway within Crystal City limits, is lined with hotels for every budget. Access Destination DC's website, click on "Places to Stay," select "All Accommodations," and then use the site's "Filters" tool to narrow the list down to accommodations in Virginia. Look for hotels with the name "Crystal City" in the name or Jefferson Davis Highway as the address and compare rates.

# ON OR NEAR CAPITOL HILL

A handful of hotels form a cluster just north of the Capitol, adjacent to Union Station; just one hotel lies on Capitol Hill itself, a few minutes' walk from the Capitol. These hotels are also within easy reach of the National Mall.

**Best for:** Travelers who have business at the Capitol and tourists who want to be close to the Capitol and other Hill attractions, as well as to the National Mall.

**Drawbacks:** These neighborhoods are in the thick of things during the day, but not so much at night.

## Expensive

**The George** ★★   The George is the best hotel closest to the Capitol. Celebrities often stay here, and not just those visiting Congress to plead the case for their pet cause. Big-name musicians (ladies and gentlemen, the Rolling Stones!) like the George, and this is interesting, because the hotel is not the most obvious choice. Its location is not the hot spot of, say, a Penn Quarter or Georgetown property. Nor is the George associated with the kind of over-the-top luxury of a Ritz-Carlton or a Four Seasons. Rather, the George offers playful personality, sumptuously comfortable guest rooms, and total discretion. The 260-square-foot guest rooms have a touch of whimsy, with their parchment and ink-stylized graphics of George Washington's inaugural address on the wallpaper, and accent pillows based on GW's original uniforms. The Capitol is a pleasant 8-minute walk from the hotel. (Turn left outside the hotel, walk up the block to North Capitol St., turn right, and then just head toward that big white building up in front of you.) The only other hotel closer to the Capitol is the Capitol Hill Hotel (see below), an entirely different kind of place. The hotel's restaurant, **Bistro Bis,** is a favorite among locals and visitors.

15 E St. NW (at N. Capitol St.). www.hotelgeorge.com. ✆ **800/546-7866** or 202/347-4200. 139 units. $159–$459 double; $459–$859 suite. Children 17 and under stay free in parent's room. Rates include hosted evening wine hour. Parking $46 plus tax. Metro: Union Station (Massachusetts Ave. exit). Pets accepted (free). **Amenities:** Restaurant; bar; children's amenity program; concierge; small exercise room w/steam rooms; room service; Wi-Fi (free when you sign up for the no-cost loyalty program).

**Residence Inn Capitol** ★   It's no accident that this Residence Inn is located within walking distance of the National Museum of the American Indian. Three Native American tribes are 49% owners of the hotel, which made it the first multi-tribal partnership with nontribal partners on land off the reservation when the hotel opened in 2005. Although certain features, like the sandstone walls in the lobby and artwork throughout, hint at its Native-American heritage, the hotel is otherwise similar to standard Residence Inns. All rooms are spacious suites (studio, one-bedroom, or two-bedroom) equipped with full kitchens. A major renovation is scheduled for 2017. All guest rooms and the lobby will be given a more modern look and furnishings (think chaise longues, stainless-steel accessories, pale teal and burgundy hues). The hotel lies close to a train track, so ask for a room on the other side.

333 E St. SW (at 4th St.). www.marriott.com/wascp. ✆ **800/331-3131** or 202/484-8280. 233 units. $179–$419 studio suite; $209–$449 1-bedroom suite; $249–$589 2-bedroom suite. Rates include hot breakfast, light fare Mon–Wed evenings, and grocery delivery service. Parking $41.30 including tax. Metro: Federal Center SW or L'Enfant Plaza. Pets accepted ($200 nonrefundable cleanup fee and an additional $10 added to room rate). **Amenities:** Concierge; fitness center; indoor pool; sundeck; Wi-Fi (free).

# Washington, D.C., Hotels

Garfield St. NW
Fulton St. NW
Woodley Rd. NW
**1**
**2**
Woodley Park–Zoo/
Adams Morgan
Calvert St. NW
**3**

**NATIONAL ZOO**
Harvard St. NW
Ontario Rd. NW
Lanier Pl.
**4**
Columbia Rd. NW
Euclid St. NW
Calvert St. NW

Observatory Circle
Woodland Dr. NW

**U.S. Naval Observatory**

**ADAMS MORGAN**

15th St.
14th St. NW

**E M B A S S Y   R O W**
Massachusetts Ave. NW

**ROCK CREEK PARK**
Rock Creek
19th St. NW
16th St.

Belmont Rd. NW
Kalorama Rd.
**5**
**6**
Wyoming Ave.
**7**
California St. NW
S St. NW

Florida Ave.
W St. NW
V St. NW
U St. NW
T St. NW

**U STREET**

**DUMBARTON OAKS PARK**

**MONTROSE PARK**

R St. NW
Reservoir Rd. NW
**GEORGETOWN UNIVERSITY**
33rd St. NW
32nd St. NW

Sheridan Circle
**8**
Massachusetts

Florida Ave. NW
18th St. NW
New Hampshire Ave. NW
17th St. NW
16th St.
15th St.

Corcoran St. NW
Q St. NW
Church St. NW
P St. NW

R St. NW

**DUPONT CIRCLE**
**17**
Dupont Circle
**16**

R St. NW
Q St. NW
P St. NW
O St. NW
Dumbarton St. NW
Wisconsin Ave. NW
31st St. NW
30th St.
29th St.
28th St.
27th St.
N St. NW

**18** **19**
**20**
**22**
Scott Circle
**21**
Thomas Circle

**GEORGETOWN**
Prospect St. NW
Francis Scott Key Bridge
**9**
**10**
M St. NW
31st St.

Rock Creek Pkwy. NW
25th St.
24th St.
23rd St.
22nd St.
21st St. NW
20th St. NW
19th St. NW

L St. NW
Farragut North
Farragut Square
McPherson Square
15th St.

Whitehurst Fwy. NW
**11**
**12**
29
**15**
K St. NW
Washington Circle
**13**
Connecticut Ave. NW
New Hampshire Ave. NW

Pennsylvania Ave. NW
Farragut West
**25**
29
**27**

**14** Foggy Bottom–GWU
**23**
Virginia Ave.
**GEORGE WASHINGTON UNIVERSITY**
I St. NW
**26**
G St. NW
**White House**
**28**
Pennsylvania

Georgetown Channel
Rock Creek and Potomac Pkwy. NW

**Theodore Roosevelt Island**

Little River
George Washington Memorial Pkwy.
66

**Kennedy Center**
**24**
E St. NW
**FOGGY BOTTOM**
18th St. NW
17th St. NW
F St. NW

C St. NW

**THE ELLIPSE**
15th St.

Theodore Roosevelt Mem. Bridge
Virginia Ave.

**Iwo Jima Memorial**

**VIRGINIA**

Constitution Ave. NW
**Vietnam Veterans Memorial**
**Lincoln Memorial**
Reflecting Pool
**WWII Memorial**
1
50
**Washington Monument**

**LADY BIRD JOHNSON PARK**
Arlington Mem. Bridge
alt.
50
Independence Ave. SW

**ARLINGTON NATIONAL CEMETERY**
Arlington Cemetery

WEST POTOMAC PARK

Washington Blvd.

Potomac River
Ohio Dr. SW

Cherry Trees
**Tidal Basin**

**FDR Memorial**
**Jefferson Memorial**

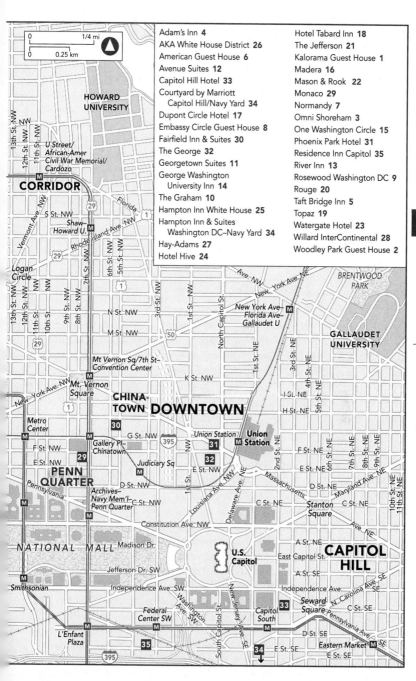

Adam's Inn **4**
AKA White House District **26**
American Guest House **6**
Avenue Suites **12**
Capitol Hill Hotel **33**
Courtyard by Marriott
    Capitol Hill/Navy Yard **34**
Dupont Circle Hotel **17**
Embassy Circle Guest House **8**
Fairfield Inn & Suites **30**
The George **32**
Georgetown Suites **11**
George Washington
    University Inn **14**
The Graham **10**
Hampton Inn White House **25**
Hampton Inn & Suites
    Washington DC–Navy Yard **34**
Hay-Adams **27**
Hotel Hive **24**

Hotel Tabard Inn **18**
The Jefferson **21**
Kalorama Guest House **1**
Madera **16**
Mason & Rook **22**
Monaco **29**
Normandy **7**
Omni Shoreham **3**
One Washington Circle **15**
Phoenix Park Hotel **31**
Residence Inn Capitol **35**
River Inn **13**
Rosewood Washington DC **9**
Rouge **20**
Taft Bridge Inn **5**
Topaz **19**
Watergate Hotel **23**
Willard InterContinental **28**
Woodley Park Guest House **2**

## Moderate

**Capitol Hill Hotel ★**  This hotel's foremost distinction is its unbeatable location: It is the only hotel in the city actually *on* Capitol Hill (on the House side of the Capitol). The property occupies two buildings on a residential street lined with old town houses. Neighbors include the Library of Congress, the Capitol, and the Supreme Court; just a block away is Pennsylvania Avenue SE's stretch of fun bars and restaurants. Guest rooms are rather ordinary in decor, but include kitchenettes with coffeemakers, microwaves, refrigerators, and utensils. Most units are studios, with the kitchenette, bed, and sofa all in the same room. Some have pullout sofas. Whatever the configuration, rooms are generally spacious, ranging in size from 320 to 510 square feet. An ample continental breakfast of baked goods, yogurt, scrambled eggs, oatmeal, sausage, cheeses, meat, and fruit is laid out each morning. A "Grab and Go" breakfast is also available in the library for guests who don't have time to linger. This is also where the hotel hosts a complimentary wine reception for guests Monday through Thursday, 5 to 6pm. Other pluses include a well-equipped fitness center and displays of original art by local artists.

200 C St. SE (at 2nd St.). www.capitolhillhotel-dc.com. ✆ 202/543-6000. 153 units. $139–$400 double. Extra person $20. Children 18 and under stay free in parent's room. Parking $50 including tax. Metro: Union Station (Massachusetts Ave. NW exit). Pets accepted ($100 fee per stay). **Amenities:** Fitness center; coin-op washer/dryers; business center; Wi-Fi (free).

**Phoenix Park Hotel ★**  This historic property, long the standard bearer for Irish fealty on Capitol Hill and throughout the capital, completed an extreme makeover in 2016. Its Irish personality still shines, in its name, in the flag of Ireland at the entrance to the Phoenix Park, and in the indomitable presence of the Irish pub, **The Dubliner** (p. 225), where the walls are paneled, the barkeep pulls drafts of Guinness and Smithwicks (pronounced "Smidicks"), and balladeers sing nightly of Molly Malone. Guest rooms remain on the small side, measuring 175 to 350 square feet. But brand-new furnishings and a fresh design make maximum use of the space: Handsome gray herringbone-patterned wood floors; simple-to-use, lightweight shades fit neatly inside the window frame; custom-made platform beds, slim desks, open shelving, and bathroom vanities; and a color scheme of steel gray and indigo blue. Other modern updates: a walk-in shower, Simmons pillowtop bedding, a 43-inch HDTV, and a mini-fridge. For best views and spaciousness, ask for a room with two queens or one king facing **Union Station** (p. 128) and/or the **National Postal Museum** (p. 125). For the quietest rooms, request a room on the top floor, to escape the sounds drifting up from both The Dubliner and traffic noise. Families appreciate the bi-level suites, with pullout sofa in the living room and, up the spiral staircase, a loft bedroom. The Phoenix Park lies just across the street from Union Station and within a short walk of the Capitol.

520 N. Capitol St. NW (at Massachusetts Ave.). www.phoenixparkhotel.com. ✆ 877/237-2082 or 202/638-6900. 149 units. $99–$359 double; $234–$599 suite. Extra person $30. Children 16 and under stay free in parent's room. Parking $50 plus tax. Metro: Union Station (Massachusetts Ave. NW exit). **Amenities:** Pub; exercise room; room service; Wi-Fi (free).

WHERE TO STAY  |  On or Near Capitol Hill

# CAPITOL RIVERFRONT

About 1 mile south of the U.S. Capitol is this up-and-coming neighborhood, its development going full throttle, spurred primarily by the opening of Nationals Park, the Washington Nationals' stadium, in 2008. The Courtyard by Marriott Capitol Hill/Navy Yard, the sole hotel here for a decade, now has three rivals, including the Hampton Inn & Suites Washington DC-Navy Yard, described below. Likewise, restaurants, apartment and office buildings, stores, bars, and parks are all on the rise. Capitol Riverfront has turned into its own destination within D.C.

**Best for:** Those with business on Capitol Hill or visitors who want to experience a young and vibrant waterfront neighborhood located just south, but within easy reach, of the city's core. And during baseball season, baseball fans!

**Drawbacks:** Sights and sounds of construction will continue on these streets for several more years to come.

## Moderate

### Courtyard by Marriott Capitol Hill/Navy Yard ★

When this hotel opened in 2006, its guests probably felt like outliers in nowheresville. No longer. This 500-acre, up-and-coming, riverfront neighborhood's beckoning features include Nationals Park, an ice rink, a waterfront walkway, pubs and breweries, an award-winning public park that stages Friday night concerts in summer and sundry festivals year-round, lots of restaurants, and a trapeze school, to boot. Glance northwards on New Jersey Avenue and you'll spot the Capitol waiting for you, just a mile away.

This Courtyard appears rather new, thanks to a 2014 renovation that replaced carpeting, wall coverings, artwork, and other features. Most rooms have king beds and a sofa bed, about 50 rooms have two queen beds, and there are 12 spacious suites. For a view of Nationals Park, ask for a room at the L Street and New Jersey corner of the hotel (for best possible views, check out the Hampton Inn & Suites Washington DC-Navy Yard, below); note, these rooms have a king bed but no pullout sofa. Other pluses: The Metro stop is 1 block away; the fitness center is available 24 hours, the pool from 5am to 11pm; a 24-hour honor-system market; and the lobby is a sea of media pods, rounded banquettes with individual TVs and outlets for charging your devices.

140 L St. SE (at New Jersey Ave.). www.marriott.com/wasny. ✆ **202/479-0027.** 204 units. $109–$359 double (rates usually are less than $250 a night). Limited parking $35 plus tax. Metro: Navy Yard/Ballpark (M St. and New Jersey Ave. exit). Service animals only allowed. **Amenities:** Restaurant; bar/lounge; fitness center; pool and hot tub; Wi-Fi (free).

### Hampton Inn & Suites Washington DC-Navy Yard ★

Baseball fans, this is your hotel. Situated directly across the street from Nationals Park, this brand new hotel has guest rooms facing the stadium from floors 9 through 14 (ask for a "park view" room), allowing for an unobstructed view of the infield, most of right field, and a bit of center field. Best rooms are nos. 1402, 1404, 1406, and 1408. Otherwise, guests and locals can enjoy an even better view, as well as cocktails and bar fare, from the rooftop Top of the Yard lounge. Here, the panoramic vista takes in not just the ballpark, but the Anacostia River, the neighborhood, and the Washington Monument and U.S. Capitol in the distance.

Year-round reasons to stay at the Hampton Inn are its location in the increasingly popular Capitol Riverfront neighborhood, not far from Capitol Hill, and its crisply new amenities and furnishings, from the ergonomic desk chair to a contemporary decor of dark woods and leather and metal accents. Everything sparkles. Meanwhile, Hampton Inn's signature features are on hand: the popular complimentary hot breakfast that includes eggs, sausage or bacon, and waffles; an "on-the-run" breakfast bag to go for those in a hurry; and a 24-hour Pavilion Pantry market in the lobby.

1265 First St. SE (at N St.). www.hamptoninnwashingtondcnavyyard.com. © **800/ HAMPTON** (426-7866) or 202/800-1000. 168 units. $155–$357 double; $195–$387 suite. (Rates are at the low end during August away games and in November and December, and at the high end during home games in baseball season.) Parking $43 including tax. Metro: Navy Yard/Ballpark (Half and M St. exit). Pets under 50 lbs. allowed (free). **Amenities:** Concierge; fitness center; coin-op laundry room; Wi-Fi (free).

# PENN QUARTER

At the center of the city is this hot locale, jammed with restaurants, bars, museums, theaters, the Verizon Center sports/concert arena, and the posh new CityCenterDC shopping arcade. The plentiful hotels include modern venues catering to convention crowds and historic properties switched up for luxury-loving funseekers.

**Best for:** Those who love being in the thick of it all. Business travelers are within easy reach of downtown offices, the convention center, and Capitol Hill. Likewise, the Penn Quarter is a prime home base for exploring tourists.

**Drawbacks:** Crowded sidewalks and noisy traffic can be annoying—even overwhelming.

## Expensive

**Hotel Monaco ★★** For deluxe accommodations in a terrific location, you can't beat the Monaco. When it was completed in 1866, this historic, four-story, marble building served as the capital's general post office and tariff building for an area that was a developing mishmash of big government and small-town buildings. Hard to imagine now. It's one of the city's top hotels, in the heart of D.C.'s hottest neighborhood, surrounded by wondrous museums, like the Smithsonian American Art/National Portrait Gallery, and trendy restaurants such as **Zaytinya** (p. 98) and **Hill Country Barbecue Market** (p. 95). A multimillion-dollar redesign in 2016 has imbued the hotel with an "elegance-meets-bold" feel. Notice the playful architectural details in each guest room, like the 5-foot lion's head medallion positioned above the bed, and the night table resembling the top of a Corinthian column, as well as the eye-catching features of the lobby/living room, with its brilliant green walls, contemporary Murano glass chandeliers, and modern art. Guest rooms are spacious, averaging about 400 square feet, and feature vaulted ceilings, long windows, and vibrant hues of bronze, plum, champagne, and royal blue. Ask for an F Street or 7th Street–facing Monte Carlo

The Willard InterContinental Hotel.

room (525 sq. ft.) for best views, or a first-floor guest room if quiet is pre-ferred (some guests call this "the basement," because it is nearly subterranean).

700 F St. NW (at 7th St.). www.monaco-dc.com. ℂ **800/649-1202** or 202/628-7177. 183 units. $179–$479 double; $459–$899 suite. Children 17 and under stay free in parent's room. Rates include complimentary coffee in morning and a hosted evening wine hour. Parking $50 including tax. Metro: Gallery Place (7th and F sts. exit). Pets welcome (free). **Amenities:** Restaurant; bar; children's amenity program; concierge; spacious fitness center; room service; Wi-Fi (free when you sign up for the no-cost loyalty program).

**Willard InterContinental** ★★★ This historic hotel's guest list has always included illustrious figures. President Abraham Lincoln actually lived here for 10 days in 1861 before moving into the White House, next door. Dr. Martin Luther King, Jr., stayed here in August 1963, finishing the writing of his historic "I Have a Dream" speech, before delivering it on August 28, from the steps of the Lincoln Memorial. And from its very start, the Willard has hosted foreign dignitaries, from Japan's first delegation to the U.S., of 3 Samurai ambassadors and their entourage of 74 in 1860 to . . . well, take a look at which head of state is on the schedule to visit President Obama, and there's a good chance that dignitary is booked at the Willard.

The spacious guest rooms are elegantly decorated with dark wood furnish-ings, shades of deep green and gold, comfortable extras like a velvet armchair and ottoman, and inviting flourishes, like the pretty, cherry blossom-embossed gold silk throw laid across the end of the plumped-up bed. Ask for courtyard-facing rooms for quiet, or Pennsylvania Avenue–facing rooms for views of the Washington Monument or the U.S. Capitol. The oval suites look directly down the avenue to the Capitol.

But you're here as much for the history and ambience as for a place to sleep. You must enjoy a cocktail at the **Round Robin Bar,** expertly mixed by

# family-friendly HOTELS

**Georgetown Suites** ★★ (p. 80)
Georgetown and all its attractions, which include not just restaurants and shops but also the C&O Canal path, tour boats on Washington Harbour, an ice-skating rink at the Harbour Complex, and even a bunch of historical sites (see the Georgetown walking tour, p. 263), are literally minutes from this hotel. Georgetown Suites has spacious suites so you can spread out, full kitchens so you can feed the hungry at any hour, and a nice complimentary breakfast down in the lobby, so you can shoo old-enough children out of the room in the morning, while you get ready for the day.

**Hotel Monaco** ★★ (p. 62)
You're in the heart of the city, literally surrounded by attractions (International Spy Museum, two Smithsonian museums, and the Verizon Center), with the National Mall just a few blocks away. The Red Line Metro stop is across the street. Meanwhile, the hotel's KimptonKids program offers welcome gifts, a list of kid-friendly activities, and the loan of high chairs, cribs, and other equipment. And as at all Kimptons, you get a goldfish delivered to your room if you so desire.

**Omni Shoreham Hotel** ★★★ (p. 81) With two pools, including a kiddie pool, loads of lawn and Rock Creek Park beyond that, the National Zoo up the street, as well as the Metro nearby, the Omni is the best hotel in town for families. The hotel sweetens the deal with its children's amenities: a backpack filled with games that your child can wear when you set off sightseeing, and cookies and milk left in the room at turndown the first night. The hotel's restaurant also offers a children's menu.

barman Jim Hewes as he tells tales about Willard guests, from Charles Dickens to Bill Clinton; stroll through the lobby and admire its mosaic floor, marble columns, and ornate ceiling; and tour the history gallery filled with memorabilia, such as a copy of Lincoln's hotel bill. Also check out the Willard's calendar. Its varied events—afternoon tea, Kentucky Derby Day soiree, Christmas tree decorating—attract as many locals as hotel guests.

1401 Pennsylvania Ave. NW (at 14th St.). www.intercontinental.com/Washington. ℂ **866/ 487-2537** or 202/628-9100. 335 units. $259–$599 double; $459–$899 basic suite. Parking $50 plus tax. Metro: Metro Center (13th and F St. exit). Small pets (up to 40 pounds) accepted ($200 nonrefundable cleaning fee). **Amenities:** Cafe w/seasonal terrace; 2 bars; seasonal afternoon tea in Peacock Alley; babysitting; complimentary chauffeur service Mon–Fri 7–9am; concierge; thoroughly equipped health club with sauna; luxurious Red Door Spa; room service; Wi-Fi (rates start at $10.95 per day).

## Moderate

**Fairfield Inn & Suites** ★★ You're really in the thick of things at this hotel, situated on a busy Chinatown street in the bustling Penn Quarter, a block north of the Verizon Center, and surrounded by hip eateries. But this is an old neighborhood, too: The bells of St. Mary Mother of God, the 1890 Catholic church across 5th Street from the Fairfield, peal from 7am to—don't worry—9pm. And if you walk down H Street to no. 604, you'll notice a historic plaque on the facade of what is now the Wok and Roll restaurant, identifying the structure as Mary Surratt's Boarding House. (Surratt conspired here with John

Wilkes Booth to assassinate President Lincoln.) The property plays up the Chinatown connection, with the color red and Chinese symbols predominating in furnishings. Most spacious are 10th-floor rooms (which also have high ceilings) and corner suites ending in "24." Fifth Street–facing rooms offer nice city views. Executive king rooms have pullout sofas. Suites and double-queen rooms have mini-fridges and microwaves, which are available upon request in king and executive king rooms. Guests also like the key-only access to elevators, the availability of a coin-operated washer/dryer, and the complimentary hot breakfast buffet, which includes eggs, sausage, and waffles.

500 H St. NW (at 5th St.). www.marriott.com/wasfc. ℂ **202/289-5959.** 198 units. $119–$399 double. Add $10 for an executive king room and $20 for a suite. Children 17 and under stay free in parent's room. Parking $42 plus tax (no oversize vehicles). Metro: Gallery Place–Chinatown (7th and H sts. exit). **Amenities:** Restaurant; bar; 24-hr. fitness center; room service; Wi-Fi (free).

# MIDTOWN

Think of the White House as center stage, with an array of hotels, law and lobbyist office buildings, and restaurants at its feet. Several historic hotels, as well as contemporary, more affordable properties, are among the options.

**Best for:** Travelers interested in a central location that's less raucous than the Penn Quarter at night. Also those on business with the executive branch or at one of the law, lobbying, or association offices that line K Street.

**Drawbacks:** Urban sounds (traffic, construction, garbage collection) may be part of the experience.

## Expensive

**The Hay-Adams ★★★** This 89-year-old hotel's tagline "Where nothing is overlooked but the White House" would be corny if it were not true. The Hay-Adams is known for its sublime service as well as for being the hotel that lies closest to the White House, and the only one with such straight-on views, best seen from guest rooms on the top floors, six through eight. (You can also see Lafayette Square, the Washington Monument, and the Jefferson Memorial.) Views in other rooms are of historic **St. John's Episcopal Church** (see p. 258) and downtown buildings. So it makes sense that views determine guest room rates. Rooms are similarly sized, about 385 square feet, and furnished with creamy white and tan toile fabrics, European linens, and marble bathrooms. The interior designs that were here when Amelia Earhart stayed at the Hay in 1928—intricate plaster moldings, walnut wainscoting, and high ceilings—are still in place. One thing that was not here then was the Off the Record bar, a regular hangout for the press and politicos. In 2015, *Travel & Leisure* magazine named the Hay-Adams to its World's Best list of top 100 hotels, coming in at #55.

800 16th St. (at H St.). www.hayadams.com. ℂ **800/853-6807** or 202/638-6600. 145 units. $329–$439 double; from $829 junior suite; from $1,299 1-bedroom suite. Two-bedroom suites available. Third person $30. Children 17 and under stay free in parent's room. Valet parking $49 plus tax. Metro: Farragut West (17th St. exit). Dogs up to 25

lbs. allowed for free; however, you will be charged for dogsitting services if you leave your dog alone in the room and for repair of any damage done to the room by your dog. **Amenities:** Restaurant; bar; concierge; state-of-the-art fitness facility; bikes (available for adults only); room service; Wi-Fi (free).

## Moderate

### Hampton Inn White House ★

Housed in the former Kiplinger Editors building located a block from the White House, the Hampton Inn opened on June 1, 2013, and started selling out immediately. Visitors, whether business or leisure, really like having a moderately priced option in this part of town, where it's possible to walk most everywhere: to the White House, the National Mall, Georgetown. For spots farther away, like the Capitol, the Metro awaits. Look for interior-design references (word plays and artful lettering) to the building's journalism roots throughout the expansive lobby, where the popular, complimentary hot breakfast includes eggs, sausage or bacon, and waffles. Another plus is

View of the White House from the Federal Suite of the Hay Adams.

the 24-hour grab-and-go market in the lobby. The hotel has 89 standard king rooms, which accommodate a maximum of two people, and 26 double queen rooms, which hold four maximum, and there are no connecting rooms (sorry, families). The hotel has a very urban feel, which means city sounds will be part of your experience and views are mainly of office buildings.

1729 H St. NW (btw. 17th and 18th sts.). www.washingtondcwhitehouse.hamptoninn.com. ✆ **800/HAMPTON** (426-7866) or 202/296-1006. 116 units. $119–$429 double. Valet parking only (height and length limits) $45 including tax. Metro: Farragut West (17th and I sts. exit). No pets. **Amenities:** Concierge; fitness center; small indoor pool; coin-op laundry room; Wi-Fi (free).

# ADAMS MORGAN

Inns and bed-and-breakfasts are far more common than hotels in Adams Morgan. In fact, the one hotel I've listed here (the Normandy) is situated just north of Dupont Circle and west of Connecticut Avenue, which is technically the Kalorama neighborhood. Oh well, it's close enough for our purposes: You just cross to the east side of Connecticut Avenue, and—presto!—you're in Adams Morgan. The B&Bs/inns, however, do lie within Adams Morgan proper.

**Best for:** Travelers who want to stay "in" the city but not downtown.

**Drawbacks:** The closest Metro stop (Dupont Circle) is several blocks away.

Travelers to Washington, D.C., who plan to visit for a week or longer should know about the centrally located **AKA White House District** ★★★ apartments/hotel, 1710 H St. NW (www.stayaka.com; ✆ **202/904-2500**). The D.C. location is one of 11 AKA properties (others are in NYC, Beverly Hills, Philadelphia, and London), all of which offer luxuriously furnished one- and two-bedroom apartments. AKA can offer tremendous value, especially when your timing is right. Check out the website to see for yourself some of the property's fine appointments and amenities, including fully equipped kitchens, stylish decor, free Wi-Fi, an on-site fitness center, and a washer/dryer in each apartment. K Street law offices, the White House, the George Washington University Museum and Textile Museum, and excellent restaurants, such as **Bombay Club** (p. 100), are just some of the property's notable neighbors. *FYI:* While AKA serves mainly as an extended stay property, it also accommodates visitors for nightly or a few nights' stay, as availability allows.

## Moderate

**The Normandy Hotel** ★★  This boutique hotel is charming, it's Parisian, and it's pretty. The six-floor Normandy lies on a tree-shaded street lined with embassies; not surprisingly, the clientele is an international mix. You're a peaceful detour right off of busy Connecticut Avenue and only minutes away, by foot, from the heart of the Dupont Circle, Adams Morgan, and Woodley Park neighborhoods. The Normandy's 75 rooms range in size, measuring between 210 and 352 square feet, and each makes good use of the space with cleverly designed and positioned furnishings: long, skinny desks; nifty little reading lamps with stems you can twist out of the walls just so; and compact Nespresso coffee machines and glass-fronted fridges placed out of the way. Front-facing rooms overlook tranquil Wyoming Avenue, while those at the back survey the courtyard. Three first-floor rooms open to a private garden terrace. Also on the first level is the parquet-floored lounge, with little sofas, armchairs, and a fireplace.

Although the Normandy is perfect for couples and solo travelers, **Avenue Suites** (see p. 76), in the same hotel family, might be a better choice for groups, large families, and those who crave a lot of space.

2118 Wyoming Ave. NW (at Connecticut Ave.). www.thenormandydc.com. ✆ **202/483-1350**. 75 units. $129–$299 double. Rates include evening wine-and-cheese hour and coffee and tea throughout the day. Extra person $20. Children 12 and under stay free in parent's room. Limited parking $34 plus tax. Metro: Dupont Circle (North/Q St. exit). Pets 20 lbs. or under allowed for a $75 non-refundable fee. **Amenities:** Free fitness passes to nearby Mint Fitness Center and 10% off services at its spa; Wi-Fi (free).

## Inexpensive

**Adam's Inn Bed & Breakfast** ★  Located on a lovely residential street, just a stone's throw from (but not within earshot of, fortunately) the rowdy Adams Morgan nightlife strip, the Adam's Inn's three 100+-year-old brick row houses hold 27 rooms that satisfy sundry needs. School groups sometimes reserve an entire house, while families with 2 or 3 children are happy to find the inn's English basement suite can accommodate them all. The more typical single and couple travelers have plenty of standard rooms from which to choose, with the option of a shared or private bath. Adam's Inn is nice but not fancy; a bed-and-breakfast, pure and simple. Guest rooms are individually decorated with comfortable furnishings, and 16 of the guest rooms have private baths. None have TVs, but there are two pleasant living rooms in which to socialize and watch TV. The inn is plumly situated close to the National Zoo, Rock Creek Park, and good restaurants and bars, and within easy access to the rest of the city. Best are its good-for-D.C. prices, especially if you take advantage of one of the discount offerings. The inn is not wheelchair accessible.

1746 Lanier Place NW (btw. Calvert St. and Adams Mill Rd.). www.adamsinn.com. ℂ **202/745-3600.** 27 units, 16 with private bath, 11 with shared bath. Rates vary widely based on room choice, shared or private bath, season, and day of week: $79–$209 room with shared bath; $89–$219 room with private bath. Rates include extensive continental breakfast. Children 8 and under free. Extra person $20. Parking $25 plus tax (only 4 spaces available), very limited street parking, plus nearby public parking garages. Pets: $100 refundable damage fee, plus $25 first pet, $10 per additional pet. Metro: Columbia Heights or Woodley Park/Adams Morgan, also DC Circulator. **Amenities:** Free computer access; Wi-Fi (free).

**American Guest House** ★ Travelers may choose this bed-and-breakfast for its appealing Dupont Circle/Adams Morgan location, its bathroom en suite guest rooms, and its reasonable rates that hold steady throughout the year. But it's chef Kevin's sumptuous breakfasts that seal the deal once they're here. (Check out the website for photos of maple bourbon banana pancakes, eggs Florentine, and lemon ginger muffins, to name a few favorites.) The B&B satisfies on other essential levels, too. The 120-year-old town house is charmingly old-fashioned, sparely decorated in places, but well maintained. Burnished paneled walls, old oak floors, and ornamental fireplaces are found throughout. The 12 guest rooms are scattered over four floors, and each room holds an antique bed with thick mattress covered in soft white linens, as well as an English secretary desk. Room 403 on the top floor is most spacious and the only room that includes a little sitting area. Rooms at the front of the house on the second and third floors nestle inside a bowed window overlooking Columbia Road. Many of the house's clientele come from around the world, say owners Lucia and Claudio Rosan, who themselves hail from Brazil. *Note:* The inn has no elevator, so is not a good choice for seniors or travelers with disabilities.

2005 Columbia Rd. NW (btw. California St. and Wyoming Ave.). www.americanguesthouse.com. ℂ **202/588-1180.** 12 units, each with private bathroom (2 have showers only). $159–$184 single; $194–$249 double. Rates include gourmet breakfast. Very limited street parking, plus nearby public parking garages. Metro: Dupont Circle (Q St. exit). **Amenities:** Free computer access in living room; Wi-Fi (free).

Guest room 16 the Taft Bridge Inn.

**Taft Bridge Inn** ★★    Housed in a 1902 Georgian-style mansion, this inn's architectural features include an exposed beam ceiling and dark-paneled wainscoting in the inviting living room, built-in china cabinets in the dining room, and high ceilings, original pine floors, and ornamental fireplaces throughout. An overall Japanese emphasis reflects the heritage of owner Yoshie Haga, who has decorated the inn with artworks and artifacts from Japan, like the framed firefighter's tunic once worn by Yoshie's father. The inn also displays remarkable items from Yoshie's many travels abroad, from Balinese placemats to a Spanish chess set with pieces (windmill, Don Quixote, and so on) that represent characters and objects from Cervantes's famous novel. Some art is Yoshie's own handiwork, such as the Japanese-fan-themed quilt hanging in the front hall. Each guest room offers unusual and lovely features, from the painted lacquered screen that hangs over the bed in room no. 18 to the spindle four-poster bed in sunny room no. 11. Perhaps room no. 20 is best favored for its roominess, built-in window seats, and cozy sitting area. Although B&Bs often pursue a warm and fuzzy ambience, this is not one of them; for example, the inn's check-in desk shuts down at 8pm, which means that if you arrive later than 8pm, the inn will charge you a late fee of $10 per hour. Also, a refrigerator on the third floor is stocked with sodas, bottled water, and juices, but guests must pay for these items. *A couple of*

*cautions:* The closest Metro stop is Dupont Circle, about 5 blocks away—a pleasant downhill stroll from the inn, a more arduous walk uphill to the inn. The inn has no elevator, so would not be a good choice for seniors or travelers with disabilities.

2007 Wyoming Ave. NW (btw. Connecticut Ave. and 20th St.). www.taftbridgeinn.com. © **202/387-2007.** 12 units, 7 with private bath, 5 with shared bath (5 bathrooms have showers only). $98–$120 single with shared bath; $179–$185 single with private bath; $140 double with shared bath; $199–$205 double with private bath. Rates include hot breakfast. Very limited parking (4 spots), $18 plus tax; otherwise limited street parking, plus nearby public parking garages. Metro: Dupont Circle (Q St. exit). **Amenities:** Free passes to nearby Washington Sports Club; vouchers for 10% discounts at select neighborhood restaurants; Wi-Fi (free).

# U & 14TH STREET CORRIDORS

Hotels abound in nearby Dupont Circle and Midtown, but in the U & 14th Street Corridors proper, only one hotel truly can claim to be in the neighborhood: Mason & Rook.

**Best for:** Travelers who prefer to stay closer to the hottest restaurants, bars, and clubs than to cultural attractions.

**Drawbacks:** Sometimes the party never ends! (Especially in pleasant weather when the hotel's rooftop lounge itself is a nightlife destination.)

## Moderate

**Mason & Rook ★★**   The conversation at check-in is all about the really good restaurants nearby, such as Le Diplomate (p. 101) and Logan Tavern (better book your restaurant reservations when you book your hotel stay). But there are plenty of other reasons to stay here: complimentary bikes, spacious guest rooms (double rooms run 300 to 425 sq. ft.; suites measure 645 sq. ft.), a rooftop pool, and the spanking-fresh newness of the property. You're meant to hang out in the living room–like lobby, with its set-up chessboard and clusters of armchairs and rounded-armed sofas; this is the site of the complimentary wine hour each evening and coffee/tea every morning. Guest rooms are equally inviting, featuring nubby gray fabrics, pumpkin-colored accents, expansive desks, enormous 65-inch TVs, large marble bathrooms with walk-in glass showers (plenty of room for two), and a truly stacked bed. The hotel's bar/lounge/restaurant includes seating around a courtyard and games to play, such as shuffleboard and checkers, and oh yeah, food: It serves breakfast, dinner, and late-night bites daily.

1430 Rhode Island Ave. NW (btw. 14th & 15th sts.). www.masonandrookhotel.com. © **800/706-1202** or 202/742-3100. 178 units, including 18 suites. $129–$429 double; $279–$599 suite. In addition to your room rate, you pay a daily "facilities fee" of $17.50 plus tax. Rates include evening wine hour 5–6pm and morning coffee and tea 6–9am weekdays/7–10am weekends. Parking $48 plus tax. Metro: McPherson Sq. (14th St. exit) or U St./Cardozo (13th St. exit). Pets allowed (free). **Amenities:** Restaurant; bar; concierge; 24-hour fitness center; rooftop pool and lounge; bikes; room service; Wi-Fi (free when you sign up for the no-cost loyalty program).

# DUPONT CIRCLE

This neighborhood of quaint town houses and beautiful embassies, bistro restaurants, art galleries, and bars is home to more hotels than any other neighborhood in the city. Boutique hotels reign supreme, though several chains have outposts here, too.

**Best for:** Travelers who love a city scene minus the office buildings. Also for gay and lesbian visitors, since Dupont Circle is GLBTQ central.

**Drawbacks:** If you have business on Capitol Hill or in the Penn Quarter, this might not be your first choice, since there are plenty of closer options.

## Expensive

**The Jefferson ★★★** If you can afford to, stay at the Jefferson, which I consider to be D.C.'s best hotel. (I'm hardly alone: *U.S. News & World Report* named the Jefferson not only the #1 hotel in D.C., but the second best hotel in the entire U.S.) And if you can't afford to, at least stop in at **Quill ★★★** (p. 227), the hotel's delightful bar, where a pianist plays jazz standards Tuesday through Saturday evenings starting at 9pm. Located slightly off the beaten track, about a half-mile north of the White House, the Jefferson exudes the ambience of a country house hotel. Decor throughout pays homage to Thomas Jefferson in all his passions, from Quill's display of 18th-century maps tracing

The Quill Bar at the Jefferson Hotel.

the oenophile's journeys through the wine regions of France, to guest-room fabrics imprinted with architectural and agricultural scenes of Monticello. A handful of rooms catch glimpses of the Washington Monument a mile away, and another few look to the White House, at the end of 16th Street; none, alas, capture the sight of the Jefferson Memorial a bit beyond. In addition to Quill and the lovely, skylit Greenhouse restaurant, the hotel's dining options include the sublime and intimate Plume restaurant, which serves seasonal menus inspired by the harvest from Thomas Jefferson's kitchen gardens at Monticello.

1200 16th St. NW (at M St.). www.jeffersondc.com. ℂ **202/448-2300.** 95 units. $320–$725 double; $800–$10,000 suite. Extra person $30. Children 18 and under stay free in parent's room. Valet parking $49 plus tax. Metro: Farragut North (L St. and Connecticut Ave. exit). Dogs welcome ($50 per stay). **Amenities:** 3 restaurants; bar/lounge; children's amenities; concierge; 24-hr. fitness center; petite spa w/massages and facials; 24-hr. room service; Wi-Fi (free).

## Moderate

**The Dupont Circle Hotel ★★**    The Dupont Circle Hotel is the sole D.C. property of the Doyle Collection, the Dublin-based hotel company. You'll hear some Irish accents here, for sure, as well as various languages of the Dupont's international clientele, some of whom have business at nearby embassies. Guest rooms are quite chic, with frosted glass doors separating bathroom from bedroom, wooden blinds on windows, and leather-wrapped headboards on beds. Level Nine is the hotel's concierge floor, offering the choice of luxury service and suites (glass balconies! hardwood floors!) at an otherwise moderately priced property. No other hotel sits right on Dupont Circle, which is the name not only for the neighborhood but also for the urban park around which the traffic swirls. The park is a performance space in its own right. So don't miss the chance to sit outside on the terrace of the Café Dupont and enjoy a drink or a meal and watch the goings-on.

1500 New Hampshire Ave. NW (across from Dupont Circle). www.doylecollection.com/hotels/the-dupont-circle-hotel. ℂ **866/534-6835** or 202/483-6000. 327 units. $130–$199 double; from $479 suite. Extra person $20. Children 17 and under stay free in parent's room. Parking $36 plus tax. Metro: Dupont Circle (either exit). Dogs 20 lb. or under allowed, with flat $150 nonrefundable fee. **Amenities:** Restaurant; bar; concierge; concierge-level rooms; state-of-the-art fitness center; room service; Wi-Fi (free).

**Embassy Circle Guest House ★★**    Housed in a turn-of-the-20th-century mansion, this upscale and sophisticated inn reflects its Embassy Row neighborhood of chancelleries and embassies and the artistic vibe of Dupont Circle. Guests enjoy complimentary wine and snacks each evening in the elegant parlor, and an extensive complimentary breakfast, including a hot entree, is served every morning in the dining room. Guest rooms take their decorative cues and their names from the antique Persian carpet displayed in each room. So room no. 124, the Pearl Gazvin, presents the carpet of that name and a creamy, tranquil decor to complement it. The Red Kashan carpet adds vivid color to its namesake, room no. 111, further enhanced by the room's brilliant paintings and furnishings. As at its sibling inn, the Woodley Park Guest

House, all of the Embassy Circle's artworks are original pieces created by artists who have stayed there. The inn also has an elevator, a rare feature of older buildings and one that comes in handy for travelers with heavy luggage or disabilities. For lovely lodging at slightly lower rates, do check out the Woodley Park Guest House (15 rooms, 11 with private bath; $125–$280 per night), located near the National Zoo. The www.dcinns.com website links you to both inns.

2224 R St. NW (at Massachusetts Ave.). www.dcinns.com. ℭ **877/232-7744** or 202/232-7744. 11 units, each with private bathroom. High season $260–$325 double, low season $180–$280 double. Limited parking; call for specific dates and information. Metro: Dupont Circle (Q St. exit). Well-behaved children 8 and older. **Amenities:** Wi-Fi (free).

**Madera ★★**   The Madera projects an earthy vibe with flashes of colorful Polynesian accents. Red, nubby terrycloth wraps the rippled headboards, and vibrant batik fabrics cover pillows and bed throws. Rooms are large and comfortable, with some offering balconies overlooking New Hampshire Avenue and the Dupont Circle neighborhood; others, on floors six and higher at the rear of the hotel, overlook some of Rock Creek Park and northwest to the Washington National Cathedral. Best are the executive king rooms, which have a small sitting area with pullout sofa. The hotel recently added four bunk-bed rooms, popular with families and girlfriends on a weekend getaway. The Madera's on-site restaurant, Firefly, remains a fave, enjoyed as much for its craft cocktails as for its seasonally driven menu.

1310 New Hampshire Ave. NW (btw. N and O sts.). www.hotelmadera.com. ℭ **800/430-1202** or 202/296-7600. 82 units. $149–$429 double; add $60 for a bunk room. Children 17 and under stay free in parent's room. Rates include complimentary morning coffee (6–9am) and hosted evening wine hour. Parking $47 plus tax. Metro: Dupont Circle (South/19th St. exit). Pets welcome (free). **Amenities:** Restaurant/bar; babysitting; bikes; children's amenity program; concierge; complimentary access to the gym at nearby sister hotel, Hotel Palomar; room service; Wi-Fi (free when you sign up for the no-cost loyalty program).

**Rouge ★**   The Rouge comes by its name honestly, as you'll note when you step across the red terrazzo tile floor in the lobby or take in the guest rooms' red faux-leather headboards and bed frames covered with red-piping-bordered white duvets. The fun continues in the dressing room, which holds a brilliant orange dresser, with a built-in minibar and goofy goodies like red wax lips. Spacious rooms easily accommodate Italian-style lounge chairs, pedestal nightstands modeled after Grecian columns, a huge mirror positioned to reflect the living-room-like space, and a 10-foot-long mahogany desk. Specialty rooms are available, including the Bunk Room, which has a space for Mom and Dad and a separate, cozy little nest of a bunk bed for the kids, with drapes to pull closed for privacy and secrets, and a tiny fridge stocked with kiddie treats.

1315 16th St. NW (at Massachusetts Ave. and Scott Circle). www.rougehotel.com. ℭ **800/738-1202** or 202/232-8000. 137 units. $109–$409 double; add $100 for the Bunk Room; $599 suite. Rates include complimentary Bloody Marys and cold pizza weekend mornings 11am–noon and hosted evening wine hour weeknights 5–6pm. Children 17 and under stay free in parent's room. Parking $45 plus tax. Metro: Dupont Circle (South-/19th St. exit). Pets welcome and pampered (free). **Amenities:** Restaurant/bar; children's amenity program; bikes; modest-sized fitness center; room service; Wi-Fi (free when you sign up for the no-cost loyalty program).

**Topaz ★★**   Other hotels may be dispensing with in-room minibars, but not Kimptons and not the Topaz; in 2017, its honor bars held goodies such as Honest Tea, Luna bars, and mineral water. And as with all Kimpton hotels, guests who sign up for the no-cost loyalty program receive a $10 credit toward minibar purchases, as well as free Wi-Fi. The minibar's exotic teas and other soothing items give you a hint that the Topaz is aiming to be an "urban oasis, a warm and tranquil escape from the hustle bustle," as the website helpfully points out. Decor throughout guest rooms leans toward tranquility, too: Comfy platform beds are triple-sheeted and topped with down comforters; furnishings are done in inky black and mesmerizing shades of purple, blue, and pale green; a yoga mat comes with the room. Rooms measure a generous 375 square feet; some have alcoves and dressing rooms. Best spots for quiet and views are N Street–facing rooms on the upper floors. Best spots for revelry are the Topaz bar to start with, then out to nearby Dupont Circle clubs for heartier times.

1733 N St. NW (btw. 17th and 18th sts., next to the Hotel Tabard Inn [see below]). www.topazhotel.com. ⓒ **800/775-1202** or 202/393-3000. 99 units. $119–$419 double; $30 more for specialty rooms; add $100–$300 for a suite. Children 17 and under stay free in parent's room. Rates include complimentary morning coffee and tea service and hosted evening wine reception. Parking $45 plus tax. Metro: Dupont Circle (North/Q St. NW). Pets welcome (free). **Amenities:** Bar/restaurant; babysitting; bikes; children's amenity program; concierge; complimentary access to nearby health club; room service; Wi-Fi (free when you sign up for the no-cost loyalty program).

## Inexpensive

**Hotel Tabard Inn ★**   Fans of quaintness and quirks will continue to find them throughout the three joined 19th-century town houses that make up the inn. Nooks, bay windows, exposed brick walls, vibrant colored walls (shades

---

### All That Jazz

For a pleasurable evening's entertainment, you sometimes need look no further than the bar/lounge or in-house restaurant of your hotel—or one nearby. The genre is usually jazz, the performers are top-notch, and the admission is free for guests and non-guests alike. So if it's a Sunday, Monday, or Tuesday night, you might want to plant yourself in the paneled parlor of the **Hotel Tabard Inn** above to listen to bassist Victor Dvoskin or another local musician play world-class jazz, usually accompanied by a guitarist or pianist. And every single night starting at 9pm (7pm on Sun), the **Phoenix Park Hotel**'s (p. 225) Dubliner restaurant is the place to be if you enjoy hoisting a pint to the tune of "Danny Boy" and rowdier Irish ballads, performed live by musicians with names like Conor Malone and Andy O'Driscoll.

of purple, or chartreuse, or periwinkle, for instance), flea-market finds, and antiques are some of the characteristics of individual guest rooms. Quaintness also means a certain creakiness throughout. There are also no televisions in guest rooms and no elevator, which can pose a challenge to those trudging upstairs with or without luggage to lodging on the third or fourth floors. The Tabard is a beloved institution to locals, who flock to the Tabard Inn's charming and highly acclaimed restaurant (p. 105) and to the adjoining paneled lounge for drinks and, on Sunday through Tuesday nights, jazz.

*Note:* Its narrow hallways and lack of elevators means the inn is not a good choice for travelers with disabilities.∂

1739 N St. NW (btw. 17th and 18th sts.). www.tabardinn.com. © **202/785-1277.** 35 units, 27 with private bathroom (6 with shower only). $125–$170 single with shared bathroom; $165–$265 single with private bathroom. Add $20 for second person. Rates include continental breakfast. Limited street parking, plus nearby public parking garages. Metro: Dupont Circle (South/19th St. exit). Small and confined pets accepted for a $25 fee. **Amenities:** Restaurant w/lounge (free live jazz Sun–Tues evenings); free computer access in lobby (printing available for small fee); free access to nearby Washington Sports Club; Wi-Fi (free).

# FOGGY BOTTOM/WEST END

This section of town is halfway between the White House and Georgetown; Foggy Bottom lies south of Pennsylvania Avenue, and the West End north. Together, the neighborhoods are home to town house–lined streets, the George Washington University, International Monetary Fund offices, World Bank headquarters, and mostly all-suites and upscale lodging choices.

**Best for:** Parents visiting their kids at GW, international business travelers, and those who desire proximity to the Kennedy Center, also located here.

**Drawbacks:** There are 10,000 undergraduate students who attend GW and who sometimes make their presence known throughout the Foggy Bottom neighborhood in ways you'd rather they wouldn't. On the flip side, the West End might seem too quiet if you like being where the action is.

## Expensive

**The Watergate Hotel** ★★★   Its design is cleverly posh but also comfortable, the service impeccable, and its Potomac River–front perch unique in the city. Nearly all guest rooms overlook the river to some degree, and 130 of the rooms have balconies. If all this sounds sweet, and if you like city sites nearby but not necessarily at your front door, you will love the Watergate. This latest iteration of the Watergate Hotel opened in June 2016, 9 years after its former self closed. New owners spent $125 million to transform the iconic structure into an "unapologetically luxurious" property, complete with a wellness floor (spa, fitness center, pool), a highly stylized modern decor (heavy on the metalwork, minimalist and streamlined furnishings, and lots of curvy artwork and other features suggesting the wavy shape of the Watergate building), and the absolute-best rooftop bar and lounge in the city. The hotel lies within the five-building Watergate complex of condos, shops, and offices, one of which made the name Watergate famous, when five men working for the Nixon presidential campaign were arrested on June 17, 1972, while breaking into and attempting to bug Democratic National Committee headquarters. Next door to the complex is the Kennedy Center. Cross Rock Creek Parkway to stroll the lovely waterfront, reaching the Lincoln Memorial if you walk south, and Georgetown harbor 5 minutes away the other direction. Thompson Boat Center, almost directly across from the hotel, rents bikes and boats. Guest rooms have minibars/fridges and large spalike bathrooms, a bathtub enclosed within the glass shower stall.

2650 Virginia Ave. NW (at Rock Creek Pkwy.). www.thewatergatehotel.com. ⓒ **844/617-1972** or 202/827-1600. 336 units, including 35 suites. Rates start in the mid-$300s for rooms and in the mid-$500s for suites. Extra person $50. Children 18 and under stay free in parent's room. Parking $44 plus tax. Pets allowed; contact hotel for exact policy. Metro: Foggy Bottom. **Amenities:** 2 restaurants; 3 bars, including seasonal rooftop bar/lounge; spa; fitness center; indoor pool; concierge; room service; Wi-Fi (free).

## Moderate

**Avenue Suites ★★** All of the 124 suites in this all-suite hotel are one-bedroom, measure a remarkably spacious 600 to 650 square feet, and include a sleeper sofa in the separate living room, a fully equipped kitchen (Whole Foods and Trader Joe's stores are nearby), and a trendy but comfortable decor, all at an affordable rate, though that varies by peak/off-peak times. I also like Avenue's prime location (on the cusp of Georgetown and within walking distance of the White House, a Metro stop, and other attractions) and that guests get pool privileges at nearby sister hotel, One Washington Circle (see below). The hotel's bar and terrace lounge, with its comfy furniture, fire pit, and green garden wall, is a charming place to enjoy the nightly happy hour, as the city's 20-somethings often do. *Note:* Interior rooms at the back of the house overlook the lounge, so during the warm seasons you might want to try for a top-floor room on the 25th Street side.

2500 Pennsylvania Ave. NW (at 25th St.). www.avenuesuites.com. ⓒ **888/874-0100** or 202/333-8060. 124 units. Peak: $276–$349, off-peak: $129–$239. Extra person $20. Children 12 and under stay free in parent's room. Parking $42 plus tax. Pets $25 per day. Metro: Foggy Bottom. **Amenities:** Bar; concierge; fitness center; room service; Wi-Fi (free).

**The River Inn ★★** Nestled among quaint town houses on a quiet side street a short walk away from the Kennedy Center, Georgetown, the White House, and the Foggy Bottom Metro station, the River Inn is a comfortable refuge for all sorts except rabble-rousers. Most of the units in the all-suite property are studios, in which the bedroom and living room are combined; 33 units are one-bedrooms, which are roomier and include either a king-size bed or two double beds, as well as a second TV in the separate bedroom. All guest rooms provide a full kitchen, bed topped with pillowtop mattress, cushy armchair, a sophisticated decor, and a sleeper sofa. Upper-floor suites offer views of the Potomac River and two, nos. 702 and 802, catch sight of the Washington

Monument. (These are always in demand, so seldom available.) Complimentary bikes (based on availability), on-site coin-operated laundry machines, a "stock-the-fridge" program that allows guests to have groceries waiting for them in advance of their stay, and an especially gracious staff are among the pluses that keep the inn steeped in bookings from happy repeat customers.

924 25th St. NW (btw. K and I sts.). www.theriverinn.com. (C) **888/874-0100** or 202/337-7600. 125 units. Peak weekdays $239–$399 double, weekends $179–$350 double; off-peak weekdays $179–$269 double, weekends $169–$259 double. Add $30 for upgrade from studio to 1-bedroom suite. Extra person $20. Children 17 and under stay free in parent's room. Rates include complimentary seasonal cocktails during nightly social hour 5–6pm. Parking $40 plus tax. Metro: Foggy Bottom. Pets welcome for $25 per day. **Amenities:** Restaurant; bar; bikes; concierge; small fitness center; room service; Wi-Fi (free).

## Inexpensive

**George Washington University Inn** ★   The GWU Inn prides itself on being old-school traditional. Rooms have flat-screen TVs, but they're housed in armoires. A tiny bar lies right off the lobby, and that's what it is, a bar, not a lounge, not a scene, not the domain of a clever mixologist (although "craft cocktails" *are* on the menu). Decor recalls Williamsburg, but you need to know that the green and gold hues are the school colors of GW, with whom the hotel is affiliated. If you're looking for easy, comfortable, and quiet lodging in a charming old neighborhood (rooms at the back of the hotel overlook quaint, colorfully painted town houses), at a rate lower than $200 a night, you'll like this place. Those affiliated with GW get a further discount of up to 18%.

Rooms are of three types: standard guest rooms with either two full beds or one king bed; studio suites that hold a king bed, sleeper sofa, and kitchenette in one room; and one-bedroom suites, in which the bedroom is separate from the living room and kitchenette. All are spacious and range in size from 400 square feet for the standard guest room to about 600 square feet for the one-bedroom.

The hotel's Notti Bianchi restaurant is quite good, and its pre-theater dinner recommended if you're headed to the nearby Kennedy Center. *Two tips:* If you've bought tickets to a Kennedy Center performance, you can take 10% off the hotel's best available rate when booking your reservation. Also, street parking is free on Sundays.

824 New Hampshire Ave. NW (btw. H and I sts.). www.gwuinn.com. (C) **202/337-6620.** 95 units. Peak (Mar–June, Sept, Oct): Mon–Wed $249–$279, Thurs–Sun $179–$209; off-peak (July–Aug, Nov–Feb): Mon–Wed $199–$229, Thurs–Sun $109–$149. Extra person $20. Children 12 and under stay free in parent's room. Parking $40 plus tax. Metro: Foggy Bottom. Pets accepted (free). **Amenities:** Restaurant; bar; fitness center; room service; Wi-Fi (free).

**Hotel Hive** ★★   The Hotel Hive is the capital's first micro-hotel, and it is adorable, from its tag line—"Buzz More. Spend Less."—to its individual decorative elements that cleverly maximize the use of space. Let's start with the guest rooms, which average 250 square feet in size, with some a little smaller, some a little larger. Most rooms have queen beds, some have bunk beds, and all rooms have their own private bathroom. Pocket doors, cubbies beneath platform beds, and built-in nightstands and plasma-screen TVs help create an uncluttered feel. Hexagonal outlines suggesting hives crop up in carpet designs, headboard fabrics, and in bathroom amenities bearing the special Hotel Hive logo. The Hive concept derived in part from the 115-year-old building's unique architectural feature, a hexagonal pocket punctuating the western end of each floor in the six-level structure. On the first floor, the hotel's cool bar occupies the space, and beyond, joining up with &Pizza, a local favorite restaurant; on the rooftop terrace, the hive area is incorporated into a seasonal cocktail lounge proffering views of the Lincoln Memorial. On all other levels, the turret holds the best rooms in the house, with six windowed walls letting in lots of light and neighborhood views, and connecting, if desired, to the bunk bed room next door: voila, instant suite. Although the budget rates and small rooms may speak most to millennials, families should consider the hotel, too. The Hive's location is pretty sweet: at the edge of George Washington University's campus, close to the Foggy Bottom Metro station, up the street from the Kennedy Center, and within walking distance of the National Mall.

2224 F St. NW (at Virginia Ave.). www.hotelhive.com. 𝄞 **888/874-0100.** 83 units. $125 to $180 year-round, with higher prices expected during peak occasions, such as cherry blossom season and the presidential inauguration. Children 16 and under stay free in parent's room. Check the website for parking rates and other details, which were still being decided at press time. Metro: Foggy Bottom. No pets. **Amenities:** Restaurant; bar; Wi-Fi (free).

## One Washington Circle Hotel ★

Even this hotel's smallest room (measuring 390 sq. ft.) is more spacious than the largest room at some other D.C. hotels. The biggest suites here encompass more than 700 feet. All of the rooms are suites, with separate full kitchens in 90% of the units and kitchenettes in the remainder. Families especially love the outdoor pool, the on-site restaurant, and the location near the Foggy Bottom Metro stations, Georgetown, and the White House. Most rooms have walkout balconies. One Washington Circle is situated, as it sounds, right on Washington Circle, and across from the George Washington University Hospital. Double-paned windows help screen some of the siren sounds, but for quietest sleep, ask for a room on the eighth or ninth floor facing L Street or New Hampshire Avenue. George Washington University–affiliated guests may be eligible for discounts.

1 Washington Circle NW (btw. 22nd and 23rd sts. NW). www.thecirclehotel.com. 𝄞 **800/424-9671** or 202/872-1680. 151 units. Weekdays $159–$299 smallest suites, $199–$339 largest suites; weekends $109–$199 smallest suites, $159–$239 largest suites. Call hotel or check the website for the best rates, including special offers. Extra person $20. Children 12 and under stay free in parent's room. Rates include complimentary wine and appetizers from 5–6pm nightly in the lobby. Parking weekdays $40 plus tax, weekends $25 plus tax. Metro: Foggy Bottom. Pets accepted (free). **Amenities:** Restaurant; bar; fitness center; outdoor pool; room service; Wi-Fi (free).

# GEORGETOWN

Bustling day and night with shoppers and tourists, Georgetown's handful of hotels range from the city's most sublime accommodations to one that offers good value, especially for families.

**Best for:** Shopaholics; tourists; and parents, students, and academics visiting Georgetown University.

**Drawbacks:** Crowds throng sidewalks; cars snarl traffic daily. College kids and 20-somethings party hearty here nightly, but especially on weekends.

## Expensive

**The Graham ★★** The Graham Georgetown is named for the inventor of the telephone, Alexander Graham Bell, who once lived and worked nearby (who knew?). The seven-story hotel holds 57 rooms, nearly half of them standard guest rooms with a king bed; the rest are suites, either junior or full, each with a king bed. Largest are king suites, which have a king-size pullout sofa in the separate living room. Each unit is similarly and stylishly decorated in shades of grays, whites, and pale blue, with white, tufted-leather headboards on beds made up in Irish linens. The pretty bathrooms feature white marbled floors and walls, Mexican accent tiles, and L'Occitane amenities. On the lower level lies the restaurant, the Alex (after you-know-who), and the seasonal (spring through fall) Observatory rooftop bar offers one of the best views in town; it wraps around the building, so you're able to take in Georgetown and the cityscape, including the Washington Monument. The bar attracts a sea of scene-seeking Washingtonians, which means 1) you must reserve a spot, and 2) you might want to consider wearing something trendy, though not too trendy: There's a dress code!

1075 Thomas Jefferson St. NW (just below M St.). www.thegrahamgeorgetown.com. ☏ **855/341-1292** or 202/337-0900. 57 units. $239–$329 king room; $349–$489 king suite. Extra person $25. Children under 8 stay free in parent's room. Parking $48 plus tax. Metro: Foggy Bottom. No pets. **Amenities:** Restaurant; rooftop bar; concierge; exercise room; room service; Wi-Fi (free).

**Rosewood Washington DC ★★★** The Rosewood is unabashedly and decadently luxurious. Butlers are at your service 24/7. The hotel has a resident stylist, who is available to take you on after-hours shopping sprees at Saks Fifth Avenue and other upscale retailers, or will shop for you. Would you like to surprise your tiny dancer with a walk-on role in the Washington Ballet's performance of *The Nutcracker,* or a chance to sit in on rehearsal? Done. And then there are the practical pluses, like the hotel's flexible check-in/checkout policy; the complimentary continental breakfast available in the hotel's Living Room; and the stock of free juice, bottled water, coffee, and sodas on hand in each guest room. The Rosewood sits alongside the C&O Canal, and some of its 49 rooms overlook the canal, as do the bar and the seasonal outdoor terrace: very nice. Rooms range in size from 359 to 504 square feet; suites go up from there. Guest-room furnishings make fashion statements with their mix of contemporary accents, dark hardwood floors, and pewter lamps. A rooftop lounge includes a fitness center, indoor/outdoor relaxation pool, and views of Georgetown, the Kennedy Center, a bit of the Potomac River, and the Washington Monument. The Rosewood's Rye Bar is a hot spot, while the Grill Room restaurant, with D.C.'s own highly acclaimed chef Frank Ruta at the helm, is considered one of the city's top 10 restaurants.

1050 31st St. NW (below M St.). www.rosewoodhotels.com/washington-dc. © **888/767-3966** or 202/617-2400. 49 units. Off-peak from $595 double, from $1,545 suite. Peak from $626 double, from $2,295 suite. Rates include complimentary continental breakfast daily. Parking $52 plus tax. Metro: Foggy Bottom. Pets accepted; fees may apply. **Amenities:** Restaurant; 2 bars; babysitting; children's programs; concierge; rooftop fitness center and relaxation pool; in-room spa services; room service; Wi-Fi (free).

## Inexpensive

**Georgetown Suites ★★**   This is a two-location hotel, with one building on 30th Street, and the second building one street over and down the block, on 29th Street.

The pros: The 30th Street address is unbeatable, just off busy M Street in Georgetown, seconds away from the picturesque C&O Canal and its towpath, but also nearby posh shops and fun restaurants and bars. Staff is cheery. Suites are quite spacious (studios measure 500 sq. ft., one-bedrooms 800 sq. ft.). All have full kitchens, which in 2014 received new flooring, cabinetry, appliances, and granite countertops. The same renovation replaced old bed frames with platform beds, changed out desks and dressers, added luxury linens, and installed a new state-of-the-art wireless Internet system. The hotel also has updated artwork, wall coverings, and color schemes in the guest rooms. The expanded and updated lobby lounge is the location for a complimentary continental breakfast. The hotel's Harbour Building on 29th Street lies just across from the Washington Harbour complex (attractions there include waterfront restaurants, tour boats that cruise the Potomac River, and an ice-skating rink that is the largest outdoor rink in the city). The Harbour Building's guest rooms and lobby underwent their own massive renovation in 2016, replacing furnishings, drapes, kitchen equipment, the works.

The cons: The 30th Street building has a whiff of college campus about it, thanks to its architecture and layout, and a clientele often made up of college-visiting students. The noise of traffic and revelers is an annoying factor for rooms on the lower floors of the 30th Street building, despite the hotel's recessed position off the street. The Harbour Building lies right next to the Whitehurst Freeway, so rooms facing the freeway get those unattractive views and the din of traffic, though double-paned and insulated windows somewhat muffle the sound. The hotel is a bit of a hike ($\frac{2}{3}$ mile) to the closest Metro station.

Conclusion: You won't find better value in Georgetown, and even in the city, especially in the summer, when weekend specials can go as low as $115 a night. At the 30th Street location, ask for a room on an upper floor, or if budget allows, consider one of the two-level, two-bedroom town houses or one of the penthouse suites, with terraces that overlook Georgetown rooftops. At the 29th Street location, ask for a courtyard-side suite or the stunning two-level penthouse suite, with a wall of windows that captures sweeping views of the Potomac, the Kennedy Center, and the bustling waterfront.

1111 30th St. NW (just below M St.) and 1000 29th St. NW (at K St.). www.georgetown-suites.com. © **800/348-7203** or 202/298-7800. 221 units. Weekdays $180 studio, $215 1-bedroom suite; weekends $155 studio, $185 1-bedroom suite; penthouse suites from $350; town houses from $425. Rollaway or sleeper sofa $10 extra. Rates include continental breakfast. Limited parking $35 including tax. Metro: Foggy Bottom. **Amenities:** Small exercise room; Wi-Fi (free).

# WOODLEY PARK

This Connecticut Avenue–centered upper northwest enclave is a residential neighborhood of little stores and restaurants, the National Zoo, and two of Washington's biggest hotels. In addition to the properties described here, consider the Woodley Park Guest House, mentioned in the writeup for its sister inn, the Embassy Circle Guest House (p. 72), in the Dupont Circle neighborhood.

**Best for:** Families who like a tamer experience than found downtown and proximity to Rock Creek Park and the zoo. Business travelers attending a meeting in one of Woodley Park's big hotels.

**Drawbacks:** This area may be a little too quiet for some, especially at night.

## Moderate

**Omni Shoreham Hotel ★★★**   Step from the jammed-up streets of D.C. into the Omni Shoreham's lovely and enormous lobby and it really does feel like you've arrived at a resort. It's the towering ceiling, the chandeliers, and the sheer expanse of lobby leading back down through the dining room and out the French doors to the terrace and the acres of landscaped lawns, all backing up to Rock Creek Park. Truly, one of the pleasures of staying here is exploring the premises. Poke your head in the Palladian Ballroom to inspect its muraled scenes of Monticello or check out the Diplomat Ballroom, which is modeled after the East Room of the White House. The Omni Shoreham was built in 1930 as a hotel and apartment building, so its guest rooms are of varying sizes and interesting shapes. For best views and quiet, ask for a park-view room at the back, preferably with a balcony (15% of the rooms have them), and within sight of the Washington Monument. You should also opt for the Omni Select Guest Loyalty program (it's free), which gets you free Wi-Fi upon signing up, plus a bundle of other privileges, such as morning beverage room service, pressing service, and shoe shine, on subsequent stays at Omni

# NEW HOTELS ARE popping up ALL OVER

Washington, D.C., is in the middle of a hotel construction boom; the *Washington Business Journal* reports that at least 21 properties (some, like the L'Enfant Plaza Hotel, undergoing a rebirth, but most of totally new construction) are in the pipeline for completion by 2018. That's a lotta lodging!

This fresh crop of hotels points to certain trends, like the introduction of the city's first "micro" hotels; that is, hotels whose guest rooms are "podlike," measuring no more than 250 square feet. The appeal? The price: $125 per night is the anticipated rate.

And then there's the new geography in which these hotels are suddenly popping up: NoMa, Southwest Waterfront, Capitol Riverfront, Mount Vernon Square. Sound familiar? Probably not. But these neighborhoods are where big things are happening, as D.C.'s economy continues to flourish, attracting developers, entrepreneurs, and residents to explore new pockets. In fact, the city's biggest new hotel (the city's biggest hotel now, period, with 1,175 rooms), the **Marriott Marquis Washington, D.C.,** is located in a freshly revitalized quarter called Mount Vernon Square, due north of the greater downtown area. The hotel, which opened in May 2014, is the Walter E. Washington Convention Center's hotel, and is connected to it by underground passage.

So be sure also to check out some of the lesser-known areas (see chapter 3 for neighborhood descriptions), where new hotels are opening all the time. Because here's the thing: You just might be able to negotiate a better rate at a hotel in an off-the-radar neighborhood, you'll enjoy individual characteristics not found elsewhere (like the Waterfront's waterfront!), and you can be assured that no matter the neighborhood, you're never far from the center of town in this compact city. Here's a rundown of some of the hotels that debuted in late 2016 or are slated to open in 2017.

**Adams Morgan:** The Line DC, 1780 Columbia Rd. NW (www.sydellgroup. com/line/washington-dc/hotel; phone number not available at time of research).

**National Mall:** L'Enfant Plaza, 480 L'Enfant Plaza SW (www.lenfantplaza hotel.com; ✆ **202/484-1000**).

**NoMa:** Homewood Suites by Hilton Washington DC NoMa Union Station, 501 New York Ave. NE (http://homewood suites3.hilton.com; ✆ **202/393-8001**).

**Southwest Waterfront:** Canopy by Hilton, Maine Ave. and 7th St. SW (www. canopybyhilton.com); Hyatt House, Maine Ave. and 7th St. SW (http://house.hyatt. com); Wharf InterContinental Hotel Washington DC, Water and 9th sts. SW (www. intercontinental.com). (Phone numbers for all three not available at time of research.)

**Capitol Riverfront:** Homewood Suites, 50 M St. SE (http://homewoodsuites3. hilton.com/en/index.html; phone number not available at time of research).

**Penn Quarter:** Pod DC, 627 H St. NW (www.modushotels.com; ✆ **202/331-3800**); Moxy Hotel by Marriott, 11th and K Sts. NW (http://moxy-hotels.marriott. com; phone number not available at time of research).

hotels. The Omni attracts a lot of groups, thanks to its size (11 acres, 836 rooms, 24 meeting rooms, several ballrooms), but families love it, too, for its large seasonal pool and smaller kiddie pool, children's amenities (backpack of games given at check-in, cookies and milk delivered on the first evening), its

A winter scene in the Woodley Park neighborhood, home to the Kalorama Guest House.

on-site restaurants, and its proximity to Rock Creek Park and the National Zoo.

2500 Calvert St. NW (near Connecticut Ave.). www.omnihotels.com/dc. © **800/843-6664** or 202/234-0700. 834 units. $159–$359 double; from $350 suite. Extra person $30. Children 17 and under stay free in parent's room. Parking $49 including tax. Metro: Woodley Park–Zoo. Pets under 25 lb. allowed; $50 cleaning fee. **Amenities:** 2 restaurants; bar and seasonal poolside bar; children's amenities program; concierge; fitness center w/heated outdoor pool, separate kids' pool, whirlpool, and spa services; room service; Wi-Fi (free when you sign up for the loyalty program).

## Inexpensive

**Kalorama Guest House ★** Kalorama's rambling red-brick house blends right in among the large town houses and family dwellings in this residential neighborhood. Built in 1910, the house retains an old-timey feeling about it. That's partly due to its 117-year-old design: old wood floors, fireplaces (decorative only) in lots of rooms, paneled wainscoting along the stairwell, a tin ceiling here and there. And it's partly due to the furnishings, which come from estate sales and antiques auctions. Owner Jack Shrestha adds to the homey feel, fussily offering cookies and coffee and pointing out the communal family room, kitchen, and laundry room facilities, even as he's pulling out photos of his 4-year-old daughter. (Speaking of children, Shrestha notes that the inn is best for well-behaved children over 6.) Least expensive rooms are two in the basement that share a bathroom; these two rooms, plus a large room on this floor with its own television, have their own entrance from the street. Basement rooms, by the way, do have windows, and are as pleasantly furnished as any upstairs. Nicest, in my opinion, is the sole room on the first floor; built-in bookcases and a sleigh bed are part of its charm. You're in a great area, with the zoo, good restaurants, Rock Creek Park, and the Woodley Park Metro stop all within a short walk.

2700 Cathedral Ave. NW (off Connecticut Ave.). www.kaloramaguesthouse.com. © **202/588-8188.** 10 units, 8 w/private bath. $99–$249 single or double. Rates include continental breakfast and afternoon refreshment of lemonade and cookies. Extra person (including children) $25. Street parking permit $20 plus tax. Metro: Woodley Park–Zoo. **Amenities:** Wi-Fi (free).

# WHERE TO EAT

Finding the cuisine of your dreams is easy in Washington, where upward of 1,000(!) restaurants present a world's choice of options, whether you crave sushi or a luscious boeuf bourguignon. Scoring a table can be the tricky part: Washingtonians dine out a lot. A LOT. Wheeler-dealers and socializing urbanistas fill restaurants throughout the city, from the U & 14th Street Corridors, where the newest and hottest eateries proliferate, to the White House neighborhood's upscale fine-dining establishments. Be sure to make a reservation.

The city is also notable for its casual dining, and often the food is as sensational in these places as at the higher-priced D.C. restaurants. If you're a fan of tacos, pizza, and burgers, you'll love the appealing versions at **Tacqueria Nacional** (p. 103), **Matchbox** (p. 96), and **Good Stuff Eatery** (p. 91). Asian cuisine is a sweeping favorite, with **Doi Moi** (p. 102) and **Daikaya** (p. 99) among the most popular eateries. The popularity of José Andrés's vegetarian fast-food joint, **Beefsteak** (p. 108), on the George Washington University campus, signals the sway of vegetable lovers in a town long associated with red meat establishments. Bistros serving "small plates" of delicious tastes are clearly here to stay, no matter whether the cuisine is Italian, as at **Graffiato** (p. 95), or the Middle Eastern *mezze* of **Zaytinya** (p. 98). Some restaurants, like **Hank's Oyster Bar** (p. 106), hedge their bets with a menu that offers both "small plates" and "large plates." Finally, you should know that a boisterous bar scene is now a dining-out fact of life. And it can get loud.

Good restaurants are in every neighborhood, and this chapter leads you to a range of options, spanning diverse cuisines and budget considerations. Be sure to get advance reservations either over the phone or through such sites as OpenTable.com.

## ATLAS DISTRICT

### Inexpensive

**Ethiopic** ★ ETHIOPIAN  The greater Washington, D.C., area is said to have the largest Ethiopian community in the world, outside of Africa. Ethiopian cuisine, likewise, has found a place for itself in D.C.'s expansive dining scene, as immigrants eager to introduce Washingtonians to the authentic tastes of their country open

# Washington, D.C., Restaurants

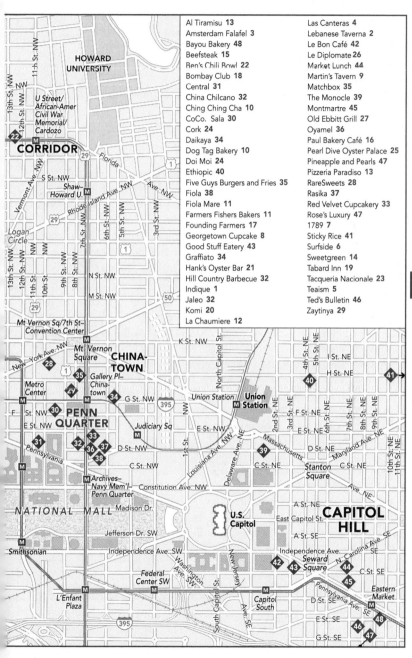

Al Tiramisu **13**
Amsterdam Falafel **3**
Bayou Bakery **48**
Beefsteak **15**
Ben's Chili Bowl **22**
Bombay Club **18**
Central **31**
China Chilcano **32**
Ching Ching Cha **10**
CoCo. Sala **30**
Cork **24**
Daikaya **34**
Dog Tag Bakery **10**
Doi Moi **24**
Ethiopic **40**
Five Guys Burgers and Fries **35**
Fiola **38**
Fiola Mare **11**
Farmers Fishers Bakers **11**
Founding Farmers **17**
Georgetown Cupcake **8**
Good Stuff Eatery **43**
Graffiato **34**
Hank's Oyster Bar **21**
Hill Country Barbecue **32**
Indique **1**
Jaleo **32**
Komi **20**
La Chaumiere **12**

Las Canteras **4**
Lebanese Taverna **2**
Le Bon Café **42**
Le Diplomate **26**
Market Lunch **44**
Martin's Tavern **9**
Matchbox **35**
The Monocle **39**
Montmartre **45**
Old Ebbitt Grill **27**
Oyamel **36**
Paul Bakery Café **16**
Pearl Dive Oyster Palace **25**
Pineapple and Pearls **47**
Pizzeria Paradiso **13**
RareSweets **28**
Rasika **37**
Red Velvet Cupcakery **33**
Rose's Luxury **47**
1789 **7**
Sticky Rice **41**
Surfside **6**
Sweetgreen **14**
Tabard Inn **19**
Tacqueria Nacionale **23**
Teaism **5**
Ted's Bulletin **46**
Zaytinya **29**

restaurants here. In other words, if you're already a fan of Ethiopian food or are curious to try it, D.C. is the place. And Ethiopic remains the best. Vegetarians, especially, rave about the vegetarian sampler: simmered collard greens; curried potatoes simmered with red onion, garlic, jalapeño pepper, olive oil, and herbs; split lentils in a spicy sauce; and yellow split peas cooked with onions and herbs. Located at the corner of H and 4th streets, it's also a great people-watching spot, as the restaurant overlooks both streets through front- and side-wall windowfronts (in good weather, ask for sidewalk seating).

401 H St. NE (at 4th St.). www.ethiopicrestaurant.com. ☏ **202/675-2066.** Reservations recommended. Main courses $14–$35, most items under $15. Tues–Thurs 5–10pm; Fri–Sun noon–10pm. Metro: Union Station, then walk, take a taxi, or ride the streetcar.

**Sticky Rice** ★ ASIAN FUSION    Turns out tater tots are a fabulous accompaniment to sushi, sashimi, noodles, and Sapporo beer. That's one of the lessons learned at Sticky Rice, one of the older restaurants in the Atlas District (it's been around for 8 years) but still one of the hottest. All sorts—girlfriend groups, families, couples, and hipsters full of attitude—flock to this sprawling, casual, three-storefront Asian eatery. Lesson #2? Entertainment along with food will keep a place popular. So when you head to Sticky Rice, expect all sorts of interesting things to be going on, like screenings of old Jamie Lee Curtis movies and karaoke nights. All of this doesn't overshadow the food, which includes elaborately presented and fresh-tasting sushi; noodle dishes of all sorts (like one with a topping of spicy shrimp and coconut, or the noodles in a mock-chicken Szechuan entree that vegetarians love); and those terrific tater tots. Order a bucket ($8.50) for the table, or a side ($5) for two people, of either regular or sweet-potato tots.

1224 H St. NE (btw. 12th and 13th sts.). www.stickyricedc.com. ☏ **202/397-7655.** Reservations recommended. Main courses at lunch/dinner/brunch $14 and under. Sun–Wed 11:30am–10:30pm; Thurs–Sat 11:30am–11pm. Metro: Union Station, then walk, take a taxi, or ride the streetcar.

# CAPITOL HILL & BARRACKS ROW

Along with the recommendations below, for solid diner fare and lively local color, I recommend **Pete's Diner and Carryout.** Also see "Eating with the Insiders" box, p. 92.

## Expensive

**The Monocle** ★ AMERICAN   Is the Monocle another branch of the U.S. government? It sometimes feels that way. Senators, representatives, Supreme Court justices, and their staffs often dine here at lunch and dinner, as they have since 1960, when the Monocle opened. (The Monocle backs up to Senate Office Building property.) Owner John Valanos, maitre'd Nick, and longtime staff greet frequent customers by name and with warmth, whether the patron is a lobbyist or a Senator. There's no other place like it in the capital. The food's pretty good, too. Usually the best picks are the specials, the salads (especially the Federal Salad and the BLT Salad), and the shrimp and asparagus orzo. Enjoy a meal at the bar after 5pm for the best deal going: a pair of cheddar cheese and bacon-topped angus beef sliders for $6.50.

107 D St. NE (at 2nd St.). www.themonocle.com. © **202/546-4488.** Reservations recommended. Main courses lunch $12–$35; dinner $16–$42. Mon–Fri 11:30am–3:45pm and 5–10pm. Metro: Union Station (Massachusetts Ave. exit).

**Pineapple and Pearls** ★★★ MODERN AMERICAN   Stop by Pineapple and Pearls during the day and you'll be introduced to the coffee bar, a bright and tiny spot with three or four stools at the windowfront, and sidewalk seating beneath an awning. Four little iced buns lie naked on the white and gray marbled counter, and there's a barista operating an impressive-looking coffee machine. Order, say, the signature pineapple and pearls bun and the fried chicken sandwich from the very short menu, and the barista's assistant disappears behind a curtain. Minutes go by. There are no smells of buns baking or fried chicken frying. Then suddenly, magically it seems, the curtain parts, the assistant reappears, and she presents you with a pretty little gold-flecked white box holding your freshly prepared sandwich and a tidy little white bakery bag holding your still-warm bun, and together they fit, just so, inside a black bag. They will turn out to be the best breakfast bun and fried chicken sandwich you have ever tasted.

The coffee bar is the teaser. What you want is to get beyond that curtain to the dining room. That's where the real magic happens. Tuesday through Friday nights, chef/owner Aaron Silverman's able staff create an improbably wondrous menu of 15 items, starting with a fennel and absinthe bonbon, going on to the likes of spring garlic egg drop and mole-smoked beef rib, and finishing with Chartreuse, Campari, Grappa, and Nardini donuts (just an example—the menu is always changing). The only way to reserve a table is to use P&P's dedicated booking system on its website. You have two price options: Pay $250 per person, everything included—meal, beverages, tax, and gratuity—and sit either at a table for two or four in the softly lit, stylishly white-and-black-toned dining room, or at the chef's counter; or pay $150 per person, everything included but the beverages, and sit at the handsome wooden bar, where you can order as much or as little to drink as you like.

5

As at Rose's Luxury (p. 90), also owned by Silverman, the overall attention to details, decor to cuisine to charming service, are likely to win you over.

715 8th St. SE (at G St.). www.pineappleandpearls.com. Reservations required. Prix fixe $250 all-inclusive (dinner, drinks, tax, and tip) per person in the dining room and at the chef's table; prix fixe $150 (includes all but the drinks) per person at the bar. Coffee bar Tues–Fri 8am–2pm, Sat 8am–4pm; dining room Tues–Fri 5–9:15pm. Metro: Eastern Market.

## Moderate

**Montmartre** ★★ FRENCH   When it opened down the street from Eastern Market in 2002, Montmartre stood out for being so good and so genuinely French. (Capitol Hill's restaurant scene wasn't much to speak of back then.) Its wooden tables, yellow-splashed walls, ceiling fans, tiny bar, and sidewalk cafe looked like a little bistro you'd find in Paris. The French owner welcomed you, and the chef served up French country specialties of duck confit, country pâté, hangar steak, mussels, braised rabbit, crème brûlée, and gratins of this and that. None of that has changed. Should you pop by without reservations and the place is full, you'll be directed next door to Seventh Hill, Montmartre's pizza bistro, which also serves fine salads, sandwiches, and soups.

327 7th St. SE (at Pennsylvania Ave.). www.montmartredc.com. ⓒ **202/544-1244.** Reservations recommended. Main courses brunch $11–$21, lunch $11–$25, dinner $20–$29. Tues–Fri 11:30am–2:30pm; Sat–Sun 10:30am–3pm; Tues–Thurs 5:30–10pm; Fri–Sat 5:30–10:30pm; Sun 5:30–9pm. Metro: Eastern Market.

**Rose's Luxury** ★★★ AMERICAN   Critics declared this quirky little labor-of-love in Barracks Row one of D.C.'s best restaurants almost as soon as it opened in October 2013. America's "best new restaurant" (*Bon Appétit* magazine 2014) and "Best Chef in the Mid-Atlantic" (2016 James Beard Foundation Award) are among the many accolades both the restaurant and its chef/owner Aaron Silverman have received. Its success comes down to endearing service, an eclectic decor of antiques and pretty fabrics and china, and a simple menu of unexpected combinations of tastes. Though the menu changes frequently, it almost always includes a pork sausage, habanero, and lychee salad among its small plates, and the smoked brisket served with white bread and horseradish, one of two dishes served family style. Rose's does not accept reservations, a policy a lot of people really hate. But the thing to do is to arrive an hour in advance of the time you'd like to eat, get on the list and give the receptionist your cellphone number, then head upstairs to the cute bar for a drink, or wander 8th Street until the restaurant calls to say your table is ready. Rose's does accept reservations for its fine-dining sibling **Pineapple and Pearls** (see above) right next door.

717 8th St. SE (btw. G and I sts.). www.rosesluxury.com. ⓒ **202/580-8889.** Small plates $13–$16, family-style plates $29–$30. Mon–Sat 5–10pm. Metro: Eastern Market.

**Ted's Bulletin** ★ AMERICAN   Ted's Bulletin calls itself a family restaurant, and it is, but many of the "children" who come here are in their 20s and

Chefs planning a meal at Rose's Luxury.

30s and they're drinking milkshakes laced with coconut rum ("Toasted Coconut") or maybe vodka and Kahlúa ("White Russian"). So it can get rowdy. What you'll enjoy, besides the retro decor, is the well-done, comfort-food menu: grilled cheese, tomato soup, fried chicken, mac and cheese, barbecued chicken, chili, sloppy joes, and breakfast items (which are served all day). Ted's Bulletin has another District location at 1818 14th St. NW (© **202/265-8337**), in the U & 14th Street Corridors.

505 8th St. SE (at E St.). www.tedsbulletin. com. © **202/544-8337.** Reservations accepted. Main courses breakfast and lunch $10–$16, dinner $17–$25. Sun–Thurs 7am–10:30pm, Fri–Sat 7am—11:30pm. Metro: Eastern Market.

## Inexpensive

**Bayou Bakery, Coffee Bar and Eatery** ★★ NEW ORLEANS CAFE Following upon the success of his first Bayou Bakery in Arlington (1515 N. Courthouse Rd.; © **703/243-2410**), New Orleans–born David Guas opened this outpost on Barracks Row in 2015. Another win. Everybody loves the Big Easy feel and the Louisiana food: buttermilk biscuits with pepper jelly, beignets, and gumbo, along with specials, like the pressed Cubano sandwich available at Wednesday lunch. Housed in a historic carriage house on the grounds of the 150-year-old Old Naval Hospital, where medic horses were once stabled, the homey Bayou eatery is not one large dining area, but a jumble of rooms, with seating in one of two cozy nooks furnished with sofas and armchairs gathered around a communal table, or in the larger sunroom overlooking the grounds, where families often sprawl on picnic blankets. A good-times ambience prevails as folks start sipping Mississippi mimosas and brandy milk punch, and dipping into grits and muffalottas, gumbo and boudin, sweet corn bread and layer cakes.

901 Pennsylvania Ave. SE (at 9th St.). www.bayoubakerydc.com. © **202/664-5307.** Reservations not accepted. All items under $18. Mon–Fri 7am–9pm; Sat 8am–9pm; Sun 8am–4pm. Metro: Eastern Market.

**Good Stuff Eatery** ★ AMERICAN This is the "baby" of Spike Mendelsohn, who shot to fame as a *Top Chef* contestant and remains renowned thanks to the scrumptiousness of his burgers, fries, and shakes. The Prez Obama Burger (with applewood bacon, onion marmalade, Roquefort cheese, and horseradish mayo sauce) is the most popular item on the menu, according

# EATING WITH THE insiders

You just can't beat the atmosphere (political) and value (cheap—your meal isn't taxed!) of the all-American food served in dining spots inside the Capitol, its office buildings, and the Supreme Court. Keep these places in mind while touring the Hill:

o The **Supreme Court** and its **Cafeteria** (© 202/479-3246), where you may spy a famous lawyer or member of the press but not any of the justices, who have their own dining room. The cafeteria is open weekdays 7:30am to 4pm (though it may be closed briefly between noon and 1pm to accommodate Supreme Court employees).

o The House of Representatives' immense, full-service **Rayburn Café** (© 202/226-9067), which is Room B357, in the basement of the Rayburn House Office Building, at 1st Street and Independence Avenue SW.

o The **Longworth Café** (Room B223, in the Longworth Building's basement, Independence Ave. and S. Capitol St. SE; © 202/225-6372), where you can grab a bite from a fairly nice food court.

o **Southside Buffet** (in the Dirksen Senate Office Building, 1st St. and Constitution Ave. NW; © 202/224-4249). The fried chicken, a carvery station, and a dessert station are highlights and popular among the Senate staffers who dine here.

All of the House and Senate eateries are open weekdays only. The carryouts usually stay open until late afternoon, while the other dining rooms close at 2:30pm. For a complete listing of **House of Representatives** dining services, go to https://thehouse.misofi.net, and for **Senate** dining services, go to http://radining.compass-usa.com/ussenate/Pages/Home.aspx.

A final, less insidery suggestion:

o The **Capitol Visitor Center's** (www.visitthecapitol.gov/plan-visit/restaurant-menu; © 202/593-1785) mammoth dining hall, which is open 8:30am to 4pm Monday through Saturday, seats 530 people and serves "meals and snacks that reflect the diverse bounty of America," which translates into the usual hamburgers and hot dogs, croissants and bagels, pizza and pasta, but also specialty sandwiches associated with different pockets of the country, like the New England lobster roll and the Chesapeake crab cake. Most items are $2 to $8. You won't see any members of Congress or other political types at the CVC restaurant, but you'll be dining in good company with fellow tourists.

to the staff; the toasted marshmallow milkshake will always be the #1 milkshake, to my mind. A second Good Stuff Eatery is located in Georgetown at 3291 M St. NW (© 202/337-4663); this location, unlike Capitol Hill's, is open daily, including Sundays. *Warning:* Good Stuff Eatery is always jumping, with people in line on the first floor and filling upstairs and outdoor patio tables. The line moves fast and table turnover is fairly quick, but just the same, you might consider getting the burgers to go, as so many do. The pizza place next door, **We The Pizza** (www.wethepizza.com; © 202/544-4008), is also Spike's.

303 Pennsylvania Ave. SE (at 3rd St.). www.goodstuffeatery.com. © **202/543-8222.** Reservations not accepted. Burgers $6.50–$8.50; milkshakes and sundaes $4–$6. Mon–Sat 11am–10pm. Metro: Capitol South.

**Le Bon Café** ★ FRENCH/CAFE   Le Bon Café comes by its French spirit honestly: Owner Sandra McCluskey studied in Paris while in college, worked in the kitchen of Le Bellecour, a Michelin-star restaurant in Paris, and has recently returned from living for 4 years in Paris. She loves all things French and her menu reflects that: croque monsieur, quiche, croissants, tuna Provençal salad, and salmon Nicoise are among the choices. But you'll also find not-so-French items, like a Southwest chicken wrap and curried turkey. I love all things French, too, and I can vouch for the tastiness of Le Bon Café's offerings, all great value for the price. The cafe is conveniently located right behind the Madison Building of the Library of Congress, a short walk from the Capitol. Look for the blue-and-white striped awning shading a cluster of round tables outside. Inside are about eight marble-topped bistro tables and, usually, a line of Hill staffers and locals from the neighborhood waiting to place their orders.

210 2nd St. SE (at Pennsylvania Ave. SE). www.leboncafedc.com. © **202/547-7200.** Reservations not accepted. Breakfast items $2.50–$8; salads/sandwiches/soups $5–$9. Mon–Fri 7am–3pm; Sat 8am–3pm; Sun 8am–2pm. Metro: Capitol South.

**Market Lunch** ★ AMERICAN/SEAFOOD   Market Lunch, like Eastern Market (p. 121), where it resides, is an institution, a little slice of D.C. life. For the best insider experience, come here on weekends and you may see senators and representatives in line with their Capitol Hill neighbors to eat the famous blueberry buckwheat pancakes ("bluebucks"), soft-shell crab sandwiches, or crab cakes. The eatery consists of a few small tables and 26 stools pulled up to a wooden counter at the end of Eastern Market's main hall. You choose what you want from the chalkboard menu and then queue to the right of the register to place your order. Once you're seated, you get to watch all that's going on in the market hall, as vendors and residents barter and chat. Market Lunch is open weekdays, too: a much quieter experience, so not nearly as much fun.

225 E. 7th St. SE, inside Eastern Market (at Pennsylvania Ave. SE). www.easternmarket-dc.org. © **202/547-8444.** Breakfast $5–$13; lunch $5–$20. Cash only. Tues–Thurs 7:30am–2:30pm; Fri 7:30am–3pm; Sat 8am–3pm; Sun 9am–3pm. Metro: Capitol South.

# DOWNTOWN & PENN QUARTER

## Expensive

**Central Michel Richard** ★★ FRENCH BISTRO   Central turns 10 in 2017 and still has that *je ne sais quoi*. Chef Michel Richard, who's won top awards over the years and owned restaurants in other cities, seems content now to focus on Central. A great Penn Quarter location on Pennsylvania

Avenue, a generous bar, a menu that speaks to both French and American cultures (devilled eggs, croque monsieur, fried chicken, mussels in white wine with garlic, hot dogs, trout almandine), and voila! Central is It. And the place is always full. The dining room can be loud, but the commotion signifies the happy time that most are enjoying. *A couple of tips:* For best value, order from the $22.50 three-course lunch special menu, or dine at the bar or on the patio for weekday happy hour 5 to 7pm, and enjoy some delicious deals from the bar menu, like french fries for $5 and a plate of three sliders for $12.

1001 Pennsylvania Ave. NW (at 11th St.). www.centralmichelrichard.com. © **202/626-0015.** Reservations recommended. Main courses lunch $16–$28, brunch $27 prix fixe, bar/patio items $5–$12, dinner $18–$34. Mon–Fri 11:30am–2:30pm and 2:30–5pm (bar/lounge & patio); Mon–Thurs 5–10:30pm; Fri–Sat 5–10:30pm, Sun 11am–2:30pm. Metro: Metro Center (12th and F sts. exit).

**Fiola** ★★★ ITALIAN   For a splash-out D.C. dining experience, book a table at Fiola, a favorite among the glitterati, but also locals who simply love inventive Italian cuisine and lively atmosphere. With its wide swath of bar at the front, white banquettes, and modern art, the dining room has a glamorous, head-turning, New York feel about it, maybe informed by chef Fabio Trabocchi's stint there not so long ago. But it's got a friendly vibe, too, helped along by Trabocchi's charming wife, Maria, who is usually on the scene. The main event is the seasonal Italian cuisine, which might include lobster ravioli in cream sauce, goat cheese fritters, lasagna with morels and truffles, or arugula salad with figs. The main menu changes frequently—and the variety of menus is always changing, too. There's a real sense that Fabio and Maria are having fun as they create the light "Maria's Menu" (available at both lunch and dinner), "Presto! Lunch@Fiola Bar," a special menu for Father's Day, a menu to celebrate spring—you get the idea: celebratory dining. Also consider the Trabocchis' casual Italian restaurant, Casa Luca, at 1099 New York Ave. NW, in the Penn Quarter, and the swank Italian seafood eatery, **Fiola Mare** (p. 109), in Georgetown's waterfront complex, Washington Harbour.

601 Pennsylvania Ave. NW (entrance on Indiana Ave., btw. 6th and 7th sts.). www.fioladc.com. © **202/628-2888.** Reservations recommended. Lunch main courses $20–$50, $28 prix-fixe (items also available a la carte) Maria's menu, and $20 prix-fixe business lunch menu; dinner main courses $24–$70, and 2-course ($80), 3-course ($95), 4-course ($115), and 5-course ($130) tasting menus. Mon–Fri 11:30am–2:30pm; Mon–Thurs 5:30–10:30pm; Fri 5:30–11:30pm; Sat 5–11:30pm. Metro: Archives–Navy Memorial or Gallery Place/Verizon Center (7th and F sts. exit).

## Moderate

**China Chilcano** ★★ PERUVIAN-CHINESE/JAPANESE   Say whaaat? Thanks to the influence of Chinese and Japanese immigrants on Peruvian culture and cuisine, Peru is known not just for its native dishes, like the *sudado de pescado* (poached red snapper), but for Chinese-Peruvian (*chifa*) and Japanese-Peruvian (*nikkei*) creations. Chef José Andrés capitalizes on all of those tastes here, and Washingtonians are loving it. For dim sum lovers, there are dumplings of shrimp, pork, jicama, and peanut, with a runny egg broken over them. Ceviches use Japanese sashimi and nigiri. A tomato stew tops rice noodles. A few of the dishes, that *sudado de pescado,* for example, require a table-side presentation that's quite dramatic and aromatic. The room is as dramatic as the cuisine, artfully brilliantly colorful.

418 7th St. NW (at D St.) www.chinachilcano.com. ℂ **202/783-0941.** Reservations accepted. Lunch, brunch, and dinner items $8–$19 each. Sun–Mon 11am–10pm; Tues–Thurs 11am–11pm; Fri–Sat 11am–midnight. Metro: Archives–Navy Memorial or Gallery Place–Chinatown (7th and F sts. exit).

**Graffiato** ★ ITALIAN  Chef/owner and *Top Chef* contestant Mike Isabella knows how to take classic Italian dishes and up the ante. At Graffiato, his pizzas are topped with gourmet ingredients, like fried calamari and cherry pepper aioli (the "Jersey Shore"), and then cooked in a wood-burning oven, just as good pizza should be. In addition, Graffiato serves flavorful small plates: charred Brussels sprouts with pancetta, wild striped bass with bourbon peaches, sweet corn agnolotti—you get the picture. Best seats in the two-floor restaurant are upstairs at the "ham counter" in front of the open kitchen, or downstairs at the back bar, where you can watch pizzas come and go from the oven. And the restaurant's location can't be beat: right across from the Verizon Center, in Chinatown/Penn Quarter. If you like Graffiato, you might want to know about Isabella's other standout restaurants: In the U & 14th Street Corridors, the Greek restaurant **Kapnos** (2201 14th St. NW) and right next door, **G by Mike Isabella** ("Sandwich Shop by Day, Tasting Menu by Night").

707 6th St. NW (at G St.) www.graffiatodc.com. ℂ **202/289-3600.** Reservations recommended. Pizzas $14–$19, small plates $7–$19 each. Sun–Thurs 11:30am–10pm; Fri–Sat 11:30am–11pm. Metro: Judiciary Square (F St. exit) or Gallery Place–Chinatown (7th and F sts. exit).

**Hill Country Barbecue Market** ★★ BARBECUE  Enter Hill Country Barbecue and you leave official Washington at the door. It's just not possible to cleave to lofty attitudes and politicking when the Red Dirt Rangers or some such band are playing up a storm, as you make your way through a mess of dry-rubbed Texas barbecued ribs ("smoked low and slow over Texas oak"), skillet corn bread, and sweet potato bourbon mash. Meats and side dishes are priced by weight, from $5 per half-pound of bbq chicken to $27.50 per pound of short ribs; and from $2.25 for 4 oz. of coleslaw to $9.75 for a pound of chili. Upstairs is where you place your order in the cafeteria/kitchen, and then carry it to your seat, either in the large dining room adjoining the cafeteria, or to your table downstairs. I recommend the downstairs. That's where the bands play and where the lively Boots Bar is. Families, however, will want to stay upstairs, and you should know about the Kids 10 & Under Combo deal: $7 for 1/8 chicken, mac and cheese or green bean casserole, and a chocolate chunk cookie.

410 7th St. NW (at D St.). www.hillcountrywdc.com. ℂ **202/556-2050.** Reservations recommended for downstairs. Main courses $5–$27.50. Sun–Tues & Thurs 11:30am–11pm; Wed & Fri–Sat 11:30am–midnight. Metro: Archives–Navy Memorial or Gallery Place–Chinatown (7th and F sts. exit).

**Jaleo** ★★★ SPANISH Jaleo, at age 24, is ancient in terms of restaurant years, but she sure doesn't act it . . . or look it. A creative re-design in 2012 added artwork by contemporary Spanish artists, foosball tables with chairs made from Vespa scooter seats, "love tables" closed off by metal curtains, and whimsical touches everywhere, even in the restrooms, where photographed faces smile up at you from the floor. Chef extraordinaire José Andrés is 24 years older as well, and in that time has grown into a culinary and personal phenomenon, with restaurants here (**Zaytinya**, p. 98; **Oyamel**, p. 98; **China Chilcano**, p. 94; and **Beefsteak**, p. 108; as well as the chef's unique and avant-garde dining experience, **minibar by José Andrés**) and elsewhere, a cooking show, courses at Harvard, and a number of cookbooks. But it all started here at Jaleo, when Andrés introduced his versions of Spanish tapas to the capital. Andrés or his staff may fiddle with the menu of some 60 individual small plates, but you always know you're enjoying the best tapas in the city (some say in the country, and some of the best dining in D.C.). Look for fried dates wrapped in bacon and served with an apple-mustard sauce; mini-burgers made from the "legendary, acorn-fed, black-footed Iberico pigs of Spain"; and roasted sweet onions, pine nuts, and Valdeón blue cheese. Be adventurous.

480 7th St. NW (at E St.). www.jaleo.com. ✆ **202/628-7949.** Reservations recommended. Tapas $4–$25 (most $7–$15), "big plates" and paellas also available $36–$65; tasting menus: $55 (classic), $70 (the Jaleo Experience), $95 (José's Way); pre-theater menu (Sun–Thurs 5–6:30pm) $30. Sun–Mon 11am–10pm; Tues–Thurs 11am–11pm; Fri–Sat 11am–midnight. Metro: Archives–Navy Memorial or Gallery Place–Chinatown (7th and F sts. exit).

**Matchbox** ★ PIZZA/AMERICAN Look for the flickering flame above the restaurant entrance and the line queuing up in front of it. That line could be people waiting for a table—Matchbox *is* awfully popular, and there's not a lot of extra space inside for hanging out. Then again, it could be the line for the Chinatown bus, which happens to pick up New York–bound passengers at this exact spot. The sight of those lines may have prompted the owners to finally accept reservations; better yet for last-minute types, you can call ahead and put your name on the list, which reduces your wait time when you arrive. Matchbox won early acclaim for its thin-crust pizzas cooked in 900°F wood-fired brick ovens (try the spicy meatball with crispy bacon and crushed red pepper), its appetizer of mini burgers on toasted brioche topped with onion "straws" (skinny fried onion strands), its chopped salad, and entrees like the pan-seared salmon, and diners keep coming back for more. Saturday and Sunday brunch is big, too. This Matchbox is the original; look for other locations on Barracks Row (521 8th St. SE) and in the U & 14th Street Corridors (1901 14th St. NW).

713 H St. NW (btw. 7th and 8th sts.). www.matchboxrestaurants.com. ✆ **202/289-4441.** Reservations accepted. Main courses $17–$31; pizzas and sandwiches $12–$23; brunch $6–$15. Mon–Thurs 11am–10:30pm; Fri 11am–11:30pm; Sat 10am–11:30pm; Sun 10am–10:30pm. Metro: Gallery Place–Chinatown (H and 7th sts. exit).

**5**

WHERE TO EAT — Downtown & Penn Quarter

Sliders and onion rings at Matchbox on Barracks Row.

**Old Ebbitt Grill** ★ AMERICAN  It's midnight and you're starving. Where are you gonna go? Or maybe it's 8am and you want to get a good jump on the day ahead. Who serves a full breakfast at this hour not too far from the National Mall? Or you want a taste of both the capital's regional dishes and insider's culture. Who brings that to the table? It's the Ebbitt.

Old Ebbitt is that rare place that attracts tourists and the city's movers and shakers in equal numbers. It could so easily be a tourist trap, with its saloon decor and old-fashioned ambience, only it's not fake. Old Ebbitt has been around since 1856, first in another nearby location, and here since 1983, and some of its furnishings date from the early days. Regulars come here precisely because they find the atmosphere genuinely comfortable. Those regulars, by the way, include Secret Service agents, as well as the people they're protecting; hotshot attorneys from nearby law firms; and politicos visiting the White House a block away.

It's comforting to have a conveniently located place that's nearly always open, with four capacious bars and a menu that's known for its untrendy dishes, like the burgers, the trout parmesan, and the house pasta, which is stuffed with spinach, mortadella ham, and three cheeses and baked in a cream sauce. Oysters are the standout, among the best and freshest in town. (Daily 3–6pm and after 11pm, all raw bar items are half off.)

675 15th St. NW (btw. F and G sts.). www.ebbitt.com. © **202/347-4800.** Reservations recommended. Main courses breakfast and brunch $13–$20, lunch and dinner $13–$30; late night $7–$30. Mon–Fri 7:30am–1am; Sat–Sun 8:30am–1am. Bar until 2am Sun–Thurs, until 3am Fri–Sat. Metro: Metro Center (13th and F sts. exit).

**Oyamel** ★★ LATIN AMERICAN/MEXICAN    Oyamel is another of José Andrés's "small plates" restaurants (see Jaleo, above, and Zaytinya, below). Another winning one, I should add. First thing you do is order a margarita and the guacamole, so you can sip and munch on dipped chips while mulling over the list of *antojitos,* or Mexican "little dishes from the streets." Need some suggestions? Try the *ceviche* (marinated seafood salad), *papas al moles* (fried potatoes in an almond and chili sauce with a touch of chocolate), house specialty *chapulines* (sauteed grasshoppers!), and *quesadilla de chicharrones* (fried pork belly in a tortilla with cheese and chile sauce). This may sound like a lot of food, but remember these are small plates meant to share. Oyamel's carnival atmosphere and whimsical decor (try to count the number of butterflies) are part of the fun. Window-fronted on two sides, Oyamel overlooks the Penn Quarter's busiest artery, 7th Street; sit at a window-side table and you're in the best spot for people-watching, inside and out.

401 7th St. NW (at D St.). www.oyamel.com. © **202/628-1005.** Limited reservations. Lunch, brunch, and dinner $4–$19. Sun–Wed 11am–midnight; Thurs–Sat 11am–2am. Metro: Gallery Place–Chinatown (7th and F sts. exit) or Archives–Navy Memorial.

**Rasika** ★★★ INDIAN    Try to get a reservation here, I dare you. It's not that it's impossible, but you do have to book far in advance. Here's why you'd want to: Rasika serves exquisite modern Indian food (Chef Vikram Sunderam won the prestigious James Beard Foundation award for Best Chef, Mid-Atlantic region, in 2014) in an intimate, soft-lit, shimmering, champagne-hued setting, that's frequented by a who's who of the capital and the world beyond. Simple as that. Its specialties are griddle, open barbecue, tandoori, and regional dishes; the *palak chaat* (crisped spinach in a yogurt sauce), black cod with honey, homestyle lamb curry, and the tandoori salmon are among the most popular dishes. Intrigued? Better get out your calendar. You can dine in the bar/lounge without advanced reservations but that, too, is usually pretty full and the lounge seating too low for comfortable eating. Rasika has a sister in the West End, at 1190 New Hampshire Ave. NW (www.rasikarestaurant.com/westend; © **202/466-2500**), a larger location with a similar menu and just as popular as the Penn Quarter Rasika.

633 D St. NW (btw. 6th and 7th sts.). www.rasikarestaurant.com. © **202/637-1222.** Reservations recommended. Main courses $16–$28; pre-theater menu $35. Mon–Fri 11:30am–2:30pm; Mon–Thurs 5:30–10:30pm; Fri–Sat 5–11pm. Lounge stays open throughout the day serving light meals. Metro: Archives–Navy Memorial or Gallery Place/Verizon Center (7th and F sts. exit).

**Zaytinya** ★★ GREEK/TURKISH/MIDDLE EASTERN    When it opened in 2002, Zaytinya, with its full-on, authentic, and wide-ranging tastes of the Middle East, Greece, and Turkey, was quite the culinary adventure for Washingtonians. (Crispy Brussels sprouts with coriander seed, barberries, and garlic, oh my! Olive-oil ice cream. How interesting!) But Washington was a different place then. Fifteen years and a boom of restaurant openings later, Zaytinya is an old friend. Those Brussels sprouts are a favorite among the dishes that appear on the four-page menu, which, in truth, has barely changed over the years. It consists, primarily, of *mezze,* which are Mediterranean small

Dining under the trees at Zaytinya.

dishes, although some entrees appear as well. Other signature dishes include scallops in yogurt and dill sauce; roasted cauliflower with sultans, caper berries, and pine-nut puree; spanakopita with house-made filo; and *kibbeh nayeh* (Lebanese-style beef tartare with bulgur wheat, radishes, mint, and pita chips). Zaytinya is enormous, seating 230 in the attractive dining rooms, another 52 on stools at the bar, and 65 outside on the patio. Best way to enjoy Zaytinya? Bring a crowd and order an array of tapas. Instant party!

701 9th St. NW (at G St.). www.zaytinya.com. © **202/638-0800.** Reservations recommended. Mezze items $6–$20 (most are $9); lunch sandwiches $11–$13; brunch items $7.50–$9. Sun–Mon 11am–10pm; Tues–Thurs 11am–11pm; Fri–Sat 11am–midnight. Metro: Gallery Place–Chinatown (9th St. exit).

## Inexpensive

**Daikaya** ★ JAPANESE   Asian cuisine is all the rage in Washington, with Daikaya being one of the top go-to hotspots. Located right next door to another local favorite, Graffiato (see p. 95), you'll know you've found Daikaya when you spot the enormous steel screen with wavelike cutouts covering the facade. The restaurant is an upstairs/downstairs affair—two different places with two separate entrances—but both offering authentic Japanese specialties. Downstairs is the tiny ramen noodle house, a 40-seat, sparsely decorated joint that lets you concentrate on slurping up one of four broths, meat-based or vegetable, filled with aged wheat noodles and topped with a bouquet of briefly stir-fried garnishes. On the second floor, which you reach via an outside staircase to the left of the ramen house, is the larger *izakaya*, or Japanese tavern. This dimly lit bar and grill's decorative woodwork and Japanese fabrics lend an exotic feel, which tastes from the menu only amplify. You might try grilled avocado with fresh wasabi, crab croquettes, miso cod with pickled carrot, monk fish liver, and finally everyone's favorite, the seaweed-covered rice balls, whose center holds a kind of sticky rice stew. Both upstairs and downstairs are always crowded, always noisy.

705 6th St. NW (at G St.). www.daikaya.com. ☏ **202/589-1600.** Reservations accepted for the upstairs izakaya. Ramen noodle soups $11.75–$13; Japanese lunch and brunch items $7–$14; Japanese small plates $2–$10. Ramen noodle house Sun–Wed 11am–10pm; Thurs–Sat 11am–11pm. Upstairs izakaya Sun 11am–3pm; Mon–Fri 11:30am–2pm; Sun–Mon 5–10pm; Tues–Wed 5–10:30pm; Thurs–Fri 5–11pm; Sat 5pm–midnight. Metro: Gallery Place (H St./Chinatown exit).

**Five Guys Burgers and Fries** ★ AMERICAN    Five Guys is taking over the world! Yeah, I know it's a chain, but it's our chain, a family operation that got started in Arlington 30 years ago. At last count, Five Guys had more than 1,200 of its joints in 48 states, Canada, Ireland, throughout the U.K., France, and the Middle East. You've got your hamburgers, cheeseburgers, bacon burgers, and bacon cheeseburgers, all of which come in two sizes; assorted hot dogs; a BLT; a veggie sandwich and a grilled cheese for vegetarians; and your choice of regular or Cajun-style fries. One immediate difference between Five Guys and most other popular burgeries, like D.C.'s Good Stuff Eatery (p. 91), is the absence of a "magic sauce." You do get to add as many as 15 toppings, grilled onions to tomatoes, for free. D.C. currently has eight Five Guys, including this Penn Quarter/Chinatown location.

808 H St. NW (at 9th St.). www.fiveguys.com. ☏ **202/393-2900.** Burgers $4.99–$8.69; fries $3.09–$5.79. Daily 11:30am–10pm. Metro: Gallery Place (H St./Chinatown exit).

# MIDTOWN
## Moderate

**Bombay Club** ★★ INDIAN    Located directly across Lafayette Square from the White House, Bombay Club has been a favorite of one administration after the other since it opened in 1988. This was Ashok Bajaj's first restaurant in D.C., and though he has added other well-reviewed dining rooms since, most notably **Rasika** (above), Bombay Club is special, a gracious veteran that seems to appeal to everyone. A pianist plays nightly in the dining room, which is decorated in hues of pale pink and yellow. You don't have to be Indian to appreciate the cuisine (although the Indians I know say it is the real thing). Among the popular dishes are the crispy spinach and arugula *chaat,* a savory snack served with date-tamarind chutney; the chicken *tikka,* prepared with coriander, cumin, garlic, black pepper, and yogurt; and tandoor-oven roasted eggplant served with sauteed onions, ginger, and yogurt. If you like spicy, try the chili- and ginger-infused duck kebab appetizer. To sample an assortment of tastes, order a house *thali.*

815 Connecticut Ave. NW (H St.). www.bombayclubdc.com. ☏ **202/659-3727.** Reservations recommended. Main courses $17–$28; Sun brunch $22. Mon–Fri and Sun brunch 11:30am–2:30pm; Mon–Thurs 5:30–10:30pm; Fri–Sat 5:30–11pm; Sun 5:30–9pm. Metro: Farragut West (17th St. exit).

## Inexpensive

**Sweetgreen** ★ LIGHT FARE   Sweetgreen was the brainchild of three eco-conscious Georgetown University students who wanted to provide home-grown, healthy options for their neighbors. The first Sweetgreen opened in 2007; today, these eateries number about 50, popping up all over D.C., and in other cities, too. The eatery "sources local and organic ingredients from farmers we know" to create seasonal salads and wraps. Choose one of the eight or so signature salads (my fave: the kale Caesar with roasted chicken) or create your own using organic greens and all sorts of interesting fresh ingredients, like spicy pickles and roasted sweet potatoes. All Sweetgreens favor the same modern and streamlined look, but size and seating capacity vary greatly. This location has seating for about 14 inside and 40 more on the sidewalk in pleasant weather. *Note:* **Teaism** (p. 107) has a location at 800 Connecticut Ave. NW, that presents another excellent option for healthy dining in, or for a carryout picnic lunch (weekdays only, and it closes at 5:30pm).

1901 L St. NW (at 19th St.). www.sweetgreen.com. ℂ **202/331-3355.** Salads $7–$12.60. Mon–Fri 10:30am–10pm. Metro: Farragut North (L St. exit).

# U & 14TH STREET CORRIDORS

The trendiest restaurants in the city are right here, making 14th Street especially, and U Street to a lesser extent, D.C.'s "Restaurant Row." Many of the hottest eateries don't take reservations, so if you're in the right mood, ready to go with the flow, wander here, stopping in at the excellent Thai/Vietnamese eatery, **Doi Moi,** or at the lively seafood joint, **Pearl Dive Oyster Palace** (see both, below), until you find the right place at the right time. And if you're not in the mood to wander? Some restaurants do take reservations.

## Expensive

**Le Diplomate** ★★ FRENCH   How hot is Le Diplomate? So hot that in the middle of a frigid winter when temperatures were in the twenties, diners were taking seats at the sidewalk tables. There were heat lamps, but still. Reservations are harder to book here than almost anywhere else in town, and it's been like that since the restaurant opened in April 2013. It looks the part of a Parisian brasserie, right down to the red banquettes, large mirrors, zinc-topped bar, little lace curtains, and windowfront opening to the sidewalk. And it tastes the part, too, with its menu of Gallic staples, from escargots to steak frites to trout almandine to crème brûlée. Le Diplomate is big and loud and fun, and though I wouldn't call it romantic, myself, others obviously do; I've noticed lots of couples, including May-December types, and there's a lot of kissing going on.

1601 14th St. NW (at Q St.). www.lediplomatedc.com. ℂ **202/332-3333.** Reservations recommended. Lunch and brunch main courses $13–$29; dinner main courses $14–$35 (most around $27; daily specials go as high as $49). Sat–Sun 9:30am–5pm; Sun–Tues 5–10pm; Wed–Thurs 5–11pm; Fri–Sat 5pm–midnight. Metro: U St./Cardozo (13th St. exit).

## Moderate

**Cork** ★ AMERICAN   If I lived in this neighborhood, I would probably hang out here all the time. It's a cozy little wine bar with 250 bottles on offer (most from unusual, small producers), and a whopping 50 wines by the glass. And because wine always tastes better with food, the menu features about 20 dishes nightly, half cold, half hot, meant to be shared. Plates of cheeses and charcuterie; white asparagus with spinach and buttermilk puree; a pan-crisped brioche sandwich of prosciutto, fontina, and Path Valley egg; duck confit with roasted strawberries; and french fries tossed with parsley, garlic, and lemon are all recommended. Consider the nightly specials, too, which on my last visit included a memorably rich moussaka. Cork was a pioneer when it opened in 2008, but just these few years later, the neighborhood has more eateries and bars than one can keep up with. Nothing like Cork, though. By the way, if you like a particular wine, you can buy it across the street, along with in-house prepared feasts to-go—pastries, sandwiches, salads, and entrees—at **Cork Market and Tasting Room,** 1805 14th St. NW (*②* **202/265-2674**).

1720 14th St. NW (at S St.). www.corkdc.com. *②* **202/265-2675.** Reservations accepted. Brunch items and dinner small plates $5–$19. Sun 11am–3pm and 5–10pm; Tues–Wed 5pm–midnight; Thurs–Sat 5pm–1am. Metro: U St./Cardozo (13th St. exit).

**Doi Moi** ★ THAI-VIETNAMESE   This stylish, window-fronted dining room is a wash of creamy white punctuated with colorful tiles and artwork. The food is anything but vanilla. Of the 40 items on the menu, nearly half are tagged as spicy, and 6 of those as "very spicy," like the ground duck and duck liver salad prepared with chilies and toasted rice powder and shallots. If you're afraid of searing your tongue, you might try the crispy pork and shrimp spring rolls, or the blue crab fried rice (both are scrumptious). Start off or end your meal with a drink at the downstairs bar, 2 Birds, 1 Stone; its cocktail menu lists such drinks as punch du jour and a pina colada made with house-spiced rum.

1800 14th St. NW (at S St.). www.doimoidc.com. *②* **202/733-5131.** Reservations not accepted. Brunch items $9–$15; dinner main courses $15–$25. Sun 11am–2pm and 5–9pm; Mon–Thurs 5–10pm; Fri–Sat 5–11pm. Metro: U St./Cardozo (13th St. exit).

**Pearl Dive Oyster Palace** ★ AMERICAN/SEAFOOD   The kitchen at Pearl's turns out some of the city's best oyster dishes, appropriately enough, including the oyster po' boy (cornmeal-fried oysters, house pickles, and aioli), oyster gumbo, and something called *mariscos de Campechana,* which is a stack of oyster, blue crab and shrimp, salsa, and avocado. But you don't have to be a bivalve lover to come here: Excellent non-oyster dishes include wood-grilled redfish and grass-fed hanger steak. The only downside (which will be an upside for some): the crowd of rambunctious 20-something patrons who fill Pearl Dive's gated front patio, like children in a playpen. Know that the dining room, with its nautical theme and friendly waitstaff, is a perfectly civilized place to eat, once you walk through the rowdy bar crowd.

1612 14th St. NW. www.pearldivedc.com. *②* **202/319-1612.** Reservations accepted nightly for dinner 5 to 7pm. Brunch main courses $7–$26; dinner main courses $16–$28.

Fri–Sun 11am–3pm; Sun–Mon 5–10pm; Tues–Sat 5–11pm. Metro: U St./Cardozo (13th St. exit).

## Inexpensive

**Ben's Chili Bowl** ★ AMERICAN    Ben's opened in 1958 and it looks like it, too, with its old-fashioned storefront, Formica counters, and red bar stools. Its staying power is impressive enough, but Ben's history is also compelling: When riots broke out throughout the city following the assassination of Dr. Martin Luther King, Jr., in April 1968, Ben's stayed open to serve police officers, firefighters, and anyone who needed sustenance, even as surrounding establishments closed or were destroyed.

On that basis alone, a visit to Ben's is warranted. You'll find yourself among a cross-section of locals: by day, workers from nearby municipal office buildings, students, and shoppers; by night, nightclubbers, cops, and neighborhood regulars. Often, it seems that everyone knows each other, and the Ali family, who own Ben's. Walls are hung with photographs that cover the history of the city and of Ben's, and include snapshots of the many celebrities who've dined here, from President Obama to Mary J. Blige.

Folks go to Ben's for the homey ambience, and for the food, which is ultra cheap and usually tasty. Most famous is the half-smoke sandwich, which is a ¼-pound, half-beef, half-pork smoked sausage, served inside a warm bun, and, if you so desire, smothered with mustard, chopped onions, and a spicy chili sauce. I went to Ben's recently with a friend and tried the half-smoke for the first time. And though it is near sacrilege in this city to admit it, I didn't care for it. My friend, who ordered the half-smoke plus cheese fries, says it's because I chose not to top off my half-smoke with the chili sauce and onions. Maybe. What I enjoy most at Ben's are other items on the menu, like the flavorful turkey burger sub and the vegetarian chili (vegetarians take note: Ben's has a few veggie-friendly options). Ben's has locations now at Nationals Park, in the Atlas District, and at National Airport.

1213 U St. NW (btw. 12th and 13th sts.). www.benschilibowl.com. © **202/667-0909.** Reservations not accepted. Main courses $4–$10. No credit cards (there's an ATM here). Mon–Thurs 6am–2am; Fri 6am–4am; Sat 7am–4am; Sun 11am–midnight. Metro: U St./Cardozo (13th St. exit).

**Tacqueria Nacional** ★ MEXICAN    Just a few steps away from noisy 14th Street is this pretty little taqueria, housed inside a former post office and decorated with beautiful Mexican tiles and grillwork, an old chandelier, and a vision of the Blessed Mother painted upon a worn plaster wall. It seats 45 max at a jumble of brightly colored tables; throughout Saturday and Sunday brunch (breakfast quesadilla, huevos rancheros, and Mexican fritters), and from happy hour on, all tables are usually occupied. The menu is short but affordable, featuring fresh, authentic tacos and custom-made quesadillas and tostadas. Favorites, like carnitas and fish tacos, are always on the menu, but the taqueria seems always to be inventing new tastes, like the shrimp, cauliflower, and cotija cheese tacos. Yucca fries, salads, guacamole, and other sides

**5**

**WHERE TO EAT**

U & 14th Street Corridors

are available. The beverage list includes full bar offerings, and features Mexican *aguas frescas* (water blended with fruit, sugar, and other ingredients) prepared in the traditional nonalcoholic form, as well as mixed with rum or tequila; locally brewed draft beer; and a $6.95 margarita.

1409 T St. NW (at 14th St.). www.tacquerianacional.com. © **202/299-1122.** Reservations not accepted. All items: $2.50–$8.50. Sun 10am–9pm; Mon–Wed noon–10pm; Thurs–Fri noon–11pm; Sat 10am–11pm. Metro: U St./Cardozo (13th St. exit) or take the DC Circulator.

# ADAMS MORGAN

## Moderate

**Las Canteras** ★ LATIN AMERICAN/PERUVIAN    This little sleeper of a restaurant is not about trendiness, thankfully. Instead, Las Canteras introduces diners to the delights of Peruvian culture in the form of food, drinks, and atmosphere. Chef/co-owner Eddy Ancasi is from southern Peru and has decorated his intimate dining room and downstairs bar with photographs of scenes from modern Peru and with colorful handcrafts of local Peruvian artisans. His menu spans both traditional and contemporary Peruvian cuisine, but I'd recommend you go the traditional route: a pisco sour cocktail to start, followed by *cebiche* (fresh white fish marinated in citrus, and garnished with sweet potatoes, roasted corn, and red onions) and *lomo saltado* (morsels of beef wok-fried in soy sauce and served with garlic rice and french fries). Try happy hour Tuesday through Friday 5 to 7:30pm or the three-course $24 early-bird special Tuesday through Thursday 5 to 7pm for best value.

2307 18th St. NW (at Kalorama Rd.). www.lascanterasdc.com. © **202/265-1780.** Reservations accepted. Main courses brunch $9–$25, lunch $12–$26, dinner $14–$26. Tues–Fri noon–3pm; Tues–Thurs and Sun 5–10pm; Fri–Sat 5–11pm; Sat–Sun brunch noon–5pm. Metro: Woodley Park–Zoo, with a walk.

## Inexpensive

**Amsterdam Falafelshop** ★ MIDDLE EASTERN/DUTCH    Inspired by the falafel shops of Holland, the owners opened their own D.C. version in 2004, and other locations since, including a shop in the U & 14th Street Corridors at 1830 14th St. NW. If you're out clubbing in the neighborhood, do what D.C.'s barhoppers do and stop here for a snack at 2, 3, even 4am. The shop does a steady business all day among people who just love these toasted pita sandwiches stuffed with fried balls of mashed chickpeas, topped with as many of the 21 self-serve garnishes as you want, from crunchy onion to hummus. You'll want to add an order of double-fried potatoes, which go best with a dab of Dutch mayo and a shake of Old Bay Seasoning. You can dine in or on the patio, but most customers carry out.

2425 18th St. NW (at Belmont Rd.). www.falafelshop.com. © **202/234-1969.** Reservations not accepted. Falafel $6.25–$9; Dutch fries $3.60–$4. Sun–Mon 11am–midnight; Tues–Wed 11am–2:30am; Thurs 11am–3am; Fri–Sat 11am–4am. Metro: Woodley Park–Zoo, with a walk, or take the DC Circulator.

# DUPONT CIRCLE
## Expensive

**Al Tiramisu** ★★ ITALIAN   Al Tiramisu is a find, and those who have found it include George Clooney and dad Nick Clooney, Hillary Clinton, Magic Johnson, Ethel Kennedy, and Catherine Zeta-Jones. I imagine celebrities like it for the same reason everyone else does: the infectious ebullience of chef/owner Luigi Diotaiuti, who bounces out from behind a curtain to greet you as you enter; the unpretentious feeling of this snug little restaurant, which is essentially one long room in the bottom of a Dupont Circle town house (people do complain that it feels cramped, but I like it); and a menu that includes excellently prepared fresh grilled fish, house-made spinach-ricotta ravioli with butter and sage sauce, and veal Milanese. This is a place to come for romance, for cheering up, for having a good time with friends, and Tiramisu has been so obliging since it opened in 1996. Check out the restaurant's website for a hint of its personality. A little hokey, maybe, but fun.

2014 P St. NW (btw. 19th and 20th sts.). www.altiramisu.com. © **202/467-4466.** Reservations recommended. Main courses $19–$30 at lunch and dinner. Mon–Fri noon–2pm, Sun–Thurs 5–10pm, Fri–Sat 5–11pm. Metro: Dupont Circle (19th St./South exit).

**Komi** ★★★ MODERN MEDITERRANEAN   Dining at Komi is a simply delicious experience in an intimate, somewhat casual dining room, where the best servers in the city make you feel fully at home and encourage you to focus on the food, your companions, and the exquisite pleasure of tasting the best cuisine in the capital. Because Komi's is among the city's top tables; critics tend to agree about that. Chef/owner Johnny Monis knows exactly what he's doing, filling dates with mascarpone, or a brioche with monkfish liver, or charring octopus with tomato and fig. There is no printed menu. Monis just sends out 15 or more tastes of his divine inspirations, and if you know what's good for you, you savor it. (Komi will accommodate those with allergies or dietary restrictions; just be sure to call ahead.) This is not a place for loud conversation, nor is it hoity-toity. I wouldn't even describe it as the domain of foodies, although foodies certainly flock here. A dinner at Komi is really about slowing down for a short while, focusing, and being renewed. You should also know that Komi serves only wine and beer, no cocktails. *FYI:* If you can't book a table at Komi, try Monis's **Little Serow,** a stools-only, walk-ins only restaurant in the basement of the building next door to Komi. The Northern Thai menu is prix-fixe, $49 for seven courses served family-style, and authentic. You'll know you've found Little Serow when you see the line.

1509 17th St. NW (near P St.). www.komirestaurant.com. © **202/332-9200.** Reservations a must (call a month in advance). Prix fixe $150 per person. Tues–Sat 5:30–9:30pm. Metro: Dupont Circle (Q St. exit).

**Tabard Inn** ★★ AMERICAN   When a brunch reservation is as difficult to get as it is here, one has to wonder what all the commotion is about. My guess? The freshly-made doughnuts served with whipped cream. The Tabard Inn bakes all its breads, pastries, and desserts in-house, and they're scrumptious.

Other items also prove a potent lure, like the buttermilk fried chicken sandwich, crab cakes with fried green tomatoes, and the eggs Benedict served with house-smoked salmon. The fact that all of this is served in an absolutely charming, sky-lit room (just past the comfy, old, wood-paneled lounge, where live jazz performances are offered on Sun through Tues evenings) and adjoining covered courtyard doesn't hurt. If you can't get in for a meal (and they serve more than brunch), do stop in for a cocktail, just so you can experience the inn's lovely ambience (it's also a hotel; see p. 74).

1739 N St. NW (at 17th St., in the Hotel Tabard Inn). www.tabardinn.com. © **202/331-8528.** Reservations recommended. Main courses breakfast $7–$11; lunch and brunch $12–$23; dinner $21–$36. Mon–Fri 7–10am and 11:30am–2:30pm; Sat–Sun 7–9am; Sat–Sun brunch 10:30am–2:30pm; Sun–Wed 5:30–9:30pm; Thurs–Sat 5:30–10pm. Metro: Dupont Circle (19th St./South exit).

## Moderate

**Hank's Oyster Bar** ★★ SEAFOOD  Around since 2005, Hank's just keeps getting better and better. Chef/owner Jamie Leeds now has three Oyster Bars, but Dupont Circle's is the original. It's a lot prettier and bigger than when it first opened: You've got a choice of patio seating, a skylit bar, a candlelit comfy lounge, the main dining room with tables and a generous swath of oyster bar, and an upstairs bar with stool seating. This is important for you to know because Hank's does not take reservations, so when you arrive at the main entrance you will inevitably note the jumble of people waiting for a table. If you're intent on sitting in the main dining room or outside, go ahead and put your name on the wait list. But if you'd be just as happy sitting at one of the bars, where food is also served, by the way, scout for vacant stools. The place always feels festive and the food is always great. *Washington City Paper* readers voted Hank's crab cake the best in the city in the paper's 2016 poll. The specials are also a safe bet, as are the po'boys, and just about anything with oyster in the name. The kitchen has a way with fresh vegetables, too. Hank's two other Oyster Bar locations are on Capitol Hill, at 633 Pennsylvania Ave. SE (© **202/733-1971**), and in Old Town Alexandria, at 1026 King St. (© **703/739-4265**). In 2016, Leeds opened Hank's Pasta Bar in Old Town, at 600 Montgomery St. (© **571/312-4117**).

1624 Q St. NW (at 17th St.) www.hanksoysterbar.com. © **202/462-4265.** Reservations not accepted. Brunch $35; Lunch small plates $8–$23, large plates $13–$25; Dinner small plates $8–$23, large plates $18–$31. Sun 11am–1am; Mon–Tues 11:30am–1am; Wed–Fri 11:30am–2am; Sat 11am–2am. Metro: Dupont Circle (Q St. exit).

## Inexpensive

**Pizzeria Paradiso** ★ PIZZA/ITALIAN  Pizzeria Paradiso has been around since before you were born. Okay, well, certainly before the gourmet pizza trend was born. It's 26 years old and remains a favorite among a wide field of contenders. Paradiso cooks its pizzas in a wood-burning, domed, stone oven that can withstand 650-degree heat, which gives the pizza a light but doughier crust than its rivals. The pies come in 9" and 12" sizes, and the 44-item toppings list includes anything you might imagine, from mussels to vegan mozzarella. Paninis and salads, too, get high marks. Pizzeria Paradiso serves wine and also has a Birreria, where patrons interested in microbrews and handcrafted beers can select from 12 drafts and 139 bottles. Paradiso's other locations are in Georgetown, at 3282 M St. NW (② **202/337-1245**), and in Old Town Alexandria, at 124 King St. (② **703/837-1245**).

2003 P St. NW (btw. 20th and 21st sts.). www.eatyourpizza.com. ② **202/223-1245.** Reservations not accepted. Pizzas $12–$21; sandwiches and salads $6–$13. Mon–Thurs 11:30am–11pm; Fri–Sat 11:30am–midnight; Sun noon–11pm. Metro: Dupont Circle (19th St./South exit).

**Teaism Dupont Circle ★** ASIAN FUSION   This homegrown teahouse enterprise currently has three D.C. locations, each similar in their menus of bento boxes, aromatic teas, savory sandwiches, and sweets, though they differ in appearance. This one, in Dupont Circle, is the original, a homey, two-level restaurant and shop tucked inside a century-old building with French windows that overlook the tree-lined street. The Penn Quarter's Teaism is busier, as you might expect from the neighborhood, and its tea shop is situated separately, one storefront away from the restaurant. No matter the Teaism, you'll find these are casual eateries, where you order from a menu that might include curried chicken, udon noodle soup, Korean beef brisket tacos, and a constantly updated inventory of about 36 teas. The menus change seasonally. All three teahouses serve an afternoon tea of savories and sweets, from 2:30 to 5:30pm, for $25 person.

Visit **Teaism Lafayette Square,** 800 Connecticut Ave. NW (② **202/835-2233**), near the White House, and **Teaism Penn Quarter ★,** 400 8th St. NW (② **202/638-6010**); both of these branches serve beer and wine, and the Penn Quarter Teaism also serves cocktails.

2009 R St. NW (btw. Connecticut and 21st sts.). www.teaism.com. ② **202/667-3827.** Reservations not accepted. All items $3–$13.75. Mon–Fri 8am–10pm; Sat–Sun 9am–10pm. Metro: Dupont Circle (Q St. exit).

# FOGGY BOTTOM/WEST END
## Moderate

**Founding Farmers ★** AMERICAN   An international clientele gathers at Founding Farmers, thanks to the fact that the restaurant is located on the ground floor of the International Monetary Fund, one block from World Bank Headquarters, and within a short walk of the Pan American Health Organization and the State Department. But the real reason for its popularity may be that it's one of only a few good dining room restaurants (as opposed to fast-food joints and delis) in this neck of the woods. So expect a full house, a frenetic ambience, and noise. That's especially true downstairs, which holds a big bar and communal farm tables, as well as booths and tables. Upstairs tends to be quieter, with silo-shaped booths and small clusters of more intimate seating. So what to order? Founding Farmers fans enthuse about the fancy cocktails, the bourbon-battered French toast available at brunch, and, at lunch and dinner, the crispy shrimp; the signature dishes, like Yankee pot roast and chicken pot pie; and the griddled farm bread topped with brie, onion jam, and sliced apples. But the options are endless and include a number of meatless entrees. The restaurant is also committed to eco-friendly practices, and uses them even in the restaurant's design. Founding Farmers has a popular sibling, **Farmers Fishers Bakers** (p. 110), on the Georgetown waterfront.

1924 Pennsylvania Ave. NW (at 20th St.). www.wearefoundingfarmers.com. © **202/822-8783.** Reservations recommended. Main courses breakfast and brunch $6–$14; lunch and dinner $11–$29 (most under $20). Mon 7am–10pm; Tues–Thurs 7am–11pm; Fri 7am–midnight; Sat 9am–midnight; Sun 9am–10pm. Metro: Foggy Bottom.

## Inexpensive

**Beefsteak** ★ VEGETARIAN   Inside the wide window-wrapped, street-level corner room of George Washington University's Engineering Building is another José Andrés culinary revelation, this one serving cheap, freshly made-to-order, vegetarian assemblages. If you've ever been to a Chipotle, you'll have an idea how it works. You step up to the counter and order one of four suggested favorites or else give instructions to the line cooks to create your own. First you choose your desired veggies from a wide assortment, then your grain (bulgur, quinoa, or rice), then your sauce (black bean, cilantro, garlic yogurt, or lemon honey), and finally, your crunchy toppings, everything from toasted almonds to chopped scallions. The counter staff flash cook the vegetables and assemble all of your ingredients in a recyclable container to eat there in the sunny eatery, or to take out. It's a simple concept, really, whose vegetarian time has come in D.C. And it's delicious. Overwhelmed by choices, I opted for the Eden on my last visit, which combined quinoa, snowpeas, edamame, green beans, asparagus, broccoli, cilantro, garlic yogurt sauce, romaine, scallions, toasted sesame seeds, and lemon honey dressing. A second Beefsteak is located at 1528 Connecticut Ave. NW (© **202/986-7597**), in the Dupont Circle neighborhood.

800 22nd St. NW (at I St.). www.beefsteakveggies.com. © **202/296-1421.** Reservations not accepted. All items under $9. Daily 10:30am–10pm. Metro: Foggy Bottom.

**Paul** ★ FRENCH BAKERY/CAFE   Talk about an appreciative audience! French expats, embassy staff, Francophiles like moi—and everybody else who loves croissants, gateau, baguettes, brioche, crepes, eclairs, and macarons—plan their runs to Paul with quiet regularity. Of the five District Pauls, I'm most partial to this one because it is so large and has so many places to perch. There are hundreds of Pauls around the world, all descendants of the one that opened in 1889 in Croix, near the city of Lille in northern France. Besides bread and pastries, Paul sells soups, salads, and sandwiches. In the D.C. area you'll find two Pauls in the Penn Quarter (801 Pennsylvania Ave. NW, © **202/524-4500,** and 555 13th St. NW, © **202/347-1606**); one in Georgetown (1078 Wisconsin Ave. NW; © **202/524-4630**); and another in Midtown (1000 Connecticut Ave. NW; © **202/524-4860**).

2000 Pennsylvania Ave. NW (entrance on 20th St.). www.paul-usa.com. © **202/524-4655.** Reservations not accepted. Breads and pastries $1–$8; sandwiches and salads $7–$14. Mon–Fri 7am–7pm; Sat–Sun 8am–6pm. Metro: Foggy Bottom.

# GEORGETOWN

The closest Metro stop to Georgetown is the Blue Line's Foggy Bottom station; from there you can walk or catch the DC Circulator bus on Pennsylvania Avenue.

## Expensive

**1789** ★★ **AMERICAN**   One of the city's top tables, the 1789 is the standard bearer for Old World charm. The restaurant's six dining rooms occupy a renovated Federal-period house on a back street in Georgetown. Equestrian and historical prints, tables laid with Limoges china and silver, and antique furnishings throughout add touches of elegance. Women usually dress up and men are advised to wear jackets (the staff have lender attire for those who forget). Romancing couples like Nicole Kidman and Keith Urban, world leaders like President Obama and German Chancellor Angela Merkel, and locals celebrating birthdays and anniversaries are among those who dine here for the intimate atmosphere and sense of momentousness the 1789 confers upon any occasion.

The kitchen has seen chefs come and go in the past few years, but the 1789, at 57 years old, is an old hand at handling change. Its cuisine has always been and always will be American, the emphasis more and more on produce purchased from local farms, and meats, seafood, and poultry bought "direct from their native regions." As classically formal as the 1789 is, wry touches of modern life pop up here and there: The smoked and roasted Icelandic cod is treated with "everything bagel spices," and there is a "beet Wellington" on the menu, with beets, mushrooms duxelles, and roasted mushrooms taking the place of beef in the puff pastry. One thing you can be sure of is that your meal will be luscious.

1226 36th St. NW (at Prospect St.). www.1789restaurant.com. © **202/965-1789.** Reservations recommended. Jackets suggested for men. Main courses $27–$47. Mon–Thurs 6–10pm; Fri 6–11pm; Sat 5.30–11pm, Sun 5:30–10pm.

**Fiola Mare** ★★★ **ITALIAN**   Strictly speaking, the Potomac River is not *Il Mare,* but as the watery view for one of the trendiest and certainly one of the finest seafood restaurants in D.C., the river certainly will do. This younger sister (opened March 2014) to Fabio Trabocchi's highly regarded **Fiola** (p. 94) in the Penn Quarter, Fiola Mare is worth a visit, if only to take in terrific river-side vistas. Sit at one of the many outdoor balcony tables and you'll be gazing out at Roosevelt Island, Key Bridge, and a slice of Georgetown's waterfront to your right, and the Watergate apartments and the Kennedy Center to your left. Great views are also available within. The sprawling, modern interior has a front bar and a back bar, and more than one dining area in between. The quietly proficient staff serve up a slate of specialty cocktails, like the standout Bellini. Trabocchi shines in his mastery of Italian seafood. A recent dinner started with a generous portion of top-grade tuna tartare, graced with a hint of tomato essence, followed by a too-generous portion of poached Alaskan halibut topped with Ossetia caviar and succulent oysters. Also done to perfection was a bowl of lobster ravioli in a simple, herb-scented lobster broth, together with juicy lobster claw and tail, tasting as if the crustacean had just been pulled from the water. End with the *bombolini:* half a dozen ricotta doughnuts dusted with sugar, complemented by a warm chocolate sauce and a generous portion of vanilla gelato bearing chocolate crunches.

3050 K St. NW, Suite 101 (at 31st St. NW & the Washington Harbour waterfront). www. fiolamaredc.com. ☏ **202/628-0065.** Reservations recommended. Lunch and dinner main courses $24–$50; prix-fixe light lunch menu $32; brunch main courses $16–$28; dinner main courses $24–$50. Tues–Fri 11:30am–2:30pm; Sat–Sun 11:30am–2pm; Sun–Thurs 5–10:30pm; Fri 5–11pm; Sat 5–11pm.

**La Chaumiere** ★ FRENCH   Sometimes you just are not in the mood for trendy. Sometimes you simply want delicious food, service that is solicitous but not in the way, a pretty but not splashy dining room, and tables set enough apart to allow for private conversation. La Chaumiere is the answer. A "grown-up" restaurant in Georgetown that's been around for 40 years, it pleases with its French-country decor, its white-tablecloth-covered tables, and rush-bottom chairs arranged around the large center hearth, where a fire crackles in winter. Le Chaumiere's menu is a joy for lovers of French classics, like French onion soup, lobster bisque, steak au poivre, and *St. Jacques a la Provençale* (sea scallops with garlic and tomatoes). The clientele usually skews older, but young couples, families, and business people are among the grateful patrons, too.

2813 M St. NW (at 28th St.) www.lachaumieredc.com. ☏ **202/338-1784.** Reservations accepted. Main courses lunch $15.50–$22; dinner $19–$37 (most under $30). Mon–Fri 11:30am–2:30pm; Mon–Sat 5:30–10:30pm.

## Moderate

**Farmers Fishers Bakers** ★ AMERICAN   Come here weekday mornings for First Bake, and you'll be among a quiet few nibbling on fresh-baked doughnuts and cinnamon rolls. By lunchtime, it's a little livelier; in the evening, the place is almost hitting its stride, with lots of young professionals gathering on the patio and inside for drinks and appetizers, most staying on for dinner. But weekend brunch is when FFB is jammed, with diners stacking plates of French toast, fried chicken, meatballs, bruléed pink grapefruit, egg scrambles, and all of the many other dishes that $29.99 covers. (Drinks are extra.) *Note:* There are no water views with your meals here. FFB is set back and down a flight of steps from the waterfront Strand, so your view is of the plaza fountain, and not the Potomac. For best view and best food, book an outdoor table at Fiola Mare (above).

3000 K St. NW (at the Georgetown waterfront). www.farmersfishersbakers.com. ☏ **202/298-8783.** Reservations accepted. First Bake items $1.50–$4; lunch/dinner main courses $10–$29 (most are under $20); brunch $29.99, $14.99 for children

**Farmers Fishers Bakers.**

# HUNGRY? MAKE LIKE A LOCAL AND FOLLOW THE food trucks

"Meet you at McPherson Square—lobster rolls!" "Time for a cupcake break—corner of 3rd and D." All day long weekdays and somewhat on weekends, D.C. workers of all trades and echelons text, tweet, e-mail, or phone friends to arrange a food-on-the-move rendezvous. They track the routes of favorite "food trucks," that most unappetizing name for the legion of mobile cook-and-serve vendors, each hocking its own irresistible specialty: gourmet macaroni and cheese, empanadas, Philly cheesesteaks, Maine lobster rolls, all sorts of desserts—you get the idea.

Traditional sidewalk and roadway merchants selling hot dogs and T-shirts still abound in all the usual sightseeing places, including in clusters around the National Mall. These are not them. This next generation of food trucks switches up street fare, tweets its location so hungry patrons know where to go, and still manages to keep prices reasonable (generally ranging from $2.25 for a vanilla-glazed doughnut from Astro Doughnuts and Fried Chicken, to $15.95

for a Red Hook Lobster Pound lobster roll). These days, more than 240 different trucks roll around town, setting up shop at designated spots before driving on to their next location. Readers of *Washington City Paper* voted the food truck Crepelove their favorite in 2016 for its assortment of breakfast, sweet, and savory crepes, like the Bombay Dhaba, a buckwheat-flour crepe stuffed with tandoori-marinated chicken strips, roasted red peppers, spicy curry aioli, and cilantro; crepes are $6 to $9 each.

For a complete list of D.C.'s food trucks, go to **www.foodtruckfiesta.com,** which also displays a map in real time of food-truck stops and messages. The website includes links to each truck's website, where menus, travel routes, and prices are posted.

Laws prohibit gourmet food trucks from parking and serving on federal property, so you won't find these trucks parked along the inside roads (Jefferson and Madison drives) of the National Mall. They're never far away, though.

ages 6–12. Mon–Fri 7:30–10am; Mon–Wed 11am–10pm; Thurs 11am–11pm; Fri 11am–midnight; Sat 9am–midnight; Sun 9am–10pm. Bar stays open later.

**Martin's Tavern** ★ AMERICAN   Martin's turns 84 in 2017, and in its lifetime has served every president from Harry Truman to George W. Bush. The tavern is best known as the place where JFK, then a U.S. Senator, proposed to Jacqueline Bouvier on June 24, 1953. Hardbacked wooden booths line the walls of the restaurant, and many bear a plaque identifying the former President or famous person who dined within; #3 is the "Proposal Booth." Fourth-generation Billy Martin is usually behind the bar, attending to the regulars who frequent the place. That's largely what Martin's is these days: a restaurant for folks from the neighborhood, many of them generational iterations of earlier customers. People who aren't regulars sometimes feel left out, but that's part of the experience, too. "Tavern" is exactly the word to describe Martin's food, which is okay American and, in some cases, Colonial American: Shepherd's pie and Brunswick stew are listed, and so is Martin's Delight, which is roasted turkey on toast, smothered in rarebit sauce. Martin's offers a

111

# chocolate LOUNGES & CUPCAKE SHOPS

Busted! Washingtonians are finally exposed for what we are: chocoholics and sweet-cake addicts. Chocolate lounges, cupcake shops, and bakery cafes continue to proliferate, forcing us to come clean. If you answer to the same passion for something desserty, join the queue at one of these five homegrown, personally vouched-for sweet shops:

**Co Co. Sala,** 929 F St. NW (www.cocosala.com; ℂ **202/347-4265**): This chocolate lounge and boutique is a sweet refuge in the heart of the Penn Quarter, dispensing coffees, cocoas, pastries, and small plates of light fare throughout the day. Dessert cocktails and chocolate-spiked liqueurs are on tap into the wee hours.

**Dog Tag Bakery,** 3206 Grace St. NW (www.dogtagbakery.com; ℂ **202/407-9609**): Both bakery and work-study program for disabled vets, this sunny Georgetown cafe makes my favorite cinnamon bun. It also serves up superb breakfast breads and pastries, bundt cake, apple pies, and non-bakery items, too, like sandwiches and soups.

**Georgetown Cupcake,** 3301 M St. NW (www.georgetowncupcake.com; ℂ **202/333-8448**): Two sisters, 12 daily flavors (chocolate ganache to vanilla birthday), plus six seasonal flavors that change monthly (November: caramel apple), darling designs and packaging, and perfect baked goods. Georgetown Cupcake is so popular that the TLC network developed a reality TV show featuring the lovely cupcake makers, Sophie LaMontagne and Katherine Kallinis. Georgetown Cupcake now has locations in New York, Los Angeles, Atlanta, and Boston.

**Rare Sweets,** 963 Palmer Alley NW (www.raresweets.com; ℂ **202/499-0077**): CityCenterDC is full of chi chi shops and big names: Dior, Hermes, David Yurman, Carolina Herrara. And then there's this tiny gem tucked away on little Palmer Alley, where pastry chef Meredith Tomason concocts variations on classic cakes, as well as seasonal specials: German chocolate, lemon and rhubarb, and lavender and buttercream, to name a few flavors. At $5 or $6 a slice, it's the best deal in the upscale complex.

**Red Velvet Cupcakery,** 505 7th St. NW (www.redvelvetcupcakery.com; ℂ **202/347-7895**): Located in the heart of the Penn Quarter, Red Velvet stays open until 11pm nightly, happy to accommodate the bar and club crowd when a yen for a sweet something hits. It also serves hot chocolate to go.

bit of old-guard Washington and Georgetown you're not going to get anywhere else, and that's mostly why I recommend it.

1264 Wisconsin Ave. NW (at N St.). www.martinstavern.com. ℂ **202/333-7370.** Reservations accepted. Main courses lunch/brunch $10–$22; dinner $16–$40. Sun 8am–1:30am; Mon–Thurs 11am–1:30am; Fri 11am–2:30am; Sat 9am–2:30am.

## Inexpensive

**Ching Ching Cha ★ CHINESE** You'd never guess this kind of place might exist in wild and woolly Georgetown, and it's right in the thick of things, too, on Wisconsin Avenue, just past Blues Alley. Although the teahouse has been here since 1998, many locals don't even know about Ching, and maybe that's why there's never a line. You're here for an authentic tearoom experience, where the emphasis is on enjoying tea in a tranquil environment. The skylit space is furnished with cushioned platform seating and chairs set at rosewood tables. Try one of the flowering teas, listed among Artisan Teas, in which the brewed tea opens up a jasmine or orange blossom. Seventy teas in all are listed: scented, black, green, oolong, decaffeinated, tisanes, you name it. Individual cups of tea, costing $6 to $20, are actually more expensive than the food items: A short list of menu options ranges from the $2 almond cookie to a $5 Mongolian dumpling to the $14 tea meal (soup, rice, marinated cold vegetables, and a main dish, such as mustard miso salmon). A fine selection of teaware products gifts is for sale.

1063 Wisconsin Ave. NW (near M St.). www.chingchingcha.com. © **202/333-8288.** Reservations not accepted. All food items $1.50–$14; tea $6–$20. Tues–Sun 11am–9pm.

**Surfside** ★ AMERICAN/LATIN/SEAFOOD At Surfside, 20- and 30-somethings gather on the rooftop deck to sip margaritas and dive into guacamole, while down in the colorful and casual eatery, their married-with-children peers, families in tow (and yes, there's a kid's menu), nosh on tacos, quesadillas, burritos, and salads. Surfside is especially known for its fresh grilled fish tacos, but its menu covers assorted options, including a pork carnitas taco served with pineapple jalapeño salsa on corn tortillas, that I like. But if the menu combinations don't appeal, you fill out a form indicating your desired ingredients so the cook can custom-prepare your order. Technically, Surfside is in a neighborhood called Glover Park, which is just north of Georgetown, so not far. *Good to know:* Surfside does a brisk takeout business, too, and it operates a 24-hour taco stand at 1800 N St. NW (© **202/466-1830**), at Connecticut Ave. NW, in the Dupont Circle neighborhood.

2444 Wisconsin Ave. NW (near Calvert St.). www.surfsidedc.com. © **202/380-9353.** Reservations accepted. Main courses dinner $8.95–$15; brunch all items $9.95. Sun–Tues 11am–9.30pm, Wed–Sat 11am–10pm. Bar daily until midnight.

# WOODLEY PARK & CLEVELAND PARK

## Moderate

**Indique** ★ INDIAN Staff from the Indian Embassy and others who know authentic Indian cuisine consider Indique's regional dishes the real deal. Favorite dishes are too many to mention, but definitely order the vegetable samosa chaat, the chicken curry, and the tandoori shrimp. The two-level town house offers two different dining spaces: Upstairs is a beautiful room of red-and-gold walls and blue-painted ceilings, with best tables overlooking the atrium; downstairs includes the lively window-fronted bar area, a good spot for watching commuters emerging from the Cleveland Park subway station and all else that's happening on busy Connecticut Avenue.

3512–14 Connecticut Ave. NW (btw. Porter and Ordway sts.). www.indique.com. © **202/244-6600.** Reservations accepted. Main courses $12–$23; Sun brunch $24. Fri–Sat noon–3pm; Sun 11am–3pm; Sun–Thurs 5:30–10:30pm; Fri–Sat 5:30–11pm. Metro: Cleveland Park (Connecticut Ave. west exit).

# family-friendly DINING SPOTS

Nearly every restaurant welcomes families, starting, most likely, with the one in your hotel. Cafes at sightseeing attractions are always a safe bet, and so are these:

**Lebanese Taverna** (below)   The taverna is located down the hill from the National Zoo. Its kids' menu doubles as a coloring book and lists chicken tenders and other items, each $7.15 and served with hummus, rice, carrots, and celery. Around for 27 years, the Taverna is a favorite among locals.

**Five Guys Burgers and Fries** (p. 100)   Duh. Burgers. Fries. Hot dogs. Sodas. Grilled cheese. Indestructible environment. And the Guys are everywhere you turn. Last but not least, the price is right: Burgers are $4.99 to $8.69, fries $3.09 to $5.79.

**Old Ebbitt Grill** (p. 97)   Well, first of all, the hours are kid-friendly: The place opens at 7:30am weekdays, 8:30am weekends, and then just stays open, there whenever you or your children need seated sustenance. Then

there's the fact that the Ebbitt's layout includes booths and nooks and different rooms and partitions and lots of strategically placed plants, which all work to contain outbursts of any sort. And finally, there's the children's menu of 13 different items, hot dogs to mac and cheese, each priced at $9, which includes a drink and ice cream.

**Ted's Bulletin** (p. 90)   This boisterous, laid-back place in the Barracks Row section of Capitol Hill, and its twin at 1818 14th St. NW, welcome children of all ages with a retro menu of comfort food, like grilled cheese, Pop-Tarts (called "Ted's Tarts"), mac and cheese, and tomato soup. Breakfast is served all day, so that might decide things right there. But kids also have their own menu of eight choices, PB&J to pasta with butter, each priced at $5.99. Or how about this: thick and creamy milkshakes ($7.99) in awesome flavors like Oreo and Heath almond. There's always a lot going on here, so you never have to worry about your children making too much noise.

**Lebanese Taverna** ★ MIDDLE EASTERN   When it opened in 1990, the family-owned Lebanese Taverna was one of the capital's few ethnic restaurants. Today, the Taverna is just one of many eateries catering to international tastes, but it hasn't lost any of its appeal. In an airy dining room whose decor has changed over the years to include a bar and lounge, wood paneling and hand-laid fieldstone walls, diners enjoy traditional Middle Eastern dishes that are presented in up-to-date ways. For instance, the hummus bar offers five flavors (traditional, spicy, garlic, with beef or lamb and pine nuts, or with marinated chicken), assorted toppings, and four dippers (crackers, vegetables, fries, and pita toasts). Entrees, such as the lamb *sharhat* (sliced lamb loin with three green-herb sauce), and mezze items, from tabbouleh to spinach pastries, continue to draw the neighborhood. All meals begin with fresh-from-the-oven puffs of pita bread with olive oil. The proper ending is an order of Lebanese doughnuts, honey-drizzled creamy pudding on the side for dipping.

2641 Connecticut Ave. NW (near Woodley Rd.). www.lebanesetaverna.com. ⓒ **202/ 265-8681.** Reservations recommended. Main courses $11–$25; mezze items $6–$13. Sun–Mon 11:30am–9:30pm; Tues–Thurs 11:30am–10pm; Fri–Sat 11:30am–11pm. Metro: Woodley Park–Zoo (Connecticut Ave. south exit).

# EXPLORING WASHINGTON, D.C.

If you've never been to Washington, D.C., your mission is clear: Get thee to the National Mall and Capitol Hill. Within this roughly 2½-by-⅓-mile rectangular plot lie the lion's share of the capital's iconic attractions (see "Iconic Washington, D.C.," in chapter 3), including presidential and war memorials, the U.S. Capitol, the U.S. Supreme Court, the Library of Congress, most of the Smithsonian museums, the National Gallery of Art, and the National Archives.

In fact, even if you have traveled here before, you're likely to find yourself returning to this part of town, to pick up where you left off on that long list of sites worth seeing and to visit new ones.

Beyond its iconic attractions lie the city's charming neighborhoods, standalone museums, historic houses, and beautiful gardens; you don't want to miss those, either. Tour national landmarks and you'll gain a sense of what this country is about, both politically and culturally. Tour off-the-Mall attractions and neighborhoods and you'll get a taste of the vibrant, multicultural local scene that is the real D.C. This chapter will help you do both.

## CAPITOL HILL

The **U.S. Capitol** and flanking Senate and House office buildings dominate this residential neighborhood of tree-lined streets, 19th-century town houses, and pubs and casual eateries. Across the street from the Capitol lie the **U.S. Supreme Court** and the **Library of Congress;** close by are the smaller but still engrossing **Folger Shakespeare Library,** the **Belmont-Paul Women's Equality National Monument,** and **Eastern Market.** A bit farther away is **Union Station,** doing triple duty as historical attraction, shopping mall, and transportation hub. But the neighborhood itself is a pleasure. Explore.

**The Capitol** ★★★ GOVERNMENT BUILDING   In Washington, D.C., one catches sight of the Capitol all around town. That's no accident: When planner Pierre L'Enfant laid out the capital in

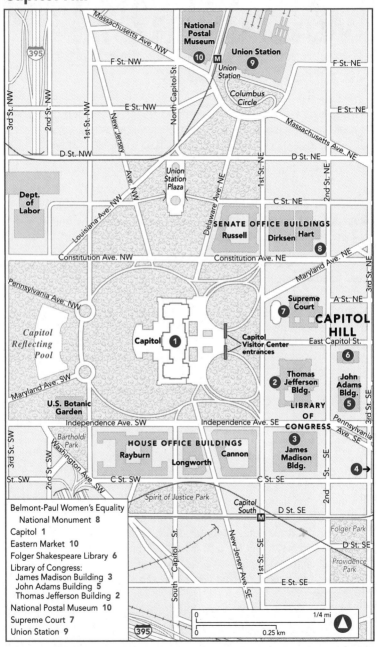

National Postal Museum
**10** M
Union Station
**9**
Union Station
F St. NW
F St. NE
395
3rd St. NW
2nd St. NW
1st St. NW
New Jersey
North Capitol St.
Massachusetts Ave. NW
E St. NW
Columbus Circle
E St. NE
D St. NW
Massachusetts Ave. NE
D St. NE
Ave. NW
Union Station Plaza
1st St. NE
C St. NE
2nd St. NE
**Dept. of Labor**
Louisiana Ave. NW
Delaware Ave. NE
**SENATE OFFICE BUILDINGS**
**Russell** **Dirksen** **Hart**
**8**
Constitution Ave. NW
Constitution Ave. NE
3rd St. NE
Pennsylvania Ave. NW
Maryland Ave. NE
*Capitol Reflecting Pool*
**Supreme Court**
**7**
A St. NE
**CAPITOL HILL**
**Capitol**
**1**
Capitol Visitor Center entrances
East Capitol St.
**6**
Maryland Ave. SW
**Thomas Jefferson Bldg.**
**2**
**John Adams Bldg.**
**5**
**U.S. Botanic Garden**
**LIBRARY OF CONGRESS**
3rd St. SE
Independence Ave. SW
Independence Ave. SE
Pennsylvania Ave. SE
*Bartholdi Park*
3rd St. SW
Washington Ave. SW
2nd St. SW
**HOUSE OFFICE BUILDINGS**
**Rayburn** **Longworth** **Cannon**
**James Madison Bldg.**
**3**
2nd St. SE
**4**→
St. SW
C St. SW
C St. SE
*Spirit of Justice Park*
Capitol South
2nd St. SE
M
D St. SE
*Folger Park*
Capitol St.
New Jersey Ave. SE
D St. SE
1st St. SE
*Providence Park*
South Capitol St.
E St. SE
395

0                    1/4 mi
0        0.25 km

The dome of the Capitol.

1791, he purposely placed "Congress House" upon this bluff, overlooking the city. Its importance, and the importance of Congress, is meant to be unmistakable.

Incontrovertible, too, is the fact that a tour of this iconic American symbol is a necessary stop on any first-time tour of D.C. When you visit here, you understand, in a very visceral way, just what it means to govern a country democratically. The fights and compromises, the din of differing opinions, the necessity of creating "one from the many" (*e pluribus unum*) without trampling on the rights of that one. It's a powerful experience. And the ideals of the Congress are not just expressed in the debates on the floor of the House and Senate (though you should try to hear those if you can; see below), but in its masterful architecture, as well as within the many historical works of art and artifacts displayed within the massive building. For 135 years it sheltered not only both houses of Congress, but also the Supreme Court and, for 97 years, the Library of Congress.

Before entering the Capitol, stand back to admire the Capitol dome, from its base up to the pedestal of the "Statue of Freedom," the 19-foot, 6-inch bronze female figure at its crown. In 2017, the 9-million-pound cast iron Capitol dome's gleaming exterior looks better than ever as it is newly restored, with 1,300 cracks sealed, and scores of finials, rosettes and other decorative ornaments recast.

**The hour-long guided tour** (for procedures, see p. 119) starts in the Capitol Visitor Center, where you'll watch a 13-minute orientation film, then takes you to the Rotunda, National Statuary Hall, down to the Crypt, and back to the Visitor Center. Here's some of what you'll see:

The **Rotunda**—a huge 96-foot-wide circular hall capped by a 180-foot-high dome—is the hub of the Capitol. The dome was completed, at Lincoln's direction, while the Civil War was being fought: "If people see the Capitol going on, it is a sign we intend the Union shall go on," said Lincoln. Eleven presidents have lain in state here, with former President Gerald Ford, in 2006, being the most recent; when John F. Kennedy's casket was displayed, the line of mourners stretched 40 blocks. On rare occasions, someone other than a president, military hero, or member of Congress receives this posthumous recognition. In October 2005, Congress paid tribute to Rosa Parks by allowing her body to lie in state here, the first woman to be so honored. (Parks was the black woman who in 1955 refused to relinquish her seat to a white man on a bus in Montgomery, Alabama, thereby helping to spark the civil rights movement. On February 27, 2013, Congress further honored Parks by adding a statue of her to **National Statuary Hall.**)

Embracing the Rotunda walls are eight immense oil paintings commemorating great moments in American history, such as the presentation of the Declaration of Independence and the surrender of Cornwallis at Yorktown. Inside the now-canopied inner dome of the Rotunda is an allegorical fresco masterpiece by Constantino Brumidi, *The Apotheosis of Washington,* a symbolic portrayal of George Washington surrounded by Roman gods and goddesses watching over the progress of the nation. Brumidi was known as the "Michelangelo of the Capitol" for the many works he created throughout the building. (Take another look at the fresco and find the woman directly below Washington; the triumphant *Armed Freedom* figure is said to be modeled after Lola Germon, a beautiful young actress with whom the 60-year-old Brumidi conceived a child.) Beneath those painted figures is a *trompe l'oeil* frieze depicting major developments in the life of America, from Columbus's landing in 1492 to the birth of the aviation age in 1903. Don't miss the sculptures in the Rotunda, including George Washington; a pensive Abraham Lincoln (sculpted from 1866 to 1870 by Vinnie Reams, the first woman artist to receive a government commission); a dignified Rev. Dr. Martin Luther King, Jr.; a ponderous trinity of suffragists, Elizabeth Cady Stanton, Susan B. Anthony, and Lucretia Mott; and a bronze statue of President Ronald Reagan, looking characteristically genial.

The **National Statuary Hall** was originally the chamber of the House of Representatives; in 1864 it became Statuary Hall, and the states were invited to send two statues each of native sons and daughters. There are 100 statues in all, New Mexico completing the original collection with its contribution in 2005 of Po'Pay, a Pueblo Indian, who in 1680 led a revolt against the Spanish that helped to save Pueblo culture. States do have the prerogative to replace statues with new choices, which is what Iowa did in 2014, swapping out the 1910 choice of Secretary of the Interior James Harlan for Nobel Peace Prize winner Norman Borlaug, known as the "father of the Green Revolution" for his work to increase food production and eliminate world hunger.

Because of space constraints, only 35 statues or so reside in the Hall, with the figures of 6 presidents displayed in the Rotunda, 24 statues placed in the Visitor Center, and the remaining 35 standing in the Crypt (directly below the Rotunda) and throughout the corridors of the Capitol. Statues include Ethan Allen, the Revolutionary War hero who founded the state of Vermont, and Missouri's Thomas Hart Benton—not the 20th-century artist famous for his rambunctious murals, but his namesake and uncle, who was one of the first two senators from Missouri and whose antislavery stance in 1850 cost him his Senate seat. Nine women are represented, including Alabama-born Helen Keller and Montana's Jeannette Rankin, the first woman to serve in Congress. The District of Columbia was finally allowed a statue in 2013: It added a full-sized bronze depiction of abolitionist Frederick Douglass who stands in Emancipation Hall of the Capitol Visitor Center. Congress has yet to recognize the District as its own state, but at least granted its constituents this representation!

In slow seasons, usually fall and winter, your public tour may include a visit to the **Old Supreme Court Chamber,** which has been restored to its mid-19th-century appearance. The Supreme Court met here from 1810 to 1860. Busts of the first four chief justices are on display—John Marshall, John Rutledge, John Jay, and Oliver Ellsworth—and so are some of their desks. The justices handed down a number of noteworthy decisions here, including in 1857 *Dred Scott v. Sandford,* which denied the citizenship of blacks, whether slaves or free, and in so doing precipitated the Civil War.

You will not see them on your tour, but the **south and north wings** of the Capitol hold the House and Senate chambers, respectively. The House of Representatives chamber is the setting for the president's annual State of the Union address. (See below for info on watching Senate and House sessions.)

**A note on the area right outside the building:** Immediately surrounding the Capitol itself are 59 acres of beautifully kept grounds, originally landscaped in 1892 by Frederick Law Olmsted, who also planned NYC's Central Park. The Capitol often offers tours of the grounds in spring.

**Procedures for Touring the Capitol:** Tours of the Capitol are free and take place year-round, Monday through Saturday between 8:50am and 3:20pm. Capitol Guide Service guides lead the hour-long, general public tours, which can include as few as 1 or 2 people or as many as 40 or 50, depending on the season. Here I must sing the praises of these guides, who are often historians in their own right, repositories of American lore, traditions, anecdotes, and, of course, actual fact. Got a question? Ask away. These guides know their stuff.

You and everyone in your party must have a **timed pass,** which you can order online at www.visitthecapitol.gov. During peak spring and summer sessions, you should order tickets at least 2 weeks in advance. Same-day passes are also available daily from the "public walk-up" near the information desks on the lower level of the visitor center—in limited supply during peak times, but plentiful at off-peak times, particularly in January and February. You can also contact your representative or senator in Congress and request passes for constituent tours, which are usually limited to groups of 15 and

# THE CAPITOL visitor center

The enormous, 4,000-person-capacity **Capitol Visitor Center** is underground, which means that as you approach the East Front of the Capitol, you won't actually see it. Look for signs and the sloping sets of steps on each side of the Capitol's central section, leading down to the center's entrances. Once inside you'll pass through security screening and then enter the two-level chamber.

Most visitors find it works best to explore the center after touring the Capitol. You can admire the 24 Statuary Hall statues scattered throughout and tour **Exhibition Hall,** which is a mini-museum of historic document displays; check out interactive kiosks that take you on virtual tours of the Capitol, filling you in on history, art, and architecture; and view exhibits that explain the legislative process. **Emancipation Hall** is the large central chamber where you line up for tours; this is also where you'll find the 26 restrooms and 530-seat restaurant.

The visitor center is open Monday through Saturday year-round from 8:30am to 4:30pm, closed on Thanksgiving, Christmas, New Year's Day, and Inauguration Day.

conducted by congressional staff, who may take you to notable places in the Capitol beyond those seen on the public tour.

The Capitol has quite a list of items it prohibits; you can read the list online at www.visitthecapitol.gov (and also make sure there that the Capitol will be open when you visit). Items ranging from large bags of any kind to food and drink are prohibited; leave everything you can back at the hotel.

The Capitol Guide Service also offers other special tours, though the specific topics might change. Recent offerings included tours of the Brumidi corridors and tours that focused on the Capitol and Congress during the Civil War.

**Procedures for Visiting the House Gallery or Senate Gallery:** Both the Senate and House galleries are open to visitors whenever either body is **in session ★–★★★**, so do try to sit in. (The experience receives a range of star ratings because a visit can prove fascinating or deadly boring, depending on whether a debate is underway and how lively it is.) Otherwise the Senate Gallery is open to visitors during scheduled recesses of 1 week or more, Monday to Friday 9am to 4:15pm, and the House Gallery is open to visitors year-round Monday to Friday 9am to 4:15pm. Children 5 and under are not allowed in the Senate gallery. You can obtain visitor passes at the offices of your representative and senators, or in the case of District of Columbia and Puerto Rico residents, from the office of your delegate to Congress. To find out your member's office location, go online at www.house.gov or www.senate.gov or call ✆ **202/225-3121.** You must have a separate pass for each gallery. Once obtained, the passes are good through the remainder of the Congress. *Note:* International visitors can obtain both House and Senate gallery passes by presenting a passport or a valid driver's license with photo ID to staff at the House and Senate appointments desks on the upper level of the visitor center.

The main, staffed offices of congressional representatives and delegates are in House buildings on the south (Independence Ave.) side of the Capitol; senators' main, staffed offices are located in Senate buildings on the north (Constitution Ave.) side. You should be able to pick up passes to both the Senate and House galleries in one place, at either your representative's office or one of your senators' offices. Visit the Architect of the Capitol's website, **www.aoc.gov,** the Visitor Center website, **www.visitthecapitol.gov,** or call your senator's or congressperson's office for more exact information about obtaining passes to the House and Senate galleries.

You'll know that the House and/or the Senate is in session if you see flags flying over their respective wings of the Capitol (*Remember:* House, south side; Senate, north side), or you can visit their websites, **www.house.gov** and **www.senate.gov,** for schedules of bill debates in the House and Senate, committee markups, and links to your Senate or House representative's page.

Capitol and Capitol Visitor Center: E. Capitol St. (at First St. NW). www.visitthecapitol. gov, www.aoc.gov, www.house.gov, www.senate.gov. ℭ **202/225-6827** (recording), 202/593-1768 (Capitol Guide Service Office), or 202/225-3121 (Capitol operator). Free admission. Year-round Mon–Sat 8:30am–4:30pm (first tour at 8:50am, last at 3:20pm). Closed for tours Sun and Jan 1, Thanksgiving, Dec 25, and Inauguration Day. Parking at Union Station or on the streets. Metro: Union Station (Massachusetts Ave. exit) or Capitol South, then walk to the Capitol Visitor Center, located on the East Front of the Capitol.

**Eastern Market** ★ MARKET  A mainstay of the historic Capitol Hill neighborhood and of the city itself, Eastern Market has been operating continuously since 1873, not even pausing after a fire in 2007 (indoor vendors moved to a parking lot across the street until the building reopened in 2009). Inside, 13 vendors in their separate stalls sell fresh produce, pasta, seafood, meats, cheeses, sweets, flowers, and pottery Tuesday through Sunday. Every Tuesday from 3 to 7pm, a farmers' market operates outside the main hall. Weekends are when things get really lively, when more than 100 arts and crafts merchants, plus an additional 20 or so farmers and open-air food vendors sell their wares on the market's outdoor plaza. The street is closed to

---

### Heads Up

Security precautions and procedures are a post-9/11 fact of life everywhere in America, but especially in the nation's capital, thanks to the preponderance of federal structures and attractions that are open to the public. What that means for you as a visitor is that you may have to stand in line to enter a national museum (like one of the Smithsonians) or a government building (like the Library of Congress). At many tourist sites, you can expect staff to search handbags, briefcases, and backpacks, either by hand or by X-ray machine. Some sites, including the National Air and Space Museum, require you to walk past metal detectors. During the busy spring and summer seasons, you may be queueing outside. Carry as little as possible, and certainly no sharp objects. Museums and public buildings rarely offer lockers for use by visitors.

## Call Ahead or Check Online

Here's a crucial piece of advice: **Call ahead or check the websites of the places you plan to tour each day before you set out.** Many of Washington's government buildings, museums, memorials, and monuments are open to the general public daily, year-round—except when they're not.

Because buildings like the Capitol, the Supreme Court, and the White House are offices as well as tourist destinations, the business of the day always poses the potential for closing one of those sites, or at least sections, to sightseers. There's also the matter of maintenance. The steady stream of visitors to Washington's attractions necessitates ongoing caretaking, which may require closing an entire landmark, or part of it, or changing the hours of operation or procedures for visiting. Washington's famous museums, grand halls, and public gardens sometimes double as settings for press conferences, galas, special exhibits, festivals, and even movie sets. You might arrive at, say, the National Air and Space Museum on a Sunday afternoon, only to find some of its galleries off-limits because a movie shoot is underway. (Have you seen *Captain America: The Winter Soldier*, by the way? Yep, the real Air and Space museum makes an appearance.) To avoid frustration and disappointment, call ahead or check online for up-to-the-minute information.

traffic in front of the market, and the block teems with families and singles doing their weekly grocery shopping, and even the occasional congressperson (many live in the neighborhood). For a real hometown experience, come for blueberry buckwheat pancakes ("bluebucks") served at Market Lunch inside the market on Saturdays (see p. 93), or for lunch Tuesday through Sunday.

225 7th St. SE (at North Carolina Ave.). www.easternmarket-dc.org. © **202/698-5253.** Free admission. Indoor market: Tues–Fri 7am–7pm, Sat 7am–6pm, Sun 9am–5pm. Closed Thanksgiving, Dec 25, and New Year's Day. Metro: Union Station or Capitol South.

**Folger Shakespeare Library** ★ LIBRARY "Shakespeare taught us that the little world of the heart is vaster, deeper, and richer than the spaces of astronomy," wrote Ralph Waldo Emerson in 1864. A decade later, Amherst student Henry Clay Folger was profoundly affected by a lecture Emerson gave similarly extolling the Bard. Folger purchased an inexpensive set of Shakespeare's plays and went on to amass the world's largest collection of the Bard's works, today housed in the Folger Shakespeare Library. When the library opened in 1932 as a gift from the Folgers to the country, the collection comprised approximately 93,000 books, 50,000 prints and engravings, and thousands of manuscripts. Today, the collection has grown to include some 255,000 books, 116,000 of which are rare (pre-1801), 55,000 manuscripts, 250,000 playbills, and a wealth of paintings, costumes, musical instruments and other materials. Sadly, Henry Folger did not live to see the library's debut, having died suddenly in June, 1930.

Most precious and best known of the Folger's possessions are its 82 copies of the **1623 First Folio of Shakespeare.** The First Folio is the first collected edition of Shakespeare's plays, and it was published in 1623, seven years after the playwright's death. As the only source for 18 of Shakespeare's works, it's likely that the world would have been without *Macbeth*, *The Tempest*, and other of the Bard's masterpieces, had the First Folio not been printed. On permanent display in the Folger's white-oak-paneled Tudor-ish **Great Hall** is one such First Folio, and right next to it, a touchscreen kiosk that allows one to flip digitally from page to page.

Scholars and qualified researchers may apply to gain access to the collection and the library's Reading Rooms. The general public may visit the Reading Rooms by signing up online for the free, hour-long, docent-led tour held every Saturday at noon. Highlights include 16th- and 17th-century tapestries and a large stained-glass window portraying the Seven Ages of Man, as described by the character Jaques in *As You Like It*.

The **Great Hall** is always open to the public and, besides its First Folio display, mounts rotating exhibits of other items from the permanent collection—Renaissance musical instruments to centuries-old playbills—that highlight a particular theme. Just off the hall is the Shakespeare Gallery, which offers an orientation video and multimedia close-up look at some of the Folgers' treasures, as well as Shakespeare's life and works. Plan on spending at least 30 minutes here. Free docent-led tours take place daily; see information below.

At the end of the Great Hall is a theater designed to suggest the yard of an Elizabethan inn, where plays, concerts, readings, and Shakespeare-related events take place (see chapter 8, p. 223 for details).

The Folger Shakespeare Library building itself has a marble facade decorated with nine bas-relief scenes from Shakespeare's plays; it is a striking example of Art Deco classicism. An **Elizabethan garden** on the east side of the building is planted with flowers and herbs of the period. Most remarkable here are eight sculptures by Greg Wyatt, each depicting figures from a particular scene in a Shakespeare play. The garden is also a nice, quiet place to have a picnic. 201 E. Capitol St. SE. www.folger.edu. ✆ **202/544-4600.** Free admission. Mon–Sat 10am–5pm; Sun noon–5pm. Free walk-in tours Mon–Sat 11am, 1 and 3pm; Sun noon and 1pm; garden tours Sat 10am, Apr–Oct. Reading Room tours held Sat at noon require reservation. Closed federal holidays. Metro: Capitol South or Union Station.

**Library of Congress ★★** LIBRARY   You're inside the main public building of the Library of Congress—the magnificent, ornate, Italian Renaissance–style **Thomas Jefferson Building.** Maybe you've arrived via the tunnel that connects the Capitol and the Library of Congress, or maybe you've climbed the Grand Staircase facing First Street and entered through the main doors. In any case, you'll likely be startled—very startled—to find yourself suddenly inside a government structure that looks more like a palace. Before you line up for the tour, take time to stroll around the building and just gape. Admire the stained-glass skylights overhead; the Italian marble floors inlaid with brass and concentric medallions; the gorgeous murals, allegorical paintings, stenciling, sculptures, and intricately carved architectural elements. This building, more than any other in the city, is a visual treasure.

The Library of Congress.

Now for the history lesson: Established in 1800 by an act of Congress, "for the purchase of such books as may be necessary for the use of Congress," the library today also serves the nation, with holdings for the visually impaired (for whom books are recorded and/or translated into Braille), scholars and researchers in every field, college students, journalists, and teachers. Its first collection was destroyed in 1814 when the British burned the Capitol (where the library was then housed) during the War of 1812. Thomas Jefferson then sold the institution his personal library of 6,487 books as a replacement, and this became the foundation of what is today the world's largest library.

The Jefferson Building was erected between 1888 and 1897 to hold the burgeoning collection and to establish America as a cultured nation with magnificent institutions equal to anything in Europe. Originally intended to hold the fruits of at least 150 years of collecting, the Jefferson Building was filled up in a mere 13 years. It is now supplemented by the **James Madison Memorial Building** and the **John Adams Building.**

Today the collection contains a mind-boggling 162 million items. Its buildings house more than 38 million catalogued books; 70 million manuscripts; millions and millions of prints and photographs, audio holdings (discs, tapes, talking books, and so on), movies, and videotapes; musical instruments from the 1700s; and the letters and papers of everyone from George Washington to Groucho Marx. Its archives also include the letters, oral histories, photographs, and other documents of war veterans from World War I to the present, all part of its **Veterans History Project;** go to www.loc.gov/vets to listen to or read some of these stories, especially if you plan on visiting the National

World War II Memorial (p. 153). Allow me to point you to the story of one soldier in particular, that of my father, Richard A. Hartman; go to http://lcweb2.loc.gov/diglib/vhp/story/loc.natlib.afc2001001.00067/.

In addition to its art and architecture, the Library displays ongoing exhibits of objects taken from its permanent collections; *Exploring the Early Americas* and *Thomas Jefferson's Library* were recent shows. Always on view are two 1450s bibles from Germany, the handwritten Giant Bible of Mainz, and the Gutenberg Bible, the first book printed with movable metal type in Europe.

The concerts that take place in the Jefferson Building's Whittall Pavilion and in the elegant **Coolidge Auditorium** are free but require tickets, which you can obtain through Eventbrite (www.eventbrite.com).

Across Independence Avenue from the Jefferson Building is the **Madison Building,** which houses venues for author readings and other events.

**Using the library:** Anyone 16 and over may use the library's collections, but first you must obtain a user card with your photo on it. You can get the process started by pre-registering online at wwws.loc.gov/readerreg/remote/. Whether pre-registered or not, you must go to Reader Registration in Room LM 140 (street level of the Madison Building) and present your driver's license or passport. Staff will verify your identity, take a photo, and present you with your user card. Then head to the Information Desk in either the Jefferson or the Madison building to find out about the research resources available to you and how to use them. Most likely, you will be directed to the Main Reading Room. All books must be used on-site.

Jefferson Building: First St. SE, between Independence Ave. and E. Capitol St. Madison Building: 101 Independence Ave. SE (at First St. SE). www.loc.gov. © **202/707-8000.** Free admission. Madison Building Mon–Fri 8:30am–9:30pm; Sat 8:30am–5pm. Jefferson Building Mon–Sat 8:30am–4:30pm. Closed federal holidays. Stop at an information desk on the ground floor of the Jefferson Building. Docent-led tours of the Jefferson Building are free, require no reservations or tickets, and take place Mon–Fri 10:30 and 11:30am, and 12:30, 1:30, 2:30, and 3:30pm; Sat 10:30 and 11:30am; and 1:30 and 2:30pm. Contact your congressional representatives to obtain tickets for congressional, or "VIP," tours (slightly more personalized tours). Metro: Capitol South.

**National Postal Museum ★ MUSEUM** This Smithsonian museum is somewhat off the standard sightseeing route (most other Smithsonians are located on or near the National Mall), so it doesn't capture as many visitors as the other attractions. If you're at all interested in the romance and adventure of the story of U.S. mail correspondence and its delivery (that's right, I said romance and adventure!), and in the international artistry and invention of that most miniature of art forms, the postage stamp, you really need to venture in.

You'll find yourself in the elegant lobby of the historic structure (home of the Old City Post Office), where a welcome center and the relatively new (opened September 22, 2013) **William H. Gross Stamp Gallery** are located. The original part of the museum, where America's postal history is on display from 1673 to the present, is downstairs. Unless you're a philatelist, I'd recommend starting your tour in the original downstairs gallery.

Children usually make a beeline to the enormous blue freightliner truck front over in the corner, and climb up into the driver's seat. This is part of the central exhibit area called **Moving the Mail,** and you'll see planes, trains, and other postal vehicles (even a handcrafted hickory Alaskan dogsled) that have been used at one time or another to transport the mail. In **Binding the Nation,** visitors can follow a path through a forest to trace the steps of mail carriers who traveled from New York to Boston in 1673, and climb into a stagecoach headed west. The exhibit introduces famous figures, like Buffalo Bill, of Pony Express renown; and founding father Benjamin Franklin in his role first as postmaster general for the British colonial post (until he was fired for his revolutionary activities), and then as postmaster general for the United Colonies.

Other exhibits cover mail's impact on city streets and rural routes (**Customers & Communities**), the journey a single letter takes through the postal system and how that process has changed over time (**Systems at Work**), and the history and current practice of getting mail delivered to and from military personnel (**Mail Call**). In June 2014, the museum added its newest permanent exhibit, **Behind the Badge,** which reveals the work of the U.S. Postal Inspection Service: Established in 1776, the federal agency is responsible for restoring mail service after disasters, spotting and preventing mail fraud, and keeping mail safe from the likes of Unabombers and lesser criminals.

Return upstairs to explore the **William H. Gross Stamp Gallery** to view the museum's 6 million–piece **National Stamp Collection,** the world's oldest intact national stamp collection. Interactive kiosks, videos, and activities keep even the non–stamp collector interested, even amused. The **World of Stamps** permanent exhibit features a hit list of famous stamps, starting with the very first postage stamp, the 1840 Penny Black, bearing a young Queen Victoria's profile. On temporary loan until November 2017 is the world's rarest and most valuable stamp, the British Guiana One-Cent Magenta, which was sold for $9.5 million in a February 2015 auction to famed shoe designer Stuart Weitzman. **Stamps Around the Globe** displays international stamps, which make up half the Postal Museum's overall collection (everything from a colorful 1965 Rwanda stamp displaying Cape buffalo to a delicate rose-tinted coat of arms on the 1859 stamp from the German state of Lübeck). Viewing these miniature artworks is a thrill.

Don't miss the last room, the **Postmasters Gallery,** housed in a gorgeous, six-sided paneled room, and reserved for special exhibits, like the one on view through March 25, 2018: "Trailblazing: 100 Years of Our National Parks," which celebrates the centennial of the Park Service with displays of relevant stamps and mail tales.

*Tip:* The Postal Museum's wall of windows features replicas of 54 historic U.S. stamps; come by at nighttime and you'll see the artwork illuminated within the building's facade.

2 Massachusetts Ave. NE (at First St.). www.postalmuseum.si.edu. © **202/633-5555.** Free admission. Daily 10am–5:30pm. Closed Dec 25. Metro: Union Station.

## Belmont-Paul Women's Equality National Monument ★ MUSEUM

Welcome to the newest national park dedicated to women's history, its status officially proclaimed by President Obama on April 12, 2016. The National Park Service roster of 410 national parks includes only a dozen or so sites focused on women's stories, so this is big news. Formerly known as the Sewall-Belmont House and Museum, this unassuming old brick house betwixt the Capitol and the Supreme Court has been the home of the National Woman's Party (NWP) since 1929. Suffragist and organizer extraordinaire Alice Paul founded the NWP in 1917 to fight for women's rights, including the right to vote. (In 1997, the NWP switched from being a political party to an organization focusing on education and advocacy.) The house is a repository of suffragist memorabilia, banners, political buttons, photos of events and main characters in the life of the women's equal rights movement, and other artifacts, 2,600 in all, of which 250 are on view. Visits here are by guided tour only, but that's a good thing, because the power and point of the site is best conveyed through hearing the stories of individual heroines. Susan B. Anthony you will have heard of. But Alva Belmont, Inez Milholland Boissevain, and Febb Burn? *Note:* The site's transition from independent museum to a national monument within the National Park System may alter its tour policies and procedures, so be sure to check the website for the latest information.

144 Constitution Ave. NE (at 2nd St.). www.sewallbelmont.org. © **202/546-1210.** Admission $8. Open for tours Fri–Sat 11am, 1pm, and 3pm. Sign up online or just show up on a scheduled day and time. Entrance is on 2nd St.—look for the signs. Closed Thanksgiving, Dec 25, and New Year's Day. Metro: Union Station or Capitol South.

## The Supreme Court of the United States ★★★ GOVERNMENT

BUILDING   On many days, the Supreme Court is the most exciting place to be in town. Beginning each annual session on the first Monday in October, the nine justices hear cases, later to render opinions that can dramatically affect every American. Visitors may attend these proceedings, in which lawyers representing opposing sides attempt to make a convincing case for their client, even as the justices interrupt repeatedly and question them sharply to clarify the constitutional principles at stake. It's a grand show, fast-paced, sometimes heated, and always full of weighty import (the justices hear only about 80 of the most vital of the 7,000 to 8,000 or so petitions filed with the Court every year). The Court's rulings are final, reversible only by an Act of Congress. And you, the visitor, get a close-up seat . . . if you're lucky (see below for info on getting in).

But even when the court isn't in session, touring the building is a worthwhile experience. During those periods, docents offer 30-minute lectures inside the Supreme Court chamber to introduce visitors of all ages to the Court's judicial functions, the building's history, and the architecture of the courtroom. Lectures take place every hour on the half-hour, beginning at 9:30am on days when the Court is not sitting and at a later time on Court days. You can also tour the building on your own. Architect Cass Gilbert, best known for his skyscrapers (such as New York's 792-ft.-high Woolworth building), designed the stately Corinthian marble palace that houses the Court today. First, stop by the ground-floor information desk to pick up a helpful flyer, view exhibits, and watch a film on the workings of the Court (the film is an excellent preliminary to the docent lecture so time your visit accordingly).

**Getting in to see a case being argued:** Starting the first Monday in October and continuing through late April, the Court "sits" for 2 weeks out of every month to hear two 1-hour arguments each day Monday through Wednesday, from 10am to noon, with occasional afternoon sessions scheduled as necessary from 1 to 2 or 3pm. You can find out the specific dates and names of arguments in advance by contacting the Supreme Court (**www.supremecourt. gov;** ℭ **202/479-3211**). The argument calendar and the "merits briefs" (case descriptions) are posted on the website.

Plan on arriving at the Supreme Court at least 90 minutes in advance of a scheduled argument during the fall and winter, and as early as 3 hours ahead in March and April, when students from schools on spring break lengthen the line. (Dress warmly; the stone plaza is exposed and can be witheringly cold.) Controversial cases also attract crowds; if you're not sure whether a particular case has created a stir, call the Court info line to reach someone who can tell you. The Court allots only about **150 first-come, first-served seats** to the public, but that number fluctuates, depending on the number of seats that have been reserved by the lawyers arguing the case and by the press. The Court police officers direct you into one line initially; when the doors finally open, you form a second line if you want to attend only 3 to 5 minutes of the argument. Seating begins at 9:30am for those attending the full argument and at 10am for those who want to catch just a few minutes.

The justices release completed opinions in the courtroom throughout the argument term, October through April, and into May and June. If you attend an oral argument, you may find yourself present as well for the release of a Supreme Court opinion, since the justices precede the hearing of new oral arguments with the announcement of their opinions on previously heard arguments, if any opinions are ready. What this means is, if you're visiting the Court on a Monday in May or June, you won't be able to attend an argument, but you might still see the justices in action, delivering an opinion, during a 10am, 15-minute session in the courtroom. To attend one of these sessions, you must wait in line on the plaza, following the same procedure outlined above.

Leave cameras, recording devices, and notebooks at your hotel—they're not allowed in the courtroom. *Note: Do* bring quarters. Security procedures require you to leave all your belongings, including outerwear, purses, books, sunglasses, and so on, in a cloak room where the coin-operated lockers accept only quarters.

1 First St. NE (btw. E. Capitol St. and Maryland Ave. NE). www.supremecourt.gov. ℭ**202/ 479-3000** or 202/479-3030 (recording). Free admission. Mon–Fri 9am–4:30pm. Closed all federal holidays. Metro: Capitol South or Union Station.

**Union Station** ★ARCHITECTURAL ICON/MARKET  When it opened in 1907, this was the largest train station in the world. It was designed by noted architect Daniel H. Burnham, who modeled it after the Baths of Diocletian and the Arch of Constantine in Rome. Its facade includes Ionic colonnades fashioned from white granite and 100 sculptured eagles. Graceful 50-foot Constantine arches mark the entryways, above which are poised 6 carved figures representing Fire, Electricity, Freedom, Imagination, Agriculture, and Mechanics. Inside is the **Main Hall,** a massive rectangular room with a 96-foot barrel-vaulted ceiling, an expanse of white-marble flooring, and a balcony adorned with 36 Augustus Saint-Gaudens sculptures of Roman legionnaires. Off the Main Hall is the **East Hall,** shimmering with scagliola marble walls and columns, a gorgeous hand-stenciled skylight ceiling, and stunning murals of classical scenes inspired by ancient Pompeiian art. (Today, this is the station's quietest shopping venue, with a handful of stores and stall vendors selling pretty jewelry and other accessories.)

Union Station.

In its time, this "temple of transport" has witnessed many important events. President Wilson welcomed General Pershing here in 1918 on his return from France. South Pole explorer Rear Admiral Richard Byrd was also feted at Union Station on his homecoming. And Franklin D. Roosevelt's funeral train, bearing his casket, was met here in 1945 by thousands of mourners.

But after the 1960s, with the decline of rail travel, the station fell on hard times. Rain caused parts of the roof to cave in, and the entire building—with floors buckling, rats running about, and mushrooms sprouting in damp rooms—was sealed in 1981. That same year, Congress enacted legislation to preserve and restore this national treasure, to the tune of $160 million. A remarkable 2-year restoration involved hundreds of European and American artisans who returned the station to its original design.

Today, several plans are in the works to both expand the station and develop the property as the linchpin for revitalizing the surrounding neighborhood. It's doubtful you will see signs of these activities when you visit in 2017. What you may observe is how bustling the place is. Union Station never closes, never pauses. At least 40 million people come through Union Station's doors yearly, more than 100,000 a day. About 100 retail and food shops on three levels offer a wide array of merchandise and dining options. Several tour-bus companies use the station as a point of arrival and departure, and operate ticket booths inside the front hall of the main concourse. (See p. 298 for more information about tours.) Amtrak, the commuter MARC trains, Metrorail trains and Metrobuses, DC Circulator buses, taxis, rental cars, local drivers and pedestrians, and the DC Streetcar all converge on Union Station; see chapter 11 for details about Union Station as a transportation hub.

50 Massachusetts Ave. NE. www.unionstationdc.com. ✆ **202/289-1908.** Free admission. Station daily 24 hr. Shops Mon–Sat 10am–9pm; Sun noon–6pm. Machines located inside the station near the exit/entrance to the parking garage will validate your ticket as follows: $3 for the first hr., $5 for 1–2 hrs., $20 for 2–12 hrs., and $24 for up to 24 hrs. Metro: Union Station.

# THE NATIONAL MALL & MEMORIAL PARKS

This one's the biggie, folks. More than one-third of the capital's major attractions lie within this complex of parkland that the National Park Service calls **National Mall and Memorial Parks.** The National Mall (see p. 145) is the centerpiece of this larger plot that extends from the Capitol to the Potomac River, and from Constitution Avenue to down and around the cherry-tree-ringed Tidal Basin. Presidential and war memorials, the Washington Monument, the Dr. Martin Luther King, Jr. Memorial, 11 Smithsonian museums, the National Gallery of Art, the National Archives, and the U.S. Botanic Garden are here waiting for you. So let's get started.

**Arts and Industries Building** ★ARCHITECTURE   Rats. Despite the near completion of a decade-long renovation, the Arts and Industries Building remains mostly closed to the public. There is at least one exception, though: During the annual 10-day Smithsonian Folklife Festival (see p. 25), the building

---

### Loop the National Mall Aboard the DC Circulator

Getting to the top attractions of the Mall is considerably easier thanks to the DC Circulator's newest route. This bus runs on a permanent, year-round, continuously looping National Mall circuit that begins and ends at Union Station, stopping at 14 points along the way. In winter, the Loop (my name for it, and I'm sticking with it) travels 7am to 7pm weekdays, 9am to 7pm weekends; in summer, the Loop operates 7am to 8pm weekdays, and 9am to 8pm weekends. As with all of the other Circulators, the buses come by every 10 minutes and you may board them at any of its stops. The route from Union Station takes you down Louisiana Avenue and loops around the Mall via the inside roads of Madison, Jefferson, West Basin and Ohio drives, as well as Constitution Avenue. Stops include the National Gallery of Art, the National Museum of American History, the Washington Monument, the Lincoln Memorial, and 10 others—every place you'd want to go, in other words. The fare is $1, as always, and if you pay with a SmarTrip Card, you'll be able to re-board for free within a 2-hour window of your first boarding. I've noted when an attraction is served by the Circulator in the listings in this section.

turns into a marketplace for arts and crafts sold by participating artisans of this year's and past Folklife Festivals. You can always admire the building's exterior. Completed in 1881 just in time to host President James Garfield's inaugural ball, this red-brick and sandstone structure was the first Smithsonian museum on the Mall, and the first U.S. National Museum. Weather permitting, a 19th-century **carousel** operates across the street on the Mall.

900 Jefferson Dr. SW (on the south side of the Mall). www.si.edu. Metro: Smithsonian (Mall exit). DC Circulator stop.

**D.C. War Memorial** ★MONUMENT/MEMORIAL    This often-overlooked memorial commemorates the lives of the 499 citizens of Washington, D.C., who died in World War I. It's worth a stop on your way to grander, more famous edifices. President Herbert Hoover dedicated the memorial in 1931; John Phillip Sousa conducted the Marine band at the event. The structure is a graceful design of 12 Doric columns supporting a classical circular dome. The names of the 499 dead are inscribed in the stone base.

On the north side of Independence Ave. SW, btw. the National World War II and Lincoln memorials. www.nps.gov/nama/planyourvisit/dc-war-memorial.htm. Metro: Smithsonian (12th St./Independence Ave. exit), with a 25-min. walk. Near DC Circulator stop at MLK Memorial.

**Enid A. Haupt Garden** ★GARDEN    Named for its donor, a noted supporter of horticultural projects, this pretty 4¼-acre garden presents elaborate flower beds and borders, plant-filled turn-of-the-20th-century urns, 1870s cast-iron furnishings, and lush baskets hung from reproduction 19th-century lampposts. The garden is planted on the rooftops of the subterranean Ripley Center and Sackler and African Art museums.

Most captivating is the **parterre** of symmetrically arranged plots whose vividly colorful and varied plantings change season by season. The ornamental garden patterns complement the Victorian architecture of the nearby Smithsonian Castle. The tranquil **Moongate Garden** near the Sackler Gallery employs water and granite in a landscape design inspired by a 15th-century Chinese temple. Two 9-foot-tall pink-granite moon gates frame a pool paved with half-rounds of granite. Benches backed by English boxwoods sit under the canopy of weeping cherry trees.

The **Fountain Garden** outside the African Art Museum replicates an Islamic garden, complete with elements of geometrical symmetry, low walls, a central fountain and water cascading down the face of a stone wall. Five majestic linden trees shade a seating area around the **Downing Urn,** a memorial to American landscapist Andrew Jackson Downing, who designed the National Mall. Elaborate cast-iron carriage gates made according to a 19th-century design by James Renwick, flanked by four red sandstone pillars, salute the Independence Avenue entrance to the garden.

10th St. and Independence Ave. SW. www.gardens.si.edu. © **202/633-2220.** Free admission. Daily dawn–dusk. Free tours May–Sept Wed 1pm. Closed Dec 25. Metro: Smithsonian (12th St. and Independence Ave. exit). DC Circulator stop.

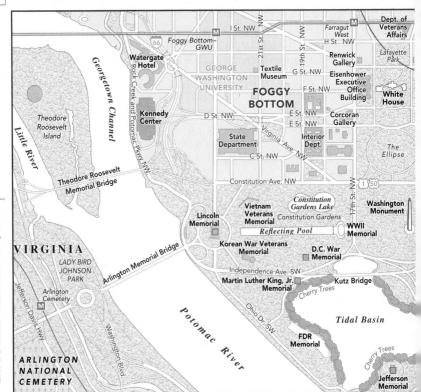

**Franklin Delano Roosevelt Memorial** ★★ MONUMENT/MEMORIAL
The FDR Memorial has proven to be one of the most popular of the presidential memorials since it opened in 1997. Its popularity has to do as much with its design as the man it honors. This 7½-acre outdoor memorial stretches out, mazelike, rather than rising up, across the stone-paved floor. Granite walls define the four "galleries," each representing a different term in FDR's presidency, from 1933 to 1945. Architect Lawrence Halprin's design includes waterfalls, sculptures (by Leonard Baskin, John Benson, Neil Estern, Robert Graham, Thomas Hardy, and George Segal), and Roosevelt's own words carved into the stone.

The many displays of cascading water can sound thunderous, as the fountains recycle an astonishing 100,000 gallons of water every minute. The presence of gushing fountains and waterfalls isn't a random choice. Instead, they reflect FDR's appreciation for the importance of $H_2O$. As someone afflicted with polio, he understood the rehabilitative powers of water exercises and established the Warm Springs Institute in Georgia to help others with polio.

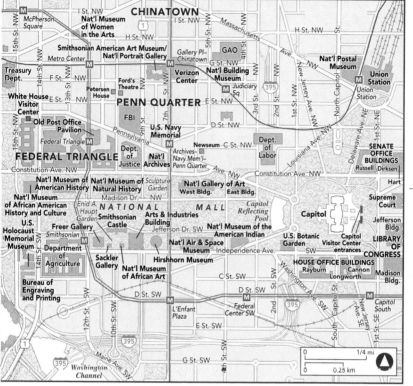

As president, FDR supported several water projects, including the creation of the Tennessee Valley Authority.

When the memorial first opened, adults and children alike arrived in bathing suits and splashed around on warm days. Park rangers don't allow that anymore, but they do allow you to dip your feet in the various pools. A favorite time to visit is at night, when dramatic lighting reveals the waterfalls and statues against the dark parkland.

Conceived in 1946, the FDR Memorial had been in the works for 50 years. Part of the delay in its construction can be attributed to the president himself: FDR had told his friend, Supreme Court Justice Felix Frankfurter, "If they are to put up any memorial to me, I should like it to be placed in the center of that green plot in front of the Archives Building. I should like it to consist of a block about the size [of this desk]." In fact, such a plaque sits in front of the National Archives. Friends and relatives struggled to honor Roosevelt's request to leave it at that, but Congress and national sentiment overrode them.

As with other presidential memorials, this one opened to some controversy. Advocates for people with disabilities were incensed that the memorial sculptures did not show the president in a wheelchair, which he used after he contracted polio. President Clinton asked Congress to allocate funding for the additional statue of a wheelchair-bound FDR; it's at the very front of the memorial, to the right as you approach the first gallery. Step inside the gift shop to view a replica of Roosevelt's wheelchair, as well as one of the rare photographs of the president sitting in a wheelchair. The memorial is probably the most accessible tourist attraction in the city; as at most of the National Park Service locations, wheelchairs are available for free use on-site. Rangers conduct tours every hour on the hour. Thirty minutes is sufficient for a visit.

**Great Depression sculpture at the FDR Memorial.**

On West Basin Dr., alongside the Tidal Basin in West Potomac Park (across Independence Ave. SW from the Mall). www.nps.gov/frde. ☏**202/426-6841.** Free admission. Ranger on duty daily 9:30am–10pm, except for Dec 25. Limited parking. Metro: Smithsonian (12th St./Independence Ave. exit), with a 20-min. walk. DC Circulator stop.

**Freer Gallery of Art** ★★ MUSEUM  The Freer Gallery is closed for renovation until the summer of 2017. You should know, however, that the Freer Gallery's arguably most famous work, and its single permanent installation, James McNeill Whistler's *Harmony in Blue and Gold: the Peacock Room,* conceived of as a dining room for the London mansion of wealthy client F. R. Leyland, receives special attention in an immersive installation on view at the Sackler Gallery of Art (p. 154).

Jefferson Dr. SW at 12th St. SW (on the south side of the Mall). www.asia.si.edu. ☏**202/633-1000.** Metro: Smithsonian (Mall/Jefferson Dr. exit). DC Circulator stop.

**George Mason Memorial** ★ MONUMENT/MEMORIAL  George Mason's name is not famous today, but it should be: He was a Virginia politician who authored the Virginia Declaration of Rights, upon which the first part of the U.S. Declaration of Independence is based, as well as the first 10 amendments to the U.S. Constitution, known as the Bill of Rights. Dedicated on April 9, 2002, the memorial consists of a bronze statue of Mason, dressed in 18th-century garb, from buckled shoes to tricorn hat, set back in a landscaped grove of trees and flower beds (lots and lots of pansies). Two stone slabs are inscribed with some of Mason's words, like these, referring to Mason's rejection of slavery: THAT SLOW POISON, WHICH IS DAILY CONTAMINATING THE MINDS & MORALS OF OUR PEOPLE. An interesting stand for a slave-owner to take, wouldn't you say? *Note:* The memorial is easy to miss, because it does not lie on the Tidal Basin path. As you approach the Jefferson Memorial from the direction of the FDR Memorial, or as you approach the FDR Memorial from the direction of the Jefferson, you'll come to the bridge that arches over the inlet leading from the Tidal Basin to the Potomac River; look straight across from the bridge, and there you'll see it.

E. Basin and Ohio drives SW (btw. the Jefferson and FDR memorials). www.nps.gov/ gemm. ℭ**202/426-6841.** Free admission. Open daily, though rangers generally are not posted here. To find out more about George Mason, visit the Jefferson Memorial, a 5-min. walk away, on the Tidal Basin, where a park ranger is on duty 9:30am–10pm. Limited parking. Metro: Smithsonian (12th St./Independence Ave. exit), with a 25-min. walk. DC Circulator stop.

### Hirshhorn Museum and Sculpture Garden ★★ ART MUSEUM
This cylindrically shaped, concrete-and-granite building holds provocative art at its best, from de Kooning to Jeff Koons. Look for Thomas Hart Benton's dizzying sprawl of figures in the 1920 painting *People of Chilmark,* Ellsworth Kelly's vivid minimalist paintings, Dan Steinhilber's sculpture made out of paper-clad wire hangers, Henri Matisse's bronze casts, and Damien Hirst's *The Asthmatic Escaped II, 1992,* in which one of two conjoined glass cases holds a camera on a tripod, and the other holds the clothing, inhaler, and other personal effects of "the escaped." The museum rotates works from its near 12,000-piece collection, 600 at any one time, so if these exact artworks are not on view, others in the avant-garde family will be.

Some of the Hirshhorn's most famous art is on display outside, on the grounds surrounding the museum plaza and across Jefferson Drive in the sunken Sculpture Garden. Sadly, a lot of people miss the garden, maybe because it's below ground. A giant red-painted steel and cable piece, *Are Years What? (for Marianne Moore),* by Mark di Suvero, stands guard at street level helping to attract attention to the sculptures planted in the lower landscape. Head down the steps to view such renowned works as Rodin's *Monument to the Burghers of Calais,* Giacometti's *Monumental Head,* and Henry Moore's *Reclining Figure No. 4,* among them. ***Note:*** The Hirshhorn's Sculpture Garden and the **National Gallery of Art's Sculpture Garden** (see p. 143), located directly across the Mall from each other, **are not the same!** It astonishes me how often people confuse the two. They offer two very different experiences, and you should visit both.

The Hirshhorn exists thanks to a man named Joseph H. Hirshhorn, who was born in Latvia in 1899 but immigrated to the United States as a boy. In 1966, Hirshhorn donated his collection of more than 6,000 works of modern and contemporary art to the United States in gratitude for the country's welcome to him and other immigrants, and bequeathed an additional 5,500 upon his death in 1981. The museum opened in 1974.

Independence Ave. at 7th St. SW (on the south side of the Mall). www.hirshhorn.si.edu. ℭ **202/633-4674.** Free admission. Museum daily 10am–5:30pm. Sculpture Garden daily 7:30am–dusk. Closed Dec 25. Metro: L'Enfant Plaza (Smithsonian Museums/ Maryland Ave. or Smithsonian exit). DC Circulator stop.

**Jefferson Memorial** ★★ MONUMENT/MEMORIAL    President John F. Kennedy, at a 1962 dinner honoring 29 Nobel Prize winners, told his guests that they were "the most extraordinary collection of talent, of human knowledge, that has ever been gathered together at the White House, with the possible exception of when Thomas Jefferson dined alone." Jefferson penned the Declaration of Independence and served as George Washington's secretary of state, John Adams's vice president, and America's third president. He spoke out against slavery—although, like many of his countrymen, he kept slaves himself. He also established the University of Virginia and pursued wide-ranging interests, including architecture, astronomy, anthropology, music, and farming.

Franklin Delano Roosevelt, a great admirer of Jefferson, spearheaded the effort to build him a memorial, although the site choice was problematic. The Capitol, the White House, and the Mall were already located in accordance with architect Pierre L'Enfant's master plan for the city, and there was no spot for such a project that would maintain L'Enfant's symmetry. So the memorial was built on land reclaimed from the Potomac River, perched upon the lip of the manmade reservoir now known as the Tidal Basin. Roosevelt laid the memorial cornerstone in 1939 and had all the trees between the Jefferson Memorial and the White House cut down so that he could see the memorial every morning.

The memorial is a columned rotunda in the style of the Pantheon in Rome, whose classical architecture Jefferson himself introduced to this country (he designed his home, Monticello, and the earliest University of Virginia buildings in Charlottesville). On the Tidal Basin side, the sculptural group above the entrance depicts Jefferson with Benjamin Franklin, John Adams, Roger Sherman, and Robert Livingston, all of whom worked on drafting the Declaration of Independence. The domed interior of the memorial contains the 19-foot bronze statue of Jefferson standing on a 6-foot pedestal of black Minnesota granite. The sculpture is the work of Rudolph Evans, chosen from among more than 100 artists in a nationwide competition. Jefferson is depicted wearing a fur-collared coat given to him by his close friend, the Polish General Tadeusz Kościuszko. If you follow Jefferson's gaze, you see that the Jefferson Memorial and the White House have an unimpeded view of each other.

Rangers present 20- to 30-minute programs throughout the day.

Ohio Dr. SW, at the south shore of the Tidal Basin (in West Potomac Park). www.nps. gov/thje. ℂ **202/426-6841.** Free admission. Ranger on duty daily 9:30am–10pm, except Dec 25. Limited parking. Metro: Smithsonian (12th St./Independence Ave. exit), with a 20- to 30-min. walk. DC Circulator stop.

**Korean War Veterans Memorial** ★ MONUMENT/MEMORIAL    This privately funded memorial, founded in 1995, honors those who served in the Korean War, a 3-year conflict (1950–53) that produced almost as many casualties as Vietnam. It consists of a circular "Pool of Remembrance" in a grove of trees and a triangular "Field of Service," highlighted by lifelike statues of 19 infantrymen who appear to be trudging across fields. A 164-foot-long

The columned rotunda of the Jefferson Memorial.

black granite wall depicts the array of combat and support troops that served in Korea (nurses, chaplains, airmen, mechanics, cooks, and others); a raised granite curb lists the 22 nations that contributed to the UN's effort; and a commemorative area honors KIAs, MIAs, and POWs. Allot 15 minutes here.

Southeast of the Lincoln Memorial, on the Independence Ave. SW side of the Mall. www.nps.gov/kowa. © **202/426-6841.** Free admission. Ranger on duty daily 9:30am–10pm, except Dec 25. Limited parking. Metro: Foggy Bottom, with 30-min. walk. DC Circulator stop.

**Lincoln Memorial ★★★** MONUMENT/MEMORIAL  When famed architect Charles Follen McKim was asked to work on the 1902 McMillan Commission to reshape the overall design for the Mall, he made his views clear on what he felt would be an important addition. "As the Arc de Triomphe crowns Place de l'Étoile in Paris, so should stand a memorial erected of the memory of that one man in our history as a nation who is worthy to be joined with George Washington—Abraham Lincoln."

Location was key, but where the monument should be was not entirely obvious: Until the late 1800s, a wider Potomac River had bumped up against the western edge of the National Mall. It was only after the Army Corps of Engineers had first reclaimed land from the river and created a mile-wide westward expanse of land, and then landscaped and engineered the muddy morass, that the choice was clear. The memorial for honoring the president who had saved the Union would preside at one end of the Mall on a direct axis to the Washington Monument honoring the nation's founding president, both sites linked on the same axis further still to the symbol of the country itself, the U.S. Capitol, at the eastern end of the Mall.

Construction began in 1914, and what a job it was, shoring up the unstable wetlands and creating a foundation strong enough to support the majestic memorial that architect Henry Bacon had designed. The foundation rests on concrete piles that extend from 44 to 65 feet from original grade to bedrock. The retaining wall, keeping the river at bay, measures 257 feet wide by 187 feet deep by 14 feet high. The Lincoln Memorial itself weighs 38,000 tons. The monument finally opened in 1922 after 8 years of construction.

The neoclassical temple-like structure, similar in architectural design to the Parthenon in Greece, has 36 fluted Doric columns representing the states of the Union at the time of Lincoln's death, plus 2 at the entrance. On the attic parapet are 48 festoons symbolizing the number of states in 1922. (Hawaii and Alaska are noted in an inscription on the terrace.) Due east is the Reflecting Pool, lined with American elms and stretching 2,000 feet toward the Washington Monument and the Capitol beyond.

The memorial chamber has limestone walls inscribed with the Gettysburg Address and Lincoln's second inaugural address. Two 60-foot-high murals by Jules Guerin on the north and south walls depict, allegorically, Lincoln's principles and achievements. On the south wall, an Angel of Truth freeing a slave is flanked by groups of figures representing Justice and Immortality. The north-wall mural portrays the unity of North and South, and is flanked by groups of figures symbolizing Fraternity and Charity.

Most powerful, however, is Daniel Chester French's 19-foot-high seated statue of Lincoln. Lincoln sits, gazing down on the visitors at his feet, the burdens of guiding the Union through the Civil War etched deeply in his face. Though 19 feet tall, the figure is eerily lifelike and exudes a fatherly compassion. Some say that his hands create the sign-language shapes for A (Abraham) and L (Lincoln), as a tribute to the fact that Lincoln signed legislation giving Gallaudet University, a school for the deaf, the right to confer college degrees. The National Park Service denies the symbolism, but it should be noted that French's son was deaf, so the sculptor *did* know sign language.

Lincoln's legacy has made his memorial the site of numerous demonstrations by those seeking justice. Most notable was a peaceful demonstration of 200,000 people on August 28, 1963, at which Martin Luther King, Jr., proclaimed, "I have a dream." Look for the words I HAVE A DREAM. MARTIN LUTHER KING, JR., THE MARCH ON WASHINGTON FOR JOBS AND FREEDOM, AUGUST 28, 1963, inscribed and centered on the 18th step down from the chamber. The inscription, which the National Park Service added in July 2003, marks the precise spot where King stood to deliver his famous speech.

Rangers present 20- to 30-minute programs as time permits throughout the day. Thirty minutes is sufficient time for viewing this memorial. *Note:* Repair and restoration work is underway through 2019, but the plan is to keep the memorial open throughout.

On the western end of the Mall, at 23rd St. NW (btw. Constitution and Independence aves.). www.nps.gov/linc. ℂ **202/426-6841.** Free admission. Ranger on duty daily

9:30am–10pm, except Dec 25. Limited parking. Metro: Foggy Bottom, then a 30-min. walk. DC Circulator stop.

## Martin Luther King, Jr. National Memorial ★★ MONUMENT/MEMORIAL

I must confess my disappointment in the Martin Luther King, Jr. Memorial, which provides little context for King's life and work as, arguably, the United States' most important civil rights activist. I would have preferred a memorial more like the one for FDR, whose panels illustrate scenes from FDR's presidency; or like Lincoln's or Jefferson's, whose remarkable words are rendered more fully in the stone walls. Still, the very fact of its existence, here on the Mall among memorials to presidents and to those who fought in U.S. wars, affirms King's critical role in American history.

Authorized by Congress in 1996, the memorial debuted on October 16, 2011. Hurricane Irene prevented it from opening on its originally planned date, August 28, exactly 48 years after the Rev. Dr. Martin Luther King, Jr., delivered his momentous "I Have a Dream" speech on the steps of the nearby Lincoln Memorial. On that original date, some 250,000 people gathered on the Mall during the March on Washington for Jobs and Freedom to pressure Congress to pass the Civil Rights Act. King was assassinated on April 4, 1968 at the age of 39.

The memorial's site along the northwest lip of the Tidal Basin is significant for the "visual line of leadership" it creates between the Lincoln Memorial, representing the principles of equality and civil rights as embodied in the personage of Abraham Lincoln and carried forward in King, and the Jefferson Memorial, which symbolizes the democratic ideals of the founding fathers. Set on a crescent-shaped, 4-acre parcel of land surrounded by the capital's famous cherry trees, the mammoth sculpture (created in China, a controversial decision) rests on 300 concrete piles driven into the muddy basin terrain. A 28-foot, 6-inch statue of Dr. King in a business suit, arms folded, stands front and center, representing the "Stone of Hope"; he is flanked by two enormous background pieces, representing the "Mountain of Despair." A curving boundary wall enclosing the grounds perhaps commemorates the slain civil rights leader best, with inscriptions of excerpts from his remarkable sermons and speeches.

Rangers hold interpretive talks and site tours throughout the day, and these are probably the best way to get the most out of a visit here. The memorial includes a bookstore, a ranger station, and restrooms.

Adjacent to the FDR Memorial, along the northwest side of the Tidal Basin, at Independence Ave. SW, in West Potomac Park. www.nps.gov/mlkm. ℂ **202/426-6841.** Free admission. Ranger on duty daily 9:30am–10pm, except Dec 25. Limited parking. Metro: Smithsonian (12th St./Independence Ave. exit), with a 25-min. walk. DC Circulator stop.

## National Air and Space Museum ★★ MUSEUM

More than eight million people. That's how many visitors this museum, and its annex near Dulles Airport, get yearly (this outlet of the museum gets a whopping seven million). This makes it, according to the Smithsonian, the most visited museum in the United States.

It's not hard to understand why. The National Air and Space Museum manages to tap into that most primordial of human impulses: the urge to fly. And it does so in a multi-layered fashion, mixing extraordinary artifacts with IMAX movies, videos, computer terminals with quizzes, even flight simulators.

The seeds of this museum were planted when the Smithsonian Institution acquired its first aeronautical objects in 1876: 20 kites from the Chinese Imperial Commission. By the time the National Air and Space Museum opened on the National Mall 100 years later, the collection had grown to tens of thousands of objects. Today, the inventory of historic aircraft and spacecraft artifacts numbers 63,000, the world's largest such collection.

Not surprisingly, the place is huge, as is much of its collection. Enormous aircraft and spacecraft dangle from the ceiling or are placed in floor exhibits throughout both levels. Visitors of all ages, but mostly families, are chattering away, taking pictures of each other against the backdrops of the towering Pershing (34.8') and SS20 (54.10') missiles, or the Apollo II Command Module *Columbia,* or just about anything in the museum, as most of the artifacts dwarf humans. Tours and demonstrations are in constant rotation.

And, unfortunately, there are often lines—many, many lines. The first is just to enter the building. Then there are lines to get tickets for **IMAX films ★,** or a show at the **Einstein Planetarium ★,** to take a ride on a flight simulator, and to enter the cockpit of the Northwest Airlines Boeing 747 on display in the **America by Air** exhibit. (*FYI:* You enter the nose of the plane from the second floor.) I have never visited the museum when it hasn't been a frenzied scene.

The National Air and Space Museum completed an extensive $30 million renovation, primarily to its **Milestones of Flight** exhibit, in July 2016, just in time for the museum's 40th anniversary. The gallery bears the name **Boeing Milestones of Flight Hall,** and new features include a more accessible Welcome Center and open floor layout, and exhibits that highlight the connections between the personal, cultural, political, social, and technical stories behind the space and aviation artifacts on display.

So take a moment when you enter to grab a flyer and strategize. Points of interest include the second floor exhibit, **Pioneers of Flight,** where Amelia Earhart's brilliant red Lockheed Vega plane is on view. Earhart piloted her "little red bus," as she called it, alone and nonstop in 1932 from Canada to Northern Ireland. Next door is the **Wright Brothers** exhibit, with the Wright brothers' 1903 Flyer, the world's first successful airplane. Additional exhibits cover **Flight and the Arts, Apollo to the Moon, Exploring the Planets, World War II Aviation,** and much more, everything in sync with the museum's mission, " . . . to commemorate the national development of aviation and spaceflight, and [to] educate and inspire the nation." Amateur astronomers should head outside to the museum's east terrace to look through the telescopes in the **Phoebe Waterman Haas Public Observatory.** The observatory is free and open to the public Wednesday to Sunday noon to 3pm for daytime sightings of moon craters and sun spots, and once or twice a month for nighttime observations; find more information on the museum's website.

The Boeing Milestones of Flight Hall at the National Air and Space Museum.

Or get off your feet for a while and take in an IMAX film, like the ever popular *To Fly,* or *Hubble 3-D,* or watch a show at the **Albert Einstein Planetarium ★**. IMAX and planetarium films require tickets, which cost anywhere from $6 to $15 per person, depending on the film, age of filmgoer, and whether or not the person is a Smithsonian Institution member. There's a charge to ride the flight simulators, as well: $6–$8 per ride per person.

This location is also home to the Smithsonian's largest gift shop (three levels, 12,000 sq. ft.), and several fast-food restaurants.

Haven't had enough? Drive the 25 miles or so to the National Air and Space Museum's companion location, the **Steven F. Udvar-Hazy Center,** which celebrated its 10th anniversary in 2013. Here you can explore one huge hangar filled with aviation objects, another with space objects, each arranged by subject (Commercial Aviation, Korea and Vietnam Aviation, Sport Aviation, and so on), and you can tour an observation tower that gives you a bird's-eye view of planes landing and departing at Washington Dulles International Airport. IMAX movies and simulator rides are options here, as well.

Mall museum: Independence Ave. SW, btw. 4th and 7th sts. (on the south side of the Mall, with 2 entrances, one on Jefferson Dr. and the other on Independence Ave.). Udvar-Hazy Center: 14390 Air and Space Museum Pkwy., Chantilly, VA. www.airand-space.si.edu. ✆ **202/633-2214** (Mall location), or **703/572-4118** (Virginia location). Free admission. Both locations daily 10am–5:30pm (Mall museum open until 7:30pm, Udvar-Hazy Center open until 6:30pm in summer). Free 1½-hr. highlight tours daily 10:30am and 1pm. Closed Dec 25. Metro: L'Enfant Plaza (Smithsonian Museums/Maryland Ave. exit) or Smithsonian (Mall/Jefferson Dr. exit). DC Circulator stop.

**National Archives Museum ★★** MUSEUM   The **Rotunda** of the National Archives displays the country's most important original documents: the Declaration of Independence, the Constitution of the United States, and the Bill of Rights (collectively known as the **Charters of Freedom**). Fourteen document cases trace the story of the creation of the Charters and the ongoing influence of these fundamental documents on the nation and the world.

It proves to be an unexpectedly thrilling experience to stand among people from all over the world and peer in this dimly lit chamber at page after page of manuscript covered top to bottom in tiny, graceful script whose forthright declarations founded our country and changed the world. It is gratifying, too, to see the documents given context within the exhibit. For example, one panel points to the role of "founding mothers" like Abigail Adams, who cautioned her husband in a letter, "If perticular [sic] care is not paid to the Ladies, we are determined to foment a Rebellion, and will not hold ourselves bound by any Laws in which we have no voice or Representation."

But the wonders don't end there: On display in the **David M. Rubenstein Gallery** is the original 1297 Magna Carta, one of only four known to exist in the world, and the only original version on public display in the United States. The Magna Carta anchors the permanent exhibit, **Records of Rights,** which presents hundreds of other landmark documents, as well as photographs, videos, and interactive items, that help visitors trace the evolution of rights in the U.S. from its founding to the present day.

Beyond famous documents are the **Public Vaults,** an area that introduces visitors to the heart of the Archives: its 10 billion records, covering 2 centuries worth of documents, from patent searches to genealogical records to copies of George Washington's handwritten inaugural address, to census records, passport applications, governmental records, and more. (Go to www.digitalvaults. org to do an at-home search.)

Using the very latest in interactive museum design—listening booths, computer terminals, videos, you name it—the curators have mined the material for drama (and often presented it in a very kid-friendly fashion). In an area on patents, for example, the process is turned into a game: You read the patent application and then try to guess what well-known gadget it was for. A section on immigration presents the search for genealogical data as a cliffhanger mystery, detailing the steps and missteps of past Archives' users. President Nixon makes several eerie appearances: You read his resignation letter and

Reading one of the many historical documents at the National Archives.

listen to disturbing excerpts from the Watergate tapes. The **Lawrence F. O'Brien Gallery** rotates exhibitions of Archives documents, often centered around a theme. On view through September 4, 2017, is "Amending America," which both celebrates the Bill of Rights and explores what it takes to pass an amendment: Out of 11,000 attempts over nearly 230 years, Congress has reached consensus to amend the Constitution only 27 times.

During the day, the **William C. McGowan Theater** continually runs dramatic films illustrating the relationship between records and democracy in the lives of real people, and at night it serves as a premier documentary film venue for the city.

Beyond its exhibits, the Archives are a vital resource for those doing research. Anyone 16 and over is welcome to use the National Archives center for genealogical research. Call for details.

The National Archives building itself is worth an admiring glance. The neoclassical structure, designed by John Russell Pope (also the architect of the National Gallery of Art and the Jefferson Memorial) in the 1930s, is an impressive example of the Beaux Arts style. Seventy-two columns create a Corinthian colonnade on each of the four facades. Great bronze doors mark the Constitution Avenue entrance, and four large sculptures representing the Future, the Past, Heritage, and Guardianship sit on pedestals near the entrances. Huge pediments crown both the Pennsylvania Avenue and Constitution Avenue entrances to the building.

In peak season, you may want to reserve a spot on a guided tour (Mon–Fri 9:45am) or simply a timed visit entry, to help avoid a long wait in line. Admission is always free, but you'll pay a $1.50 convenience fee when you place your order online at www.recreation.gov. Enter "National Archives DC."

700 Constitution Ave. NW (btw. 7th and 9th sts. NW; tourists enter on Constitution Ave., researchers on Pennsylvania Ave.). www.archives.gov/nae. © **202/357-5000.** Free admission. Daily 10am–5:30pm. Call for research hours. Closed Dec 25. Metro: Archives–Navy Memorial. DC Circulator stop.

**National Gallery of Art ★★★** ART MUSEUM   Best. Art museum. Ever. That's my opinion, but let me quickly say that world-renowned critics also consider the National Gallery of Art, which celebrated its 75th anniversary in 2016, to be among the best museums in the world. Its base collection of more than 130,000 paintings, drawings, prints, photographs, sculpture, decorative arts, and furniture trace the development of Western art from the Middle Ages to the present in a manner that's both informative and rapturously beautiful.

The original West Building is devoted to works by European (13th to early-20th-century) and American (18th to early-20th-century) artists; across the street from the West Building is a Sculpture Garden that features 20 sculptures created by an international roster of artists in the last few decades, as well as a stunning Chagall mosaic.

The I. M. Pei–designed East Building, which showcases modern and contemporary art, re-opened in September 2016 following a grand renovation that added 12,260 square feet of new exhibit space and two skylit tower galleries, connected by an outdoor sculpture terrace.

Now let me tell you why this is my favorite art museum, even one of my favorite places in Washington. I love the many ways the Gallery's design and programs make the artworks and the museum itself accessible to the ordinary visitor. Architect John Russell Pope (of Jefferson Memorial fame, see p. 136) modeled his design after the Pantheon in Rome, anchoring the main floor's interior with a domed rotunda, and then centered a colonnaded fountain beneath the dome. The overall feeling is of spaciousness and grace, especially when the huge fountain is encircled with flowers, as it often is. Extending east and west of this nexus are long and wide, light-filled, high-ceilinged halls, off which the individual **paintings galleries** lie, nearly 100 in all, leading eventually to lovely garden courts and more places to sit.

One hundred galleries? Yes, but the 1,000-some paintings are arranged in easy to understand order, in separate rooms by age and nationality: 13th-century Italian to 18th-century Italian, Spanish, and French artists on the west side; 18th- and 19th-century Spanish, French, British, and American masters on the east side. You may recognize some names: Leonardo da Vinci (whose painting, *Ginevra de' Benci,* which hangs here, is the only da Vinci painting on public view in the Americas), Rubens, Raphael, Cassatt, El Greco, Brueghel, Poussin, Vermeer, van Dyck, Gilbert Stuart, Winslow Homer, Turner, and so on.

Down the sweep of marble stairway lie the ground floor's fewer chambers. The light-filled, vaulted ceilinged sculpture galleries include standouts by Bernini, Rodin, Degas, and Honoré Daumier, whose 36 small, bronze busts of French government administrators are highly amusing caricatures. Other galleries display decorative arts, prints and drawings, photographs, even Chinese porcelain.

If you exit the West Building onto 7th Street, you are directly across from the **Sculpture Garden.** Go! Positioned throughout its lushly landscaped 6 acres you'll find a stalking *Spider* by Louise Bourgeois, a shiny stainless steel and concrete tree called *Graft,* by Roxy Paine, and 17 other modern sculptures. In the northwest corner is a delightful, large (10×17 ft.) glass and stone mosaic by Marc Chagall. Chagall created the work for his friends Evelyn and John Nef, who displayed the mosaic in the garden of their Georgetown residence for 4 decades (it joined the National Gallery collection in November, 2013).

At the center of the Sculpture Garden is an expansive pool, which turns into an ice rink in winter. The garden is famous for its summer Friday Jazz in the Garden series of concerts, which are free and draw a crowd.

The National Gallery also mounts killer special exhibits, like the "Stuart Davis: In Full Swing" show of 100 works by the American modernist (through March 5, 2017). And then there's the robust schedule of films, tours, talks, and Sunday concert series (now in its 75th year), plus four recommendable dining options, the best of which are the Garden Café (its menu is often tied to the theme of a current exhibit), and the Sculpture Garden's Pavilion Café. So add it all up: world-class art, gorgeous setting, jazz concerts, films, classical music performances, good eats, and ice skating—every bit of this free, except for the food and ice skating, and just see whether the National Gallery of Art isn't one of your favorite places, too.

One other thing you should know is that we have a man named Andrew W. Mellon to thank for the museum. The financier/philanthropist, who served as ambassador to England (1932–1933), was inspired so much by London's National Gallery that he decided to give such a gift to his own country. The National Gallery of Art's West Building opened in Washington, D.C., in 1941, the East Building in 1978, and the Sculpture Garden in 1999.

Constitution Ave. NW, btw. 3rd and 7th sts. NW (on the north side of the Mall). www. nga.gov. ℂ **202/737-4215.** Free admission. Gallery: Mon–Sat 10am–5pm; Sun 11am–6pm. Sculpture Garden: Memorial Day to Labor Day Mon–Thurs and Sat 10am–7pm, Fri 10am–8:30pm, Sun 11am–6pm; Labor Day to Memorial Day Mon–Sat 10am–5pm, Sun 11am–6pm. Ice Rink: Mid-Nov to mid-Mar Mon–Thurs 10am–9pm, Fri–Sat 10am–11pm, Sun 11am–11pm. Rink fees: $8.50 adults, $7.50 children, plus $3 skate rental. Closed Dec 25 and Jan 1. Metro: Archives–Navy Memorial, Judiciary Square (either exit), or Gallery Place/Verizon Center (Arena/7th and F sts. exit). DC Circulator stop.

**National Mall ★★★ ICON**   As part of his vision for Washington, Pierre L'Enfant conceived of the National Mall as a bustling ceremonial avenue of embassies and other distinguished buildings. Today's 2-mile, 700-acre stretch of land extending westward from the base of the Capitol to the Potomac River, just behind the Lincoln Memorial, fulfills that dream to some extent. Eleven Smithsonian buildings, including the newest, the National Museum of African American History and Culture, plus the National Gallery of Art and its Sculpture Garden, and a stray government building (Department of Agriculture), stake out the Mall's northern border along Constitution Avenue and southern border along Independence Avenue. More than 2,000 American elm trees shade the pebbled walkways paralleling Jefferson and Madison drives. In a single year, more than 29 million tourists and locals crisscross the Mall as they visit the Smithsonian museums; hustle to work; exercise; participate in whatever festival, event, or demonstration is taking place on the Mall that day; or simply go for a stroll—just as L'Enfant envisioned, perhaps.

What L'Enfant did not foresee was the toll that all of this activity might take on this piece of parkland. In recent years, visitors to the Mall often have been dismayed to see an expanse of brown rather than green grass, crumbling walkways, and an overall worn appearance. The National Park Service maintains the land but struggles to keep up with needed repairs and preservation work, mostly due to lack of sufficient funds, despite money from Congress and from the Trust for the National Mall (**www.nationalmall.org**), the Park Service's official fundraising partner. A third organization called the National Coalition to Save Our Mall (**www.savethemall.org**), made up of professional and civic groups as well as assorted concerned artists, historians, and residents, advocates for a public voice in Mall enhancement decisions, and for more support from Congress.

These organizations don't necessarily agree on their visions for the Mall. Nevertheless, by the time you visit in 2017, the National Mall should be looking pretty spiffy, now that turf restoration of the grounds has been completed.

Other improvement projects that may be underway include the construction of a new amphitheater and wooded canopy for performances on the grounds of the Washington Monument, and a complete overhaul of the area known as Constitution Gardens, which sits between Constitution Avenue and the Lincoln Memorial Reflecting Pool.

From the foot of the Capitol to the Lincoln Memorial. www.nps.gov/nama.✆ **202/426-6841.** Public space, open 365/24/7. Metro: Smithsonian. DC Circulator stop.

### National Museum of African American History and Culture ★★★

**MUSEUM** A most profound and essential American experience awaits you at the Smithsonian's newest museum, which opened on September 24, 2016. Conceived as a place where visitors of all backgrounds might comprehend America's narrative through an African-American lens, the National Museum of African American History and Culture succeeds on every level. History exhibits, culture galleries, and the museum's architecture and design each express critical elements of the story.

Located across from the Washington Monument, within view of the Lincoln Memorial and the White House, not far from the National Archives, and next door to the National Museum of American History, the museum's very placement nudges the visitor toward a contextual appreciation. The building belongs within this panoply, but it speaks for itself, a remarkable standout in this landscape of white stone structures. A three-tiered shell of bronze-colored panels, the "corona," sheaths the museum's glass-walled exterior, angling outward and upward, suggesting designs found in traditional West African sculpture and headware. The filigreed pattern of the corona mimics the ornate ironwork crafted by slaves in 19th-century New Orleans and Charleston. The museum's main entrance is on Madison Drive, across from the Washington Monument; called "the Porch," the entrance functions as a kind of outdoor room meant to welcome all inside.

When you enter the museum, you are stepping inside a 400,000-square-foot space, 60% of which lies below ground. The History Galleries, or "crypts," are subterranean, as are the theater named after Oprah Winfrey, a cafe, an atrium and a contemplative court. On floors two and three above ground, "the Attic," are exhibits that highlight African-American struggles and achievements in the arts and within communities. You'll want to stop at the welcome desk and the orientation theater on the first floor to ask questions, pick up maps, and find out about that day's events. Museum staff may tell you that you can start your tour on any level, but really it makes most sense on your first visit to travel chronologically through the museum, beginning with the History Galleries, and ending up in the Arts and Culture Galleries. As you move along, you will notice cutouts in the building's bronze scrim, which allow glimpses of surrounding landmarks, including the White House, Lincoln Memorial, and Arlington Cemetery, reinforcing the museum's emphasis on viewing the American experience through the eyes of an African American.

The museum covers more than 500 years of history, its crypt exhibits starting in the 15th century with the transatlantic slave trade and continuing on to slavery in the U.S., the Civil War, Reconstruction, segregation, the Civil Rights movement, and America since 1968. Ramps lead from one exhibit area and level to the next, creating different vantage points for viewing the artifacts and for connecting the gradual progression of events in time. Among the artifacts on hand are shackles used by an enslaved child, an early 1800s weatherboard-clad slave cabin from Edisto Island, South Carolina; Harriet Tubman's shawl and hymn book; an 1874 log house from Poolesville, Maryland, built and inhabited by free slaves after the Civil War; a Jim Crow–era, 1920s Southern Railway car; a vintage, open-cockpit biplane used at Tuskegee Institute to train African-American pilots for Army service during World War II; the Greensboro, North Carolina, Woolworth's lunch counter stools occupied on a February day in 1960 by four black college students who refused to move after being denied service; and assorted documents and artifacts that capture more recent developments, from the election and presidency of Barack Obama to the Black Lives Matter movement.

Exhibits in the Community Galleries on the third floor explore stories of place, region, and migration; how African Americans carved a way for themselves in a world that denied them opportunities; and African Americans' contributions in sports and the military. The fourth floor's Arts and Culture Galleries showcase African-American contributions in music, fashion, food, theater, and the visual arts. Displayed artifacts on these floors range from the outfit that Marian Anderson wore when she sang at the Lincoln Memorial in 1939, to Chuck Berry's red Cadillac convertible, to artworks by Romare Bearden and Elizabeth Catlett.

The story of the museum itself is worth telling, too, and it is told here on the concourse level of the museum. "A Century in the Making" reveals that a group of black Civil War veterans are said to have proposed the idea for an African-American history museum in 1915. Congress took up the cause from time to time over the ensuing decades, finally enacting The NMAAHC Act in December 2003, establishing the museum within the Smithsonian Institution. The Smithsonian Board of Regents approved the current 5-acre site in 2006, a four-firm architectural unit won the design competition in 2009, groundbreaking took place on February 22, 2012, and construction began. Meanwhile, staff, starting from scratch, were traveling around the country amassing artifacts for exhibits. Today, more than half of the museum's collection of 34,000 objects are donations.

Given the NMAAHC's multi-layered chronicling of African-American history from its very beginnings, it is significant that President Barack Obama, the country's first black president, was finishing up his second term in office when he cut the ribbon signaling the opening of the National Museum of African American History and Culture. But, say officials, that's not the end of the story for African-American progress, nor for the museum. This is a living museum and it will continue to tell the ongoing story of African-American history and culture, which at this particular time in America is more necessary than ever.

*Note:* In a certain way, the touring trajectory of the National Museum of African American History and Culture, where you start at the bottom and move upward (from slavery to today), offers a symbolic converse of that in place at the United States Holocaust Memorial Museum (p. 161), where you begin at the top floor and descend (from the rise of Hitler and Nazism to the Final Solution). Exhibits at both museums reveal history through chronological storytelling that focuses on the lives of ordinary and heroic individuals. And both museums provide areas of contemplation and reflection, where visitors can sit and take everything in, from the tragic facts to celebrations of the indomitable human spirit.

1400 Constitution Ave. NW, btw. 14th and 15th sts. NW, next to the Washington Monument, with entrances on Madison Dr. (main entrance) and Constitution Ave. www.nmaahc.si.edu. © **202/633-1000.** Free admission. Daily 10am–5:30pm, with possible extended hours into 2017. Closed Dec 25. Metro: Smithsonian or Federal Triangle. DC Circulator stop.

**National Museum of African Art** ★ MUSEUM   This inviting little museum does not get the foot traffic of its larger, better-known sister Smithsonians, but that only makes for a happier experience for those who do visit. Find it by strolling through the Enid A. Haupt Garden, under which the subterranean museum lies, and enter via the domed pavilions to descend to the galleries, picking up a self-guided tour flyer at the information desk as you go.

Traditional and contemporary African music plays lightly in the background as you tour the dimly lit suite of rooms on three sublevels. The galleries rotate works from the museum's 10,000-piece permanent inventory of ancient and modern art, spanning art forms and geographic areas. (The museum owns the largest public holdings of contemporary African art in the United States.) Sometimes the museum emphasizes a particular region in its choice of exhibited art, as a 2016 exhibit that showcased historic photos of West African rituals and pageantry in the early- to mid-20th century. The photographs were taken from the museum's permanent photo collection, numbering more than 350,000 items.

A tour of the museum at any time turns up diverse discoveries: a circa 13th- to 15th-century ceramic equestrian figure from Mali; face masks from Congo and Gabon; a 15th-century Ethiopian manuscript page; and a commanding, mixed-media sculpture of Haiti's liberator, Toussaint Louverture, *Toussaint Louverture et La Vieille Esclave,* by Senegalese artist Ousmane Sow.

The African Art Museum was founded in 1964, joined the Smithsonian in 1979, and moved to the Mall

The National Museum of African American History and Culture.

in 1987. If you descend to sublevel 3, you will reach the subterranean passage that takes you to the **Ripley Center** (p. 154).

950 Independence Ave. SW. www.africa.si.edu. © **202/633-4600.** Free admission. Daily 10am–5:30pm. Closed Dec 25. Metro: Smithsonian. DC Circulator stop.

**National Museum of American History ★★★** MUSEUM How does one museum possibly sum up the history of a nation that is 240 years old, 3.8 million square miles in size, and has a population of 319 million people? And how does the museum sort through its collection of 3.3 million artifacts, which include every imaginable American object, from George Washington's uniform to an 1833 steam locomotive, from the Star-Spangled Banner to a 1960s lunchbox, and choose which to display? And finally, how does the museum serve it up in such a way as to capture both the essence of American history and culture, and the attention of a diverse and international public?

As the National Museum of American History celebrates 53 years in 2017, it is in the midst of reinventing itself so as to live up to these daunting but joyful challenges. And though the strategic plan involves another few years to complete, I can tell you that a visit to the National Museum of American History today is already much more fun and interesting than it ever was before.

I recommend you head to the **Flag Hall** first, because this is the location of the museum's star (or should I say "starred"?) attraction: the original Star-Spangled Banner. This 30×34-foot wool and cotton flag is the very one that Francis Scott Key spied at dawn on September 14, 1814, flying above Fort McHenry in Baltimore's harbor, signifying an American victory over the British during the War of 1812. Key memorialized that moment in a poem, which became the country's official National Anthem in 1931. The threadbare 202-year-old treasure is on view behind a window in an environmentally controlled chamber, just beyond the atrium wall; terrific, interactive displays bring to life the significance and grandeur of this important artifact.

From Flag Hall, stay on the second floor to see Dorothy's ruby slippers, a fragment of Plymouth rock, and 100 other objects in **American Stories.** The other highlight of the second floor is a partially reconstructed, 200+-year-old house transplanted from Ipswich, Massachusetts, the centerpiece of **Within These Walls . . . ,** which tells the stories of the families who lived here. Scheduled to open in 2017 on this floor are exhibits on American democracy that explore the idea of what it means to be American.

American ingenuity is celebrated in first-floor exhibits, which include excellent offerings for children of all ages. **Wegmans Wonderplace,** geared toward children under age 6, is a large learning playroom where kids can "cook" in a kitchen inspired by Julia Child's (on display in the first floor's east wing, see below) and find owls hidden in a miniature replica of the Smithsonian Castle. A revamped and much improved version of an old favorite attraction, the **Lemelson Center,** features **Places of Invention** and **Spark!Lab,** where interactive exhibits allow for hands-on learning about inventors and inventiveness. This west wing of the museum was oddly quiet when I visited, sharply in contrast to the east wing and the other floors of the museum. It seems that parents have yet to discover the wonderful, fairly new, family-oriented exhibits. Well, now you know!

In the same area as the children's galleries is the **Wallace H. Coulter Performance Stage and Plaza,** where cooking demonstrations, jazz concerts, and other programs frequently take place. Around the corner from this area, just inside the Constitution Avenue entrance to the museum is the Jazz Café, where you can power up with ice cream cones, pastries, and sandwiches.

Other first-floor exhibits focused on American ingenuity display patent models of inventions by Samuel Morse, Alexander Graham Bell, and Thomas Edison, as well as the **workshop of Ralph Baer,** the progenitor of video games. Stop by the museum's fresh exhibit on business history, **American Enterprise,** a kind of companion piece to the **Value of Money** exhibit here.

Assorted transportation vehicles command a lot of space and attention in the exhibit **America on the Move,** but to my mind they're not nearly as interesting as the exhibit titled *FOOD: Transforming the American Table, 1950–2000.* Its *piece de resistance* is **Julia Child's home kitchen,** kitchen sink to favorite skillet, which Child donated to the museum in late 2001.

If you're interested in American wars and politics, you should make your way to the third floor, which holds the museum's most visited exhibit: **The First Ladies** features 26 first ladies' gowns and more than 1,000 objects, which round out our perceptions about the roles and personalities of these singular women. Also on this floor is **The American Presidency: A Glorious Burden,** which displays 900 objects, including Thomas Jefferson's lap desk, shining a more personal light on those who have held the office. Continue on to **The Price of Freedom: Americans at War,** which explores military history and the idea of wars as defining episodes in American history.

Constitution Ave. NW, btw. 12th and 14th sts. NW (on the north side of the Mall, with entrances on Constitution Ave. and Madison Dr.). www.americanhistory.si.edu.ⓒ **202/ 633-1000.** Free admission. Daily 10am–5:30pm (until 7:30pm in summer). Closed Dec 25. Metro: Smithsonian or Federal Triangle. DC Circulator stop.

**National Museum of the American Indian ★** MUSEUM    This striking building, located at the Capitol end of the National Mall, stands out for the architectural contrast it makes with neighboring Smithsonian and government structures. It is the first national museum in the country dedicated exclusively to Native Americans, and Native Americans consulted on its design, both inside and out; the main architect was a Blackfoot Indian. The museum's rippled exterior is clad in golden sand-colored Kasota limestone, the building standing 5 stories high within a landscape of wetland grasses, water features, and 40 large uncarved rocks and boulders known as "grandfather rocks."

Although the interior design is breathtaking (you enter into a 120-ft.-high domed "Potomac," or rotunda, whose central atrium shows off beautiful boats, each representing the handcrafted boatbuilding traditions of different native peoples), the experience of visiting here can be bewildering, thanks to the vast number of artifacts (approximately 8,500) and the variety of tribes and tribal traditions portrayed. Perhaps this dizzying effect is intentional, but I've found that going through on one of the highlights tours is far superior to navigating the museum on your own.

But if a tour isn't starting when you arrive, or you prefer exploring on your own, begin with the 13-minute *Who We Are* orientation film that plays throughout the day in the Lelawi Theater on the fourth level. It offers a good introduction to the diversity of traditions and contemporary Native-American life that the museum explores. You'll add to that understanding of Native culture by visiting two other exhibits on the fourth floor: **Our Universes,** which focuses on Native cosmologies and the spiritual connection between man and nature, and **Nation to Nation,** which explores the history of treaty-making between the United States and American Indian nations, using 125 objects, such as wampum belts and peace medals, three videos, and four interactive touch-based media stations.

The second floor's **"Return to a Native Place"** tells the more local story of the Algonquian peoples of the Chesapeake Bay region (today's Washington, D.C., Maryland, Virginia, and Delaware). **"Window on the Collections"** (found on both the third and fourth levels) is for art lovers, showcasing 4,500 objects arranged in 7 categories, including animal-themed figurines and objects, beadwork, dolls, and peace medals. Also look for displays of totem poles and other landmark objects and art throughout the museum.

A special exhibit that should be on view while you're at the museum is "The Great Inka Road: Engineering an Empire" (until June 1, 2018), which presents the fascinating story behind the 20,000-mile road, a century in the making, traversing mountains, lowlands, rivers and deserts to link places that are now part of Columbia, Bolivia, Peru, Argentina, Ecuador, and Chile.

When you return to the first floor, consider stopping by the museum's restaurant, **Mitsitam,** which features the native foods of five different regions.

4th St. and Independence Ave. SW. www.americanindian.si.edu. © **202/633-1000.** Free admission. Daily 10am–5:30pm. Closed Dec 25. Metro: Federal Center Southwest or L'Enfant Plaza (Smithsonian Museums/Maryland Ave. exit). DC Circulator stop.

**National Museum of Natural History ★★** MUSEUM   I'll be blunt: This museum is just too much. And I mean that in, unfortunately, a negative way. Not only is it the most popular museum in town (get ready to fight the crowds!), but there are so many exhibits, and so many items within the exhibits, that the average visitor experiences an uncomfortable sensory overload.

Let me give you some numbers: The museum's collection has more than 127 million artifacts and specimens (only a small percentage on display); the building measures 1.32 million square feet, of which 325,000 square feet is public space; and about 7 million people visit annually, making this the most visited natural history museum *in the world.*

Best advice: Know before you go. That is, visit the museum's website and click on "Plan Your Visit," which in turn allows you to click on "Discover the Museum's Must-Sees," "Navigate the Museum," and other options that will help you develop a strategy before you arrive. And if you still find yourself feeling overwhelmed on arrival, do as I did on a recent visit to the crowded

The National Museum of Natural History rotunda.

museum: Go up to one of the green vested "Visitor Concierges" you'll see roaming the exhibit areas and ask them to name the two must-see things they would recommend in the particular exhibit (naturally, you should tailor this to your liking: five must-sees, or the concierge's particular favorites, or the ones best for children, and so on). A concierge I approached in the Sant Ocean Hall responded immediately with the "live coral reef" and the "shark mouth," pointing me to them in the vast hall. Perfect suggestions. The variously colored coral reef tank holds fish of brilliant blue, purple, yellow, and pink hues. The enormous jaw of a *Carcharodon megalodon,* a shark that lived 5 million years ago, is enclosed in a glass case; the idea is for you to pose behind the glass case so that it appears as if you're "inside the mouth" of the sharp-toothed shark and your partner/mom/friend/passing guidebook writer snaps a photo of you.

The museum has 16 different galleries, with exhibits that cover the story of natural history from the earliest beginnings of life to the present. An extreme makeover of the popular fossils and dinosaurs exhibit means that that gallery is closed, not to reopen until the new Dinosaur and Fossils Hall debuts . . . in 2019! Until 2019, dinosaur lovers can get their fix by touring interim dinosaur-focused exhibits, including one called "The Last American Dinosaurs: Discovering a Lost World."

But forget the dinosaurs for a moment and look to the giant squids swimming in **Ocean Hall** and a rearing African bush elephant greeting you in the museum's central Rotunda. And there's more: a gems and geology exhibit that displays the Hope Diamond and other fine bling; a live butterfly pavilion, where exotically colored butterflies alight upon you; a discovery room of hands-on exhibits for young children; and simulator rides and 2-D and 3-D IMAX movies (*Dinosaurs Alive 3-D* was one shown in 2016) for thrill seekers.

And that doesn't even cover the special exhibits on tap in 2017, like "Primordial Landscapes: Iceland Revealed," to name just one.

What to pick? That's up to you. Good luck.

Constitution Ave. NW, btw. 9th and 12th sts. (on the north side of the Mall, with entrances on Madison Dr. and Constitution Ave.). www.naturalhistory.si.edu. ℘ **202/633-1000,** or 633-4629 for information about IMAX films. Free admission. Daily 10am–5:30pm (until 7:30pm in summer). Closed Dec 25. Metro: Smithsonian (Mall/Jefferson Dr. exit) or Federal Triangle. DC Circulator stop.

## National World War II Memorial ★★ MONUMENT/MEMORIAL

When this memorial was dedicated on May 29, 2004, 150,000 people attended: President Bush; members of Congress; Marine Corps General (retired) P. X. Kelley, who chaired the group that spearheaded construction of the memorial; actor Tom Hanks and now-retired news anchor Tom Brokaw, both of whom had been active in soliciting support for the memorial; and last, but most important, thousands of World War II veterans and their families. These legions of veterans—some dressed in uniform, many wearing a cap identifying the name of their division—turned out with pride, happy to receive the nation's gratitude, 60 years in the making, expressed profoundly in this memorial.

Designed by Friedrich St. Florian and funded mostly by private donations, the memorial fits nicely into the landscape between the Washington Monument grounds to the east and the Lincoln Memorial and its Reflecting Pool to the west. St. Florian purposely situated the 7½-acre memorial so as not to obstruct this long view down the Mall. Fifty-six 17-foot-high granite pillars representing each state and territory stand to either side of a central plaza and the Rainbow Pool. Likewise 24 bas-relief panels divide down the middle so that 12 line each side of the walkway leading from the entrance at 17th Street.

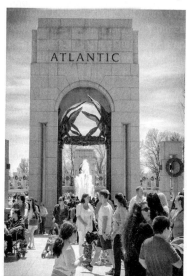

The panels to the left, as you walk toward the center of the memorial, illustrate seminal scenes from the war years as they relate to the Pacific front: Pearl Harbor, amphibious landing, jungle warfare, a field burial, and so on. The panels to the right are sculptured scenes of war moments related to the Atlantic front: Rosie the Riveter, Normandy Beach landing, the Battle of the Bulge, the Russians meeting the Americans at the Elbe River. Architect and sculptor Raymond Kaskey sculpted these panels based on archival photographs.

Large open pavilions stake out the north and south axes of the memorial, and semicircular fountains create waterfalls on either side. Inscriptions

The World War II Memorial.

at the base of each pavilion fountain mark key battles. Beyond the center Rainbow Pool is a wall of 4,048 gold stars, 1 star for every 100 American soldiers who died in World War II. People often leave photos and mementos around the memorial, which the National Park Service gathers up daily for an archive. Rangers give tours every hour on the hour, 10am to 11pm. For compelling, firsthand accounts of World War II experiences, combine your tour here with an online visit to the **Library of Congress's Veterans History Project,** at www.loc.gov/vets; see the Library of Congress entry (p. 123) for more information.

From the 17th Street entrance, walk south around the perimeter of the memorial to reach a ranger station, where there are brochures as well as registry kiosks for looking up names of veterans (also at **www.wwiimemorial.com**).

17th St., near Constitution Ave. NW. www.nps.gov/nwwm. ℡**800/639-4992** or 202/426-6841. Free admission. Ranger on duty daily 9:30am–10pm, except Dec 25. Limited parking. Metro: Farragut West, Federal Triangle, or Smithsonian, with a 20- to 25-min. walk. DC Circulator stop.

**Ripley Center** ★CULTURAL INSTITUTION    Part of the Smithsonian complex but not officially counted as a museum, the S. Dillon Ripley Center is notable for hosting **Smithsonian Associates** arts, education, and entertainment programs (the programs are open both to members and to the general public; there's usually an admission fee) and **Discovery Theater's** children's plays and entertainment. The center also mounts small rotating exhibits of works from various Smithsonian museums. Look for the copper-domed, hutlike structure next to the Smithsonian Castle. Its galleries and the Discovery Theater are subterranean and connect to the Freer, Sackler, and African Art museums.

1100 Jefferson Dr. SW. www.si.edu/museums/ripley-center. ℡**202/633-1000.** Free admission. Daily 10am–5:30pm. Closed Dec 25. Metro: Smithsonian (Mall exit). DC Circulator stop.

**Sackler Gallery** ★MUSEUM    The Sackler is one-half of what is formally known as the National Museum of Asian Art in the United States (the Freer Gallery, p. 134, is the other half). Though the two museums are connected by purpose, research, staff—and subterranean passageway—they occupy separate buildings. The Freer Gallery is closed for renovation until summer 2017, but be assured, the Sackler is open.

The Sackler Gallery exists because primary benefactor Arthur M. Sackler gave the Smithsonian Institution 1,000 works of Asian art and $4 million to put toward museum construction. When it opened in 1987, the gallery held mostly ancient works, including early Chinese bronzes and jades, centuries-old Near East ceramics, and sculpture from South and Southeast Asia. Pieces from that stellar permanent collection continue to be on rotating view in several underground galleries, along with other precious works acquired over the years, like an assemblage of Persian book artistry and 20th-century Japanese ceramics and works on paper. The collection now numbers nearly 9,000 objects. Especially recommended is *Vietnam's Ceramics: Depth and Diversity* (continuing indefinitely), which displays 23 examples of centuries-old stoneware vessels that reflect the variety of form and artistry at work in a country that holds 54 ethnic groups.

But a big focus today is on the works of contemporary Asian and Asian-diaspora artists, often showcased in the museum's street-level pavilion. ***Perspectives,*** as the series is known, hosts an exhibit through July 9, 2017, of Korean-American artist Michael Joo's monumental installation combining painting, sculpture, photography, digital scanning, and printmaking to represent the movement of Korean red-crowned cranes.

Once you've viewed Perspectives, descend the stairs to tour exhibits on sublevels 1, 2, and 3 that include the arts of China and sculptures of South Asia and the Himalayas. The monumental sculpture suspended from the skylit atrium, through the stairwell, and down to the reflecting pool at bottom is called *Monkeys Grasp for the Moon* and was designed specifically for the gallery by Chinese artist Xu Bing. The work links 21 laminated wood pieces, each of which spells the word "monkey" in one of a dozen languages.

1050 Independence Ave. SW. www.asia.si.edu. ✆ **202/633-4880.** Free admission. Daily 10am–5:30pm. Closed Dec 25. Metro: Smithsonian (Mall/Jefferson Dr. exit). DC Circulator stop.

### Smithsonian Information Center ("The Castle") ★ MUSEUM   This 1855 Medieval-style building, with its eight crenellated towers and rich red sandstone facade, lives up to its nickname, at least from the exterior. Its Great Hall interior is pretty unattractive, but that doesn't matter, because you're just here for information, possibly restrooms, and perhaps a bite to eat. Watch the 10-minute orientation video, take a look at the National Mall models in the middle of the room, and, most important, stop by the information desk to ask the multilingual staff of volunteers to help you plan your Smithsonian itinerary.

There's not much else in this big building that's open to the public. The remains of Smithsonian benefactor James Smithson are buried in that big crypt in the Mall-side entrance area, which includes a small exhibit about the man. The pretty south-side entrance has been repainted to appear as it did in the early 1900s, when children's exhibits were displayed here. On the east side of the building is the **Castle Café,** which opens at 8:30am, earlier than any other building on the Mall. Coffee, pastries, sandwiches, and even beer and wine are sold. Situate yourself at a table inside, where there's free Wi-Fi, or outdoors in the lovely Enid A. Haupt Garden, and plot your day.

1000 Jefferson Dr. SW. www.si.edu. ✆**202/633-1000.** Daily 8:30am–5:30pm (info desk 9am–4pm). Closed Dec 25. Metro: Smithsonian (Mall exit). DC Circulator stop.

### United States Botanic Garden ★ GARDEN   For the feel of summer in the middle of winter and the sight of lush, breathtakingly beautiful greenery and flowers year-round, stop in at the Botanic Garden, located at the foot of the Capitol and next door to the National Museum of the American Indian. The grand conservatory devotes half of its space to exhibits that focus on the importance of plants to people, and half to exhibits that focus on ecology and the evolutionary biology of plants. But those finer points may escape you as you wander through the various chambers, outdoors and indoors, upstairs and down, gazing in stupefaction at so much flora. Throughout its 10 "garden rooms" and 2 courtyards, the conservatory holds about 1,300 living species, or about 3,000

plants. Individual areas include a high-walled enclosure, called "the Jungle," of palms, ferns, and vines; an Orchid Room; a garden of plants used for medicinal purposes; a primeval garden; and seasonal gardens created especially with children in mind. Stairs and an elevator in the Jungle take you to the top of this windowed tower, where you can admire the sea of greenery 24 feet below and, if condensation on the glass windows doesn't prevent it, a view of the Capitol Building rising up on Capitol Hill. Just outside the conservatory is the National Garden, which includes the First Ladies Water Garden, a formal rose garden, a butterfly garden, an amphitheater, and a lawn terrace. Tables and benches make this a lovely spot for a picnic, though much of the garden is unshaded.

Ask at the front desk about guided tours, which don't follow a regular schedule. The USBG sometimes offers entertainment and special programs, like the popular American Roots summer concert series that features twice-monthly performances by Americana, blues, folk, zydeco, and country bands.

Also visit the garden annex across the street, the newly renovated **Bartholdi Park,** which is about the size of a city block, with a cast-iron classical fountain created by Frédéric Auguste Bartholdi, designer of the Statue of Liberty. Flower gardens bloom amid tall ornamental grasses, benches are sheltered by vine-covered bowers, and a touch and fragrance garden contains such herbs as pineapple-scented sage.

100 Maryland Ave. SW (btw. First and 3rd sts. SW, at the foot of the Capitol, bordering the National Mall). www.usbg.gov. ℭ **202/225-8333.** Free admission. Conservatory and National Garden daily 10am–5pm. Bartholdi Park dawn–dusk. Metro: Federal Center SW (Smithsonian Museums/Maryland Ave. exit). DC Circulator stop.

**Vietnam Veterans Memorial** ★★ MONUMENT/MEMORIAL    The Vietnam Veterans Memorial is possibly the most poignant sight in Washington: two long, black-granite walls in the shape of a V, each inscribed with the names of the men and women who gave their lives, or remain missing, in the longest war in American history. Even if no one close to you died in Vietnam, it's moving to watch visitors grimly studying the directories to find out where their loved ones are listed, or rubbing pencil on paper held against a name etched into the wall. The walls list close to 60,000 people, most of whom died very young.

Because of the raging conflict over U.S. involvement in the war, Vietnam veterans had received almost no recognition of their service before the memorial was conceived by Vietnam veteran Jan Scruggs. The nonprofit Vietnam Veterans Memorial Fund raised $7 million and secured a 2-acre site in tranquil Constitution Gardens to erect a memorial that would make no political statement about the war and would harmonize with neighboring memorials. By separating the issue of the wartime service of individuals from the issue of U.S. policy in Vietnam, the VVMF hoped to begin a process of national reconciliation.

Yale senior Maya Lin's design was chosen in a national competition open to all citizens ages 18 and over. Erected in 1982, the memorial's two walls are angled at 125 degrees to point to the Washington Monument and the Lincoln Memorial. The walls' mirrorlike surfaces reflect surrounding trees, lawns, and monuments. The names are inscribed in chronological order, documenting an

Vietnam Veterans Memorial.

epoch in American history as a series of individual sacrifices from the date of the first casualty in 1959. The National Park Service continues to add names as Vietnam veterans die eventually of injuries sustained during the war. Catalogs near the entrances to the memorial list names alphabetically and the panel and row number for each name that is inscribed in the wall. Elsewhere on the grounds of the Vietnam Veterans Memorial, though not part of Maya Lin's design, are two other sculptures honoring the efforts of particular servicemen and women: the Three Servicemen Statue and the Vietnam Women's Memorial.

Northeast of the Lincoln Memorial, east of Henry Bacon Dr. (btw. 21st and 22nd sts. NW, on the Constitution Ave. NW side of the Mall). www.nps.gov/vive. ⓒ 202/426-6841. Free admission. Ranger on duty daily 9:30am–10pm, except Dec 25. Limited parking. Metro: Foggy Bottom, with 25-min. walk. DC Circulator stop.

**Washington Monument ★★★** MONUMENT/MEMORIAL  The idea of a tribute to George Washington was first broached 16 years before his death, by the Continental Congress of 1783. But the new nation had more pressing problems and funds were not readily available. It wasn't until the early 1830s, with the 100th anniversary of Washington's birth approaching, that any action was taken.

First there were several fiascos. A mausoleum under the Capitol Rotunda was provided for Washington's remains, but a grandnephew, citing Washington's will, refused to allow the body to be moved from Mount Vernon. In 1830, Horatio Greenough was commissioned to create a memorial statue for the Rotunda. He came up with a bare-chested Washington, draped in classical Greek garb. A shocked public claimed he looked as if he were "entering or leaving a bath," and so the statue was relegated to the Smithsonian. Finally, in

The Washington Monument, with the U.S. Capitol in the distance.

1833, prominent citizens organized the Washington National Monument Society. Treasury Building architect Robert Mills's design was accepted.

The cornerstone was laid on July 4, 1848, and construction continued for 6 years, until declining contributions and the Civil War brought work to a halt at an awkward 153 feet (you can still see a change in the color of the stone about one-third of the way up). It took until 1876 for sufficient funds to become available, thanks to President Grant's authorization for use of federal moneys to complete the project, and another 4 years after that for work to resume on the unsightly stump. The Washington Monument's dedication ceremony took place in 1885, and the monument finally opened to the public in 1888.

**Visiting the Washington Monument:** When you have your ticket (see below for details), stand in line to enter the Monument. Once inside you'll pass through a small screening facility before boarding the Monument's large elevator, which whisks you upward for 70 seconds.

You won't arrive at the pinnacle of the 555-foot, 5⅛-inches-tall obelisk, but close to it: the 500-foot level of the world's tallest free-standing work of masonry. At this height, you'll see that the Washington Monument lies at the very heart of Washington, D.C., landmarks. Its 360-degree views are spectacular. Due east are the Capitol and Smithsonian buildings; due north is the White House; due west are the World War II and Lincoln memorials (with Arlington National Cemetery beyond); due south are the Martin Luther King, Jr. and Jefferson memorials, overlooking the Tidal Basin and the Potomac River. On a clear day, you can see 20 miles in any direction.

Once you've gotten your fill of the views, head down the steps to the small museum (at level 490 ft.), where you can peer at bent lightning rods removed from the top of the Monument after it had been struck, discover that Pierre L'Enfant had hoped to honor George Washington with an equestrian statue, and read the prophetic quote by Senator Robert Winthrop, at the 1885 dedication of the Washington Monument: "The lightening of Heaven may scar and blacken it. An earthquake may shake its foundations . . . But the character which it commemorates and illustrates is secure."

(Oh yeah. Remember the earthquake that hit this area on Aug 23, 2011? The monument's marble and granite walls were damaged inside and out, causing the monument to be closed for repairs until May 12, 2014.)

When you re-board the glass-walled elevator, you'll have the chance during the 2-minute descent to view some of the 194 carved stones inserted into the interior walls that are gifts from foreign countries, all 50 states, organizations, and individuals. One stone you usually get to see is the one given by the state of Alaska in 1982—it's pure jade and worth millions. There are stones from Siam (now Thailand), the Cherokee Nation, the Vatican, and the Sons of Temperance, to name just a few.

**Ticket Information:** Admission is free, but you'll need a ticket. Since day-of tickets are often gone by 9am in peak season, I strongly encourage you to get tickets in advance, by at least 6 weeks, through the **National Park Reservation Service** (www.recreation.gov (search for "Washington Monument"; © **877/444-6777**). Visitors can reserve up to six tickets at a time. You'll pay $1.50 per ticket in a service fee if you order in advance, plus $2.85 for shipping and handling if you want the tickets mailed to you; otherwise, you can pick up the tickets at the "will call" window at the ticket kiosk that everyone goes to. That booth is located in the Monument Lodge, at the bottom of the hill from the monument, on 15th Street NW between Madison and Jefferson drives; it opens daily at 8:30am. If you don't get advanced tickets, plan to get there by 7:30 or 8am, especially in peak season. The tickets grant admission at half-hour intervals between the stated hours on the day you visit.

*Important:* Travel light! Large backpacks, strollers, and open containers of food or drink are not allowed inside the Monument.

15th St. NW, directly south of the White House (btw. Madison Dr. and Constitution Ave. NW). www.nps.gov/wamo. © **202/426-6841.** Free admission. Labor Day to Memorial Day 9am–4:45pm; Memorial Day to Labor Day 9am–9pm (until noon July 4). Last elevators depart 15 min. before closing (arrive earlier). Closed Dec 25. Limited parking. Metro: Smithsonian (Mall/Jefferson Dr. exit), with a 10-min. walk. DC Circulator stop.

# SOUTHWEST OF THE MALL

Two top attractions are located on 15th Street SW, across Independence Avenue from the National Mall. These sites are not National Park Service properties, so I separate them from other attractions located nearby in the southwest section of the National Mall and Memorial Parks category.

### Bureau of Engraving & Printing ★ GOVERNMENT BUILDING
This is where they will literally show you the money: A staff of about 2,000 works round-the-clock Monday through Friday churning it out at the rate of nearly $500 million a day. Everyone's eyes pop as they walk past rooms overflowing with new greenbacks. But the money's not the whole story. The bureau prints security documents for other federal government agencies, including military IDs and passport pages.

A 40-minute guided tour begins with a short introductory film. Large windows allow you to see what goes into making paper money: designing, inking, engraving, stacking of bills, cutting, and examining for defects. The process combines traditional, old-world printing techniques with the latest technology to create counterfeit-proof currency. Additional exhibits display bills no longer

# JAMES SMITHSON & the smithsonians

You must be wondering by now: How did the Smithsonian Institution come to be? It's rather an unlikely story, concerning the largesse of a wealthy English scientist named James Smithson (1765–1829), the illegitimate son of the Duke of Northumberland. Smithson willed his vast fortune to the United States, to found "at Washington, under the name of the Smithsonian Institution, an establishment for the increase and diffusion of knowledge." Smithson never explained why he left this handsome bequest to the United States, a country he had never visited. Speculation is that he felt the new nation, lacking established cultural institutions, most needed his funds.

Smithson died in Genoa, Italy, in 1829. Congress accepted his gift in 1836; 2 years later, half a million dollars' worth of gold sovereigns (a considerable sum in the 19th c.) arrived at the U.S. Mint in Philadelphia. For the next 8 years, Congress debated the best possible use for these funds. Finally, in 1846, James Polk signed an act into law establishing the Smithsonian Institution and authorizing a board to receive "all objects of art and of foreign and curious research, and all objects of natural history, plants, and geological and mineralogical specimens . . . for research and museum purposes." In 1855, the first Smithsonian building opened on the Mall, not as a museum, but as the home of the Smithsonian Institution. The red sandstone structure suffered a fire and underwent several reconstructions over the years, to serve today as the Smithsonian Information Center, known by all as "the Castle." Smithson's remains are interred in the Crypt located inside the north vestibule (National Mall side).

Today, the Smithsonian Institution's 20 museums and galleries (D.C. has 18), 9 research centers, and the National Zoological Park comprise the world's largest museum complex. Millions of people visit the Smithsonians annually—more than 28 million toured the museums in 2015. The Smithsonian's collection of 138 million objects spans the entire world and all of its history, its peoples and animals (past and present), and our attempts to probe into the future.

So vast is the collection that Smithsonian museums display only about 1% or 2% of the collection's holdings at any given time. Artifacts range from a 3.5-billion-year-old fossil to inaugural gowns worn by the first ladies. Thousands of scientific expeditions sponsored by the Smithsonian have pushed into remote frontiers in the deserts, mountains, polar regions, and jungles of the world.

Individually, each museum is a powerhouse in its own field. The National Museum of Natural History and the National Air and Space Museum are the most visited of the Smithsonians, each welcoming about seven million people in 2015. The National Air and Space Museum maintains the world's largest collection of historic aircraft and spacecraft. The Smithsonian American Art Museum is the nation's first collection of American art and one of the largest in the world. And so on.

To find out information about any of the Smithsonian museums go to **www. si.edu,** which helps you get to their individual home pages.

in circulation and a $100,000 bill designed for official transactions. (Since 1969 the largest-denomination bill issued for the general public is $100.)

After you finish the tour, allow time to explore the **visitor center,** open from 8:30am to 7pm, with additional exhibits and a gift shop, where you can buy bags of shredded money, uncut sheets of currency in different denominations, and copies of historic documents, like a hand-engraved replica ($200) of the Declaration of Independence.

**Ticket Tips:** Many people line up each day to get a peek at all the moolah, so arrive early, especially during the peak tourist season. To save time and avoid a line, consider securing VIP, also called "congressional," tour tickets from one of your senators or your congressperson; email or call at least 3 months in advance for tickets. These tours take place April through August at 8:15 and 8:45am, and between 4 and 4:45pm.

Tickets for general public tours are generally not required from September to February; simply find the visitors entrance at 14th and C streets. March through August, however, every person taking the tour must have a ticket. To obtain a ticket, go to the ticket booth on the Raoul Wallenberg (formerly 15th St.) side of the building. You will receive a ticket specifying a tour time for that same day and be directed to the 14th Street entrance of the bureau. You are allowed as many as four tickets per person. The ticket booth opens at 8am and closes when all tickets are dispersed for the day. *Note:* Renovation of the building underway through March 2017 may affect touring procedures, so be sure to check the website before your visit.

14th and C sts. SW. www.moneyfactory.gov. (✆) **866/874-2330.** Free admission. Mon–Fri 9am–2pm Sept to mid-March, 9am–6pm mid-March through Aug. Closed weekends, federal holidays, and Dec 25–Jan 1. Metro: Smithsonian (Independence Ave. exit). DC Circulator stop.

**United States Holocaust Memorial Museum** ★★ MUSEUM   The Holocaust Museum documents Nazi Germany's systematic persecution and annihilation of six million Jews and others between 1933 and 1945, and presents visitors with individual stories of both horror and courage in the persecuted people's struggle to survive. The museum calls itself a "living memorial to the Holocaust," the idea being for people to visit, confront the evil of which mankind is capable, and leave inspired to face down hatred and inhumanity when they come upon it in the world. A message repeated over and over is this one of Holocaust survivor and author Primo Levi: "It happened. Therefore it can happen again. And it can happen everywhere." Since the museum opened in 1993, approximately 39 million visitors have taken home that message, and another: "What you do matters."

You begin your tour of the permanent exhibit on the first floor, where you pick the identity card of an actual Holocaust victim, whose fate you can learn about in stages at different points in the exhibit. Then you ride the elevator to the fourth floor, where "Nazi Assault, 1933–1939" covers events in Germany, from Hitler's appointment as chancellor in 1933 to Germany's invasion of Poland and the official start of World War II in 1939. You learn that anti-Semitism was nothing new, and observe for yourself in newsreels how Germans were bowled over by Hitler's powers of persuasion and propaganda. Exhibits tell stories of desperation, like the voyage of the St. Louis passenger liner in May 1939, which sailed from Germany to Havana with 900 Jews, but was turned away and returned to Europe.

The middle floor of the permanent exhibit covers the years 1940 to 1945, revealing the horrors of the Nazi machine's "Final Solution" for the Jews, including deportations, the ghetto experience, and life and death within

## UPDATE ON NEW bills

You may have heard about the coming redesigns of the $20, $10, and $5 bills and may wonder whether you will see these new notes being printed during your tour. No, you will not. The task of redesigning the bills and incorporating the new designs into the Bureau's secure printing process takes time. The plan is for the Treasury Department to unveil the new $20, $10, and $5 notes in 2020, in conjunction with the 100th anniversary of the ratification of the 19th Amendment, giving women the right to vote. The $20 bill will feature abolitionist Harriet Tubman on the front and Andrew Jackson on the back; the $10 bill will keep Alexander Hamilton on the front but will depict suffragettes Lucretia Mott, Susan B. Anthony, Alice Paul, Elizabeth Cady Stanton, and Sojourner Truth on the reverse; and the $5 note will keep Abraham Lincoln on the face, but the flip side will depict historic events at the Lincoln Memorial involving First Lady Eleanor Roosevelt, singer Marian Anderson, and civil rights leader Dr. Martin Luther King, Jr.

concentration camps. You listen to survivors tell their stories in taped recordings, and view artifacts such as transport rail cars, reconstructed concentration camp barracks, and photographs of "killing squad" executions. One of the most moving exhibits is the "Tower of Faces," which contains photographs of the Jewish people who lived in the small Lithuanian town of Eishishok for some 900 years, before the Nazis killed nearly all, in two days in September 1941.

"The Last Chapter," on the second floor, documents the stories of heroes, like the king of Denmark, who was able to save the lives of 90% of Denmark's Jewish population. Exhibits also recount the Allies' liberation of the concentration camps and aftermath events, from Jewish emigration to America and Israel, to the Nuremberg trials. At exhibit's end is the hour-long film, *Testimonies,* in which Holocaust survivors tell their stories. The tour finishes in the **Hall of Remembrance,** a place for meditation and reflection and where you may light a memorial candle.

*Note:* You should know that a group of about 80 Holocaust survivors volunteers at the museum, usually two each day. The volunteers stand near the information desk on the first floor and are there to answer questions.

Don't overlook the first-floor and lower-level exhibits. Always on view are **"Daniel's Story: Remember the Children,"** for children 8 and older, and the **"Wall of Remembrance"** (Children's Tile Wall), which commemorates the 1.5 million children killed in the Holocaust. The lower

"Tower of Faces" exhibit at the United States Holocaust Memorial Museum.

## Holocaust Museum Ticket Tips

Because so many people want to visit the museum (it has hosted as many as 10,000 visitors in a single day), passes specifying a visit time (in 15-min. intervals) are required during the busiest months, March through August. You can obtain same-day passes, as many as 20 per person, by arriving early and standing in line on the 14th Street side of the museum's alley, where museum staff distribute passes. (If there's no line, head inside to the information desk.) The museum also offers a limited number of same-day passes available online, starting at 6am on the day you hope to visit; or you can reserve as many as 55 tickets in advance at www.etix.com (search for "Holocaust"), for $1 per pass (you print your own tickets). Passes are valid for entry within a 1-hour time frame from the time stamped on your pass. **Note:** The passes are for the museum's permanent exhibition on the first three floors. No passes are needed to see the lower-level exhibits.

level is also the site for special exhibits. On view through 2017 is "Some Were Neighbors: Collaboration and Complicity in the Holocaust," which explores the role of ordinary citizens in carrying out Nazi policies.

The museum also houses a Resource Center that includes a registry of Holocaust survivors and victims, a library, and archives, all of which are available to anyone who wants to research family history or the Holocaust.

The museum's permanent exhibit is not recommended for children 11 and under; for older children, it's advisable to prepare them for what they'll see.

There's a cafeteria and museum shop on the premises.

100 Raoul Wallenberg Place SW (formerly 15th St. SW; near Independence Ave., just off the Mall). www.ushmm.org. © **202/488-0400.** Free admission. Daily 10am–5:20pm, open later in peak seasons. Closed Yom Kippur and Dec 25. Metro: Smithsonian (12th St. and Independence Ave. SW exit). DC Circulator stop.

# MIDTOWN

The **White House** is midtown's main attraction and offers reason enough to visit this part of town, even if you're only able to admire it from the outside. Midtown is where you'll find an off-the-Mall Smithsonian museum, the **Renwick Gallery,** and smaller and more specialized art collections and several historic houses. Pick and choose from the offerings below, or follow the walking tour of the neighborhood outlined in chapter 10.

**Art Museum of the Americas** ★ ART MUSEUM    Contemporary Latin and American artworks are on display inside this picturesque, red-tiled-roofed, Spanish-colonial-style structure. The museum rotates art from its permanent collection of 2,000 to encapsulate a theme, like the 2016 exhibit, "Streams of Being," which explored ideas and identities emerging in contemporary Latin American art. The Organization of American States opened the museum in 1976 as a gift to the U.S. in honor of its bicentennial.

201 18th St. NW (at Virginia Ave.). www.museum.oas.org. © **202/458-6016.** Free admission. Tues–Sun 10am–5pm. Closed federal holidays and Good Friday. Metro: Farragut West (18th St. exit) or Farragut North (K St. exit).

### Daughters of the American Revolution (DAR) Museum ★ MUSEUM

The DAR Museum gives visitors a glimpse of pre-1840 American life through its displays of folk art, rocking chairs, quilts and other furnishings, silverware, samplers, and everyday objects. Its Americana Collection showcases the paperwork of each period, from Colonial days through the Revolutionary War, up to the country's beginnings: diaries, letters, and household inventories. Be sure not to miss the Period Rooms. See p. 261 for further information. From time to time, the museum hosts a special exhibit, like its 2016 show, "Remembering the American Revolution, 1776–1890," which highlighted the ways that citizens saved and created objects to maintain a connection with the Revolution.

1776 D St. NW (at 17th St.). www.dar.org/museum. ☏ **202/628-1776.** Free admission. Museum Mon–Fri 9:30am–4pm; Sat 9am–5pm. Period Rooms Mon–Fri 9:30am–4pm; Sat 9am–5pm. Americana Collection Mon–Fri 8:30am–4pm. Closed on federal holidays. Metro: Farragut West (17th St. exit) or Farragut North (K St. exit).

### Octagon House ★ HISTORIC HOME

This is the country's oldest museum dedicated to architecture and design. Dr. William Thornton, first architect of the Capitol, designed the house in 1801. As its name suggests, the structure is an architectural marvel. Eight sides, though? Nope, try six. Thornton designed the house for Colonel John Tayloe III, a Virginia planter, breeder of racehorses and friend of George Washington, who would come by to inspect the construction site from time to time. Upon its completion (which Washington did not live to see), the Octagon became a favorite social scene, the Tayloes welcoming John Adams, Thomas Jefferson, James Madison, James Monroe, Daniel Webster, Henry Clay, and their ilk.

1799 New York Ave. NW (at 18th St.). www.architectsfoundation.org/preservation. ☏ **202/626-7439.** Free admission for walk-in, self-guided tours, or $5–$10 for guided tours (by appointment only). Thurs–Sat 1–4pm. Metro: Farragut West (17th St. exit).

### Renwick Gallery of the Smithsonian American Art Museum ★

ART MUSEUM The Renwick Gallery is the city's go-to venue for lovers of American decorative arts, traditional and modern crafts, and architectural design. Reopened in November 2015 after a 2-year renovation, the Renwick's inaugural exhibit, *Wonder,* attracted lines out the door for months, as word spread about the brilliantly innovative, immersive, room-size installations created by nine major contemporary artists. Two of the nine pieces remain on display indefinitely: that of Leo Villareal, whose work, *Volume,* flashes 23,000 LEDs in endless variations above the Grand Staircase; and that of Janet Echelman, *1.8,* in which a colorful handwoven net hangs suspended over the expanse of the Grand Salon, replicating the surge of energy that was released across the Pacific Ocean during the Tohoku earthquake and tsunami.

Also ongoing is an exhibit of 80 objects from the permanent collection; some are old favorites, such as Wendell Castle's *Ghost Clock,* and others are new acquisitions, such as Marie Watt's *Edson's Flag,* but all celebrate contemporary craft. An exhibit in the elegant Octagon Room uses photographs, documents, and art objects to chronicle the history of the building.

The Renwick Gallery.

Designed by and named for James W. Renwick, Jr., architect of the Smithsonian Castle (p. 155), the Renwick was built in 1859, an example of French Second Empire–style architecture. The recent renovation restored the original 19th-century window configurations, and turned up some surprises, like the long-concealed vaulted ceilings on the second floor. Located directly across the street from the White House, the Renwick originally was built to house the art collection of William Wilson Corcoran. The collection quickly outgrew the space, which led to the opening of the Corcoran Gallery of Art (currently closed) just down the street, in 1874.

1661 Pennsylvania Ave. NW (at 17th St.). www.americanart.si.edu/renwick. © **202/633-7970.** Free admission. Daily 10am–5:30pm. Closed Dec 25. Metro: Farragut West or Farragut North.

**The White House** ★★★ GOVERNMENT BUILDING   It's amazing when you think about it: This house has served as residence, office, reception site, and world embassy for every U.S. president since John Adams. The White House is the only private residence of a head of state in the world that is open year-round to the public, free of charge, a practice that Thomas Jefferson inaugurated. On a typical day, you'll be one of some 1,600 people touring the White House, knowing that meanwhile, somewhere in this very building, the president and White House staff are meeting with foreign dignitaries, congressional members, and business leaders, and hashing out the most urgent national and global decisions. For tour info, see box, p. 168.

An Act of Congress in 1790 established the city now known as Washington, District of Columbia, as the seat of the federal government. George Washington and city planner Pierre L'Enfant chose the site for the president's house

and staged a contest to find a builder. Although Washington picked the winner—Irishman James Hoban—he was the only president never to live in the White House. The structure took 8 years to build, starting in 1792, when its cornerstone was laid. Its facade is made of the same stone used to construct the Capitol. The mansion quickly became known as the "White House," thanks to the limestone whitewashing applied to the walls to protect them, later replaced by white lead paint in 1818. In 1814, during the War of 1812, the British set fire to the White House and gutted the interior; the exterior managed to endure only because a rainstorm extinguished the fire. What you see today is Hoban's basic creation: a building modeled after an Irish country house (in fact, Hoban had in mind the house of the Duke of Leinster in Dublin).

*Note:* Tours of the White House exit from the North Portico. Before you descend the front steps, look to your left to find the window whose sandstone sill remains unpainted as a reminder both of the 1814 fire and of the White House's survival.

Additions over the years have included the South Portico in 1824, the North Portico in 1829, and electricity in 1891, during Benjamin Harrison's presidency. In 1902, repairs and refurnishing of the White House cost nearly $500,000. No other great change took place until Harry Truman's presidency, when the interior was completely renovated after the leg of Margaret Truman's piano cut through the dining room ceiling. The Trumans lived at Blair House across the street for nearly 4 years while the White House interior was shored up with steel girders and concrete.

In 1961, First Lady Jacqueline Kennedy spearheaded the founding of the White House Historical Association and formed a Fine Arts Committee to help restore the famous rooms to their original grandeur, ensuring treatment of the White House as a museum of American history and decorative arts. "It just seemed to me such a shame when we came here to find hardly anything of the past in the house, hardly anything before 1902," Mrs. Kennedy observed.

Every president and first family put their own stamp on the White House. The Obamas installed artworks on loan from the Hirshhorn Museum and from the National Gallery of Art in their private residence, and chose works to hang in the public rooms of the White House. (Changing the art in the public rooms requires approval from the White House curator and the Committee for the Preservation of the White House.) Michelle Obama planted a vegetable garden on the White House grounds, and President Obama altered the outdoor tennis court so that it could be used for both basketball and tennis games.

Highlights of the public tour include the gold and white **East Room,** the scene of presidential receptions, weddings, major presidential addresses, and other dazzling events. This is where the president entertains visiting heads of state and the place where seven of the eight presidents who died in office (all but Garfield) laid in state. It's also where Nixon resigned. The room's early-18th-century style was adopted during the Theodore Roosevelt renovation of 1902; it has parquet Fontainebleau oak floors and white-painted wood walls with fluted pilasters and classical relief inserts. Note the famous Gilbert Stuart portrait of George Washington that Dolley Madison saved from the British

# THE "HOW TO'S" OF TOURING
## THE white house

You must have a reservation to tour the White House. At least 21 days and as far as 3 months in advance of your trip, call one of your senators' or your representative's office with the names of the people in your group and ask for a specific tour date. The tour coordinator consults with the White House on availability and, if your date is available, contacts you to obtain the names, birth dates, Social Security numbers (for those 14 and over), and other info for each of the people in your party. The Secret Service reviews the information and clears you for the tour, putting the names of the people in your group on a confirmed reservation list; you'll receive a confirmation number and the date and time of your tour well in advance of your trip. (**Note:** International visitors should contact their embassy to submit a tour request.)

**Hours:** White House tours are available to the general public year-round from 7:30 to 11:30am Tuesday through Thursday and 7:30am to 1:30pm Friday and Saturday, and at other times as well, depending on the president's schedule. If the president is out of town, it's possible that more tours will be allowed past the usual cutoff time.

**Format and timing:** Tours are self-guided. Most people take no more than an hour to go through. Arrive about 15 minutes before your scheduled tour time.

**Entry and ID:** You'll enter at the side of East Executive Avenue, near the Southeast Gate of the White House. Bring valid, government-issued photo IDs whose information exactly matches that which you provided to your congressional member's office. Everyone in your party who is 18 or older must have an ID.

**Important:** On the day of your tour, call ℂ **202/456-7041** to make sure the White House is still open to the public that day and that your tour hasn't been cancelled.

**Do not bring the following prohibited items:** Backpacks, book bags, handbags, or purses; food and beverages; strollers; video recorders; tobacco products; personal grooming items, from cosmetics to hairbrushes; any pointed objects, whether a pen or a knitting needle; aerosol containers; guns; ammunition; fireworks; electric stun guns; maces; martial arts weapons/devices; or knives of any kind. Smartphones are okay, as are small cameras. The White House does not have a coat-check facility, so there is no place for you to leave your belongings while you go on the tour. There are no public restrooms or telephones in the White House. **Best advice:** Leave everything but your wallet and camera back at the hotel.

torch during the War of 1812; the portrait is the only object to have remained continuously in the White House since 1800 (except during reconstructions).

You'll visit the **Green Room,** which was Thomas Jefferson's dining room but today is used as a sitting room. Mrs. Kennedy chose the green watered-silk-fabric wall covering. In the **Oval Blue Room,** decorated in the French Empire style chosen by James Monroe in 1817, presidents and first ladies have officially received guests since the Jefferson administration. It was, however, Martin Van Buren's decor that began the "blue room" tradition. The walls, on which hang portraits of five presidents (including Rembrandt Peale's portrait of Thomas Jefferson and G. P. A. Healy's of John Tyler), are covered in reproductions of early-19th-century French and American wallpaper.

Grover Cleveland, the only president to wed in the White House, was married in the Blue Room. This room was also where the Reagans greeted the 52 Americans liberated after being held hostage in Iran for 444 days, and every year it's the setting for the White House Christmas tree.

The **Red Room,** with its red-satin-covered walls and Empire furnishings, is used as a reception room, primarily for afternoon teas. Several portraits of past presidents and a Gilbert Stuart portrait of Dolley Madison hang here. Dolley Madison used the Red Room for her famous Wednesday-night receptions.

From the Red Room, you'll enter the **State Dining Room.** Modeled after late-18th-century neoclassical English houses, this room is a superb setting for state dinners and luncheons. Below G. P. A. Healy's portrait of Lincoln is a quote taken from a letter written by John Adams on his second night in the White House (FDR had it carved into the mantel): I PRAY HEAVEN TO BESTOW THE BEST OF BLESSINGS ON THIS HOUSE AND ON ALL THAT SHALL HERE-AFTER INHABIT IT. MAY NONE BUT HONEST AND WISE MEN EVER RULE UNDER THIS ROOF.

1600 Pennsylvania Ave. NW (visitor entrance gate at E St. and E. Executive Ave.). www. whitehouse.gov. ✆ **202/456-7041** or 202/208-1631. Free admission. Tours for groups of 10 or more who have arranged the tour through their congressional offices; otherwise tours are self-guided. Closed federal holidays. Metro: Federal Triangle.

**The White House Visitor Center ★** MUSEUM   The Visitor Center is highly recommended now, following a major renovation (completed in fall of 2014) that has added a wide range of intriguing offerings. These include a state-of-the-art theater that continuously runs the newly commissioned 14-minute film, "White House: Reflections from Within," featuring the personal stories of the current and former First Family occupants of the White House; interactive exhibits that allow you to explore inside and outside the White House with a touch of the screen; and exhibits of some 100 artifacts, like the mahogany desk that White House architect James Hoban fashioned out of the wood scraps left over from the construction of the White House. National Park Service rangers staff the information desks, and the White House Historical Association mans its large gift shop here—this is a great place to purchase mementos and presents, like the annually designed White House Christmas tree ornament. Whether or not you're able to tour the White House, try to stop here for a behind-the-scenes understanding of the history and everyday life inside the executive mansion. And here's a fact you might just want to know: The center has public restrooms.

1450 Pennsylvania Ave. NW (in the Department of Commerce Building, btw. 14th and 15th sts.). http://www.nps.gov/whho/planyourvisit/white-house-visitor-center.htm. ✆ **202/208-1631.** Free admission. Daily 7:30am–4pm. Closed Jan 1, Thanksgiving, and Dec 25. Metro: Federal Triangle.

# PENN QUARTER

Most of this bustling downtown neighborhood's attractions congregate near the Verizon Center, on or just off 7th Street, the main artery. The ones that aren't there, like Ford's Theatre and the National Museum of Women in the Arts, are just a short walk away. If you enjoy layering your touring experience with stops for delicious meals or snacks, this is your neighborhood. The Penn Quarter is loaded with great restaurants, bars, and bakeries (see chapter 5, p. 93).

**Ford's Theatre National Historic Site** ★★ HISTORIC SITE   On April 14, 1865, President Abraham Lincoln was in the audience at Ford's Theatre, one of the most popular playhouses in Washington. Everyone was laughing at a funny line from Tom Taylor's celebrated comedy, *Our American Cousin,* when John Wilkes Booth crept into the President's Box, shot the president, and leapt to the stage, shouting, *"Sic semper tyrannis!"* ("Thus ever to tyrants!") With his left leg broken from the jump, Booth mounted his horse in the alley and galloped off. Doctors carried Lincoln across the street to the house of William Petersen, where the president died the next morning.

The theater was closed after Lincoln's assassination and used as an office by the War Department. In 1893, 22 clerks were killed when three floors of the building collapsed. It remained in disuse until the 1960s, when the National Park Service remodeled and restored Ford's to its appearance on the night of the tragedy. Grand renovations and developments completed in phases between 2009 and 2012 have since brought about a wholly new experience for visitors.

Ford's Theatre today stands as the centerpiece of the **Ford's Theatre National Historic Site,** a campus of three buildings straddling a short section of 10th Street and including the **Ford's Theatre** and its **Ford's Theatre Museum; Petersen House,** where Lincoln died; and the **Center for Education and Leadership,** which debuted in 2012 and is dedicated to exploring Lincoln's legacy and promoting leadership.

I recommend visiting all four attractions if you have the time. Briefly, here's what you'll see at the Ford's Theatre National Historic Site:

**The box at Ford's Theatre where President Lincoln was assassinated.**

**The Ford's Theatre:** The National Park Service presentations vividly recreate the events of that night, so try for a tour that includes one of these. The President's Box is still on view, but no, you are not allowed to enter it and sit where Lincoln sat. A portrait of George Washington hangs beneath the President's Box, as it did the night Lincoln was shot. Ford's remains a working theater, so consider returning in the evening to attend a play. Ford's productions lean toward historical dramas and classic American plays and musicals; the 2016–17 season includes Charles Dickens's *A Christmas Carol* and Edward Albee's *Who's Afraid of Virginia Woolf?* The production schedule means that the theater, and sometimes the museum, may be closed to sightseers on some days; check the online schedule before you visit.

The **Ford's Theatre Museum,** on the lower level of the theater, displays artifacts that tell the story of Lincoln's presidency, his assassination, and what life was like in Washington and in the United States during that time. Unfortunately, when the museum is crowded, as it often is, it can be hard to get close enough to (and have enough time at) each of the exhibits to properly absorb the information. An exhibit about life in the White House shines a little light on Mary Todd Lincoln; a display of artifacts that includes the Derringer gun used by John Wilkes Booth connects the dots between the assassin and those who aided him.

Across 10th Street from the theater and museum is **Petersen House.** The doctor attending to Lincoln and other theatergoers carried Lincoln into the street, where boarder Henry Safford, standing in the open doorway of his rooming house, gestured for them to bring the president inside. So Lincoln died in the home of William Petersen, a German-born tailor. Now furnished with period pieces, the dark, narrow town house looks much as it did on that fateful April night. You'll see the front parlor where an anguished Mary Todd Lincoln spent the night with her son, Robert. In the back parlor, Secretary of War Edwin M. Stanton held a cabinet meeting and questioned witnesses. From this room, Stanton announced at 7:22am on April 15, 1865, "Now he belongs to the ages." Lincoln died, lying diagonally because he was so tall, on a bed the size of the one in the room. (The Chicago History Museum owns the actual bed and other items from the room.) The exit from Petersen House leads to an elevator that transports you to the fourth floor of the:

**At the Center for Education and Leadership,** your tour begins with the sights and sounds of the capital in the days following the assassination of Lincoln. You hear church bells tolling and horseshoes clopping and view exhibits of mourning ribbons, coffin handles, and newspaper broadsheets announcing the tragic news. Details convey the sense of piercing sorrow that prevailed: Twenty-five thousand people attended Lincoln's funeral on April 21, 1865, though not Mary Todd Lincoln, who was too overcome with grief. A staircase that winds around a sculptured tower of some 6,800 books all to do with Lincoln leads down to the center's third floor. Here, a short film, videos, and exhibits explore Lincoln's influence and legacy: Lincoln's name and image pop up on all sorts of commercial products, from the children's building game of Lincoln Logs to jewelry. Following the staircase another level down takes you to a gallery on real-life examples of brave individuals, such as Rosa Parks, to pose the question "What Would You Do?" in their circumstances.

*The how to:* You'll need a timed ticket to tour any part of the campus. Tickets are free and tours take place daily. Visit the website, www.fords.org, for a list of offerings, which can range from a simple museum and theater walkthrough (45 min.) to a full tour encompassing the museum; the theater, including either a National Park Service ranger's interpretive program or a mini-play (highly recommended); Petersen House; and the Center for Education and Leadership (for a total of about 2 hr. and 15 min.).

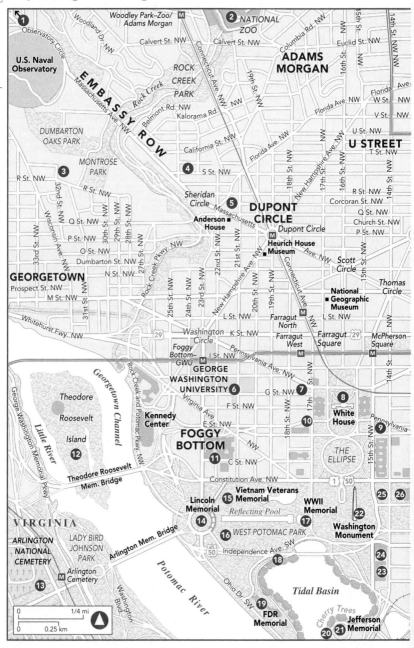

U.S. Naval Observatory

Observatory Circle

Woodland Dr. NW

Woodley Park–Zoo/ Adams Morgan Ⓜ

NATIONAL ZOO

Calvert St. NW

Calvert St. NW

Columbia Rd. NW

Euclid St. NW

ADAMS MORGAN

EMBASSY ROW

Massachusetts Ave. NW

ROCK CREEK PARK

Rock Creek

Belmont Rd. NW

Kalorama Rd. NW

Florida Ave.

W St. NW

V St. NW

DUMBARTON OAKS PARK

California St. NW

Florida Ave. NW

U St. NW

U STREET

T St. NW

MONTROSE PARK

R St. NW

R St. NW

S St. NW

Sheridan Circle

DUPONT CIRCLE

Corcoran St. NW

Q St. NW

Church St. NW

P St. NW

32nd St. NW

Wisconsin Ave. NW

33d St. NW

31st St. NW

30th St. NW

29th St. NW

28th St. NW

27th St. NW

Q St. NW

P St. NW

O St. NW

Dumbarton St. NW

N St. NW

Massachusetts

Anderson House

Dupont Circle Ⓜ

Heurich House Museum

Scott Circle

Thomas Circle

GEORGETOWN

Prospect St. NW

M St. NW

25th St. NW

24th St. NW

23d St. NW

New Hampshire Ave. NW

22nd St. NW

21st St. NW

20th St. NW

19th St. NW

Connecticut Ave. NW

National Geographic Museum

L St. NW

L St. NW

McPherson Square Ⓜ

Whitehurst Fwy. NW

Rock Creek Pkwy. NW

Washington Circle

K St. NW

Pennsylvania Ave. NW

Farragut North Ⓜ

Farragut West Ⓜ

Farragut Square

Foggy Bottom– GWU Ⓜ

I St. NW

GEORGE WASHINGTON UNIVERSITY

Virginia Ave.

G St. NW

17th St. NW

White House

8th St. NW

15th St. NW

Pennsylvania

Georgetown Channel

Theodore Roosevelt Island

Kennedy Center

F St. NW

E St. NW

FOGGY BOTTOM

C St. NW

THE ELLIPSE

Theodore Roosevelt Mem. Bridge

George Washington Memorial Pkwy.

Little River

Constitution Ave. NW

Vietnam Veterans Memorial

Lincoln Memorial

Reflecting Pool

WWII Memorial

Washington Monument

VIRGINIA

ARLINGTON NATIONAL CEMETERY

LADY BIRD JOHNSON PARK

Arlington Cemetery Ⓜ

Arlington Mem. Bridge

WEST POTOMAC PARK

Independence Ave. SW

Washington Blvd.

Potomac River

Ohio Dr. SW

Tidal Basin

Cherry Trees

FDR Memorial

Jefferson Memorial

0    1/4 mi

0    0.25 km

172

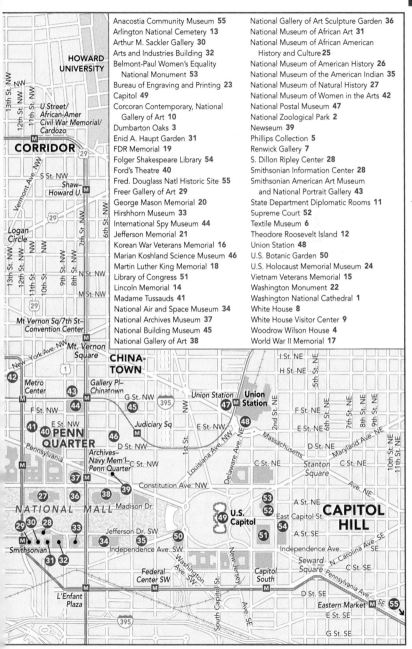

Anacostia Community Museum **55**
Arlington National Cemetery **13**
Arthur M. Sackler Gallery **30**
Arts and Industries Building **32**
Belmont-Paul Women's Equality
National Monument **53**
Bureau of Engraving and Printing **23**
Capitol **49**
Corcoran Contemporary, National
Gallery of Art **10**
Dumbarton Oaks **3**
Enid A. Haupt Garden **31**
FDR Memorial **19**
Folger Shakespeare Library **54**
Ford's Theatre **40**
Fred. Douglass Natl Historic Site **55**
Freer Gallery of Art **29**
George Mason Memorial **20**
Hirshhorn Museum **33**
International Spy Museum **44**
Jefferson Memorial **21**
Korean War Veterans Memorial **16**
Marian Koshland Science Museum **46**
Martin Luther King Memorial **18**
Library of Congress **51**
Lincoln Memorial **14**
Madame Tussauds **41**
National Air and Space Museum **34**
National Archives Museum **37**
National Gallery of Art **38**

National Gallery of Art Sculpture Garden **36**
National Museum of African Art **31**
National Museum of African American
History and Culture **25**
National Museum of American History **26**
National Museum of the American Indian **35**
National Museum of Natural History **27**
National Museum of Women in the Arts **42**
National Postal Museum **47**
National Zoological Park **2**
Newseum **39**
Phillips Collection **5**
Renwick Gallery **7**
S. Dillon Ripley Center **28**
Smithsonian Information Center **28**
Smithsonian American Art Museum
and National Portrait Gallery **43**
State Department Diplomatic Rooms **11**
Supreme Court **52**
Textile Museum **6**
Theodore Roosevelt Island **12**
Union Station **48**
U.S. Botanic Garden **50**
U.S. Holocaust Memorial Museum **24**
Vietnam Veterans Memorial **15**
Washington Monument **22**
Washington National Cathedral **1**
White House **8**
White House Visitor Center **9**
Woodrow Wilson House **4**
World War II Memorial **17**

A single ticket admits you to all parts of the campus, so don't lose it! Ford's really wants you to order tickets in advance online—only 20% of the daily allotment of tickets are available for same-day pickup. And even though Ford's says tours are free, the fact is online tickets cost $4.25 each to cover processing fees; if you want an audio tour, you'll pay $10.25 per ticket. You order the tickets online and can print them yourself or pick them up at the theater's will-call booth. *Good to know:* When the Ford's Theatre website shows same-day tickets as unavailable, that just means they are unavailable to order online; go in person to the box office and you may score one of those same-day passes.

Spring through early fall, Ford's also sells tickets ($17 each, plus $5.50 processing fee, available online) to its popular "History on Foot" 2-hour walking tours. A costumed actor brings to life the events of April 14 and 15, 1865, leading tourists on a 1½-mile traipse to about eight historically significant locations.

511 10th St. NW (btw. E and F sts.). www.fords.org. © **202/426-6925.** Daily 9am–5pm. Closed Thanksgiving, Christmas, and other days subject to the theatre's schedule. Timed tickets required for the free tours offered throughout the day. See above for details. Metro: Metro Center (11th and G sts. exit).

**International Spy Museum** ★★ MUSEUM  A visit to this museum takes on a whole new meaning following the disclosures of the National Security Agency's far-flung phone and internet surveillance practices. One can easily believe the claim made in the museum's 5-minute introductory film that Washington, D.C., has more spies than any other city in the world. Yikes.

Well, if you can't flee them, join them. The International Spy Museum gives you the chance to do just that, learning about the best in the trade and tricks of the trade in interactive exhibits that allow you to test your powers of observation and pretend to be a spy. (Is that a gun in your pocketbook or a lipstick tube?) The history section reveals that the most unlikely of people have acted as spies in their time. Would you believe Moses? George Washington? Julia Child?

The International Spy Museum's inventory of international espionage artifacts numbers about 2,400, one-third of which are on display at any one time, in exhibits that cover history, as noted, as well as training, equipment, the "spies among us," legendary spymasters, spying during the Civil War, and 21st-century cyber-spying. "Exquisitely Evil: 50 Years of Bond Villains," originally conceived as a temporary show, continues due to popular demand. The attraction here is, basically, you get to be Agent 007. Interactive props allow you to use surveillance cameras, design a villain's hideout, and match your skills against the real James Bond. On display throughout the show are 110 artifacts from James Bond movies.

The Spy Museum is a three-floor affair, its main exhibit occupying the top level, and the James Bond exhibit consuming most of the first floor. Your general admission ticket grants you access to both of these areas. The second floor is devoted to providing the **Operation Spy** experience, which requires a separate ticket and admission fee. Here, participants immerse themselves in spy activities, like decrypting audio conversations and searching for evidence, as they work as part of a team to accomplish a mission.

*Note:* Operation Spy participants must be 12 or older. In fact, although the museum doesn't specify an age requirement for touring its main exhibits, I think children 10 and older have the most fun here (and they have a *lot* of fun).

For an extra $3 convenience fee, you can order advance tickets online and print your tickets at home or pick them up at the box office. You can also purchase advance tickets, including for same-day tours, at the box office.

800 F St. NW (at 8th St. NW). spymuseum.org. ℂ **866/779-6873** or 202/393-7798. Admission $21.95 plus tax ages 12–64, $15.95 plus tax seniors (65 and over), $14.95 plus tax ages 7–11. Operation Spy $14.95 plus tax ages 12 and over (combined admission fee $28.95 plus tax). Open daily 9 or 10am to 6pm, sometimes later, rarely earlier; check website for details. Closed Jan 1, Thanksgiving, and Dec 25. Metro: Gallery Place–Chinatown (9th and G sts. exit) or Archives–Navy Memorial.

**Madame Tussauds Washington, D.C.** ★ MUSEUM  Calling all tweens! Justin Bieber's in the house! And OMG, is that Rihanna? On display throughout this museum are upwards of 100 lifelike wax figures, dressed and poised true to form, and grouped by theme: The Presidents' Gallery, Sports, Glamor, Civil Rights, Media Room, and Behind the Scenes. You can pretend to play golf with Tiger Woods, mingle with Johnny Depp, dance with Beyoncé, and shake hands with President Barack Obama. Said to be the most interactive of the 20 Madame Tussauds around the world, the D.C. Madame's best feature is its **3-D Presidential Gallery,** which arranges each of the 44 presidents with important historical figures of that day, at important moments in their presidencies. With the use of interactive devices and fun props, the gallery creates an entertaining learning experience targeted to children. Kids can try on period costumes and join George Washington in his boat crossing the Delaware River, or stand next to Woodrow Wilson and listen to the crowds cheer his arrival at the end of World War I.

1001 F St. NW (btw. 10th and 11th sts.). www2.madametussauds.com/washington-dc/en/. ℂ **866/823-9565** or 202/942-7300. Walk-up admission $22 plus tax ages 13 and over, $17.50 plus tax ages 4–12, children 3 and under free. Purchase advance tickets online and receive a 20% or higher discount. Open daily, but hours fluctuate; call or check the website for exact hours on the day you wish to visit. Metro: Metro Center (11th and G sts. exit).

**Marian Koshland Science Museum** ★ MUSEUM  As small as the **National Museum of Natural History** (p. 151) is large, the Koshland Science Museum serves as a perfect (and quieter) counterpoint to the Smithsonian museum's experience. This museum is about helping people use science to solve problems in their community. High-tech, interactive exhibits aim to provoke critical thinking about science and how it can be applied to looming issues, from climate change to healthy aging to understanding how the brain works. A popular feature is a driving simulator that crystallizes the dangers of distracted driving. In the "Earth Lab Exhibit: Degrees of Change," museum-goers use interactive tools to devise possible energy policy solutions in order to reduce $CO_2$ emissions. Families with scientifically inclined children 14 and over should bop by this museum on weekend afternoons for hands-on science activities, like "Feel the Energy," in which you learn to use your own muscles to power a lightbulb. Check out the museum's calendar online to learn about other fun events.

525 E St. NW. www.koshland-science-museum.org. © **202/334-1201.** Admission $5, $3 students and military (with ID). Wed–Mon 10am–6pm. Closed Jan 1, Thanksgiving, and Dec 25. Metro: Gallery Place–Chinatown or Judiciary Square.

**National Building Museum ★ MUSEUM** The first thing you notice about the National Building Museum is the actual building, its pressed red-brick exterior and decorative terra cotta frieze, and its *size,* 400 feet by 200 feet, big enough to hold a football field. Inside the impressive **Great Hall** is an Italian Renaissance courtyard, colossal Corinthian columns, 15-story-high ceiling, and central fountain. The structure, modeled after an Italian palazzo, was designed to house the Pension Bureau (its offices were located in those upper arcaded areas, overlooking the atrium) and to serve as a venue for grand galas. The building hosted its first event, President Grover Cleveland's inaugural ball, in 1885, even before construction was completed in 1887, and it's been the site of such balls and other events ever since.

In the 1980s, the site took on a new purpose as a museum dedicated to architecture, landscape architecture, engineering, urban planning, and historic preservation and opened to the public in 1985 as the National Building Museum. The museum charges a fee to tour its exhibits, which are mounted in the galleries off the Great Hall on the first and second floors and change year to year. A typical topic is the one covered in the show "Small Stories" (May 21, 2016–Jan 16, 2017), which displays 12 dollhouses on loan from London's Victoria & Albert Museum of Childhood and invites visitors to imagine the everyday lives of people who would have lived in these kinds of houses, throughout the 300 year history that the dwellings represent. The museum's year-round Building Zone exhibit is a favorite for families with children ages 2 to 6, who can build a tower, drive a bulldozer, and explore a life-size playhouse.

If you're here in summer, you've got to stop by to experience the super-fun, interactive "Summer Block Party" that takes over the entire expanse of the Great Hall; one year it was two 9-hole mini golf courses designed and built by area experts in the building arts; in 2014, the museum fabricated a giant maze. In 2016 the museum installed "Icebergs," using reusable construction materials to create the effect of icebergs, ranging as high as 56 feet, or up to the third-floor balcony in the Great Hall, and along the ocean floor below; visitors ascend to the top of the tallest berg, cross an undersea bridge, roam among caves and grottos, and lap up shaved-ice snacks. *Note:* There's a charge to visit the Summer Block Party; otherwise you can tour the Great Hall for free. The museum gift shop is an especially good one, as is the on-site eatery Firehook Bakery, a local favorite.

401 F St. NW (btw. 4th and 5th sts.). www.nbm.org. © **202/272-2448.** Free admission to view the inside of the building. Exhibit tour: $10 adults; $7 students (with ID), children 3–17, and seniors 60 and over. Building Zone only: $3. Summer Block Party: $16 adults; $13 students, children, and seniors. Mon–Sat 10am–5pm; Sun 11am–5pm. Closed Thanksgiving and Dec 25. Metro: Gallery Place (7th and F sts. exit) or Judiciary Square (F St. exit).

**National Museum of Women in the Arts** ★ ART MUSEUM If you've never heard of Clara Peeters, a 16th-century Flemish painter of superbly rendered still-lifes; or Renaissance painter Lavinia Fontana; or Russian artist Sonia Delaunay, whose mastery of murals, theater sets, and ceramics led the Louvre in 1964 to choose her as its first living female artist to hold a retrospective there . . . well, as I say, if you've never heard of these wondrous artists, it's a shame, but not surprising, given the historical short shrift accorded women's contributions to art. Here in Washington, D.C., we have an answer for that: Visit the National Museum of Women in the Arts, where more than 1,000 works by women, 16th century to the present, are on display at any one time. Open since 1987, the museum remains the world's only major museum solely dedicated to recognizing women's creative accomplishments.

Inside the white marble Renaissance Revival 1908 museum building, originally a Masonic temple, is a space so elegant it's frequently in demand as a wedding reception venue. Some of the artwork is on display in the Grand Hall, but most exhibits are in upstairs galleries, accessed via the sweeping marble double stairways. Among the works from the permanent collection that you might see are those by Rosa Bonheur, Mary Cassatt, Helen Frankenthaler, Barbara Hepworth, Georgia O'Keeffe, Lilla Cabot Perry, and Elaine de Kooning. Most popular is Frida Kahlo's self-portrait, the only Frida Kahlo on view in Washington. The museum mounts several special exhibits annually, which from October 14, 2015, to February 26, 2017, includes "Wanderer/Wonderer: Pop-Ups by Colette Fu," which presents oversize pop-up images of landscapes that incorporate elements of fantasy and folklore.

Also recommended is the museum's gift shop, which sells clever little items like a Dorothy Parker martini glass. And if you're hungry, dine in view of artworks at the Mezzanine Café, Monday to Friday 11am to 2pm.

1250 New York Ave. NW (at 13th St.). www.nmwa.org. ✆ **800/222-7270** or 202/783-5000. Admission $10 adults, $8 students (with ID) and seniors 65 and over, free for youths 18 and under (general admission rates; special exhibition prices may be higher). Mon–Sat 10am–5pm; Sun noon–5pm. Closed Jan 1, Thanksgiving, and Dec 25. Metro: Metro Center (13th St. exit).

**Newseum** ★★ MUSEUM With newspapers closing every other week, it seems, a visit to the Newseum takes on not just added poignancy, but may raise feelings of alarm. That's because at the core of this entertaining yet erudite enterprise there's an important message: that journalism is an integral part not just of democracy, but of civilization itself. And the museum makes its case in a much less heavy-handed way than I just have, while at the same time acknowledging the myriad ways that journalists can screw up! In a town of absorbing museums, this one more than holds its own.

The seven-level museum has 15 galleries highlighting subjects from ethics in journalism to Pulitzer Prize photographs, 15 theaters, 130 interactive game stations, and 2 broadcast studios, including one that has the real-life Capitol as its backdrop. When you enter, staff usually direct you to the lower level to watch orientation films. I'd say you can skip the 4-minute introductory film

Washington's museum shops hold a treasure trove of unusual gifts. Right now I'm loving the set of coffee mugs I bought my husband for Christmas at the **Folger Shakespeare Library** (p. 122) gift shop. They're covered in Shakespeare quotes, both for when you're in a foul mood ("Bolting-hutch of beastliness," "Thou art a boil, a plague sore") and for when you're feelin' the love ("Love is a smoke raised with the fume of sighs"). I've always had a weakness for the shop at the **National Building Museum** (p. 176), which is jammed with surprising, useful, and cleverly designed housewares and interesting games, including bookends embossed with Celtic designs, Bauhaus mobiles, and collapsible strainers. And I can never visit the **National Gallery of Art** (p. 143) without lingering a little while in the store to admire captivating catalogue books, note cards, posters, children's games, and a slew of other things. The Smithsonian's **National Museum of African Art** (p. 148) has unusual items from all over Africa, but I especially liked the bright colors and interesting designs of the dishtowels, handbags, and headbands from Ghana. And then there's the woman-centric **National Museum of Women in the Arts** (p. 177) gift shop, which has fab Frida Kahlo notecards and leaning lady bookends.

and head instead to the theater showing the 8-minute *What's News?*, a topical film that explores the boundaries of journalism. Also on this level is the **Berlin Wall** exhibit, which includes eight 12-foot-high concrete sections of the original wall and an East German guard tower. Future crime reporters might want to tour the **FBI exhibit's** display of artifacts related to big-name cases from the past 100 years.

From here, take the glass elevator to the sixth floor and stroll the outdoor terrace to admire the view of Pennsylvania Avenue and the Capitol (great photo op). If you have time, peruse the timeline that's posted along the length of this promenade, tracing the history of events that took place along the avenue.

Also on this level until July 31, 2017, is a special exhibit, "Louder than Words: Rock, Power and Politics." The Newseum partnered with the Rock and Roll Hall of Fame in Cleveland to mount this show that uses video, multimedia, photographs, periodicals, and artifacts to explore the intersection between rock and politics, and music's influence on the civil rights and gender equality movements, the Vietnam War, and income inequality issues. Exhibited first in Cleveland during and after the Republican National Convention, the show debuts at the Newseum on January 13, 2017, just in time for the inauguration. Look for such priceless items as the guitar John Lennon used to introduce the anti-war song "Give Peace A Chance."

Now walk down the stairs to level five to explore the **History Gallery,** which serves up 5 centuries of journalism and more than 300 historic front pages. The 100-foot-wide video wall plays original programming and breaking news throughout the day.

Down another flight to the fourth floor finds you in the Newseum's technology hub gallery, where the subject changes with current events, but social media and interactive tools are always a focus. For example, continuing until

January 22, 2017, "CNN Politics Campaign 2016" is the joint presentation of CNN and the Newseum, allowing visitors an immersive experience in the ways that digital and social media have transformed political campaigns and the reporting on them. Elsewhere on this floor, the **First Amendment Gallery** tells the stories of real people whose experiences illustrate the value of our five First Amendment freedoms. The **9/11 Gallery** highlights the challenges faced by journalists reporting on 9/11 in a seriously moving fashion.

The third floor's **Journalists Memorial** honors the more than 2,271 journalists who have died in the course of reporting their stories since 1837. Also on this floor are two state-of-the-art broadcast studios frequently in use by media organizations.

Pull up to one of 48 interactive kiosks in the second floor's **NBC News Interactive Newsroom** and test your prowess as a photojournalist, reporter, or editor. Sit in as a news anchor and read from a teleprompter, then play back the tape to see how well you did.

The gallery of **Pulitzer Prize–winning photographs** on the first floor includes a documentary film and interactive kiosks featuring interviews with some of the photographers.

Finish up on the concourse level with a viewing of *I-Witness,* whose 4-D film features put you in the picture with legendary journalists Isaiah Thomas (radical printer, not basketball legend), Nellie Bly, and Edward R. Murrow.

If it's before 3pm, you might want to visit the food court, which has a very kid-friendly (and adult-friendly; wine and beer are on offer) menu designed by Wolfgang Puck. The museum also has several gift shops.

555 Pennsylvania Ave. NW (at 6th St.). www.newseum.org. © **202/292-6100.** Admission $23 plus tax ages 19–64, $19 plus tax seniors (65 and over), $14 plus tax ages 7–18, free for children 6 and under. Buy tickets online and receive a 15% discount. Daily 9am–5pm. Closed Jan 1, Thanksgiving, and Dec 25. Metro: Judiciary Square (4th St. exit), Gallery Place/Verizon Center (7th and F sts./Arena exit), or Archives–Navy Memorial.

### Old Post Office Clock Tower ★ HISTORIC SITE

Donald Trump bought the historic Old Post Office Pavilion and turned the building into a hotel, the Trump International Hotel Washington, D.C., which opened in fall 2016. The Clock Tower, however, is untouchable. The National Park Service, which operates and maintains the building's 1899 Clock Tower, confirms that the tower is off limits to Trump family designs, but open to the general public for tours, once again offering its fabulous view, 315 feet up, of Pennsylvania Avenue, from the Capitol to the White House, and all around the town. Check the website for touring details, which were not available at the time of this writing.

1100 Pennsylvania Ave. NW (at 12th St.). www.nps.gov/opot. Metro: Federal Triangle.

### Smithsonian American Art Museum and National Portrait Gallery ★★★ ART MUSEUM

Walt Whitman called this historic Greek Revival structure "the noblest of Washington buildings," and if he were around today, he'd likely stick with that opinion. If you've been flitting around the Penn Quarter, you had to have noticed it, with its porticoes modeled after the Parthenon in Athens, and its monumental footprint (405×274 ft.).

But it's the inside we're interested in. The magnificent landmark, which served as the nation's patent office in the mid–19th century, now houses two distinct Smithsonian museums: the American Art Museum and the National Portrait Gallery, each occupying three levels of galleries that enclose a stunning, light-filled inner courtyard, museum wings meeting seamlessly.

Walt Whitman's name crops up again. He is here, yes he is, in portrait form, painted by John White Alexander in 1889, appearing rather old and tired, with blindingly white hair, full beard, and fluffy eyebrows, sitting at an angle and staring into the distance. Whitman's portrait hangs in the National Portrait Gallery's first floor section, **American Origins,** a chronological arrangement of paintings of American notables that tells the country's story, from Pocahontas to Harriet Beecher Stowe to Thomas Edison, in compelling fashion. Other permanent exhibits feature **20th Century Americans** and **America's Presidents.** A temporary exhibit on view through May 21, 2017, is "One Life: Babe Ruth," which displays prints, photographs, personal paraphernalia, and advertising memorabilia that reveal the kind of marketing frenzy that surrounded the baseball legend in the first half of the 20th century.

The American Art Museum resides within these skylit, vaulted halls, too. Its collection of American art is one of the largest in the world, and most diverse, with folk art, modern, African-American, and Latino art well represented. Standouts include Georgia O'Keeffe's take on *Manhattan;* Albert Bierstadt's idealized vision of the American West, *Among the Sierra Nevada;* a Nam June Paik video installation, *Electronic Superhighway: Continental U.S., Alaska, Hawaii;* and intriguing folk art, like James Hampton's creation of artwork out of garbage, *The Throne of the Third Heaven of the Nations' Millennium General Assembly.* You'll either love it or hate it, but you won't be able to look away from it.

In all, about 2,000 works are on display throughout both the American Art and Portrait galleries. You'll want to tour the top floor's two-level **Luce Foundation Center for American Art,** too, where thousands more works are stored but still on view, from walking canes to sculptures to dollhouses. In the adjacent **Lunder Conservation Center,** conservators work to preserve art pieces. Finally, make time to visit the museum's courtyard cafe, the setting for concerts including the monthly free jazz series of performances, *Take Five!*

*Note:* These two museums are open later than most in D.C., so you can schedule a visit for the end of the day.

8th and F sts. NW. www.americanart.si.edu or www.npg.si.edu. ℂ **202/633-1000.** Free admission. Daily 11:30am–7pm. Highlights tours are offered; check online or call for exact schedule. Closed Dec 25. Metro: Gallery Place–Chinatown (7th and F sts. exit, or 9th and G sts. exit).

# DUPONT CIRCLE

In a city of national this-and-that attractions, Dupont Circle provides a charmingly personal counterpoint. Within this lively residential neighborhood of old town houses, trendy boutiques, and bistros are mostly historic houses (such as the Christian Heurich House), embassy buildings, and beloved art galleries (such as the Phillips Collection). Follow the walking tour of Dupont Circle and Embassy Row, p. 272, for a fuller picture of the neighborhood.

**Anderson House** ★ HISTORIC HOME   A visit to Anderson House is about marveling over the palatial architecture and interior design (love the ballroom), the display of artwork—from Flemish tapestries to Asian and European paintings and antiquities to Revolutionary War artifacts. A bit of background: This limestone-veneered Italianate mansion, fronted by twin arches and a Corinthian-columned portico, was built between 1902 and 1905. Its original owners were career diplomat Larz Anderson III, who served as ambassador to Japan in 1912 and 1913, and his wife, heiress and philanthropist Isabel Weld Perkins, who as a Red Cross volunteer cared for the dying and wounded in France and Belgium during World War I, and who authored at least 40 books. The couple traveled a lot and filled their home with beautiful purchases from those journeys. Larz and Isabel were popular hosts in the capital and counted presidents and foreign dignitaries among their guests. Upon Larz's death in 1937, Isabel donated the house to the Society of the Cincinnati, and it has served ever since as headquarters and museum for the Society, founded in 1783 for descendants of Revolutionary War army officers. Anderson's great-grandfather was a founder and George Washington the organization's first president-general. Anderson House hosts exhibits, concerts, and lectures throughout the year; all are free and open to the public.

2118 Massachusetts Ave. NW (at Q St.). www.societyofthecincinnati.org. ✆ **202/785-2040.** Free admission. Tues–Sat 10am–4pm, Sun noon–4pm; highlights tours hourly, at 15 minutes past the hour. Closed Thanksgiving, Dec 25, and Jan 1. Metro: Dupont Circle (Q St. exit).

**Heurich House Museum** ★ HISTORIC HOME   Wealthy German businessman and brewer Christian Heurich built this turreted, four-story brownstone and brick Victorian castle in 1894, and lived here with his family until he died in 1945. Old Heurich was a character, as a tour of the 31-room mansion/museum reveals. Allegorical paintings cover the ceilings, silvered plaster medallions festoon the stucco walls, and there's a *bierstube* (tavern room) in the basement sporting the brewer's favorite drinking mottos—written in German, but here's one translation: "There is room in the smallest chamber for the biggest hangover." The Castle Garden is a good place to pause for a picnic or to page through your guidebook. Enter the garden through the east gate on Sunderland Place NW.

1307 New Hampshire Ave. NW (at 20th St.). www.heurichhouse.org. ✆ **202/429-1894.** Garden free admission; house tours $5, reservations required. Tours Thurs–Sat 11:30am, 1pm, and 2:30pm. Garden weekdays 9am–5pm. Metro: Dupont Circle (19th St. exit).

**National Geographic Museum** ★ MUSEUM   You don't have to be an adventurer to appreciate the exhibits mounted at the National Geographic Society's headquarters. It does help, though, if you're a curious soul and admire the natural world. Consider the recent exhibit, "Crocs: Ancient Predators for a Modern World." From time to time, National Geo mounts a blockbuster that nobody can resist, like the 2016 show "The Greeks, from Agamemnon to Alexander the Great," which displayed 550 artifacts from the national collections of 22 museums in Greece, surveying 5,000 years of Greek history and culture. National Geographic always presents at least one free photography exhibit in its M Street lobby location; otherwise, exhibits and most lectures, films, and performances charge admission.

1145 17th St. NW (at M St.). www.nationalgeographic.com/museum. © **202/857-7700.** Special exhibit admission $15 adults, $12 students and seniors, $10 children 5–12. Daily 10am–6pm. Closed Dec 25. Metro: Farragut North (Connecticut Ave. and L St. exit).

**Phillips Collection** ★★ ART MUSEUM    The Phillips is beloved in Washington, mostly because of its French Impressionist and Post-Impressionist paintings by van Gogh, Bonnard, Cezanne, Picasso, Klee, and Renoir, whose *Luncheon of the Boating Party* is the most popular work on display. But as familiar and traditional as these paintings may seem now, the works and their artists were considered daring and avant garde when Duncan Phillips opened his gallery in 1921. The Phillips Collection, indeed, was America's first official museum of modern art.

Founder Phillips's vision for "an intimate museum combined with an experiment station" is one that the museum continually renews, through programs like its *Intersections* series of contemporary art projects that explore links between old and new artistic traditions; and in exhibits of provocative art. Let me give you a good example:

On March 2, 2013, the Phillips Collection debuted the **Wolfgang Laib Wax Room,** its first permanent artwork installation since its opening of the Rothko Room in 1960. The Laib Room is also the first beeswax chamber that artist Laib has created for a specific museum. That's right: beeswax. You actually smell it before you see it, kind of a musty, faintly honey-ish, cloying scent. The artwork is the size of a powder room, with a single light bulb dangling to illuminate walls and ceiling slathered thickly with wax that has the yellow hue of the fruit of a peach, flecked with bits of orangey brown. I sooo wanted to touch it, but that's not allowed. And a staff sentry stands just outside the entrance to make sure you don't. What is the Wax Room but an experiment station?

Today, the museum's 3,000-work collection includes European masterpieces, treasures by American masters Dove, Homer, Hopper, Lawrence, and O'Keeffe; and works by living artists, such as Susan Rothenberg and Sean Scully. The Phillips resides in a complex that joins the original 1897 Georgian Revival mansion that served initially as both Phillips family home and public art gallery, with a modern gallery annex that doubles the space. The elegant mansion's graceful appointments—leaded- and stained-glass windows, elliptical stairway, oak-paneled Music Room, and tiled fireplaces—provide a lovely backdrop to the art and add to the reasons that locals love the Phillips.

Other reasons include blockbuster temporary shows, like "People on the Move – Beauty and Struggle in Jacob Lawrence's Migration Series" (October 8, 2016 to January 8, 2017), bringing together all 60 panels of the seminal work. Also consider gallery talks, Sunday concerts in the Music Room (Oct–May; admission $30); and the Phillips After Five events that take place on the first Thursday of each month, combining live music, cash bar, and food ($12 admission and you must make a reservation—very popular). The museum also has a charming cafe and a small gift shop.

1600 21st St. NW (at Q St.). www.phillipscollection.org. ✆ **202/387-2151.** Admission: Permanent collection free (donation welcome) on weekdays; weekends when no special exhibits are on view $10 adults; $8 seniors 62 and older and students 18 and older; free ages 18 and under. Ticketed special exhibits: $12 adults; $10 seniors 62 and older and students 18 and older; free ages 18 and under. Admission price allows entry to both permanent and special exhibits. Tues–Sat 10am–5pm (Thurs until 8:30pm); Sun noon–7pm. Closed Mon and federal holidays. Metro: Dupont Circle (Q St. exit).

**Woodrow Wilson House Museum** ★ HISTORIC HOME America's 28th president was too ill to attend the inauguration of his successor. Instead he was driven to his new home in the prestigious Kalorama neighborhood. His final residence is preserved as he left it. The story here focuses on Wilson's Washington years (1912–24), examining his public persona while allowing a peek behind the draperies into his personal life. Furnishings, White House objects, personal memorabilia, and elaborate gifts of state help tell the story. A mosaic of St. Peter hangs in the drawing room, a gift from Pope Benedict XV when the Wilsons toured Europe at the conclusion of World War I. Edith's portrait hangs above the mantle. The only presidential home open to the public in Washington, it's a natural stop for students of diplomacy.

2340 S St. NW (at Massachusetts Ave.). www.woodrowwilsonhouse.org. ✆ **202/387-4062.** Jan–Feb Fri–Sun 10am–4pm; Mar–Dec Wed–Sun 10am–4pm. Guided tours only. Admission $10 adults, $8 seniors, $5 students, free for ages 11 and under. Tues–Sun 10am–4pm. Closed federal holidays. Metro: Dupont Circle (Q St. exit).

# FOGGY BOTTOM

Known primarily as the locale for the George Washington University campus, the State Department, the International Monetary Fund, and the World Bank, Foggy Bottom is home also to the new George Washington Museum and the Textile Museum, the John F. Kennedy Center for the Performing Arts (see p. 220) and the State Department's Diplomatic Reception Rooms. Expected to open here in 2017 is the State Department Diplomacy Center, dedicated to telling the story of American diplomacy through interactive exhibits.

**The George Washington Museum and the Textile Museum** ★ MUSEUM The Textile Museum, long located in the Dupont Circle neighborhood, up and moved in 2015 to this new and larger location at the intersection of G and 21st streets, on the George Washington University campus. In relocating from its charming town-house location off of Embassy Row to a prime spot on GW's urban campus in Foggy Bottom, the nearly century-old Textile Museum tripled its space and was, in a sense, reborn within this custom-designed, 46,000-square-foot gallery. Curators pull from the museum's collection of some 20,000 textiles spanning 5,000 years and five continents to mount exhibits that in one way or another ask: How do clothes, adornments, and fabric furnishings articulate self and status within cultural, political, social,

## Albert Einstein Memorial, 22nd Street & Constitution Avenue NW

In a grove of holly and elm trees at the southwest corner of the National Academy of Science grounds, you'll find this dear memorial displaying the slouching figure of brilliant scientist, great thinker, and peace activist Albert Einstein. He sits slightly bent and sideways upon a granite bench, leaning on one hand and holding in the other a bronze sheet of paper on which are written mathematical equations for which he is famous. At his feet is a celestial map. His gaze looks worn and warm. The statue measures 12 feet in height and weighs 4 tons, yet children cannot resist crawling up on it and leaning up against this man.

religious, and ethnic frameworks? How do textiles reveal identities? Here's an example: An exhibit running through January 31, 2017, "Bingata! Only in Okinawa," displays the brightly colored, traditional resist-dyed fabrics of the southernmost prefecture in Japan, which was once an independent kingdom with its own language, culture, and distinctive textile techniques. The choice of colors and patterns used in the labor-intensive process of creating bingata often revealed information about the wealth and status of those who wore them.

Meanwhile, on the second floor of the building, stemming off the Textile Museum's large gallery, is the Albert H. Small Washingtoniana Collection, totally unrelated to textiles but fascinating in its own right for the display of maps, prints, old photos, and rare letters that fill you in on life in the capital from the 17th to the 20th centuries.

701 21st St. NW (at G St.). https://museum.gwu.edu. ☏ **202/994-5200.** $8 suggested donation. Mon and Wed–Fri 11am–6:30pm; Sat 10am–5pm; Sun 1–5pm. Metro: Foggy Bottom.

**State Department Diplomatic Reception Rooms** ★ GOVERNMENT BUILDING   This is a fine-arts tour of rooms that serve as our country's stage for international diplomacy and official entertaining. The rooms house a collection of early American paintings, furniture, and decorative arts dating from 1740 to 1850. The tour is not recommended for children under 12. You must bring a valid picture ID, such as a driver's license, to enter the building.

2201 C St. NW (entrance on 23rd St. NW). www.state.gov/m/drr. ☏ **202/647-3241.** Free admission. Guided tours only: Mon–Fri 9:30am, 10:30am, and 2:45pm. Advance reservations required. Metro: Foggy Bottom.

# U & 14TH STREET CORRIDORS

In these old stomping grounds of Duke Ellington and his fellow Black Broadway jazz greats, the main attractions are of the nightlife and dining variety—jazz clubs, like Twins Jazz, that carry Duke's legacy forward, and many restaurants and bars that cater to a range of appetites and interests. The two museums located here reflect the neighborhood's identity as a stronghold of African-American history and heroes. *Note:* These two museums are located about half a mile from each other.

**African American Civil War Memorial and Museum** ★ MUSEUM
This modestly sized museum displays old photographs, maps, letters, and
inventories, along with ankle shackles worn by slaves and other artifacts
accompanied by text to tell the stories of the United States Colored Troops
and the African American involvement in the American Civil War. Not everyone knows that thousands of African Americans, mostly slaves, fought during
the Civil War. Walk across the street to view the African American Civil War
Memorial. A semicircular Wall of Honor curves behind the sculpture; etched
into the stone are the names of the 209,145 United States Colored Troops who
served in the Civil War.

1925 Vermont Ave. NW (at 10th St.; in the Grimke Building). www.afroamcivilwar.org.
© **202/667-2667.** Free admission. Tues–Fri 10am–6:30pm; Sat 10am–4pm; Sun noon–
4pm. Metro: U St./Cardozo (10th St. exit).

**Mary McLeod Bethune Council House National Historic Site** ★
HISTORIC HOME   This town house is the last D.C. residence of African-American activist/educator Bethune, who was a leading champion of
blacks' and women's rights during FDR's administration. Born in South Carolina in 1875, the 15th of 17 children of former slaves, Mary McLeod grew
up in poverty but learned the value of education through her schooling by
missionaries. It was a lesson she passed forward. By the time she died in 1955
at the age of 79, McLeod—now Bethune, from her marriage in 1898 to Albert
Bethune—had founded a school for "Negro girls" in Daytona Beach, Florida,
that would later become the Bethune-Cookman College, today Bethune-
Cookman University; received 11 honorary degrees; served on numerous
government advisory commissions, including the National Child Welfare
Commission; and acted as Special Advisor on Minority Affairs to President
Franklin Delano Roosevelt from 1935 to 1944. Bethune also established this
headquarters of the National Council of Negro Women to advance the interests of African-American women and the black community. Maintained by
the National Park Service, the Bethune House exhibits focus on the professional achievements of this remarkable woman.

1318 Vermont Ave. NW (at O St.). www.nps.gov/mamc. © **202/673-2402.** Free admission. Open daily 9am–5pm. Metro: U St./Cardozo (13th St. exit).

# UPPER NORTHWEST D.C.: GLOVER PARK, WOODLEY PARK & CLEVELAND PARK

A handful of attractions lie in these just-beyond-downtown enclaves.

**Hillwood Museum and Gardens** ★ HISTORIC HOME   This magnificent estate of Post cereal heiress, businesswoman, and socialite Marjorie
Merriweather Post, includes the beautiful mansion, where she lived from 1955
until her death in 1973, and 13 acres of gardens. The Georgian-style manse is
filled with Post's collections of art and artifacts from 18th-century France and

18th- and 19th-century Russia, from Fabergé eggs to tapestries. The spectacular gardens include a Japanese-style plot, a Russian dacha, a French parterre, and a pet cemetery. A rather nice conclusion to your visit here is lunch, or on Sundays, afternoon tea, at Hillwood's Café, especially spring through fall, when the Café opens its terrace overlooking the gardens.

4155 Linnean Ave. NW (at Connecticut Ave.). www.hillwoodmuseum.org. © **202/686-5807.** Admission $18 adults, $15 seniors, $10 college students, $5 students 18 and under. Tues–Sun 10am–5pm. Metro: Van Ness/UDC (east side of Connecticut Ave. exit), with a 20-minute walk.

**National Zoological Park** ★★ ZOO   The National Zoo was created by an act of Congress in 1889 and became part of the Smithsonian Institution in 1890. A leader in the care, breeding, and exhibition of animals, the zoo occupies 163 lushly landscaped and wooded acres and is one of the country's most delightful zoos. In all, the park is home to about 300 species—some 1,800 animals, many of them rare and/or endangered. You'll see cheetahs, zebras, gorillas, elephants, monkeys, brown pelicans, orangutans, a bison, and, of course, lions, tigers, and bears. The zoo's biggest draws continue to be its **giant pandas,** Mei Xiang and Tian Tian, and their cub, Bao Bao, born August 2013.

Enter the zoo at the Connecticut Avenue entrance; you'll be right by the Education Building, where you can pick up a map and find out about feeding times and any special activities. *Note:* From this main entrance, you're headed downhill; the return uphill walk can prove trying if you have young children and/or it's a hot day. Unfortunately, waiting for families at the *bottom* of the hill is the **Kids' Farm** with ducks, chickens, goats, cows, and miniature donkeys, plus a vegetable garden and pizza sculpture. Let's face it: You might not get that far. But just in case, keep in mind that the zoo rents strollers, and that snack bars and ice-cream kiosks are scattered throughout the park.

The zoo animals live in large, open enclosures—simulations of their natural habitats—along easy-to-follow paths. The **Olmsted Walk** winds from the zoo's Connecticut Avenue entrance all the way to the zoo's end, at Rock Creek Park. Stemming off the central Olmsted Walk is the **Asia Trail,** which takes you past sloth bears, those frolicking giant pandas, fishing cats, clouded leopards, and Japanese salamanders. You can't get lost, and it's hard to miss a thing.

Like the big old **elephants.** Just across from the giant panda yard is **Elephant Trails,** the zoo's high-tech, environmentally friendly habitat for its seven Asian elephants. The enclosure includes 4 acres of indoor and outdoor space, a wading

---

**Early Risers?**

Zoo grounds open daily at 6am, which might be too early for a lot of tourists, but not for families whose young children like to rise at the crack of dawn. If you find yourselves trapped and restless in the hotel room, hop on the Red Line Metro, which opens at 5am weekdays, 7am Saturday and Sunday (or drive—the zoo parking lot opens at 6am, too), get off at the Woodley Park–Zoo station, and walk up the hill to the zoo. A Starbucks, which opens at 5:30am weekdays, 6am Saturday and Sunday, is directly across from the zoo's entrance on Connecticut Avenue. Good morning.

pool, a walking path for exercise, a barn with soft flooring for sleeping and geothermal heating, and, for real, a community center that offers the elephants the chance to socialize!

Moving on from there takes you to the **American Trail.** Located dead center in the zoo, American Trail is home to animals native to the United States and Canada that were once in danger of becoming extinct. Bald eagles, ravens, seals, sea lions, gray wolves, beavers, and river otters are among the creatures living here. An artificial tidal pool is now part of the display, and visitors are welcome to dip their toes in and touch model sea creatures.

I also recommend **Amazonia,** where you can hang out and observe enormous 7-foot-long arapaima fish and itty-bitty red-tailed catfish, and look for monkeys hiding in the 50-foot-tall trees.

Not far from the Amazonia exhibit, stationed in front of the **Great Cats** habitat, is the zoo's solar-powered carousel, whose canopy is carved with 58 species of animals. Rides are $3.

The zoo offers many dining options, stroller rental stations, a handful of gift shops, a bookstore, and several paid-parking lots. The lots fill up quickly, especially on weekends, so arrive early or take the Metro.

3001 Connecticut Ave. NW (adjacent to Rock Creek Park). www.nationalzoo.si.edu. © **202/633-4888.** Free admission. Apr–Oct (weather permitting) grounds daily 8am–7pm, animal buildings daily 9am–6pm; Nov–Mar grounds daily 8am–5pm, animal buildings daily 9am–4pm. Closed Dec 25. Metro: Woodley Park–Zoo or Cleveland Park.

**Washington National Cathedral ★★** CATHEDRAL   Pierre L'Enfant's 1791 plan for the capital city included "a great church for national purposes." Possibly because of early America's fear of mingling church and state, more than a century elapsed before the foundation for Washington National Cathedral was laid. Its actual name is the Cathedral Church of St. Peter and St. Paul. The church is Episcopal, but it has no local congregation and seeks to serve the entire nation as a house of prayer for all people. It has been the setting for every kind of religious observance, from Jewish to Serbian Orthodox.

A church of this magnitude—it's the sixth-largest cathedral in the world, and the second largest in the U.S.—took a long time to build. Its principal (but not original) architect, Philip Hubert Frohman, worked on the project from 1921 until his death in 1972. The foundation stone was laid in 1907 using the mallet with which George Washington set the Capitol cornerstone. Construction was interrupted by both world wars and by periods of financial difficulty. The cathedral was completed with the placement of the final stone on the west front towers on September 29, 1990, 83 years (to the day) after it was begun.

English Gothic in style (with several distinctly 20th-c. innovations, such as a stained-glass window commemorating the flight of *Apollo 11* and containing a piece of moon rock), the cathedral is built in the shape of a cross, complete with flying buttresses and 110 gargoyles. Along with the Capitol and the Washington Monument, it is one of the dominant structures on the Washington skyline. Its 59-acre landscaped grounds have two lovely gardens (the lawn is ideal for picnicking), three schools, and two gift shops.

Among the many historic services and events that have taken place at the cathedral are: celebrations at the end of World Wars I and II; the burial of President Wilson; funerals for Presidents Eisenhower, Reagan, and Ford; the burials of Helen Keller and her companion, Anne Sullivan, inside the cathedral; the Rev. Dr. Martin Luther King, Jr.'s final sermon; a round-the-clock prayer vigil in the Holy Spirit Chapel when Iranians held American hostages captive, and a service attended by the hostages upon their release; and President Bush's National Prayer and Remembrance service on September 14, 2001, following the cataclysm of September 11.

Washington National Cathedral.

The best way to explore the cathedral is to take a 30-minute **guided highlights tour** (the tour is included in your admission price); the tours leave continually from the west end of the nave. You can also walk through on your own, using a self-guiding brochure available in several languages. Visit the website to find out about group and special-interest tours, which require reservations and fees. Allow additional time to tour the grounds and to visit the **Pilgrim Observation Gallery ★,** where 70 windows provide panoramic views of Washington and its surroundings. Among the most popular special-interest tours are the Tuesday and Wednesday afternoon **Tour and Tea** events, which start at 1:30pm with an in-depth look at the cathedral and conclude in the Observation Gallery with a lovely "high tea," in both the British and literal sense—you're sitting in the cradle of one of the highest points in Washington, gazing out at the cathedral and the city below, while noshing on scones and Devon cream. The cost is $30 per person, and reservations are required. Call ✆ **202/537-2228** or book online at https://tix.cathedral.org.

The cathedral hosts numerous events: organ recitals and other types of concerts; choir performances; an annual flower mart; and the playing of the 53-bell carillon. And open daily 7am to 6pm is the Cathedral's new coffeehouse/cafe, **Open City at the National Cathedral,** operated by the owners of **Tryst** (p. 227) in Adams Morgan. This is the Cathedral's first eatery and it is located inside the restored Old Baptistry, near the Bishop's Garden.

*Note:* When you visit in 2017, there's a good chance you'll see exterior scaffolding. The earthquake of August 23, 2011, damaged some of the pinnacles, flying buttresses, and gargoyles at the very top of the cathedral's exterior, as well as some minor areas of the interior ceiling. Interior repair work was completed in 2015, so you'll see a fully restored nave, looking better than ever, in truth, because the restoration included cleaning clerestory windows and stones, the first time ever. Much exterior repair work remains, but the cathedral is completely safe to visit, and its programs continue as usual.

3101 Wisconsin Ave. NW (at Massachusetts Ave.). www.cathedral.org. © **202/537-6200.** Admission: $11 adults, $7 children and seniors. Cathedral Mon–Fri 10am–5pm; Sat 10am–4pm; Sun 1–4pm. Gardens daily until dusk. Regular tours Mon–Fri 10:15–11:15am and 1–3:30pm; Sat 10:15–11:15am and 1–3:30pm; Sun 1–3:30pm. No tours on Palm Sunday, Easter, Thanksgiving, Dec 25, or during services. Services vary throughout the year, but Mon–Fri Evensong service at 5:30pm is usually on throughout the academic year. Check the website for all other service times. Metro: Tenleytown, with a 20-min. walk. Bus: Any N bus up Massachusetts Ave. from Dupont Circle, or any 30-series bus along Wisconsin Ave. This is also a stop on the Old Town Trolley Tour. Parking garage $6 per hr./$22 maximum weekdays until 11pm and a flat rate of $7 if you arrive after 4pm; flat rate of $9 on Sat; free on Sun.

# GEORGETOWN

One of the oldest parts of the city has long been best known for its major shopping opportunities, but we think the better reason to come here is to experience its rich history. A walking tour in chapter 10 will lead you to centuries-old estates and dwellings, including **Tudor Place, the Old Stone House, Dumbarton House Museum and Gardens,** and **Dumbarton House.** The **Georgetown** walking tour in chapter 10 includes a stop at the **Mount Zion United Methodist Church,** whose black congregation is the oldest in the city. Whether or not you take one of the walking tours, you might want to seek out one other place included in this chapter: the **Kreeger Museum,** located slightly northwest of Georgetown proper and most easily accessible by car or taxi. But very cool.

**Dumbarton House** ★ HISTORIC HOME   Built between 1799 and 1805, Dumbarton House is the headquarters for the National Society of Colonial Dames of America. Stop here to admire gorgeous architecture and antique decorative arts, and to glean a bit of early American history. Self-guide your way or call to arrange in advance for a docent-guided tour.

2715 Q St. NW (at 27th St.). www.dumbartonhouse.org. © **202/337-2288.** Admission $5; free for students. Tues–Sun 11am–3pm. Closed federal holidays. Metro: Dupont Circle (Q St. exit, with a 20-min. walk) or take the DC Circulator bus, two of whose routes run close by the house.

**Dumbarton Oaks** ★ GARDEN & MUSEUM   One block off the main drag of Wisconsin Avenue in upper Georgetown delivers you far from the madding crowds, to the peaceful refuge of Dumbarton Oaks. The estate includes a museum devoted to Byzantine and pre-Columbian art, a research center and library, and 10 acres of formal and informal gardens. Frankly, many people skip the museum altogether to wander along the garden's hedge-lined walkways, into the orangery, past the weeping cherry trees, and all around the garden plots, admiring what's in bloom as they go. If it's February, you may see English daisies. April? Bluebells. August? Dahlias. (Just to name a few.) The gardens are romantic, have several pretty places to perch, and also are adorned here and there with garden ornaments and artwork. The gardens can get crowded in spring and early summer, when they are at their loveliest.

## 6 MUSEUMS IN anacostia

This historic, largely black residential neighborhood located east of the Capitol and away from the center of the city is not a typical tourist destination, but two attractions do draw visitors. The **Frederick Douglass National Historic Site** (1411 W St. SE, at 14th St. SE; www.nps.gov/frdo; ✆ **202/426-5961**) is by far the more compelling. Born a slave in 1818, Frederick Bailey escaped his Maryland plantation, became an abolitionist and gifted orator, changed his name to Douglass to avoid capture, and fled to Britain, where he purchased his freedom. Back in the United States a free man, Douglass picked up where he had left off, fighting against slavery and for equal rights for all, including women. This house, known as Cedar Hill, was Douglass's home for the last 18 years of his life. A National Park Service ranger begins your tour on the verandah, where you can see that the house crowns one of the highest hills in Washington. Then your guide takes you upstairs and down, and fills you in on the life of the brilliant, brave, and charismatic abolitionist here at this house, but with detours to Douglass's life story: his love of reading, his escape from slavery, his married life, and his embrace of emancipation for all oppressed people. See website for hours and admission, which is free, but by guided tour only. Also see the African American History itinerary, p. 41, in chapter 3.

The **Anacostia Community Museum** (1901 Fort Place SE, off Martin Luther King Jr. Ave.; www.anacostia.si.edu; ✆ **202/633-4820**) is a Smithsonian museum that primarily serves the neighborhood and the local black community with exhibits that focus on social, cultural, and historical themes that resonate with area residents.

Do try to make time for the museum, whose newly renovated galleries display 1,200 Byzantine artifacts, including jewelry, lamps, icons, and illuminated manuscripts from the 4th to the 15th centuries; and pre-Columbian objects such as Aztec stone carvings, Inca gold ornaments, and Olmec heads. Other highlights include the Flemish tapestries and an El Greco painting, *The Visitation,* on display in the Renaissance-style Music Room. Like the Phillips Collection (p. 182), the museum's mansion setting adds to its charm.

The country house and gardens, which are situated at the highest point of Georgetown, belonged to a couple named Mildred and Robert Woods Bliss, who initiated these collections and gardens in the first half of the 20th century.

1703 32nd St. NW (garden entrance at 31st and R sts.). www.doaks.org. ✆ **202/339-6401.** Gardens admission Mar 15–Oct 31 $10 adults, $5 children 12 and under, $8 seniors; free Nov–Mar 14. Museum free admission. Gardens Tues–Sun year-round (weather permitting): Mar 15–Oct 31 2–6pm; Nov 1–Mar 14 2–5pm. Museum Tues–Sun year-round 11:30am–5:30pm. Closed national holidays and Dec 24. Metrobus nos. 31, 32, 36, D1, D2, D3, D6, and G2, plus the DC Circulator bus all have stops close to the site.

**Kreeger Museum** ★ ART MUSEUM  You have to make an effort to visit the Kreeger, because it's located in a residential neighborhood away from downtown and public transportation. But if you don't mind driving, taking a taxi, or riding the D6 bus from Dupont Circle, then walking a half-mile up the hill to the museum, you'll be well rewarded. On view throughout this unique Philip Johnson–designed building, besides the stunning architecture itself, are paintings, sculptures, prints, and drawings by 19th- and 20th-century European artists, Picasso (early and late works), Kandinsky, Monet, Renoir, Munch, Pissarro, Rodin among them. American works are on view, too, including some by Washington, D.C., artists such as Sam Gilliam and Gene Davis. Downstairs lies a small collection of traditional African masks and figures and Asian pieces. Outdoors is a sculpture terrace, where large works by Maillol and Henry Moore, and the sight of the distant Washington Monument, are some of the pleasures at hand. On the museum's north lawn is the separate sculpture garden, where works by the likes of George Rickey rise up. This summit-situated, 5½-acre estate, once the residence of collectors Carmen and David Kreeger, opened to the public in 1994. On view around the museum's reflecting pool through April 2017 are six large-scale sculptures by John L. Dreyfuss, who created this "Inventions" series in celebration of the Kreeger's 20th anniversary in 2014.

2401 Foxhall Rd. NW (off Reservoir Rd.). www.kreegermuseum.org. © **202/337-3050.** Museum: Admission $10 adults, $7 seniors and students, free for children 12 and under. Fri–Sat 10am–4pm; Tues–Thurs by reservation only for guided tours at 10:30am and 1:30pm. Sculpture Garden: Free admission, Tues–Sat 10am–4pm. Closed federal holidays and Aug. About 2 miles from Reservoir Rd. and Wisconsin Ave. in Georgetown (a pleasant walk on a nice day); otherwise drive, take a taxi, or ride the D6 bus from Dupont Circle.

**Old Stone House ★** HISTORIC HOME    This 1765 structure is said to be the oldest in Washington. The National Park Service owns and operates the house, and National Park Service rangers provide information and sometimes demonstrations related to the site's pre-Revolutionary history. See p. 307.

3051 M St. NW (at 30th St.). www.nps.gov/olst. © **202/895-6070.** Free admission. Daily 11am–6pm. Garden open during daylight hours. Closed Dec 25. Metro: Foggy Bottom with a 15-min. walk, or take the DC Circulator.

**Tudor Place ★** HISTORIC HOME    Designed by Dr. William Thornton, architect of the Capitol, Tudor Place was constructed between 1796 and 1816 for Martha Parke Custis, who was George Washington's step-granddaughter. Family descendants lived here until 1983. Tour the garden on your own; house tours are docent-led only. See p. 298.

1644 31st St. NW (at R St.). www.tudorplace.org. © **202/965-0400.** Mar–Dec: House admission $10 adults, $8 seniors and college students, $3 children 5–17. Garden admission $3. Feb: Half-price admission to house and to garden. House and Garden Feb–Dec, Tues–Sat 10am–4pm; Sun noon–4pm. Closed Dec 25. Metro: Dupont Circle (Q St. exit, with a 20-min. walk).

# NORTHERN VIRGINIA

## Arlington

The land that today comprises Arlington County, Virginia, was included in the original parcel of land demarcated as the nation's capital. In 1847 the state of Virginia took its territory back, referring to it as "Alexandria County" until 1920, when Arlington at last became "Arlington," a name change made to avoid confusion with the city of Alexandria.

And where did the county pick up the name "Arlington"? From its famous estate, Arlington House, built by a descendant of Martha Washington, George Washington Parke Custis, whose daughter married Robert E. Lee. (Before that, "Arlington" was the name of the Custis family estate in Tidewater Virginia.) The Lees lived in Arlington House on and off until the onset of the Civil War in 1861. The beginnings of Arlington National Cemetery date from May 1864, when four Union soldiers were buried here, in the area now known as section 27, the oldest section in the cemetery.

The Arlington Memorial Bridge leads directly from the Lincoln Memorial to the Robert E. Lee Memorial at Arlington House, symbolically joining these two figures into one Union after the Civil War.

Beyond Arlington the cemetery is Arlington, a residential community from which most residents commute into Washington. In recent years, however, the suburb has come into its own, booming with businesses, restaurants, and nightlife, giving tourists more incentive to visit. Below are its worthwhile sites.

**Arlington National Cemetery** ★★ CEMETERY   Arlington National Cemetery is, without hyperbole, the United States' most important burial ground. This shrine occupies approximately 624 acres on the high hills overlooking the capital from the west side of Memorial Bridge. More than 400,000 people are buried here, including veterans of all national wars, from the American Revolution to the Iraq and Afghanistan conflicts; Supreme Court justices; literary figures; slaves; presidents; astronauts; and assorted other national heroes. Many graves of the famous at Arlington bear nothing more than simple markers.

A visit to Arlington National Cemetery is a considerably more informative and organized experience than in past years, thanks to changes made in 2015. As always, upon arrival, head to the Welcome Center, where you can view exhibits, pick up a detailed map, and use the restrooms (there are no others until you get to Arlington House). The Welcome Center also offers kiosks where you can access the cemetery's app, ANC Explorer, newly updated, to find locations of and directions to individual gravesites plus self-guided tours of the cemetery. (Or download the free app ahead of time at the iTunes store or from Arlington National Cemetery's website.)

If you're here to visit a particular grave, you'll be gratified to know that the cemetery now operates a free shuttle to individual gravesites. And if you're here as a tourist, and you've got plenty of stamina and it's a nice day, consider touring all or part of the cemetery on foot. Plenty of people do. I'd say it's worth it to spring for the narrated tour: It's a hop-on, hop-off tour that makes six stops on weekdays, with an additional three stops included on weekend tours, for those who so desire. All tours include stops at the gravesites of **Pres. John F. Kennedy, Gen. John J. Pershing,** the **U.S. Coast Guard Memorial,** the **Memorial Amphitheater** and **Tomb of the Unknowns, Arlington House,** and the **Marine Corps Memorial.** The weekend add-ons are **Sections 54** and **55,** the **Columbarium** and **Niche Wall,** and the **9/11 Memorial.** The tour lasts an hour or more, depending on how many times you hop on and off, and how long you stay at each site. Service is continuous, and the narrated commentary is lively and informative. You can buy tickets online in advance (www.arlingtontours.com) or at the ticket counter in the Welcome Center. Tickets are $12 adults, $9 seniors, $6 children 4 to 12; military and active-duty personnel receive discounted prices and disabled and active-duty military in uniform are free (with proper ID).

Remember as you go that this is a memorial frequented not just by tourists, but also by those attending burial services or visiting the graves of beloved relatives and friends who are buried here.

Cemetery highlights include the **Tomb of the Unknowns,** which contains the unidentified remains of a service member from World War I in a massive, white marble sarcophagus; just west of the sarcophagus are three white marble slabs flush with the plaza, marking the graves of unknown service members from World War II, the Korean War, and the Vietnam War. But the crypt for the Vietnam War service member contains no remains. In 1998 the entombed remains of the unknown soldier from Vietnam were disinterred and identified as those of Air Force 1st Lt. Michael Blassie, whose A-37 was shot down in South Vietnam in 1972. The Blassie family buried Michael in his hometown of St. Louis. A 24-hour honor guard watches over the marble Tomb of the Unknowns and its companion gravesites with the changing of the guard taking place every half-hour April to September, every hour on the hour October to March, and every hour at night year-round.

Within a 20-minute walk, all uphill, from the Welcome Center is **Arlington House, The Robert E. Lee Memorial** (www.nps.gov/arho; ✆ **703/235-1530**), which was begun in 1802 by Martha and George Washington's adopted grandson, George Washington Parke Custis. Custis's daughter, Mary Anna Randolph, inherited the estate, and she and her husband, Robert E. Lee, lived here between 1831 and 1861. When Lee headed up Virginia's army, Mary fled, and federal troops confiscated the property. Restoration work is ongoing throughout the grounds and house, but will not interfere with your visit. The house, fully furnished with Lee and Custis family artifacts, is open to the public for self-guided tours. Slave quarters and a small museum adjoin. Park rangers are on-site to answer your questions. Admission is free. It's open October to February from 9:30am to 4:30pm; March to May and September from 9am to 5pm; and June to August 9am to 5:30pm. (closed December 25 and January 1).

The view of the capital is spectacular from Arlington House's hilltop, but just below the house, look for **Pierre Charles L'Enfant's grave** at a spot that is believed to offer the best view of Washington, the city he designed.

Below Arlington House is the **gravesite of President John Fitzgerald Kennedy,** which is a 3-acre lawn terrace paved with irregular-sized stones of Cape Cod granite, bits of grass growing between the stones. At the head of the gravesite is a 5-foot, circular fieldstone, with the Eternal Flame burning in the center. Embracing the terrace is a low crescent wall inscribed with quotations from President Kennedy's presidency. Slate headstones mark the actual graves for President Kennedy, Jacqueline Kennedy Onassis, and two infant children. President Kennedy's two brothers, Senators Robert Kennedy and Edward

Kennedy, are buried close by. The Kennedy graves attract streams of visitors. Arrive close to 8am to contemplate the site quietly; otherwise, it's often crowded.

In 1997, the **Women in Military Service for America Memorial** (www. womensmemorial.org; ℂ **800/222-2294** or 703/533-1155) was added to Arlington Cemetery to honor the more than 2.5 million women who have served in the armed forces from the American Revolution to the present. The impressive memorial lies just beyond the gated entrance to the cemetery, a 3-minute walk from the visitor center. As you approach, you see a large, circular reflecting pool, perfectly placed within the curve of the granite wall rising behind it. Arched passageways within the 226-foot-long wall lead to an upper terrace and dramatic views of Arlington National Cemetery and the monuments of Washington; an arc of large glass panels (which form the roof of the memorial hall) contains etched quotations from famous people about contributions made by servicewomen. Behind the wall and completely underground is the **Education Center,** housing a **Hall of Honor,** a gallery of exhibits tracing the history of women in the military; a theater; and a computer register of servicewomen, which visitors may access for the stories and information about 250,000 individual military women, past and present. Hours are 8am to 5pm. Stop at the reception desk for a brochure with a self-guided tour through the memorial. The memorial is open every day except Christmas.

Just across the Memorial Bridge from the base of the Lincoln Memorial. www.arlington cemetery.mil. ℂ **877/907-8585.** Free admission. Apr–Sept daily 8am–7pm; Oct–Mar daily 8am–5pm. Metro: Arlington National Cemetery. If you come by car, parking is $1.75/hr. for the 1st 3 hrs., $2.50/hr. thereafter. The cemetery is also accessible as a stop on several tour bus services, including Old Town Trolley.

**The Pentagon** ★ GOVERNMENT BUILDING   Completed in January 1943 after a mere 16 months of construction, the structure is the world's largest low-rise office building in the world. The Capitol could fit inside any one of its five wedge-shaped sections. Twenty-five-thousand people work at the Pentagon, which holds 17½ miles of corridors, 19 escalators, 284 restrooms, and 691 water fountains. Tours of this headquarters for the American military establishment were suspended for a while following the September 11, 2001, attack in which terrorists hijacked American Airlines Flight 77 and crashed it into the northwest side of the Pentagon, killing 125 people working at the Pentagon and 59 people aboard the plane. In the years since, the Pentagon has been completely restored and its tour program reinstated, in accordance with certain procedures (see below). More than 106,000 visitors tour the Pentagon annually.

An active duty staff person from the National Capital Region's ceremonial unit conducts the free, 60-minute tour that covers 1½ miles. Your tour guide is required to memorize 20 pages of informational material, outlining the mission of each military branch. It's a fascinating introduction, as is seeing the building itself, its corridors commemorating the history, people, and culture of the Air Force, Navy, Army, Marine Corps, and Coast Guard. You'll see historical photos, the Hall of Heroes for Medal of Honor recipients, an exhibit recognizing

U.S. prisoners of war and the missing in action, and paintings depicting the country's founding fathers and the signing of the Declaration of Independence.

The tour does not include a visit to the two-acre **Pentagon Memorial,** better known as the **9/11 Memorial,** which is located outside, on the northwest side of the building near where the plane crashed. The memorial opened to the public on the seventh anniversary of the 9/11 attacks, September 11, 2008. On view are 184 granite-covered benches, each engraved with a victim's name, and arranged in order of birth date. The names are written in such a way on each bench that you must face the Pentagon to be able to read the names of those killed there and face away from the Pentagon, toward the western sky, to read the names of those who perished on the plane. *Note:* You do not need to sign up for a Pentagon tour to visit the 9/11 Memorial, which is outside and open to the public 24 hours a day, every day. The best way to reach the memorial is to take the Metro to the Pentagon station and walk the half-mile, following the signs that lead from the station to the northwest side of the Pentagon. *FYI:* A Visitor Education Center is in the works; when completed in 2018, the center will include interactive exhibits that explain the impact of 9/11, provide bios of the 184 people who were killed aboard Flight 77 and at the Pentagon, and offer a children's area. The education center will be located across the highway from the 9/11 Memorial, with shuttles transporting visitors between the two locations, and to the Metro station.

Pentagon tours are available Monday to Friday 9am to 3pm, and you must book your tour no sooner than 14 days and no later than 90 days in advance. You request the tour online at **https://pentagontours.osd.mil,** providing your Social Security number, birth date, and other information for each of the people in your party. There is no public parking at the Pentagon, so it's best to arrive by Metro, because the Pentagon has its own Metro stop. Once you exit the Pentagon Metro station, look for the Pentagon Visitors Center near the station entrance and go to the Pentagon Tour Window.

Department of Defense, 1400 Defense Pentagon. https://pentagontours.osd.mil and www.pentagonmemorial.org. ✆ **703/697-1776.** Free admission, but reservations required; guided tours only. Pentagon Mon–Fri 9am–3pm. Pentagon Memorial daily 24 hr. Metro: Pentagon.

# PARKS

More than 27% of Washington, D.C.'s land space is national parkland. When you add in the parks and gardens maintained by the D.C. Department of Parks and Recreation, as well as private estates that are open to the public, you're talking thousands and thousands of green acres!

## Potomac Park ★★★

The National Mall and Memorial Parks' individual spaces known as West and East Potomac parks are 720 riverside acres divided by the Tidal Basin. The parkland is most famous for its display of **cherry trees,** which bloom for a mere 2 weeks, tops, every spring, as they have since the city of Tokyo first gave the U.S. capital the gift of the original 3,000 trees in 1912. Today there are more than 3,750 cherry trees planted along the Tidal Basin in West Potomac Park, East Potomac Park, the Washington Monument grounds, and other pockets of the city.

The sight of the delicate cherry blossoms is so special that the whole city joins in cherry-blossom-related hoopla, throwing the **National Cherry Blossom Festival** (the 2017 festival is scheduled for March 20 through April 16). The National Park Service devotes a home page to the subject, **www.nps.gov/cherry,** and the National Cherry Blossom Festival officially has another: **www.nationalcherryblossomfestival.org.** The trees usually begin blooming sometime between March 20 and April 17; April 4 is the average date at which the blooms reach their peak, defined as the point at which 70% of the Tidal Basin–sited cherry trees have blossomed.

To get to the Tidal Basin by car (*not* recommended in cherry-blossom season—actually, let me be clear: *impossible* in cherry-blossom season), you want to get on Independence Avenue and follow the signs posted near the Lincoln Memorial that show you where to turn to find parking. If you're walking, you'll want to cross Independence Avenue where it intersects with West Basin Drive and follow the path to the Tidal Basin. There is no convenient Metro stop near here. If you don't want to walk or ride a bike, your best bet is a taxi.

**West Potomac Park** encompasses Constitution Gardens; the Vietnam, Korean, Lincoln, Jefferson, World War II, and FDR memorials; the D.C. World War I Memorial; the Reflecting Pool; the Tidal Basin and its paddleboats; and countless flower beds, ball fields, and trees. More than 1,500 cherry trees border the Tidal Basin, some of them Akebonos with delicate pink blossoms, but most are Yoshinos with white, cloudlike flower clusters.

**East Potomac Park** has 1,701 cherry trees in 10 varieties. The park also has picnic grounds, tennis courts, three golf courses, a large swimming pool, and biking and hiking paths by the water. East Potomac Park's **Hains Point** is located on a peninsula extending into the Potomac River; locals love to ride their bikes out to the point; golfers love to tee up in view of the Washington Monument. See "Outdoor Activities," p. 200, for further information.

Part of National Mall and Memorial Parks, bordering the Potomac River along the west and southwest ends. www.nps.gov/nama. ✆ **202/426-6841.** Free admission. Daily 24 hr. Metro: Smithsonian (12th St./Independence Ave. exit).

## Rock Creek Park ★★★

Created in 1890, **Rock Creek Park** was purchased by Congress for its "pleasant valleys and ravines, primeval forests and open fields, its running waters, its rocks clothed with rich ferns and mosses, its repose and tranquility, its light and shade, its ever-varying shrubbery, its beautiful and extensive views," according to a Corps of Engineers officer quoted in the National Park Service's administrative history. A 1,750-acre valley within the District of Columbia, extending 12 miles from the Potomac River to the Maryland border, it's one of the biggest and finest city parks in the nation. Parts of it are still wild;

Cyclists cruise through Rock Creek Park.

coyotes have been sighted here, joining the red and gray foxes, raccoons, and beavers already resident. Most tourists encounter its southern tip, the section from the Kennedy Center to the National Zoo, but the park widens and travels much farther from there. Among the park's attractions are playgrounds; an extensive system of hiking and biking trails; sports facilities; remains of Civil War fortifications; and acres and acres of wooded parklands.

For full information on the wide range of park programs and activities, visit the **Rock Creek Nature Center and Planetarium,** 5200 Glover Rd. NW (© **202/895-6070**), Wednesday through Sunday from 9am to 5pm. To get to the center by public transportation, take the Metro to Friendship Heights and transfer to bus no. E2 to Military Road and Oregon Avenue/Glover Road, then walk up the hill about 100 yards.

The Nature Center and Planetarium is the scene of numerous activities, including weekend planetarium shows, nature films, crafts demonstrations, live animal demonstrations, guided nature walks, plus a mix of lectures, films, and other events. Self-guided nature trails begin here. All activities are free, but for planetarium shows you need to pick up tickets a half-hour in advance. The Nature Center is closed on federal holidays.

At Tilden Street and Beach Drive, you can see the recently refurbished, water-powered 1820s gristmill, used until not so long ago to grind corn and wheat into flour. It's called **Peirce Mill** (a man named Isaac Peirce built it). The mill is open for tours (Nov 1–Mar 31 Sat–Sun noon to 4pm; Apr 1–Oct 31 Wed–Sun 10am–4pm); the mill seldom operates, however. Check the website, www.nps.gov/pimi, or call © **202/895-6070.**

You'll find convenient free **parking** throughout the park.

In addition to the circumscribed 1,750 acre park, Rock Creek Park's charter extends to include the maintenance of other parks, gardens, and buildings throughout the city.

In Georgetown, the park's offerings include D.C.'s oldest standing structure, the 1765 **Old Stone House** (see p. 191) located on M St. NW, Georgetown's busy street; the 10-acre, Potomac River–focused **Georgetown Waterfront Park** (www.georgetownwaterfrontpark.org), a swath of greenways, plazas, and walkways, with benches, a labyrinth, and overlooks—you owe it to yourself to take a stroll here; and in upper Georgetown, the family-friendly **Montrose Park,** a favorite place for picnicking and playing tennis; and **Dumbarton Oaks Park,** a 27-acre rustic preserve. Both Montrose and Dumbarton Oaks parks adjoin each other and the Dumbarton Oaks estate and formal gardens (p. 189).

Along 16th northwest, about 1 mile north of the White House, is **Meridian Hill Park** (www.nps.gov/mehi), 12 acres in size, and located between the Adams Morgan and Columbia Heights neighborhoods. Meridian Hill Park is worth a visit for several reasons: Its view serves up the White House, the Washington Monument, and the Jefferson Memorial in the distance; its cascading fountain is the longest in North America; and planted amidst its landscaped gardens are a potpourri of statues of famous people: Joan of Arc, Dante, President Buchanan. Best of all is the mix of people you'll find here, mostly from the nearby diverse neighborhoods, and the assorted activities they get up to: yoga lessons, soccer matches, and Sunday afternoon through evening, spring through fall, an African drum circle.

From the Potomac River near the Kennedy Center northwest through the city into Maryland. www.nps.gov/rocr. ✆ **202/895-6070.** Free admission. Daily during daylight hours. Metro: Access points near the stations at Dupont Circle, Foggy Bottom, Woodley Park–Zoo, and Cleveland Park.

## Theodore Roosevelt Island Park ★

A serene, 88.5-acre wilderness preserve, Theodore Roosevelt Island is a memorial to the nation's 26th president in recognition of his contributions to conservation. During his administration, Roosevelt, an outdoor enthusiast and expert field naturalist, set aside a total of 234 million acres of public lands for forests, national parks, wildlife and bird refuges, and monuments.

Native American tribes were here first, inhabiting the island for centuries until the arrival of English explorers in the 1600s. Over the years, the island passed through many owners before becoming what it is today—an island preserve of swamp, marsh, and upland forest that's a haven for rabbits, chipmunks, great owls, foxes, muskrats, turtles, and groundhogs. It's a complex ecosystem in which cattails, arrow arum, and pickerelweed grow in the marshes, and willow, ash, and maple trees root on the mud flats. You can observe these flora and fauna in their natural environs on 2.5 miles of foot trails.

In the northern center of the island, overlooking a terrace encircled by a water-filled moat, stands a 17-foot bronze statue of Roosevelt. Four 21-foot granite tablets are inscribed with tenets of his conservation philosophy.

To drive to the island, take the George Washington Memorial Parkway exit north from the Theodore Roosevelt Bridge. The parking area is accessible only from the northbound lane; park there and cross the pedestrian bridge that connects the lot to the island. You can also rent a canoe at Thompson Boat Center or Key Bridge Boathouse (p. 202) and paddle over, making sure to land at the north or northeast corner of the island; there is no place to secure the boat, so you'll need to stay with it. Or take the Metro to the Rosslyn Metro station, walk toward Key Bridge, and follow the short connecting trail leading downhill from the downstream side of the river and across the parkway into the parking lot. Expect bugs in summer and muddy trails after a rain.

In the Potomac River, btw. Washington and Rosslyn, VA (see above for access information). www.nps.gov/this. ℂ **703/289-2500.** Free admission. Daily 6am–10pm. Metro: Rosslyn, then follow the trail to the island.

## Chesapeake & Ohio Canal National Historical Park ★

One of the great joys of living in Washington is the **C&O Canal** and its unspoiled 184.5-mile towpath. You leave urban cares and stresses behind while hiking, strolling, jogging, cycling, or boating in this lush natural setting of ancient oaks and red maples, giant sycamores, willows, and wildflowers. But the canal wasn't always just a leisure spot for city people. It was built in the 1800s, when water routes were considered vital to transportation. Even before it was completed, though, the canal was being rendered obsolete by the B&O Railroad, which was constructed at about the same time and along the same route. Today its role as an oasis from unrelenting urbanity is even more important.

You can enter the towpath in Georgetown below M Street via Thomas Jefferson Street. If you hike 14 miles, you'll reach **Great Falls,** a point where the Potomac becomes a stunning waterfall plunging 76 feet. This is also where the National Park Service runs its **Great Falls Tavern Visitor Center,** 11710 MacArthur Blvd., Potomac, MD (ℂ **301/767-3714**). The center is open Wednesday through Sunday year-round, 9am to 4:30pm. At this 1831 tavern, you can see museum exhibits and a film about the canal; there's also a bookstore on the premises. The park charges an entrance fee: $10 per car, $5 per walker or cyclist.

The park offers many opportunities for outdoor activities (see below), but if you or your family would prefer a less strenuous form of relaxation, consider the park's **mule-drawn 19th-century canal-boat trip,** led by Park Service rangers in period dress. They regale passengers with canal legend and lore and sing period songs. Boats operate at Great Falls spring through fall, Saturday and Sunday at 11am, 1:30pm, and 3pm; in summer, the boats operate on Fridays as well, at the same times. Barge rides last about 1 hour and 10 minutes, and cost $8 per adult, $6 for seniors, $5 per child, and free for children 3 and under.

Enter the towpath in Georgetown below M St. via Thomas Jefferson St. www.nps.gov/choh. ℂ **301/767-3714.** Free admission. Daily during daylight hours. Metro: Foggy Bottom, with a 20-min. walk to the towpath in Georgetown.

# ESPECIALLY FOR KIDS

As far as I know, Pierre L'Enfant and his successors were not thinking of children when they incorporated the long, open stretch of the Mall into their design for the city. But they may as well have been. This 2-mile expanse of lawn running from the Lincoln Memorial to the Capitol is a playground, really, and a backyard to the Smithsonian museums and National Gallery of Art, which border it. You can visit any of these sites assured that if one of your little darlings starts to misbehave, you'll be able to head right out the door to the National Mall, where numerous distractions await. Vendors sell ice cream, soft pretzels, and sodas. Festivals of all sorts take place on a regular basis, whether it's the busy **Smithsonian Folklife Festival** for 10 days at the end of June into July (see "Washington, D.C., Calendar of Events," in chapter 2, p. 25), or the **Kite Festival** in spring. Weather permitting, a 19th-century carousel operates in front of the Arts and Industries Building, on the south side of the Mall. Right across the Mall from the carousel is the children-friendly National Gallery Sculpture Garden, whose shallow pool is good for splashing one's feet in summer and for ice-skating in winter. The Smithsonian's comprehensive calendar of events page (www.si.edu/events) allows you to screen for children's activities, which is a great timesaver, producing a daily list of family-friendly fun going on at all 18 locations.

The truth is that many of Washington's attractions hold various enchantments for children of all ages. It might be easier to point out which ones are not recommended for your youngest: the Supreme Court, the chambers of Congress, the U.S. Holocaust Memorial Museum, and the Marian Koshland Science Museum; the International Spy Museum is now recommending that its museum is most suitable for children 10 and over. Generally speaking, the bigger and busier the museum, the better it is for kids (see box below).

For more ideas, consult the online or print version of the Friday "Weekend" section of the *Washington Post,* which lists numerous activities (mostly free) for kids: special museum events, children's theater, storytelling programs, puppet shows, video-game competitions, and so forth. View the websites for the Kennedy Center and the National Theatre to find out about children's shows; see chapter 8 for details. Also see p. 35 for a family-themed tour of the capital.

# OUTDOOR ACTIVITIES

For information about spectator-sports venues, see chapter 8. But if you prefer to work up your own honest sweat, Washington offers plenty of pleasant opportunities in many lush surroundings. See "Parks," earlier in this chapter, for complete coverage of the city's loveliest green spaces.

## Biking

Biking is big in D.C., not just as a leisure activity but as an environmentally friendly form of transportation. So much of the city is flat, and paths are everywhere, notably around the National Mall and Memorial Parks. Rock

# FAVORITE children's ATTRACTIONS

Check for special children's events at museum information desks when you enter. I especially recommend a visit to the **National Building Museum** (p. 176), which has activities going on every day for different age groups. Here's a run-down of overall great kid-pleasers in town:

o **Discovery Theater, inside the S. Dillon Ripley Center** (p. 154): Right next to the Smithsonian Castle is this underground children's theater that puts on live performing arts entertainment for the kiddies, about 30 productions each season, including puppet shows, storytelling, dances, and plays.

o **Lincoln Memorial** (p. 137): Kids know a lot about Lincoln and enjoy visiting his memorial. A special treat is visiting after dark.

o **Madame Tussauds Washington, D.C.** (p. 175): There are two kinds of people in this world: those who think wax museums are hokey, and children. Yeah, watch your offspring pretend to sing with Beyoncé, box with Evander Holyfield, stand tall next to George Washington, and whoop it up with Whoopi. Maybe you'll find your inner child and start loving these wax figures, too.

o **National Air and Space Museum** (p. 139): Spectacular IMAX films (don't miss), thrilling flight simulators, planetarium shows, missiles, rockets, and a walk-through orbital workshop.

o **National Museum of American History** (p. 149): This museum's got all your kids covered: the fabulous Wegmans Wonderplace is a playground for infants to 6-year-olds; the Lemelson Center

introduces visitors of all ages to the stories of inventors and inventions (Places of Invention), and invites kids ages 6 to 12, especially, to experiment and test their curiosity with plenty of hands-on activities (Spark!Lab). And the museum has gotten into simulators, offering rides on machines that make you believe you're driving a race car or riding on a roller coaster.

o **National Museum of the American Indian** (p. 150): Children, and their parents, too, enjoy themselves in the museum's imagiNATIONS Activity Center, where visitors learn basket weaving, kayak balancing, and other Native American skills, and play games to discover more about American Indian culture.

o **National Museum of Natural History** (p. 151): A Discovery Room just for youngsters, the Butterfly Pavilion and exhibit, an insect zoo, shrunken heads, dinosaurs, and the IMAX theater showing 2-D and 3-D films.

o **National Zoological Park** (p. 186): Pandas! Cheetahs! Kids always love a zoo, and this is an especially good one.

o **Newseum** (p. 177): Proceed directly to one of two areas: the interactive newsroom on the second floor, where your children will happily, endlessly play computer games while testing their news knowledge and journalism skills, and where they'll have the chance to play an on-camera reporter; or to the New Media Gallery for similar activities.

o **Washington Monument** (p. 157): Spectacular 360-degree views from the center of Washington, D.C.—unbeatable.

Creek Park has an **11-mile paved bike route** ★ from the Lincoln Memorial through the park into Maryland. For a less-crowded ride, check out the **Anacostia Riverwalk Trail;** its 19 miles (of a planned 28-mile stretch) take you from the Tidal Basin to the Capitol Riverfront neighborhood, and along the Anacostia River into other waterfront communities. Capital BikeShare stations are located conveniently near the Tidal Basin and the National Mall, and signage in these areas clearly directs you to the path. Or you can follow the bike path from the Lincoln Memorial and go over Memorial Bridge to pedal to Old Town Alexandria and on to Mount Vernon (see chapter 9). On weekends and holidays, a large part of Rock Creek Parkway is closed to vehicular traffic. The C&O Canal park's towpath, described in "Parks," earlier in this chapter, is a popular bike path. The **Capital Crescent Trail** takes you from Georgetown to the suburb of Bethesda, Maryland, following a former railroad track that parallels the Potomac River for part of the way and passes by old trestle bridges and pleasant residential neighborhoods. You can pick up the trail at the **Thompson Boat Center** in Georgetown, and at **Fletcher's Cove** along the C&O Canal; visit **www.cctrail.org** for maps and more information. If you like to bike and you're here for more than a few days, consider a Capital BikeShare membership (see p. 297).

Bike rental locations include:

o The **Boat House at Fletcher's Cove,** 4940 Canal Rd. NW (www.fletcherscove.com; ℰ **202/244-0461**).

o **Bike and Roll/Bike the Sites** (www.bikethesites.com; ℰ **202/842-2453**), with four locations: the National Museum of American History, tours only, leaving from the south entrance, or Mall side, of the museum (Metro: Smithsonian); Union Station, rentals, service, and repairs (no tours) (Metro: Union Station); near the National Mall, at 955 L'Enfant Plaza SW, North Building Suite 905, tours and limited rentals (Metro: L'Enfant Plaza); and Old Town Alexandria, Cameron Street at the waterfront, self-guided tours and advance reservations only (Metro: King St.). See p. 301 for information about Bike and Roll's guided tours. Rates vary depending on the bike you choose but always include helmet, bike, lock, and pump; there's a 2-hour minimum. *Note:* The Union Station location is the only year-round operation, subject to the weather; the other locations close for the winter.

o **Thompson Boat Center,** 2900 Virginia Ave. NW, at Rock Creek Parkway (www.thompsonboatcenter.com; ℰ **202/333-9543;** Metro: Foggy Bottom, with a 10-min. walk). Both Fletcher's and Thompson rent bikes, weather permitting, from about mid-March to the end of October.

o **Big Wheel Bikes,** 1034 33rd St. NW, near the C&O Canal just below M Street (www.bigwheelbikes.com; ℰ **202/337-0254**). You can rent a bike here year-round Tuesday through Sunday.

## Boating & Fishing

Look to the same places that rent bikes for rental boats: **Thompson Boat Center** and the **Boat House at Fletcher's Cove** (see above for both); they follow the same schedule as their bike rental season, basically March to November. Thompson has canoes, kayaks, and rowing shells (recreational and racing), and is open for boat and bike rentals daily in season from (generally) 7am to 7pm. Fletcher's is right on the C&O Canal, about 2 miles from Key Bridge in Georgetown. In addition to renting bikes, canoes, rowboats, and kayaks, Fletcher's sells fishing licenses, bait, and tackle. Open daily 7am to 7pm in season, and as late as 8:30pm in June and July, Fletcher's is accessible by car (west on M St. NW to Canal Rd. NW) and has plenty of free parking.

Key Bridge Boathouse, 3500 Water St. NW (www.boatingindc.com; ⓒ 202/337-9642), located along the Georgetown waterfront beneath Key Bridge, is open daily mid-April to November (check website for hours) for canoe and kayak rentals. Foggy Bottom is the closest Metro station. There is a second boathouse in the Capital Riverfront neighborhood, at Potomac Avenue SE and First Street SE.

From mid-March to mid-October, weather permitting, you can rent **paddleboats ★** on the north end of the Tidal Basin off Independence Avenue (www.tidalbasinpaddleboats.com; ⓒ 202/479-2426). Four-seaters are $26 an hour, two-seaters $16 an hour, from 10am to 6pm daily mid-March to Labor Day, Wednesday to Sunday Labor Day to mid-October. New as of spring 2016 are motorized two-seater "swan boats," for those who need a little help in getting around on the water; the charge is $30 an hour.

## Golf

The District's best and most convenient public golf course is the historic **East Potomac Golf Course** on Hains Point, 972 Ohio Dr. SW, in East Potomac Park (www.golfdc.com; ⓒ 202/554-7660). Golfers use the Washington Monument to help them line up their shots. The club rents everything but shoes. In addition to its three courses, one 18-hole and two 9-hole greens, the park offers a miniature golf course; open since 1930, this is the oldest continually operating miniature golf course in the country.

## Hiking & Jogging

Washington has numerous **hiking paths.** The C&O Canal offers 184.5 miles stretching from D.C. to Cumberland, Maryland; hiking any section of the flat dirt towpath or its more rugged side paths is a pleasure (and it's free). There are picnic tables, some with barbecue grills, about every 5 miles on the way to Cumberland. Theodore Roosevelt Island has more than 88.5 wilderness acres to explore, and Rock Creek Park boasts 20 miles of hiking trails (visit www.nps.gov/rocr/planyourvisit/brochures.htm for maps).

**Joggers** can enjoy a run on the National Mall, along the path in Rock Creek Park, and around the 3.5-mile roadway that loops the 327-acre **East Potomac Park** (part of National Mall and Memorial Parks, www.nps.gov/nama/planyourvisit/outdooractivities.htm) and takes you to Hains Point, the East Potomac Golf Course (see above) and Tennis Courts (see below).

# Ice Skating

Georgetown's waterfront complex, **The Washington Harbour,** at 3050 K St. NW (www.thewashingtonharbour.com/ice-skating; ✆ **202/706-7666**), opened an ice rink in 2012 that, at 11,800 square feet, is the largest outdoor skating venue in the city. (The view of the Potomac River ain't bad either.) The season runs November to March, and the rink is open Monday and Tuesday noon to 7pm, Wednesday and Thursday noon to 9pm, Friday noon to 10pm, Saturday 10am to 10pm, and Sunday 10am to 7pm.

For a truly memorable experience, head to the **National Gallery Sculpture Garden Ice Rink ★,** on the Mall at 7th Street and Constitution Avenue NW (✆ **202/289-3360**), where you can rent skates, twirl in view of the sculptures, and enjoy hot chocolate in the Pavilion Café next to the rink. This ice rink is also open daily, November into March.

The Capitol Riverfront neighborhood has its own figure-eight-shaped ice rink in **Canal Park,** www.canalparkdc.org, open daily in winter.

Each of these ice rinks charges for skate rentals and skating.

# Swimming

If it's summer and your hotel doesn't have a **pool,** you might consider one of the neighborhood pools, including a large outdoor pool at 25th and N streets NW (✆ **202/727-3285**) and the Georgetown outdoor pool at 34th Street and Volta Place NW (✆ **202/645-5669**). Keep in mind that these are likely to be crowded.

One of the best places open to the public for swimming in summer and for other outdoor sports year-round (see sections on golf and jogging, above, and tennis, below) is **Hains Point,** in **East Potomac Park,** which lies within walking distance of Independence Avenue and has a large outdoor swimming pool (✆ **202/727-6523**).

For a list of public indoor and outdoor pools in D.C., access the DC Parks and Recreation website, www.dpr.dc.gov, and click on the "Aquatic Facilities" link within the "Parks and Facilities" tab.

# Tennis

**Hains Point** also has 24 tennis courts (10 clay, 9 outdoor hard courts, and 5 indoor hard courts), including three illuminated at night; the park rents rackets as well; contact East Potomac Park Tennis (www.eastpotomactennis.com; ✆ **202/554-5962**). Fees vary with court surface and time of play.

Finally, one other tennis option: **Montrose Park,** right next to Dumbarton Oaks (p. 189), in Georgetown, has several courts available free on a first-come, first-served basis, but they're often in use.

# SHOPPING

Washington, D.C.'s shopping scene is thriving, thanks to the city's strong economy. With its low unemployment rate, high-income population, and vigorous spending statistics for both visitors and residents, Washington continues to attract major retailers to open stores here. Local entrepreneurs, meanwhile, are also doing quite nicely, thank you very much. Wherever you are in the city, shops present a variety of wares, prices, and styles. This chapter leads you to some of the best.

## THE SHOPPING SCENE

Most Washington-area stores are open from 10am to 5 or 6pm Monday through Saturday. Sunday hours vary, with some stores opting not to open at all and others just from noon to 5 or 6pm. Many stores in Georgetown and at Union Station keep later hours and are also open on Sunday. Other exceptions include antiques stores and art galleries, which tend to keep their own hours.

Sales tax on merchandise is 5.75% in the District, 6% in Maryland, and 6% in Northern Virginia. Most gift, arts, and crafts stores, including those at the Smithsonian museums, will handle shipping; clothing stores generally do not.

## GREAT SHOPPING AREAS

**UNION STATION**   It's a railroad station, a historic landmark, an architectural marvel, and a shopping mall. Yes, the beauteous Union Station offers some fine shopping opportunities; it's certainly the best on Capitol Hill, with more than 60 clothes, specialty, and souvenir shops. **Metro:** Union Station.

**PENN QUARTER**   The area bounded east and west by 7th and 14th streets NW, and north and south by New York and Pennsylvania avenues NW, continues to develop as a central shopping area. At the northern end of the quarter, the residential/office/dining/retail complex, CityCenterDC (on H St. NW, between 9th and 11th sts.), beckons 1 percenters and the curious to its high-end shops, Dior to David Yurman; but local enterprises are also here, including a weekly farmers' market and outdoor yoga classes. Plus, the design of the site is cool, so check it out. The Penn Quarter has plenty of national chains such as Urban Outfitters; Bed, Bath & Beyond; H&M; Forever 21; and Anthropologie, as well as one-of-a-kind

An art stall in the Penn Quarter's holiday market.

stores like the museum shops at the National Building Museum, the Smithsonian American Art Museum and Portrait Gallery, and the International Spy Museum. Macy's (formerly "Hecht's") at 12th and G streets, continues as the sole department store downtown. **Metro:** Metro Center, Gallery Place–Chinatown, or Archives–Navy Memorial.

**ADAMS MORGAN**   Centered on 18th Street and Columbia Road NW, Adams Morgan is a neighborhood of ethnic eateries and nightclubs interspersed with the odd secondhand bookshop and eclectic collectibles stores. It's a fun area for walking and shopping. For the closest **Metro,** you have a few choices: Woodley Park–Zoo/Adams Morgan, then walk south on Connecticut Avenue NW until you reach Calvert Street, cross Connecticut Avenue, and follow Calvert Street across the Duke Ellington Memorial Bridge until you reach the junction of Columbia Road NW and 18th Street NW. Second choice: Dupont Circle; exit at Q Street NW and walk up Connecticut Avenue NW to Columbia Road NW. Best bet: the DC Circulator bus, which runs between the McPherson Square and the Woodley Park–Zoo/Adams Morgan Metro stations.

**CONNECTICUT AVENUE/DUPONT CIRCLE**   Running from K Street north to S Street, Connecticut Avenue NW is the place to find clothing, from traditional goods at Brooks Brothers to casual duds at Gap to haute couture at Rizik's. The area closer to Dupont Circle is known for its art galleries; funky boutiques; gift, stationery, and book shops; and stores with a gay and lesbian slant. **Metro:** Farragut North at one end, Dupont Circle at the other.

**U & 14TH STREET CORRIDORS**   Urbanistas have been promoting this neighborhood for years, but now the number of cool shops has hit critical mass, winning the area widespread notice. If you shun brand names and box stores, you'll love the vintage boutiques and affordable fashion shops along U and 14th streets. Look for provocative handles, like Miss Pixie's Furnishings and Whatnot. **Metro:** U Street/African American Civil War Memorial/Cardozo.

**GEORGETOWN**  If you don't want to mess around, just head to Georgetown. This is and always will be the city's main shopping area. There are more than 150 clothes and accessories stores, over 70 interior-design stores and art galleries, and 40+ salons and spas. Most of the stores sit on the two main, intersecting streets, Wisconsin Avenue and M Street NW. You'll find both chain and one-of-a-kind shops, chic as well as thrift. Sidewalks and streets are almost always crowded, and parking can be tough. **Metro:** Foggy Bottom, then catch the DC Circulator bus from the stop at 22nd Street and Pennsylvania Avenue (see p. 296 for more information). Metro buses (the no. 30 series) travel through Georgetown from different parts of the city. Otherwise, consider taking a taxi.

**UPPER WISCONSIN AVENUE NORTHWEST**  In a residential section of town known as Friendship Heights on the D.C. side and Chevy Chase on the Maryland side (7 miles north of Georgetown, straight up Wisconsin Ave.) is a quarter-mile shopping district that extends from Saks Fifth Avenue at one end to Sur La Table at the other. In between are malls, department stores, and top designer boutiques. The street is too wide and traffic always too snarled to make this a pleasant place to stroll, although teenagers do love to loiter here. Drive if you want and park in the garages beneath the Mazza Gallerie, Chevy Chase Pavilion, or Bloomingdale's. Or take the **Metro;** the strip is on the Red Line, with the "Friendship Heights" exits leading directly into each of the malls.

**OLD TOWN ALEXANDRIA**  Old Town, a Virginia neighborhood beyond National Airport, resembles Georgetown in its picturesque location on the Potomac, streets lined with historic homes, and plentiful shops, as well as in its less desirable aspects: heavy traffic, crowded sidewalks, difficult parking. Old Town extends from the Potomac River in the east to the King Street Metro station in the west, and from about 1st Street in the north to Green Street in the south, but the best shopping is in the center, where King and Washington streets intersect. Weekdays are a lot tamer than weekends. It's always a nice place to visit, though (see chapter 9, p. 240); the drive alone is worth the trip. **Metro:** King Street, then take a free King Street Trolley to reach the heart of Old Town.

# SHOPPING A TO Z

## Antiques

Georgetown has a concentration of great antiques stores, but Adams Morgan and the U and 14th Street Corridors are worth scoping out.

**Brass Knob Architectural Antiques** ★  When old homes and office buildings are demolished in the name of progress, these savvy salvage merchants spirit away salable treasures, from lots and lots of light fixtures and chandelier glass to wrought-iron fencing. 2311 18th St. NW. www.thebrassknob. com. ✆ **202/332-3370.** Metro: Woodley Park or Dupont Circle, with a 20 min. walk, or take the DC Circulator bus.

**Cote Jardin Antiques ★★**   This very pretty shop just off busy Wisconsin Avenue specializes in 18th- and 19th-century French formal and country antique home furnishings and late-19th- to early-20th-century antique French garden ornaments and furniture. 3218 O St. NW. www.cotejardinantiques.com. ℂ **800/505-3067** or 202/333-3067. Metro: Foggy Bottom, then take the DC Circulator bus.

**Marston Luce Antiques ★★**   The shop's focus since opening in 1981 has been on 18th- and 19th-century painted furniture, folk art, pottery, and garden items, specifically from Sweden and France. The owner lives more than half the year in Dordogne, France, and his inventory often reflects that provenance. 1651 Wisconsin Ave. NW. www.marstonluce.com. ℂ **202/333-6800.** Metro: Foggy Bottom, then take the DC Circulator bus.

**Old Print Gallery ★★**   Open since 1971, this gallery carries original American and European prints from the 17th to the 19th centuries, including political cartoons, maps, and historical documents. It's one of the largest antique print and map shops in the U.S. Prices range from $45 to $10,000. 1220 31st St. NW. www.oldprintgallery.com. ℂ **202/965-1818.** Metro: Foggy Bottom, then take the DC Circulator bus.

## Art Galleries

Art galleries used to center on the Dupont Circle neighborhood, but now are scattered throughout the city. The following are among the best.

**Addison/Ripley Fine Art ★**   Representing internationally, nationally, and regionally recognized artists, Addison/Ripley hosts frequent exhibits. Works include paintings, sculpture, photography, and fine art. 1670 Wisconsin Ave. NW (Reservoir Rd.). www.addisonripleyfineart.com. ℂ **202/338-5180.** Metro: Foggy Bottom, then take the DC Circulator bus.

**Foundry Gallery ★**   Established in 1971, Foundry is non-profit and artist-owned and -operated. It features the pieces of local artists, who work in various media and styles, from abstract painting on silk to mixed-media collages. The gallery moved in summer 2015 from the Dupont Circle neighborhood to the U and 14th Street Corridors. 2118 8th St. NW (between U and V sts.). www.foundrygallery.org. ℂ **202/232-0203.** Metro: U St./Cardozo (10th St. exit).

**Hillyer Art Space ★**   Situated in a restored historic carriage house, this hip three-room gallery lies in an alley behind the Phillips Collection. Its shows of contemporary art fulfill its mission to "increase cross-cultural understanding and exposure to the arts internationally." Hillyer hosts First Friday events that draw social 20-somethings. 9 Hillyer Court NW (21st St.). www.hillyerartspace.org. ℂ **202/338-0325.** Metro: Dupont Circle (Q St. exit).

**Studio Gallery ★**   Studio is the city's oldest and most successful cooperative gallery, in existence for 61 years. Studio represents American and international artists, whose works are in all mediums: paintings, sculpture, installations, video, and mixed media. Don't miss the sculpture garden. Open Wednesday through Saturday. 2108 R St. NW (20th St.). www.studiogallerydc.com. ℂ **202/232-8734.** Metro: Dupont Circle (Q St. exit).

**Susan Calloway Fine Arts** ★   On display are antique European and American oil paintings; contemporary art by local, regional, and international artists; and a carefully chosen selection of 17th- to 19th-century prints. 1643 Wisconsin Ave. NW (Q St.). www.callowayart.com. ℂ **202/965-4601.** Metro: Foggy Bottom, then take the DC Circulator bus.

## Beauty

The city's best hair salons and cosmetic stores are in Georgetown, while spas are more evenly scattered throughout the city.

**Blue Mercury** ★   Half "apothecary," half spa, this chain's five D.C. locations offer a full selection of facial, massage, waxing, and makeup treatments, as well as a smorgasbord of high-end beauty products, from Acqua di Parma fragrances to Kiehl's skincare line. Very popular. www.bluemercury.com. Georgetown: 3059 M St. NW; ℂ **202/965-1300;** Metro: Foggy Bottom, then take the DC Circulator bus. Dupont Circle: 1619 Connecticut Ave. NW (ℂ **202/462-1300**) and 1145 Connecticut Ave. NW (ℂ **202/628-5567);** Metro: Dupont Circle (Q St. exit). **Union Station:** ℂ **202/289-5008**; Metro: Union Station. U and 14th St. Corridors: 1425 P St. NW (ℂ 202/238-0001).

**George at the Four Seasons** ★★   If you have a hair emergency or just need a cut or styling and don't want to take any chances, George is a safe bet. The salon has been the Four Seasons Hotel's in-house salon for so long—at least 30 years—that one might wonder if there really is a George at George. Of course! George Ozturk has a devoted following, as do his team of nine. In addition to hair services, the salon offers waxing, makeup, and nail treatments. 2828 Pennsylvania Ave. NW (in the Four Seasons Hotel). www.georgefourseasonssalon.com. ℂ **202/342-1942.** Metro: Foggy Bottom, then take the DC Circulator bus.

**Gloria's Hair Salon** ★   Gloria Piedra, formerly of Interiano Salon, is gifted in coloring, cutting, and styling hair. I should know: I've been going to her for at least 25 years, and my husband has been going to Gloria for probably 35 years. Gloria concentrates on hair only, with coloring a specialty (no nail or spa services). She counts local politicians and known-names among her clientele, but that's all I'm saying. 3058 M St. NW. ℂ **202/333-3455.** Metro: Foggy Bottom, then take the DC Circulator bus.

## Books

Real live bookstores still have many fans. Here are some favorite shops in general, used, and special-interest categories.

**Bridge Street Books** ★   A small, serious shop specializing in politics, poetry, literature, history, philosophy, and publications you won't find elsewhere. Bestsellers and discounted books are not its specialty. 2814 Pennsylvania Ave. NW (next to the Four Seasons Hotel). ℂ **202/965-5200.** Metro: Foggy Bottom, then take the DC Circulator bus.

**Capitol Hill Books** ★   This longtime, local favorite used-book store has books piled in every possible bit of space throughout the two-story shop located directly across the street from Eastern Market. Look for foreign language books in the bathroom, cookbooks in the kitchen sink; mysteries get their own Mystery Room, fiction its own Fiction Room. Open daily. 657 C St. SE. www.capitolhillbooks-dc.com. ℭ **202/544-1621.** Metro: Eastern Market.

**Kramerbooks & Afterwords Cafe ★★★**   Opened in 1976, Kramer's was the first bookstore/cafe in Washington, maybe in this country, and has launched countless romances. It's jammed and often noisy, stages author readings and other events, and is open until 3am on weekends. Paperback fiction takes up most of its inventory, but the store carries a little of everything. 1517 Connecticut Ave. NW. www.kramers.com. ℭ **202/387-1400** or 202/387-3825 for information. Metro: Dupont Circle (Q St. exit).

**Politics and Prose Bookstore ★★★**   Located a few miles north of downtown in a residential area, this much-cherished two-story shop may be

worth going out of your way for. It has vast offerings in literary fiction and nonfiction alike and an excellent children's department. The store has expanded again and again over the years to accommodate its clientele's love of books in every genre, as well as a growing selection of greeting cards, journals, and other gift items. The shop hosts author readings nearly every night of the year. A warm, knowledgeable staff will help you find what you need. Downstairs is a cozy coffeehouse. 5015 Connecticut Ave. NW. www.politics-prose.com. ℭ **202/ 364-1919.** Metro: Van Ness–UDC, and walk, or transfer to an "L" bus to take you the ¾ mile from there.

Enjoy author readings at Politics and Prose bookstore in Cleveland Park.

**Reiter's Bookstore ★**   Open since 1936, Reiter's is D.C.'s oldest independent bookstore. Located in the middle of the George Washington University campus, it's the go-to place for scientific, technical, medical, and professional books. The store is also known for its intriguing, sometimes amusing, mathematical and scientific toys in the children's section. 1900 G St. NW (19th St.). www.reiters.com. ℭ **202/223-3327.** Metro: Foggy Bottom.

**Second Story Books ★**   If it's old, out of print, custom bound, or a small-press publication, you'll find it here. The store also specializes in used CDs and vinyl and has an interesting collection of campaign posters. 2000 P St. NW. www.secondstorybooks.com. ℭ **202/659-8884.** Metro: Dupont Circle (South/19th St. exit).

## Cameras & Computers

**Apple Store ★**   Come to hang out and fool around on the floor samples, to check out the merchandise, and to get your questions answered by techy geeks roaming the room. 1229 Wisconsin Ave. NW. www.apple.com/retail/georgetown. © **202/572-1460.** Metro: Foggy Bottom, then take the DC Circulator bus.

**Leica Camera** ★   This store is one of only six that the German company has opened in the U.S. If you know your way around cameras and don't mind spending a bit of money, this shop will likely take you to paradise. *FYI:* This store also sells used equipment and occasionally sponsors photo walks at beauteous locations around the city. 977 F St. NW. www.leicastoredc.com. © **202/787-5900.** Metro: Gallery Place (9th and G sts. exit).

# Clothing

## CHILDREN'S CLOTHING

Also consider **Macy's** department store at 1201 G St. NW (© **202/628-6661**), in the Penn Quarter; and **GapKids** at 1258 Wisconsin Ave. NW (© **202/333-2657**) in Georgetown, and at 664 11th St. NW (© **202/347-0258** in the Penn Quarter.

**Little Birdies Boutique** ★   This precious little shop sells precious little clothes for precious little children, newborns to size 10. Young Versace, Darling Betty, and Petite Lucette are among the brands on sale. 1526 Wisconsin Ave. NW. www.shoplittlebirdies.com. © **202/333-1059.** Metro: Foggy Bottom, then take the DC Circulator bus.

## MEN'S & WOMEN'S CLOTHING

See the "Great Shopping Areas" (p. 205) section if you're interested in such chain stores as **Urban Outfitters, Gap, Brooks Brothers,** or **Zara.** Below are stores that speak more to the fashion zeitgeist of D.C.

**Avenue Jack** ★   *Washington City Paper* staff in 2016 named this newcomer the city's best men's apparel shop. It's about casual men's clothes, both known lines such as Bread & Boxers and LaCoste, and independent brands such as Bluebuck and Keyway. The shop also stocks D.C.-themed gifts, like Washington Monument–illustrated iPhone cases. 1301 Connecticut Ave. NW. www.avenuejack.myshopify.com. © **202/887-5225.** Metro: Dupont Circle (South/19th St. exit).

**Betsy Fisher** ★★   A walk past the store is all it takes to know that this shop is a tad different. Its windows and racks show off whimsically feminine fashions, shoes, and accessories by new American, French, and Italian designers. Access the website to find out about upcoming events; Betsy Fisher often hosts an evening cocktail hour to introduce a new line or inventory. 1224 Connecticut Ave. NW. http://betsyfisher.com. © **202/785-1975.** Metro: Dupont Circle (South/19th St. exit).

**Maketto** ★★   It's a cafe, it's a bar, it's a store, it's an award-winning restaurant—it's all of that and more. Maketto the shop is primarily about menswear, its inventory of international footwear, clothing, and accessories laid out in glass display cases and on open shelving. Puma, Comme des Garcons, Vans, and Born X Raised are among the brands. Walk to the rear of the shop on the first floor to reach the courtyard where, in nice weather, you can have a bite to eat while you admire your purchases. 1351 H St. NE. www.maketto1351.com. ©**202/838-9972.** Metro: Union Station, then catch the DC Streetcar to the Atlas District.

**Proper Topper ★★** For the longest time, I thought this store was just a hat boutique. Then my husband came home satisfied at Christmas time, delighted at finding this "one-stop shop" for stocking presents and bigger gifts for his girls, me included. I totally approve: lovely designs by Velvet and Nanette Lepore, pretty jewelry, adorable clothes for children, stationery, all sorts of gifty things, and yes, hats. 1350 Connecticut Ave. NW. www.propertopper.com. ©**202/842-3055.** Metro: Dupont Circle (19th St. exit).

**Rizik's ★★** Rizik's is 109 years old, and still working it. This downtown high-fashion store sells bridal dresses and other high-toned fashions by European and American designers such as Carolina Herrera, Sylvia Heisel, and Lourdes Chavez, but lately has expanded to sell designer sportswear and more casual lines. 1100 Connecticut Ave. NW. www.riziks.com. ©**202/223-4050.** Metro: Farragut North (L St. exit).

**Sherman Pickey ★** This store is prep to the max, but also a little fey: Think red corduroys. Both men's and women's clothes are on sale here, including Bills Khakis and Dapper Classics socks for men; Lily Pulitzer, Gigi NY, embroidered capris, and ribbon belts for women. 1647 Wisconsin Ave. NW. www.shermanpickey.com. ©**202/333-4212.** Metro: Foggy Bottom, then take the DC Circulator bus.

**Violet Boutique ★** This Adams Morgan shop is a favorite of fashionistas on a budget. Feminine and trendy, the offerings range from cocktail dresses to colorful tee shirts, everything priced under $100. 2439 18th St. NW. www.violetdc.com. ©**202/621-9225.** Metro: Woodley Park or Dupont Circle, with a 20 min. walk, or take the DC Circulator bus.

### VINTAGE SHOPS

**Meeps ★★** Meeps is aimed at male and female urbanistas attracted to local designer ware and vintage clothes, from 1930s gabardine suits to 1950s cocktail dresses to satiny lingerie. 2104 18th St. NW. www.meepsdc.com. ©**202/265-6546.** Metro: U St./Cardozo (13th St. exit) or Woodley Park–Zoo, with a bit of a walk from either station.

**Secondi Inc. ★** On the second floor of a building right above Starbucks is this high-style consignment shop that sells women's clothing and accessories, including designer suits, evening wear, and more casual items—everything from Kate Spade to Chanel. Open since 1986, Secondi is the longest-running designer consignment shop for women in D.C. 1702 Connecticut Ave. NW (btw. R St. and Florida Ave.). www.secondi.com. ©**202/667-1122.** Metro: Dupont Circle (Q St. exit).

## Crafts

**A Mano ★★** Owner Adam Mahr frequently forages in Europe and returns with the unique handmade French and Italian ceramics, linens, and other decorative accessories for home and garden that you'll covet here. 1677 Wisconsin Ave. NW. www.amano.bz. ✆ **202/298-7200.** Metro: Foggy Bottom, then take the DC Circulator bus.

**Appalachian Spring** ★   Country comes to Georgetown. This store sells pottery, jewelry, newly made pieced and appliqué quilts, stuffed dolls and animals, candles, rag rugs, handblown glassware, an incredible collection of kaleidoscopes, glorious weavings, and wooden kitchenware. Everything is made by hand in the United States. 1415 Wisconsin Ave. NW (at P St.). www.appalachianspring.com. ✆ **800/763-4293** or 202/337-5780. Metro: Foggy Bottom, then take the DC Circulator bus. There's another branch in Union Station (✆ **202/682-0505**).

**Indian Craft Shop** ★★   The Indian Craft Shop has represented authentic Native-American artisans since 1938, selling their handwoven rugs and hand-crafted baskets, jewelry, figurines, pottery, and other items. Since the shop is situated inside a federal government building, you must pass through security and show a photo ID to enter. Use the C Street entrance on Saturday, the C or E Street entrance on weekdays. The shop is open weekdays and the third Saturday of each month. Department of the Interior, 1849 C St. NW, Room 1023. www.indiancraftshop.com. ✆ **202/208-4056.** Metro: Farragut West (17th St. exit), with a bit of a walk from the station.

**The Phoenix** ★   Around since 1955, the Phoenix sells high-end Mexican folk and fine art; handcrafted sterling silver jewelry from Mexico and all over the world; clothing in natural fibers from Mexican and American designers like Eileen Fisher and Flax; collectors' quality masks; and decorative doodads in tin, brass, copper, and wood. Oaxaca folk and fine art are a specialty. 1514 Wisconsin Ave. NW. www.thephoenixdc.com. ✆ **202/338-4404.** Metro: Foggy Bottom, then take the DC Circulator.

**Torpedo Factory Art Center** ★★   Once a munitions factory, this three-story building built in 1918 now houses more than 82 working studios, 7 galleries, and the works of about 165 artists, who tend to their crafts before your very eyes, pausing to explain their techniques or to sell their pieces. Artworks include paintings, sculpture, ceramics, glasswork, and textiles. 105 N. Union St., Alexandria, VA. www.torpedofactory.org. ✆ **703/838-4565.** Metro: King St., then take the free King Street Trolley or the DASH bus (AT2, AT5) eastbound to the waterfront.

## Farmers' & Flea Markets

**Dupont Circle FreshFarm Market** ★   About 50 local farmers sell their flowers, fruits, vegetables, meat, poultry, fish, bread, eggs, and cheeses here. The market sometimes features kids' activities, live music, and guest appearances by chefs of some of D.C.'s best restaurants. Sundays rain or shine, year-round, from 10am to 1pm January through March and 8:30am to 1:30pm the rest of the year. The FreshFarm Market organization stages other farmers' markets on other days around town; see the website for info. On 20th St. NW (btw. Q St. and Massachusetts Ave.) and in the adjacent PNC Bank parking lot. www.freshfarmmarkets.org. ✆ **202/362-8889.** Metro: Dupont Circle (Q St. exit).

**Eastern Market ★★★** Historic Eastern Market has been in continuous operation since 1873. Today Eastern Market's restored South Hall is a bustling bazaar, where area farmers, greengrocers, bakers, butchers, and others sell their wares Tuesday through Sunday, joined by a second line of farmers outside on Tuesdays 3 to 7pm; on the weekend, 100 or so local artisans hawk jewelry, paintings, pottery, woodwork, and other handmade items. Best of all is the Saturday morning ritual of breakfasting on blueberry pancakes at the Market Lunch counter. The indoor market is open Tuesday to Friday 7am to 7pm, Saturday 7am to 6pm, and Sunday 9am to 5pm. 225 7th St. SE (North Carolina Ave.). www.easternmarket-dc.org. ℭ **202/698-5253.** Metro: Eastern Market.

Eastern Market.

**Old Town Alexandria Farmers' Market ★** The oldest continuously operating farmers' market in the country (since 1753), this market offers locally grown fruits and vegetables, along with delectable baked goods, cut flowers, and more. Open year-round, Saturday mornings from 7am to noon. 301 King St. (at Market Square in front of the city hall), in Alexandria, VA. www.alexandriava.gov/market. ℭ **703/746-3200.** Metro: King St., then take the free King St. Trolley or the DASH bus (AT2, AT5) eastbound to Market Sq.

**Union Market ★** Worth a detour from sightseeing is this year-round indoor market, whose offerings include pop-up marketers hawking their particular specialty, like small-batch pickles. At least 40 vendors set up in stalls or at counters selling fresh produce, flowers, cheeses, artworks—everything from olive oil to oysters. Stop by Salt & Sundry for lovely handcrafted gifts; visit Sundays at noon and join a yoga class. There's always something popping up. Open Tuesday to Friday 11am to 8pm, Saturday and Sunday 8am to 8pm. 1309 Fifth St. NE. www.unionmarketdc.com. ℭ 202/347-3998. Metro: NoMA–Gallaudet–U St.

## Gifts/Souvenirs

See also "Crafts," earlier in this chapter, the Eastern Market listing above (weekend artisans sell excellent take-home gifts, like Jeannette Landphair's glazed tile coasters each bearing an image of an iconic D.C. scene), and Hill's Kitchen under "Home Furnishings," below. Museum gift shops (see chapter 6) are another good source. Also check out the **White House Historical Association Gift Shops** (www.whitehousehistory.org, then click on "Our Museum

Shops" at the bottom of the page) at Decatur House (1610 H St. NW; © **202/ 218-4337**) and at the White House Visitor Center (1450 Pennsylvania Ave. NW; © **202/208-7031**); see p. 169. The shops sell interesting memorabilia, such as the White House Christmas tree ornament newly designed each year, and sundry items related to the White House and its history.

**America!** ★ Stop here if you want to pick up a baseball cap with COM-MANDER IN CHIEF printed across its bill; a T-shirt proclaiming I LOVE MY COUNTRY, IT'S THE GOVERNMENT I'M AFRAID OF; White House guest towels or coasters; or other impress-the-folks-back-home items. Union Station. © **202/842-0540**. www.marshallretailgroup.com. Metro: Union Station. Or save your shopping for the airport; America! has at least one location at National, two at BWI, and two at Dulles.

**Chocolate Moose** ★ Its website welcomes browsers with the words "Serving weirdly sophisticated Washingtonians since 1978, but now attempting to reach out to the rest of you!" I guess my family qualifies as weirdly sophisticated, because we're longtime fans. My husband endears himself to me and our daughters when he brings home gifts from this shop: a Wonder Woman daybook; chunky, transparent, red heart-shaped earrings; wacky cards; kimonocovered hair clips; eccentric clothing; and other funny presents. 1743 L St. NW. www.chocolatemoosedc.com. © **202/463-0992**. Metro: Farragut North (L St. exit).

## Home Furnishings

You may not have come to Washington to shop for housewares or furnishings, but step inside the shops of Cady's Alley or Home Rule and you may change your mind.

**Cady's Alley** ★ Cady's Alley refers not to a single store, but to the southwest pocket of Georgetown, where about 20 stores reside in and around said alley, which lies south of M Street. Look for tony, big-name places such as Waterworks and Design within Reach; European outposts, such as the hip kitchen furnishings of Bulthaup; and high-concept design stores, such as Contemporaria. 3318 M St. NW (btw. 33rd and 34th sts.). www.cadysalley.com. Metro: Foggy Bottom, then take the DC Circulator bus.

**Hill's Kitchen** ★★ This gourmet kitchenware store occupies an 1884 town house adjacent to the Eastern Market Metro station on Capitol Hill. Precious take-homes are cookie cutters shaped like the Washington Monument and the Capitol dome; topflight cooking utensils; colorful aprons and towels; and specialty foods. 713 D St. SE. www.hillskitchen.com. © **202/543-1997**. Metro: Eastern Market.

**Home Rule** ★ Unique housewares; bath, kitchen, and office supplies; and gifts cram this tiny store. You'll see everything from French milled soap to martini glasses. 1807 14th St. NW (at S St.). www.homerule.com. © **202/797-5544**. Metro: U St./Cardozo (13th St. exit).

**Miss Pixie's Furnishings & Whatnot** ★ The name says it all. Vintage home furnishings from armoires to old silver cram the space. The owner buys only from auctions and only things that are in good shape and ready to use. New inventory arrives every Wednesday. 1626 14th St. NW. www.misspixies.com. © **202/232-8171.** Metro: U St./Cardozo (13th St. exit).

## Jewelry

**Bloom ★**   Shop here for costume jewelry that doesn't look like costume jewelry, at prices that are actually affordable, say $30 for a fine necklace, $10 for stud earrings. The shop also sells sterling silver pieces and semiprecious stones, and assorted other items, like soaps and towels. 1719 Connecticut Ave NW. www.yelp.com/biz/bloom-washington-7. © **202/621-9049.** Metro: Dupont Circle (Q St. exit).

**Mia Gemma ★**   This pretty boutique sells the original designs of American and European artists, including Judy Bettencourt, Sarah Richardson, and Randi Chervitz. All pieces are handcrafted, either of limited edition or one of a kind. If you'd like a customized design, Mia Gemma can do that, too. 933 F St. NW. www.miagemma.com. © **202/393-4367.** Metro: Gallery Place/Verizon Center (9th St. exit).

**Tiny Jewel Box ★★**   Opened and owned by the same family since 1930, this jewelry store is the first place Washingtonians go for estate and antique jewelry, engagement rings, and the finest brands of watches. Tiny Jewel Box also sells the pieces of many designers, from Links of London to Alex Sepkus, as well as crystal and other house gifts. In the month leading up to Mother's Day, the Tiny Jewel Box holds its top-to-bottom sale, where you can save anywhere from 10% to 75% on most merchandise. The four-story store near the Mayflower Hotel expanded in 2015 to twice its original size, so that now the store extends down the block, rounding the corner of Connecticut Avenue and M Street. 1147 Connecticut Ave. NW. www.tinyjewelbox.com. © **202/393-2747.** Metro: Farragut North (L St. exit).

## Shoes

**Comfort One Shoes ★**   This locally owned family business was founded in Old Town Alexandria in 1993. Its three D.C. stores (of about 20 in the area) sell a great selection of popular styles for both men and women, including Doc Martens, Birkenstocks, and Ecco. You can always find something that looks good and actually feels comfortable. 1630 Connecticut Ave. NW. www.comfortoneshoes.com. © **202/328-3141.** Metro: Dupont Circle. Also at 1625 Connecticut Ave. NW (© **202/667-5789**), Union Station (© **202/898-2430**), and several other locations.

**Hu's Shoes ★**   Fashion models in every D.C. photo shoot wear Hu's shoes, it seems. The Georgetown shop sells designer ready-to-wear footwear, handbags, and accessories. Owner Marlene Hu Aldaba travels to New York, Paris, and Milan in search of elegant specimens to suit her discriminating eye. Across the street, at 2906 M St. NW, is Hu's Wear, a two-level store selling designer outfits to accompany the darling shoes. 3005 M St. NW. www.husonline.com. © **202/342-0202.** Metro: Foggy Bottom, then walk or take the DC Circulator bus.

# Wine & Spirits

**Barmy Wines & Liquors** ★   Located near the White House, this store sells it all, but with special emphasis on fine wines and rare cordials. 1912 L St. NW. www.barmywines.com. ℂ **202/833-8730.** Metro: Farragut North (L St. exit).

**Central Liquors** ★   This store, which opened in 1934, is like a clearing-house for liquor: Its great volume allows the store to offer the best prices in town. The store carries more than 250 single-malt scotches. 625 E St. NW. www.centralliquors.com. ℂ **202/737-2800.** Metro: Gallery Place (9th and F sts. exit).

**Schneider's of Capitol Hill** ★   Two blocks south of Union Station is this family-run liquor store, in business for nearly 70 years. With a knowl-edgeable and enthusiastic staff, a 12,000-bottle inventory of wine, and a fine selection of spirits and beer, this shop is a find on Capitol Hill. 300 Massachu-setts Ave. NE. www.cellar.com. ℂ **800/377-1461** or 202/543-9300. Metro: Union Station.

# ENTERTAINMENT & NIGHTLIFE

Nightlife in the capital is rollicking and diverse. You can play putt-putt golf and shuffleboard at the H Street Country Club in the Atlas District (p. 226), dance your heart out at Marvin (p. 226) on 14th Street, take a turn at live-band karaoke at Hill Country Barbecue (p. 226) in the Penn Quarter, or settle in for top-notch jazz at Blues Alley (p. 228) in Georgetown. The internationally renowned John F. Kennedy Center for the Performing Arts (p. 220) is the city's crown jewel, hosting more than 3,000 world-class performances annually in every genre, opera to dramatic theater. But smaller, excellent venues abound, too, offering a variety of experiences in stage productions, live music, nightclubs, comedy, and, of course, serious drinking. Washington's nightlife scene serves up something for everyone.

The truth is that D.C. nightlife is not only vigorous but also competitive. One-third of the city's population is between 20 and 35; thanks to the capital's strong economy, most people have jobs and are ready to party. But in this hard-charging city, most everyone, from government wonks to expense-account attorneys, are ready to seek entertainment after a long day at the desk.

The best neighborhoods for nightlife are **Adams Morgan;** the **U & 14th streets NW crossroads** (U St. between 16th and 9th sts., and 14th St. btw. P and V sts.); north and south of **Dupont Circle** along Connecticut Avenue; all over the **Penn Quarter; Georgetown; the Atlas District;** and **Columbia Heights,** an area east of Adams Morgan and north of the U Street district.

Most of D.C.'s clubs and bars stay open until 1 or 2am Monday through Thursday and until 3am Friday and Saturday; what time they open varies. It's best to call ahead or check the website.

For current concert and club offerings, check the **Washington Post's** online "Going Out Guide" (www.washingtonpost.com/goingoutguide), which covers all entertainment options, including nightlife, reported minute by minute, venue by venue, by the paper's "going out gurus." If you're here on a weekend, try to pick up a copy of the *Post's* Friday "Weekend" section. **Washington City Paper,** available free at restaurants, bookstores, and other places around town, and online at **www.washingtoncitypaper.com**, is another excellent resource. (The printed version is actually easier to read, so it's worth getting your hands on one.)

# THE PERFORMING ARTS

Washington's performing-arts scene has an international reputation. We have not just one, but two Shakespeare theaters. Our **Arena Stage** is renowned for its innovative productions of American masters and new voices. As noted above, the **Kennedy Center** reigns over all, staging something for everyone. Don't assume that these theaters present only classic renditions from a performing-arts hit list; no, they are each wildly creative in their choices and their presentations. On the other hand, for most avant-garde theater, seek out smaller stages, like **Woolly Mammoth** and **Studio** theaters.

The Kennedy Center's and Arena Stage's seasons run year-round; the Shakespeare Theatre's and the smaller theaters' seasons are nearly year-round, taking a 4- to 6-week break July into August. The Kennedy Center often has performances going on throughout the day, but all theaters hold their major productions at 7:30pm or 8pm nightly, with Saturday and Sunday matinee performances at 2pm and occasional mid-week matinee performances on the schedule, especially at Arena Stage.

The bad news is that as popular as theater-going is in the capital, **ticket prices** have gone through the roof in the past couple of years. A lot of locals subscribe to the big three (Kennedy Center, Shakespeare, Arena), which leaves fewer one-off tickets available. Expect to pay $75 to $100-plus for a ticket—unless you're able to obtain a discounted ticket directly from the theater or from a discounted ticket service; see the "Getting Tickets" box, p. 223.

## Major Theaters & Companies

**Arena Stage ★★★**    Arena Stage is located in the Southwest Waterfront neighborhood of D.C., away from the downtown area. You'll see much construction underway that will very soon make this neighborhood a happenin' place: Scheduled to open by late 2017 are at least eight restaurants, a 6,000-person-capacity concert hall run by owners of the 9:30 Club (p. 229), an Irish pub, and a couple of hotels, with many more projects in the works. Until then, Arena Stage is the neighborhood's main attraction.

And an attraction it is, drawing 300,000 people annually to its productions dedicated to "putting the American spirit in the spotlight." A major expansion in 2010 made Arena Stage D.C.'s second-largest theater space after the Kennedy Center. Officially called "The Mead Center for American Theater," the venue's three staging areas are the theater-in-the-round Fichandler, the fan-shaped Kreeger, and the intimate (200-seat), oval-shaped Kogod Cradle. Founded in 1950, Arena Stage was a pioneer and remains a leader in the regional theater movement.

Arena's 2016–17 season highlights include a Lillian Hellman Festival in which *The Little Foxes* and *Watch on the Rhine* take the stage; world-premiere

political thriller *Intelligence* by Jacqueline E. Lawton; Lorraine Hansberry's American classic *A Raisin in the Sun;* and the musical *Carousel.*

1101 6th St. SW (at Maine Ave.). www.arenastage.org. ℂ **202/488-3300** for tickets, or 202/554-9066 for general information. Tickets $40–$110; discounts available for students, those under the age of 30, patrons with disabilities, families, veterans, groups, and others. Metro: Southwest/Waterfront.

Arena Stage.

### John F. Kennedy Center for the Performing Arts ★★★

The capital's most renowned theater covers the entire realm of performing arts: Presentations of ballet, opera, plays, musicals, modern dance, jazz, comedy, classical and chamber music, and children's theater all take the stage at this magnificent complex overlooking the Potomac River. The setting is gorgeous, the productions superb. As a living memorial to President John F. Kennedy, the Center considers itself the nation's theater and is committed to fulfilling the president's mission to make the performing arts available to everyone. The Center's 3,000+ annual productions draw more than three million people.

But 2017 is a special year for the KenCen, marking the centennial of President Kennedy's birth on May 29, 1917. The Center is in the midst of a year-long celebration, partnering with three acclaimed artists, Yo-Yo Ma, Renee Fleming, and Q-Tip, to help advance new initiatives, and launching thousands of performances, including 25 commissioned or co-commissioned works and projects. But let's cut to the chase, shall we: season highlights.

The lineup is staggering, but here's a hint: musicals *Into the Woods, Wicked,* and *Cabaret;* the American Ballet's performance of *Swan Lake* and the annual engagement of the Alvin Ailey American Dance Theatre; the National Symphony Orchestra's classical series covering the masters, Tchaikovsky to

---

### Longer Than the Washington Monument Is Tall

Most Kennedy Center performances take place in theaters that lie off the Grand Foyer. But even if the one you're attending is on the Roof Terrace level, one floor up, make sure you visit the foyer anyway. The Grand Foyer is one of the largest rooms in the world. Measuring 630 feet long, 40 feet wide, and 60 feet high, the foyer is longer than the Washington Monument is tall (555⅝ ft.). Millennium Stage hosts free performances here nightly at 6pm, the famous Robert Berks sculpture of President John F. Kennedy is here, and just beyond the foyer's glass doors is the expansive terrace, which runs the length of the building and overlooks the Potomac River.

Beethoven; the Washington National Opera's premiere presentation of *The Dictator's Wife;* the New York City Public Theater's timely production of *The Gabriels: Election Year in the Life of One Family;* a robust schedule of 50 jazz concerts; a tribute concert to Pete Seeger; and several one-nighter shows featuring comics such as Kevin Nealon and Adam Carolla. And this too: The Kennedy Center, newly but permanently, is embracing hip-hop, staging several shows including **Top Notch,** a break-dance competition, and **/peh-LO-tah/,** a world premiere performance that layers poetry, movement, music, and visuals based on hip-hop culture. Honestly, you need to check out the KenCen's website.

Within this 17-acre arts facility lie eight different theaters and stages: the Opera House, the Concert Hall, the Terrace Theater, the Eisenhower Theater, the Theater Lab, the Terrace Gallery, the Family Theater, and Millennium Stage. By 2018, the theater will have expanded to include three pavilions housing additional performance and education spaces, as well as a pedestrian bridge arching over Rock Creek Parkway, connecting the Kennedy Center to the Potomac Riverfront.

Visit the KenCen to attend a performance, for sure, but also consider stopping by for one of the free guided tours, which take place throughout the day. Finish the visit by attending the free "Millennium Stage" performance, mostly concerts, but also dance, theater, comedy, and other forms of entertainment, staged every single evening at 6pm in the Grand Foyer, each night featuring a different act, local artists sometimes, but nationally known and international performers, too, and often performers appearing on stage later that evening in one of the Center's main theaters.

Otherwise, expect to pay ticket prices that range from $15 for a family concert to $300 for opera; most tickets cost between $45 and $100.

Whatever performance you attend, make sure you head out to the terrace for a grand view of the Potomac.

2700 F St. NW (at New Hampshire Ave. NW and Rock Creek Pkwy.). www.kennedy-center.org. ☎ **800/444-1324** or 202/467-4600; 50% discounts are offered (for select performances) to students, seniors 65 and over, travelers with permanent disabilities, enlisted military personnel, and persons with fixed low incomes (☎ **202/416-8340** for details). Garage parking $23 (or pay $20 online in advance). Metro: Foggy Bottom (though it's a fairly short walk, there's a free shuttle btw. the station and the Kennedy Center, departing every 15 min. 9:45am–midnight Mon–Fri, 10am–midnight Sat, and noon–midnight Sun). Bus: 80 from Metro Center.

**National Theatre ★**    Open since 1835, the National is the capital's oldest continuously operating theater and the country's third oldest. In earlier days, the like of Sarah Bernhardt, Helen Hayes, and John Barrymore took the stage, and presidents Lincoln and Fillmore and others were among those in the audience. These days, the National is almost entirely about Broadway musicals. Among the productions coming our way in the 2016–17 season are *Once, How the Grinch Stole Christmas, Fun Home,* and *Rent.* The 1,672-seat National continues its free, family-oriented, public-service programs: Saturday-morning children's theater (puppets, clowns, magicians, dancers, and singers), and free screenings of classic films shown on select Monday nights throughout the year. 1321 Pennsylvania Ave. NW (at 13th and E sts.). www.thenationaldc.com. ✆ **202/628-6161** for general information, 202/783-3370 for info about free programs, and call 800/514-3849 or go to www.etix.com to charge tickets. Tickets $38–$153 (most are in the $70–$90 range). Metro: Metro Center (13th and G sts. exit) or Federal Triangle.

**Shakespeare Theatre Company at the Lansburgh Theatre and Sidney Harman Hall ★★★** So popular are the Shakespeare Theatre Company's productions that the company has two downtown locations (literally within a stone's throw of each other, the 451-seat **Lansburgh Theatre,** at 450 7th St. NW, and the 775-seat **Sidney Harman Hall,** at 610 F St. NW (across the street from the Verizon Center), and both houses frequently sell out. You can count on imaginative and superb performances, though not all of them are Shakespeare's works. The 2016–17 season includes tragedies *Romeo and Juliet* and *Macbeth,* but also a comedy, *The School for Lies,* based on Moliere's 17th-century masterpiece *The Misanthrope;* a musical, *The Secret Garden,* based on the children's novel of the same name, by Frances Hodgson Burnett; *King Charles III,* a modern history play by Mike Bartlett; and *The Select,* an adaptation of Ernest Hemingway's novel *The Sun Also Rises.* The Shakespeare Theatre also screens live performances of London's National Theatre productions, Shakespeare plays and otherwise.

An annual plum presentation is the "Free For All," which stages free performances of a Shakespeare play for 2 weeks in late August into September; *The Tempest* was the feature in 2016.

Also check out the many other events happening at the Shakespeare; the theater hosts all kinds of talks, dance performances, discussions, cocktail hours, workshops, and other events, many of which seem to target the 20- to 30-somethings. Best deal for the under-35s is the sale of $25 tickets available online with the promo code provided on the website. Lansburgh Theatre: 450 7th St. NW (btw. D and E sts.). Sidney Harman Hall: 610 F St. NW. www.shakespearetheatre.org. ✆ **202/547-1122.** Tickets $25–$110; discounts available for students, military, patrons 21–35, seniors, and groups. Metro: Archives–Navy Memorial or Gallery Place/Verizon Center (7th St./Arena exit).

## Smaller Theaters

Smaller but no less compelling, these theaters stage productions that are consistently professional and often more contemporary and daring than those you'll find in the better-known theaters. These more intimate theaters, each in a different neighborhood, have their own strong followings, which means their performances often sell out.

**Studio Theatre ★★** at 1501 14th St. NW, at P Street (www.studiotheatre.org; ✆ **202/332-3300**), since its founding in 1978, has grown in leaps and bounds into a four-theater complex, helping to revitalize this downtown neighborhood in the process. Productions are provocative and the season jam-packed, with nine plays on tap for the 2016–17 calendar. Former artistic director Joy Zinoman, who retired in 2010, helped to create buzz for

# GETTING tickets

Most performing-arts and live-music venues mentioned in this chapter require tickets, which you can purchase online at the venue's website, in person at the venue's box office, or through one of the ticket vendors listed below.

The best deals in town might be those posted on the website **www.goldstar.com.** It costs nothing to subscribe, and you'll immediately start receiving e-mail notices of hefty discounts on admission prices to performances and venues, including museums, all over the city.

**TICKETPLACE** sells discounted tickets to the arts in metropolitan Washington, D.C., online only, at **www.ticketplace.org.** TICKETPLACE is a program of the nonprofit organization, culturecapital.org.

Ticket sellers **Live Nation** (www.live-nation.com) and **Ticketmaster** (www.ticketmaster.com; ℂ **800/745-3000**) merged in January 2010, which means that you can buy full-price tickets for many performances in town from either operation. Expect to pay taxes plus a service charge, an order-processing fee, and a facility fee (if a particular venue tacks on that charge). For the same kinds of performances, also check out **www.ticketfly.com** (ℂ **877/435-9849**).

Washington's theater scene as well as for the U & 14th Street neighborhood in which Studio resides. Her legacy lives in Studio's continuing success in showcasing contemporary plays and in nurturing Washington acting talent.

The **Woolly Mammoth Theatre Company** ★★ (www.woollymammoth.net; ℂ 202/393-3939) offers as many as seven productions every year, specializing in new, offbeat, and quirky plays, often world premieres. The Woolly resides in a 265-seat, state-of-the-art facility at 641 D St. NW (at 7th St. NW), in the heart of the Penn Quarter.

In addition, I highly recommend productions staged at the **Folger Shakespeare Library** ★★, on Capitol Hill, 201 E. Capitol St. SE, at 2nd Street (www.folger.edu; ℂ 202/544-7077), which celebrates its 85th anniversary in 2017. Plays take place in the library's Elizabethan Theatre, which is styled after the inn-yard theater of Shakespeare's time. The theater is intimate and charming, the theater company is remarkably good, and an evening spent here guarantees an absolutely marvelous experience. The Elizabethan Theatre is also the setting for musical performances, lectures, readings, and other events.

## Headliner Concert Venues

When Demi Lovato, Sting, or Beyoncé come to town, they usually play at the 20,600-seat **Verizon Center,** 601 F St. NW, at 7th Street (www.verizoncenter.com; ℂ 202/628-3200). Situated in the center of downtown, the Verizon Center hosts plenty of concerts and is also Washington's premier indoor sports arena. Occasionally in summer and fall, when the Washington Nationals baseball team doesn't have a home game, headliners like Billy Joel, Taylor Swift, and Bruce Springsteen play at the 41,000-seat **Nationals Park,** 1500 S. Capitol St. SE (http://washington.nationals.mlb.com/was/ballpark/index.jsp; ℂ 202/675-6287), in the Capitol Riverfront neighborhood.

A concert at the Verizon Center.

**DAR Constitution Hall** ★★ on 18th Street NW, between C and D streets (www.dar.org; ☏ **202/628-4780**), is housed within a beautiful turn-of-the-20th-century Beaux Arts building and seats 3,746. Its excellent acoustics have supported an eclectic group of performers, from John Legend to John Fogerty.

Under management by the 9:30 Club (see p. 229), the historic **Lincoln Theatre** ★, 1215 U St. NW, at 13th Street (www.thelincolndc.com; ☏ **202/328-6000**), is once again a vital venue. Look for indie favorites such as Natalie Merchant and Neko Case in the lineup. Once a movie theater, vaudeville house, and nightclub featuring black stars such as Louis Armstrong and Cab Calloway, the theater closed in the 1970s, then reopened in 1994 after a renovation restored it to its former elegance. But somehow the theater's appeal just never took off, until the 9:30 Club stepped in, in 2013.

The **Warner Theatre** ★, 513 13th St. NW, between E and F streets (www.warnertheatredc.com; ☏ **202/783-4000**), opened in 1924 as the Earle Theatre (a movie/vaudeville palace) and was restored to its original, neoclassical-style appearance in 1992. It's worth coming by just to see its ornately detailed interior. The 2,000-seat auditorium offers year-round entertainment, alternating dance performances, like the Washington Ballet's Christmas performance of the *Nutcracker,* with comedy acts including Russell Brand, Margaret Cho, or Wanda Sykes, and seasoned rockers like The Go-Go's.

# THE BAR SCENE

Washington has a thriving and varied bar scene. But just when you think you know all the hot spots, a fresh batch pops up. Lately, it is homegrown breweries and rooftop bars that draw the largest crowds. Here's a smattering of some favorites, old and new.

**Black Jack** ★ Downstairs is the super popular **Pearl Dive Oyster Palace** (p. 102) restaurant, and upstairs is its super-cool bar. Red-velvet curtains part to reveal the fully stocked bar, and old movies project black-and-white images

Bluejacket Brewery.

on the brick walls. Other bars may have pool tables and DJs; Black Jack has two full-size bocce courts, with 19 stadium seats for spectators. Lots of comfortable red-vinyl seating, crafty cocktails, and "really good house-made pies," as in pizzas, make Black Jack everyone's favorite hangout. 1612 14th St. NW (at Corcoran St.). www.blackjackdc.com. ⓒ **202/319-1612.** Metro: U St./Cardozo (U and 13th sts. exit).

**Bluejacket Brewery ★★** A Washington Nationals baseball game at Nationals Park is one reason to visit the Capitol Riverfront neighborhood. Bluejacket is another. Opened in October 2013 by Greg Engert and his band of master brewers, the same team behind ChurchKey (see below), Bluejacket brews 20 unique ales and lagers at its three-story site, from dry-hopped ales to barleywine. You can hang out at the bar in Bluejacket's restaurant, the Arsenal, and sample a few homebrews, dine here, or take a tour. Bluejacket offers four options: a free tour ending in a complimentary tasting; a $29 per person taste-as-you-go tour on Saturday or Sunday; a $35 per person Friday night taste, snack, and tour; and a $99 per person food-and-beer tour, which concludes with a beer-pairing dinner served in the Arsenal. No tours on Nationals home game days. 300 Tingey St. SE (at 4th St.). www.bluejacketdc.com. ⓒ **202/524-4862.** Metro: Navy Yard/Ballpark (New Jersey Ave. exit).

**ChurchKey ★** This mellow hangout draws a diverse mix, boomers to their 20-something children, all sprawled upon loungey banquettes or perched on stools at the long bar. This is a haven for beer lovers with its 50 drafts, 500 bottles, and 5 cask ales on tap. ChurchKey's downstairs sibling, Birch & Barley, is a popular restaurant. 1337 14th St. NW (at Rhode Island Ave.). www.church keydc.com. ⓒ **202/567-2576.** Metro: McPherson Sq. (14th St. exit) or U St./Cardozo (U and 13th sts. exit).

**The Dubliner ★** Capitol Hill big names and the media that cover them, as well as neighborhood regulars, hang here for no other reason but that the atmosphere's Irish and the bar's got Guinness on tap. Open from breakfast through last call, the Dubliner features live Irish music nightly. In the Phoenix Park Hotel, 520 N. Capitol St. NW (separate entrance on F St. NW). www.dublinerdc.com. ℂ **202/737-3773.** Metro: Union Station.

**The Gibson** ★★ If the word "mixologist" is in your vocabulary, you'll like the Gibson, where expert drink-makers will concoct a libation just for you, based on your taste preferences. You can throw anything at them: smoky and tequila or citrusy and sweet, or cinnamon and scotchy, and presto! A cocktail answering to those very whims is placed before you. It's clear that they are having fun, and so will you. You'll need to know that the speakeasy is small, dark, and requires a reservation for entry. On busy nights, you're only allowed 2 hours here, but that ought to do it. 2009 14th St. NW (at U St.). www.thegibsondc.com. ℂ **202/232-2156.** Metro: U St./Cardozo (13th St. exit).

**H Street Country Club** ★ The Atlas District has come into its own, with new restaurants, bars, and theaters opening all the time, and at last a streetcar to get you there (see p. 294 for info about streetcar service). This one's been around from the beginning, which is to say, 2009, when the neighborhood started morphing from low-key commercial and residential into a nightlife district. H Street's main draw as a bar is its assortment of play activities: Skee-ball, shuffleboard, and the District's only indoor miniature golf course; up top is a huge rooftop deck. H Street serves pretty good Mexican food, too. 1335 H St. NE (at 13th St.). www.hstreetcountryclub.com. ℂ **202/399-4722.** Metro: Union Station, then take a cab, or the DC Streetcar, or walk.

**Hill Country Barbecue** ★★ Everybody knows to go to this Penn Quarter restaurant for awesome barbecue, strong drinks, and, downstairs, live music nearly nightly. The music tends toward outlaw country and honkytonk. But one of the most popular acts in town is one that patrons themselves deliver here every Wednesday night (usually after tossing back a couple of tequilas). The Hari-Karaoke Band provides live backup as a singer takes the microphone and "rocks 'n twangs" her heart out. 410 7th St. NW (at D St.). www.hillcountrywdc.com. ℂ **202/556-2050.** Metro: Gallery Place/Chinatown (7th and F sts. exit) or Archives–Navy Memorial.

**Lucky Bar** ★ You looking for a good old-fashioned bar with booths, couches, a pool table, a jukebox, and cheap beer? Lucky Bar's the place. It's also Soccer Central, with TV screens broadcasting soccer matches from around the globe. Monday through Wednesday and Friday, Lucky Bar's happy hour runs from 3 to 8pm. And there are nightly specials, like 50¢ chicken wings on Tuesday nights and half-price burgers on Wednesdays. 1221 Connecticut Ave. NW (at N St.). www.luckybardc.com. ℂ **202/331-3733.** Metro: Dupont Circle (South/19th St. exit) or Farragut North (L St. exit).

**Marvin** ★★ Downstairs is a Belgian bistro, upstairs is the bar, which includes a lounge, rooftop beer garden, and DJ space. Washington's 20-somethings come here to dance, and it's always crowded after 10pm. 2007 14th St. NW (at U St.). www.marvindc.com. ℂ **202/797-7171.** Metro: U St./Cardozo (13th St. exit).

**The Observatory** ★★ Crowning Georgetown's Graham Hotel is this seasonal rooftop bar, which wraps around the entire building, so you're able

# CHEAP EATS: happy hours TO WRITE HOME ABOUT

Good-value promotions are often available at area bars and nightclubs, like Lucky Bar's half-price burgers (your choice: beef, turkey, or vegetarian; comes with fries!) every Wednesday night, 50¢ wings on Tuesdays, and $2 sliders on Fridays. A step above these are certain restaurants around town that set out tasty bites during happy hour, either free or for an astonishingly low price. Here are several you might like:

In the bar only at **BLT Steak,** 1625 I St. NW, between 16th and 17th streets (http://bltrestaurants.com/blt-steak/washington-d-c/; ℂ **202/689-8999**), not far from the White House, a swell 5@5 happy hour offers six delicious snacks, burgers, grilled cheese and broiled oysters among them, at $5 each, to pair with your choice of a pomegranate gimlet, a glass of wine, or a beer, each $5. The 5@5 deal runs Monday to Friday from 5 to 6:30pm, in the bar area only.

In Georgetown, **Morton's Steakhouse,** 3251 Prospect St. NW, just off Wisconsin Avenue NW (www.mortons.com/georgetown; ℂ **202/342-6258**), serves up "Power Hours" bar bites in its bar, Sunday to Friday 5pm to closing. Drinks are specially priced—$5.50 for beer, $7.50 for wine, and $8.50 for certain cocktails—and the bar-bites menu features a variety: cheeseburger trio, four petite filet mignon sandwiches, blue cheese french fries, and so on, each priced at $7 or $8 per plate.

Finally, Penn Quarter's **Oyamel,** at 401 7th St. NW (www.oyamel.com; ℂ **202/628-1005**), has happy-hour specials 4 to 6pm Sunday through Friday featuring $5 margaritas, Dos Equis, Tecate, or Mexican wine, and, for another $4, two of Oyamel's superb tacos; a late-night menu Sunday through Wednesday 10pm to midnight and Thursday through Saturday 11pm to 2am offers the same deal on tacos, Dos Equis and Tecate.

to view Georgetown and the city, including the Washington Monument. The fact that the bar is open not just to hotel guests but to Washington's drinking crowd means you should reserve a spot (reservations are recommended though not required), and you must pass the bar's "Georgetown chic" dress-code inspection (though we're not sure what that means). It's a comfortable place to lounge, too, with pretty teal-colored cushions and a partially protected bar area. The Observatory also serves a light bites menu of charcuterie, cheese, that sort of thing. At the Graham Hotel, 1075 Thomas Jefferson St. NW (just below M St.). www.thegrahamgeorgetown.com. ℂ **202/337-0900.** Metro: Foggy Bottom, with a 20-min. walk.

**Quill ★★★** A pianist plays Tuesday through Saturday starting at 9pm, the perfect accompaniment to that Swept Away cocktail you're sipping and plate of charcuterie you're nibbling, at this chicest of lounges inside the city's chicest hotel. In the Jefferson Hotel, 1200 16th St. NW (at M St.). www.jeffersondc.com. ℂ **202/448-2300.** Metro: Dupont Circle (19th St./South exit) or Farragut North (L St. exit).

**Tryst ★** Tryst is a coffeehouse bar. Coffee to charge you up in the a.m., drinks to get you going later in the day. It's got a good vibe, too: loungey in the pre-hipster sense of a comfort zone. Morning, noon, and night, customers sprawl on comfy old furniture, juggling laptops and beverages. Tryst also runs the cafes at the Phillips Collection (p. 182) and at the Washington National Cathedral (p. 187). 2459 18th St. NW (at Columbia Rd.). www.trystdc.com. ℂ **202/232-5500.** Metro: U St./Cardozo or Woodley Park/Zoo/Adams Morgan, then the DC Circulator.

**Tune Inn** ★   Open since 1955, this Capitol Hill inn is a veritable institution. The divey Tune Inn is open from early morning 'til late at night serving police officers, Hill staffers and their bosses, and folks from the neighborhood. Sometimes they eat here, too: burgers, fries, and crab cakes. 331 Pennsylvania Ave. SE (at 4th St.). ℂ **202/543-2725.** Metro: Capitol South.

# THE CLUB & MUSIC SCENE

## Live Music

If you're looking for a tuneful night on the town, Washington offers everything from hip jazz clubs to DJ-driven dance halls—both places where you sit back and listen and places where you can get up and rock out.

### JAZZ & BLUES

If you're a jazz fan and are planning a trip to D.C. in early to mid-June, check out **www.dcjazzfest.org** for exact dates of the fabulous, 10 day-long **DC Jazz Festival,** which showcases the talents of at least 100 musicians in various venues around town, including many free events. And if you're a jazz or blues fan and you're coming to town at some other time of the year, check out the following venues.

**The Birchmere Music Hall and Bandstand** ★★★   This place started out 40 years or so ago showcasing bluegrass and country acts primarily. Take a look at the calendar now and you'll see the range stretches from Maysa & Her Jazz Funk Soul Symphony to John Hiatt. Located in Alexandria, 6 miles and a $12 cab fare from downtown D.C., the Birchmere is well worth the trip. The hall seats 500 and serves food. Purchase tickets at the box office or online from www.ticketmaster.com. 3701 Mt. Vernon Ave. (off S. Glebe Rd.), Alexandria, VA. www.birchmere.com. ℂ **703/549-7500.** Tickets $17–$60. Take a taxi or drive.

**Blues Alley** ★★★   An inconspicuous alley off of busy Wisconsin Avenue in Georgetown delivers you to the door of Blues Alley and another world entirely. Jazz greats like Wynton Marsalis and Ahmad Jamal and lesser-known artists play here nightly, usually two sets a night, at 8 and 10pm, with the occasional midnight show thrown in on weekends. Blues Alley is a tiny joint filled with small, candlelit tables, so reservations are a must for the first-come-first-served seating. The supper club has been around since 1965 and looks it, but that's part of its charm. Its Creole menu features dishes named after stars (try Dizzy Gillespie's Jambalaya). 1073 Wisconsin Ave. NW (in an alley below M St.). www.bluesalley.com. ℂ **202/337-4141.** Tickets $16–$75 (most $20–$40), plus a $12-per-person food or drink minimum, plus $4.50 per-person ticket surcharge. Metro: Foggy Bottom, then walk or take the DC Circulator.

**Gypsy Sally's ★**   One of D.C.'s newest live-music venues features blue-grass and "Americana" acts. Performances take place in the Music Room, which holds 300 people, and follow a Wednesday through Saturday schedule. Most shows offer a mix of reserved seating and general-admission standing. The club incudes the Vinyl Lounge bar, which hosts free open mic nights most Tuesdays, and a private event space; food and full bar are offered throughout. Gypsy Sally's is located in Georgetown, right down by the waterfront, under-neath the Whitehurst Freeway. 3401 K St. NW (at 34th St.). www.gypsysallys.com. ✆ **202/333-7700.** Most tickets $10–$15. Metro: Foggy Bottom, then walk or take the DC Circulator.

**The Hamilton ★★**   Located on the subterranean level of a large restaurant is this live-music venue, with blues, rock, jazz, R&B, and folk performances staged nightly. You sit at communal tables and dine from a pizza, sandwich, and sushi menu (not great). Located in the heart of the Penn Quarter, the Hamilton's great sight lines, eclectic lineup (world music, jazz, blues, you name it), and excellent sound system make it a club always worth checking out. 600 14th St. (at F St.). www.thehamiltondc.com. ✆ **202/787-1000.** Live music acts $15–$50; most main courses under $20. Metro: Metro Center (13th St. exit).

**Howard Theatre ★★**   A $29-million renovation of this historic arts land-mark theater, built in 1910, has helped restore not just the building but also a piece of history. The Howard Theatre of old was the Black Broadway show-case for musicians such as Duke Ellington and Ella Fitzgerald, and later hosted performances by Marvin Gaye and the Supremes. The theater reopened in April 2012, with a lineup of stars from the Roots to Mos Def. With its 1,200 seats arranged at tables, the venue is both supper club and concert venue. Cuisine is American with a soul influence, naturally, and food and drink are served throughout the show. 620 T St. NW (at 7th St.). www.thehowardtheatre.com. ✆ **202/588-5595.** Tickets $15–$95 (most $25–$55). Metro: Shaw/Howard University (7th and S sts. exit).

**Madam's Organ Restaurant and Bar ★★★**   Everyone stops by the legendary Madam's at some point. There's a lot going on throughout its eclec-tically decorated three levels and it's all fun: live music nightly on the first floor, from funk/jazz/blues on Sunday and Monday to regional blues bands on weekends; the second floor Big Daddy's Love Lounge & Pick-Up Joint (it is what it is); and the year-round rooftop deck, for mingling, playing darts, and taking in the fine view. 2461 18th St. NW (at Columbia Rd.). www.madamsorgan.com. ✆ **202/667-5370.** Cover $3–$7. Metro: U St./Cardozo or Woodley Park–Zoo, then catch the DC Circulator.

## ROCK, HIP-HOP & DJS

Below are primarily live-music clubs, but also a sprinkling of nightclubs known for their DJs and dance floors.

**9:30 Club ★★★**   The 9:30 rules over the live-music scene. It's a 1,200-person-capacity concert hall with excellent sightlines, state-of-the-art sound system, four bars, and of course most important, a nightly concert schedule that features every possible star, rising or arrived, in today's varied rock world, from The Struts to Adele. The 9:30 Club is frequently voted the best live music venue, certainly in D.C., but also countrywide. Unless advertised as seated, all shows are standing room only, general admission. Tickets generally $12 to $40. 815 V St. NW (at 9th St.). www.930.com. © **202/265-0930.** Metro: U St./ Cardozo (10th St. exit).

**Black Cat ★★★** This club is D.C.'s flagship venue for alternative music. When it opened on 14th Street in 1993, the neighborhood was a red-light district and D.C. was not a major player when it came to a vibrant live-music scene. So hats off to the Black Cat, who played a part in the changes that have happened since. Local, national, and international groups play here, everyone from the Arcade Fire to Black Lips. The Black Cat has two stages: its main concert hall, which holds more than 600 people, and Backstage, the place for soloists, smaller bands, DJs, film screenings, and poetry readings. The Red Room Bar features pinball machines, a pool table, and a jukebox. Concerts are nightly, sometimes twice in a single night, on different stages. 1811 14th St. NW (btw. S and T sts.). www.blackcatdc.com. © **202/667-4490.** Purchase tickets ($5–$25) online for concerts or arrive with cash, since the club does not accept credit cards; no cover in the Red Room Bar. Metro: U St./Cardozo (13th and U sts. exit).

**Eighteenth Street Lounge ★★** Ever the hotspot, ESL is the place to go for dressing sexy and dancing to live music and DJ-spun tunes, a range of acid jazz, hip-hop, reggae, Latin jazz, soul, and party sounds. The setting is somewhat surprising: a restored, century-old mansion, once the home of Teddy Roosevelt, with fireplaces, high ceilings, and an outside deck. It's open Tuesday through Friday from 5pm, Saturday and Sunday from 9pm. 1212 18th

**A performance at the Black Cat.**

Washington is home to more than 180 embassies and international culture centers, which greatly contribute to the city's cosmopolitan flavor. There are a number of ways to soak up this international scene, starting with a detailed walking tour of Embassy Row, in chapter 10 of this book. The tour takes you past the embassies, but not inside them, because few embassies are open to the public on a walk-in basis. If you're in D.C. in May, however, you may have the opportunity to tour embassies that participate in one of two programs, the Around the World Embassy Tour, held on the first Saturday in May, and the Shortcut to Europe Open House, held on the second Saturday in May (go to www.culturaltourismdc.org and click on "Passport DC" for more information). In fact, the European Union Delegation to the United States sponsors a month-long celebration (www.euintheus.org/event/european-month-of-culture/) of its 28 member countries, with cultural events taking place throughout May at embassies as well as at the National Gallery of Art, the Library of Congress, and other DC Institutions. On the third Saturday in May, the National Asian Heritage Festival stages its Fiesta Asia Street Fair, on Pennsylvania Avenue in the Penn Quarter, introducing all to Asian culture.

The helpful website www.embassy.org provides a list of all the embassies with links to their websites. If you explore these individual websites, you'll find that lots of embassies host events that are open to the public—sometimes for free, sometimes at minimal cost. In my opinion, the **French Embassy's La Maison Française** (www.frenchculture.org) and the Swedish Embassy's **House of Sweden** (www.swedenabroad.com/washington; then click on "Current Affairs," and then on "Events") offer the most interesting events. A highlight is the Nordic Jazz Fest, cosponsored by the embassies of Sweden, Denmark, Norway, Finland, and Iceland every June, with the best performances staged on the roof of the House of Sweden building on the Georgetown waterfront overlooking the Potomac River. The cost is usually $35 per person per concert; the experience is priceless.

Finally, you can buy tickets for **Embassy Series** (www.embassyseries.org; ℂ **202/625-2361**) program events. These are world-class, mostly classical-music performances hosted by individual embassies, held at the embassy or at the ambassador's residence. Tickets are expensive for the intimate experience. For instance, on June 23, 2016, the Portuguese ambassador hosted an evening of Portuguese music and culinary tastes at his residence, where pianist Julio Resende's multimedia performance crossed modern jazz with traditional Fado. It was $150 per ticket, but totally worth it!

St. NW (at Jefferson Place and Connecticut Ave.). www.eighteenthstreetlounge.com. ℂ **202/466-3922.** No cover Tues–Thurs; cover varies on weekends, but usually $5–$15 after 10pm. Metro: Dupont Circle (South/19th St. exit) or Farragut North (L St. exit).

**Rock & Roll Hotel** ★ Located in the Atlas District, this club features a second-floor pool hall, 400-person concert hall, a separate comfy bar for hanging out, and year-round rooftop deck and bar. Nightly acts range from local garage bands to national groups on tour. *FYI:* Don't expect to stay overnight; despite its name, the hotel is just a club. 1353 H St. NE (at 14th St.). www.rockandrollhoteldc.com. ℂ **202/388-7625.** Cover $8–$20. Metro: Union Station, then take the D.C. Streetcar, a taxi, or walk.

## Comedy Clubs

In addition to the Kennedy Center's growing presence on the comedy circuit, as mentioned earlier in this chapter, the **Warner Theatre** features big-name comedians or troupes.

**The Capitol Steps** ★   *What to Expect When You're Electing* is the name of the latest album released by this musical political satire troupe, following fast on the heels of *Mock the Vote* and *How to Succeed in Congress Without Really Lying*—just three out of the more than 30 albums the troupe has produced since it debuted in 1981. But really, it's best to see them perform their songs and skits in person, which you can do nearly every weekend at the Ronald Reagan Building and International Trade Center. The performers are former congressional staffers, and therefore well equipped to satirize politicians. In the Ronald Reagan Building, 1300 Pennsylvania Ave. NW (at 13th St.). www.capsteps.com. ℂ **202/312-1555.** Tickets $41. Metro: Federal Triangle.

**The Improv** ★   The Improv features headliners on the national comedy-club circuit as well as comic plays and one-person shows. Shows are about 1½ hours long and generally include three comics (an emcee, a feature act, and a headliner). Showtimes are 7:30 or 8pm Tuesday through Sunday, with a second show at 9:45pm or later on Friday and Saturday. Acts also take place in the more intimate 60-person lounge. You must be 18 to enter. 1140 Connecticut Ave. NW (btw. L and M sts.). www.dcimprov.com. ℂ **202/296-7008.** Tickets $15–$35, plus a 2-item minimum per person. Metro: Farragut North (L St. exit).

# THE GLBT SCENE

**Dupont Circle** is the gay and lesbian hub of Washington, D.C., with at least 10 gay or lesbian bars within easy walking distance of one another. Here are two from that neighborhood, plus another a few blocks away.

**Cobalt** ★   This is "D.C's premier gay bar and nightspot." So says Cobalt's owners, but so does everyone else, too. Cobalt is actually the name of the club's third-floor dance space, while the first floor holds the club's Level One restaurant and the second floor its 30 Degrees lounge. The club hosts karaoke and other themed and popular events. 1639 R St. NW (at 17th St.). www.cobaltdc.com. ℂ **202/232-4416.** Metro: Dupont Circle (Q St. exit).

**J.R.'s Bar and Grill** ★   This friendly place is always packed, whether it's Thursday night between 5 and 8pm, when $15 gets you all you can drink, or on "Showtunes Monday" nights. The all-male Dupont Circle club attracts an attractive crowd, here to play pool, participate in sing-alongs, or simply hang out. 1519 17th St. NW (btw. P and Q sts.). www.jrsbar-dc.com. ℂ **202/328-0090.** Metro: Dupont Circle (Q St. exit).

**Nellie's Sports Bar** ★   *Washington City Paper's* **2016 Best of D.C.** issue reported that readers voted Nellie's Sports Bar their favorite in three different categories: best sports bar, best trivia bar, and best gay bar. Clearly, Nellie's has her fans, and they aren't necessarily all gay. But if the idea of drag brunch or drag bingo appeals, or if you happen to be a whiz at trivia, or if you enjoy an entertaining social scene while you watch your favorite team play on TV, or if you fancy a cocktail on Nellie's roof deck overlooking U Street, you're bound to be happy at Nellie's. 900 U St. NW (at 9th St.). www.nelliessportsbar.com. ☎ **202/332-6355.** Metro: U St./Cardozo (10th St. exit).

# SPECTATOR SPORTS

Washington, D.C., has professional football, basketball, baseball, ice hockey, and soccer teams, and of those five, it's the Capitals, the ice-hockey team, whose fans are the most passionate. And visible: In season you'll see the red-jersey'd devotees swarming downtown before and after the match at the Verizon Center. Tickets to the Caps games are attainable but not cheap. It's the tickets to the Redskins football games that remain most elusive, thanks to a loyal subscription base.

## Annual Sporting Events

### Citi Open (formerly known as the Legg Mason Tennis Classic)
This U.S. Open series event attracts more than 72,000 people to watch tennis pros compete for big bucks. A portion of the profits benefits the Washington Tennis and Education Foundation. The tournament takes place for about 9 days in mid-July at the Rock Creek Park Tennis Center in Rock Creek Park. www.citiopentennis.com. ☎ **202/721-9500.**

**Marine Corps Marathon** Thirty thousand runners compete in this 26.2-mile race (the third-largest marathon in the United States), which winds past major memorials. The race takes place the last Sunday in October; 2017 marks its 42nd year. www.marinemarathon.com. ☎ **800/786-8762.**

## General Spectator Sports

**Baseball** Washington, D.C.'s Major League Baseball team, the **Nationals,** play at the finely designed **Nationals Ballpark** (www.nationals.com; 1500 S. Capitol St. SE ☎ **202/675-6287**), located in southeast Washington. The 41,000-seat stadium has sparked much development in this waterfront neighborhood, which now goes by the name "Capitol Riverfront."

**Basketball** The 20,600-seat **Verizon Center,** 601 F St. NW, where it meets 7th Street (www.verizoncenter.com; ☎ **202/628-3200**) in the center of downtown, is Washington's premier indoor-sports arena, where the **Wizards** (NBA), the **Mystics** (WNBA), and the **Georgetown University Hoyas** basketball teams play.

**Football** The **Redskins** National Football League team plays at the 85,000-seat stadium **FedEx Field,** outside of Washington, in Landover, Maryland. Obtaining tickets is difficult thanks to season-ticket holders, but if you want to try, visit www.redskins.com/fedexfield.

**Ice Hockey**   The **Capitals** of the National Hockey League are beloved in this city. The team rink is inside the 20,600-seat **Verizon Center,** 601 F St. NW (www.verizoncenter.com; © **202/628-3200**), in the center of downtown.

**Soccer**   D.C.'s men's soccer team, **D.C. United** (www.dcunited.com), has been around since 1994, playing its matches at the increasingly creaky 55,000-seat **Robert F. Kennedy Memorial Stadium,** 2400 E. Capitol St. SE (© **202/547-9077**). A new stadium is in the works(!), but won't open until 2018.

**Tennis**   World Team Tennis franchise team, the Washington Kastles (www.washingtonkastles.com), plays at the **Kastles Stadium at the Smith Center,** 600 22nd St. NW, on the campus of George Washington University. WTT is a coed professional tennis league; the Kastles team includes Martina Hingus, Madison Brengle, and Leander Paes (© **202/483-6647**).

# DAY TRIPS FROM D.C.

Y ou've come as far as Washington, D.C.—why not travel just a bit farther to visit Mount Vernon, the home of the man for whom the capital is named? "Washington slept here" is a claim bandied about by many a town. "Washington lived here for 45 years" is a claim only Mount Vernon can make. Located 16 miles south of Washington, D.C., the estate was George Washington's home from 1754 until his death in 1799 (as much as the American Revolution and Washington's stints as the new republic's first president would allow). And where did Washington go to sell his produce, kick up his heels, or worship? In nearby Old Town Alexandria. Its cobblestone streets and historic churches and houses still stand, surrounded now by of-the-moment eateries and chic boutiques. Make time, if you can, for visits to both Old Town and Mount Vernon.

## MOUNT VERNON

Only 16 miles south of the capital, George Washington's Southern plantation dates from a 1674 land grant to the president's great-grandfather.

### Essentials

**GETTING THERE**   If you're going by car, take any of the bridges over the Potomac River into Virginia and follow the signs pointing the way to National Airport/Mount Vernon/George Washington Memorial Parkway. Travel south on the George Washington Memorial Parkway, the river always to your left, and pass by National Airport on your right. Continue through Old Town Alexandria, where the parkway is renamed "Washington Street," and head 8 miles farther, until you reach the large circle that fronts Mount Vernon.

You might also take a narrated bus or boat tour to Mount Vernon; their prices include the price of admission to Mount Vernon. Tour buses that travel to Mount Vernon include **Gray Line Buses** (www.graylinedc.com; © **202/779-9894**), which offers a daily half-day tour ($55 per adult, $20 per child; see website for special offers) only of Mount Vernon, and a daily 9-hour tour ($90 per adult, $30 per child) that includes a tour of Arlington Cemetery on the return

Though few people realize it, the George Washington Memorial Parkway is actually a national park. The first section was completed in 1932 to honor the bicentennial of George Washington's birth. The parkway follows the Potomac River, running from Mount Vernon, past Old Town and the nation's capital, and ending at Great Falls, Virginia. Today the parkway is a major commuter route leading into and out of the city. Even the most impatient driver, however, can't help but notice the beautiful scenery and views of the Jefferson and Lincoln memorials and the Washington Monument that you pass along the way.

from Mount Vernon. Both tours depart and return to Union Station, allow you to explore Mount Vernon on your own, and drive through, but don't stop in, Old Town Alexandria. The bus company **OnBoard Sightseeing** (http://washingtondctours.onboardtours.com/mount-vernon-tour/; ✆ **301/839-5261**) offers a daily 6-hour tour ($79.99 per adult, $69.99 per child Mon–Thurs; $89.99 per adult, $79.99 per child Fri–Sun) of Mount Vernon and Arlington Cemetery, via a drive-through of Old Town Alexandria, but on this tour, your OnBoard tour guide not only narrates your experience on the bus but also escorts and narrates your tour of Mount Vernon and Arlington Cemetery. The tour picks you up at 10am at the White House Gifts shop at 15th Street NW and New York Avenue NW, and returns you to the same location.

The **Spirit of Washington Cruises'** *Spirit of Mount Vernon* (www.cruisetomountvernon.com; ✆ **866/302-2469**) is a seasonal operation, cruising to Mount Vernon March through October (check online for daily schedules, which can vary). The vessel leaves from Pier 4 (6th and Water sts. SW; 3 blocks from the Green Line Metro's Waterfront station) at 8:30am, returning by 3pm. The cost is $46.95 plus tax/adult, $41.95 plus tax/child (ages 6–11).

*Miss Christin,* run by the **Potomac Riverboat Company** (www.potomacriverboatco.com; ✆ **877/511-2628** or 703/684-0580), operates Tuesday through Sunday April through August, Friday to Sunday September to mid-October, and Saturday and Sunday mid-October until late October. It departs at 10:30am for Mount Vernon from the pier adjacent to the Torpedo Factory, where Union and Cameron streets intersect, at Old Town Alexandria's waterfront. The rate is $42/adult, $22/child (ages 6–11), free for children under 6. Arrive 30 minutes ahead of time at the pier to secure a place on the boat. The narrated trip takes 90 minutes each way, stopping at Gaylord's National Harbor to pick up and discharge passengers. The boat departs Mount Vernon at 4pm to return to Old Town by 5:30pm, via Gaylord's.

And here's a clever way to travel to and from Mount Vernon: The Potomac Riverboat Company and **Bike & Roll** (book through www.bikeandrolldc.com; more on p. 301) have teamed up to offer **Bike & Boat,** which includes bike rental from Bike & Roll's Old Town Alexandria location at the waterfront, admission to Mount Vernon, and a narrated return trip back to Old Town aboard the *Miss Christin.* You pedal your own way along the Mount Vernon

**George Washington's Mount Vernon.**

Trail (see the box, "Biking to Old Town Alexandria & Mount Vernon," p. 246) to reach the estate. The package costs $68 for ages 13 and older, $40 ages 6 to 12, and $20 ages 2 to 5.

If you're up for it, you can rent a bike and pedal the 18-mile round-trip distance at your own pace any time of year.

Finally, it is possible to take **public transportation** to Mount Vernon by riding the Metro to the Yellow Line's Huntington station and proceeding to the lower level, where you catch the Fairfax Connector bus #101 to Mount Vernon.

## Touring the Estate

**Mount Vernon Estate and Gardens ★★★** You could easily spend a full day soaking in the life and times of our first president, George Washington, when he lived at Mount Vernon. The 500-acre estate includes the centerpiece mansion, George and Martha Washington's home, and so much else: gardens, outbuildings, a wharf, slave quarters and burial grounds, a greenhouse, a working farm, an orientation center, education center, museum and, about 3 miles down the road, a working distillery and grist mill.

The plantation was passed down from Washington's great-grandfather, who acquired the land in 1674, to George's half-brother, and eventually to George himself in 1754. Washington proceeded over the next 45 years to expand and fashion the home to his liking, though the American Revolution and his years as president kept Washington away from his beloved estate much of the time.

What you see today is a remarkable restoration of the mansion, the oldest part of which dates from the 1740s. Interiors appear as they would have in 1799, with walls painted in the original colors chosen by George and Martha, and with original furnishings and objects used by the Washington family on display. Historical interpreters stationed through the house answer your questions as you pass through.

If time allows, visit the **Ford Orientation Center** and the **Donald W. Reynolds Museum and Education Center,** located not far from the mansion. The Orientation Center's 25-minute film, "We Fight to Be Free," offers some insight into Washington's character and career. The Education Center's 23 galleries, theater presentations, and display of 700 original artifacts further help round out the story of this heroic, larger-than-life man.

But given the choice of visiting those centers or the historic sites scattered throughout the estate, I'd direct you to those historic sites, especially April through October, when Mount Vernon's shuttle operates (see information box, below) and the weather is most pleasant. Conversely, during the months of

November through March, and in inclement weather, visits to the museum and education and orientation centers might prove a better idea.

If you can then, start with the **Outbuildings:** the kitchen, slave quarters, storeroom, smokehouse, overseer's quarters, coach house, stables, and working blacksmith shop with daily demonstrations. Walk or take the shuttle to the 4-acre **Pioneer Farm,** which includes a replica of Washington's 16-sided barn and fields of crops that he grew (corn, wheat, oats, and so forth). Historical interpreters in period costumes demonstrate 18th-century farming methods. At its peak, Mount Vernon was an 8,000-acre working farm, which reminds us that Washington considered himself first and foremost a farmer.

Not too far from the Pioneer Farm is the wharf, where you can learn about Washington's boat building and fisheries, and take a 45-minute narrated excursion on the Potomac ($11 per adult, $7 per child). Back on land, you have more to cover: the slave burial ground, the greenhouse, and the tombs of George and Martha Washington. Down the road from the estate are Washington's fully functioning distillery and gristmill. The shuttle travels the 2.7 miles to the site, which is open April through October, and operated by costumed staff. Admission to the distillery and gristmill, as well as the shuttle to and from Mount Vernon, are included in your ticket. Samplings of the whiskey produced here are not included in your admission price, alas, but you can purchase Mount Vernon–made whiskey and stoneground products at the Shops at Mount Vernon. If you're not visiting Mount Vernon, the admission here is $5 per adult and $2 per child; kids under 6 free.

Mount Vernon belongs to the Mount Vernon Ladies' Association, which purchased the estate for $200,000 in 1858 from John Augustine Washington III, great-grandnephew of the first president. Without the group's purchase, the estate might have crumbled and disappeared, for neither the federal

## tips FOR TOURING MOUNT VERNON

1. Buy your admission tickets online, which automatically reduces the price by $3 for adults, $1 for children.

2. Your admission ticket is also your timed entry ticket to tour the mansion, so choose a tour time that allows you to first visit the Ford Orientation Center, where a 25-minute movie provides some good background for your visit.

3. You will also be given the choice of buying a standard tour ticket or, for $10 more, a premium tour ticket. Again, consider the timing, and if it works, opt for the premium ticket. The difference is worth it: Instead of self-guiding your way through two floors of the mansion, usually a 15- to 20-minute experience, you'll receive a guided, 1-hour tour that takes you beyond the usual tourable rooms, with all your questions answered by your guide as you go.

4. During the online ticketing process, you will have the chance to add on specialty tours covering areas beyond the mansion—for instance, a 1-hour "Enslaved People of Mount Vernon Tour" for an additional $4. If you can manage it, add on a specialty tour. These tours truly bring history to life.

Throughout the year, but especially April through October, Mount Vernon offers many special tours, demonstrations, activities, and events, some, but not all, included in your price of admission. Every imaginable topic is covered: 18th-century gardens, slave life, Colonial crafts, food and dining at Mount Vernon, archaeology, and, for children, hands-on history programs. Check the website for details.

government nor the Commonwealth of Virginia wanted to buy the property when it was earlier offered for sale.

Today, more than a million people tour the property annually. The best time to visit is off season; during the heavy tourist months (especially in spring, when schoolchildren descend in droves), it's best to arrive in the afternoon, weekdays, or weekends, because student groups will have departed by then.

3200 Mount Vernon Memorial Hwy. www.mountvernon.org. © **703/780-2000.** Admission $20 adults, $19 seniors, $9 children 6–11, free for children 5 and under. Purchase tickets online for $3 off adult prices, $1 off children's prices. Apr–Oct daily 9am–5pm; Nov–Mar daily 9am–4pm.

# Dining & Shopping

Mount Vernon's comprehensive **Shops at Mount Vernon Complex** offers a wide range of books, children's toys, holiday items, Mount Vernon private-label food and wine, whiskey produced at the distillery, stoneground flour made at the gristmill, and Mount Vernon licensed furnishings. The Orientation Center and the slave quarters/greenhouse hold much smaller gift shops. A **food court** features a menu of baked goods, deli sandwiches, coffee, grilled items, pizza, and cookies. Although you can't **picnic** on the grounds of Mount Vernon, you can drive a mile north on the parkway to Riverside Park, where there are tables and a lawn overlooking the Potomac. However, I recommend the Mount Vernon Inn restaurant.

**Mount Vernon Inn** ★ AMERICAN TRADITIONAL   Lunch or dinner at the inn is an intrinsic part of the Mount Vernon experience. It's a quaint and charming Colonial-style restaurant, complete with period furnishings and three working fireplaces. The waiters are all in 18th-century costumes. Lunch entrees range from Colonial turkey "pye" (a sort of early-American stew served with garden vegetables in an open pieshell) to a pulled-pork barbecue sandwich. There's a full bar, and premium wines are offered by the glass. At dinner, tablecloths and candlelight make this a more elegant setting. The menu is mostly modern, but you may still see colonial references in starters like the homemade peanut and chestnut soup. By the way, Mount Vernon has joined the happy-hour trend and now serves discounted beer, wine, and spirits, along with very un-Colonial appetizers (fried calamari, buffalo wings) Tuesday through Friday from 4 to 8pm, at the bar and in the tavern.

Near the entrance to Mount Vernon Estate and Gardens. www.mountvernon.org/inn. © **703/780-0011.** Reservations recommended for dinner. Main courses lunch $10–$17, brunch $10–$25, dinner $16–$34. Sun 11am–5pm; Mon–Sat 11am–3:30pm; Tues–Thurs 4–8:30pm; Fri 4:30–9pm; Sat 5–9pm.

> ### The Mount Vernon Shuttle
>
> Good news! Mount Vernon offers free shuttle service around its estate, as well as to the gristmill and distillery, 2.7 miles down the road. The shuttle operates in high season only, from April to October, running every 30 minutes between the Museum and Education Center and the Pioneer Farm, near the Wharf, with a separate shuttle running back and forth between Mount Vernon Estate and its gristmill and distillery.

# OLD TOWN ALEXANDRIA

Old Town Alexandria is about 8 miles S of Washington.

The city of Washington may be named for our first president, but he never lived there. No, he called this other side of the Potomac home from the age of 11, when he joined his half-brother Lawrence, who owned Mount Vernon. Washington came to Alexandria often, helping to map out the 60-acre town's boundaries and roads when he was 17, training his militia in Market Square and selling produce there from his Mount Vernon farm, worshipping at Christ Church, and dining and dancing at Gadsby's Tavern.

The town of Alexandria is actually named after John Alexander, the Scot who purchased the land of the present-day town from an English ship captain for "six thousand pounds of Tobacco and Cask." Incorporated in 1749, the town soon grew into a major trading center and port, known for its handsome houses.

Today, thanks to a multimillion-dollar urban renewal effort, some 200 structures from Alexandria's early days survive in Old Town's historic district. (Four thousand structures, in all, are deemed historic.) Market Square is the site of the oldest continuously operating farmers' market in the country. (Catch it on Sat btw. 7am and noon, and you'll be participating in a 264-year-old tradition.) Christ Church and Gadsby's Tavern are still open and operating. Many Alexandria streets still bear their original Colonial names (King, Queen, Prince, Princess, Royal), while others, like Jefferson, Franklin, Lee, Patrick, and Henry, are obviously post-Revolutionary.

Twenty-first-century America thrives in Old Town's many shops, boutiques, art galleries, bars, and restaurants. But it's still easy to imagine yourself in Colonial times as you listen for the rumbling of horse-drawn vehicles over cobblestone (portions of Prince and Oronoco sts. are still paved with cobblestone), dine on Sally Lunn bread and other 18th-century grub in the centuries-old Gadsby's Tavern, and learn about the lives of the nation's forefathers during walking tours that take you in and out of their houses.

## Essentials

**GETTING THERE** For spectacular views, consider biking to Old Town Alexandria (see the box, "Biking to Old Town Alexandria & Mount Vernon," on p. 246). But if you're driving from the District, take the Arlington Memorial Bridge or the 14th Street Bridge to the George Washington Memorial

# Old Town Alexandria

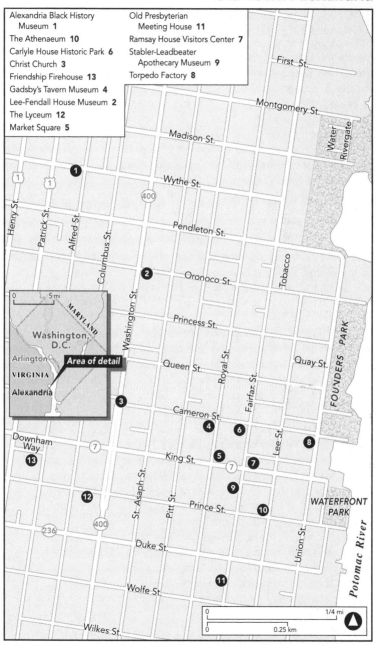

Alexandria Black History
 Museum **1**
The Athenaeum **10**
Carlyle House Historic Park **6**
Christ Church **3**
Friendship Firehouse **13**
Gadsby's Tavern Museum **4**
Lee-Fendall House Museum **2**
The Lyceum **12**
Market Square **5**

Old Presbyterian
 Meeting House **11**
Ramsay House Visitors Center **7**
Stabler-Leadbeater
 Apothecary Museum **9**
Torpedo Factory **8**

First St.

Montgomery St.

Water
Rivergate

Madison St.

Wythe St.

1  1  400

Henry St.
Patrick St.
Alfred St.
Columbus St.

Pendleton St.

**1**

Tobacco

Oronoco St.

**2**

Washington St.

Princess St.

0  5 mi

MARYLAND

Washington,
D.C.

Arlington

**Area of detail**

VIRGINIA

Alexandria

Royal St.

Fairfax St.

Queen St.

Quay St.

FOUNDERS PARK

**3**

Cameron St.

**4**   **6**

Lee St.

**8**

Downham
Way

7

**13**

King St.

**5**   7   **7**

**9**

**12**

Prince St.

**10**

WATERFRONT
PARK

236   400

Duke St.

St. Asaph St.
Pitt St.
Union St.

Potomac River

**11**

Wolfe St.

0                    1/4 mi

0          0.25 km

Wilkes St.

Parkway south, which becomes Washington Street in Old Town Alexandria. Washington Street intersects with King Street, Alexandria's main thoroughfare. Turn left from Washington Street onto one of the streets before or after King Street (southbound left turns are not permitted from Washington St. onto King St.), and you'll be heading toward the waterfront and the heart of Old Town. If you turn right from Washington Street onto King Street, you'll still be in Old Town, with King Street's long avenue of shops and restaurants awaiting you. Parking is inexpensive at nearby garages and at street meters, but if you want to pay nothing, drive a couple of blocks to streets off King Street, north of Cameron Street or south of Duke Street, where you can park for 2 or 3 hours for free. The town is compact, so you should be able to get around on foot.

The easiest way to make the trip is by Metro (www.wmata.com); Yellow and Blue Line trains travel to the King Street station. From the station, catch the free King Street Trolley, which operates Sunday to Wednesday 10am to 10:15pm, Thursday to Saturday 10am to midnight, making frequent stops between the Metro station and the Potomac River. The eastbound AT2 or AT5 blue-and-gold DASH bus (www.dashbus.com; ✆ **703/746-3274**) marked OLD TOWN or BRADDOCK METRO will also take you up King Street. Ask to be dropped at the corner of Fairfax and King streets, across the street from Alexandria Visitors Center at Ramsay House. The fare is $1.60 in cash, or free if you are transferring from Metrorail or a Metrobus and using a SmarTrip card (see p. 291). Or you can walk, and shop, the 1½ miles from the station into the center of Old Town.

Or consider taking a **water taxi,** operated by the Potomac Riverboat Company April until November, and running between the Alexandria dock and Washington, D.C.'s waterfront, at West Basin Drive and Ohio Drive SW, near the FDR Memorial. The 30-minute ride is not cheap: $28 per adult, $16 per child, round-trip, but is scenic for sure. Check the website, www.potomacriverboatco.com, for schedule and reservations.

**VISITOR INFORMATION** The **Alexandria Convention and Visitors Association's Visitors Center at Ramsay House,** 221 King St., at Fairfax Street (www.visitalexandriava.com; ✆ **800/388-9119** or 703/746-3301), is open April through September Sunday to Wednesday 10am to 6pm and Thursday to Saturday 10am to 8pm; October through March it's open daily 10am to 5pm (closed Thanksgiving, Dec 25, and Jan 1). Here you can obtain a map/self-guided walking tour and brochures about the area, get tickets for special events, and receive answers to any questions you might have. Consider purchasing in advance online, or at the visitor center, a $10 per person "Key to the City" pass, which covers admission to nine historic sites, and discounts at many attractions, shops, and restaurants. Valued at $26, the pass saves you $16 on admission prices alone, and more if you take advantage of the special offers.

**ORGANIZED TOURS** Though it's easy to see Alexandria on your own and with the help of Colonial-attired guides at individual attractions, you might consider taking a comprehensive walking tour. Architecture and history tours leave from the visitor center garden March through mid-November, at least once a day, weather permitting. Tours depart at 10:30am Monday through Saturday and at 2pm on Sunday, with additional tours during busy seasons. Call **Alexandria Tours** (𝒸 **703/329-1122**) for more information or to book a tour, which lasts 90 minutes and costs $15 per person (free for ages 6 and under). Or you can just show up at the appointed time, and pay the guide when you arrive.

A slew of other organized tours is available, each focused on a particular subject. Ghosts tours may be the most popular. Check out **Alexandria Colonial Tours'** (www.alexcolonialtours.com; 𝒸 **703/519-1749**) **Ghosts and Graveyard Tour,** which is offered March through November (weather permitting) at various times and days—best to call for exact schedule. This 1-hour tour departs from Ramsay House and costs $13 for adults, $7 for children ages 7 to 17; it's free for children 6 and under. Reservations are recommended, though not required, for these tours; or you can purchase tickets from the guide, who will be dressed in Colonial attire and standing in front of the visitor center.

**CITY LAYOUT**   Old Town is very small and laid out in an easy grid. At the center is the intersection of Washington Street and King Street. Streets change from north to south when they cross King Street; for example, North Alfred Street is the part of Alfred north of King Street (closest to Washington, in other words). Guess where South Alfred Street is.

# Alexandria Calendar of Events

The **Alexandria Convention and Visitors Association** posts its calendar of events online. Unless otherwise noted, you should visit the association's website, www.visitalexandriava.com, or call 𝒸 **800/388-9119** or 703/746-3301, for details about the following event highlights.

## FEBRUARY

**George Washington's Birthday** is celebrated over the course of the entire month of February, including Presidents' Weekend, which precedes the federal holiday (the third Mon in Feb). Festivities typically include a Colonial-costume or black-tie banquet, followed by a ball at Gadsby's Tavern, a 10km race, special tours, a Revolutionary War encampment at Fort Ward Park (complete with uniformed troops engaging in skirmishes), the nation's largest George Washington Birthday Parade, and 18th-century comic opera performances. Most events, such as the parade and historical reenactments, are free. The Birthnight Ball at Gadsby's Tavern requires tickets for both the banquet and the ball. www.washingtonbirthday.com.

## MARCH

**St. Patrick's Day Parade** takes place on King Street on the first Saturday in March.

## APRIL

**Historic Garden Week in Virginia** is celebrated with tours of privately owned local historic homes and gardens the third or fourth Saturday of the month. Call the Visitor Association (𝒸 **703/746-3301**) in early 2017 for more information about tickets and admission prices for the tour.

## JULY

**Alexandria's birthday** (its 268th in 2017) is celebrated with a concert performance by the Alexandria Symphony Orchestra, fireworks, birthday cake, and other festivities. The Saturday following the Fourth of July. All events are free.

## SEPTEMBER

**Alexandria Festival of the Arts** features the ceramics, sculpture, photography, and other works of more than 200 juried artists. On a Saturday and Sunday in early September. Free.

**Ghost tours** take place year-round but pick up around **Halloween.** A lantern-carrying guide in 18th-century costume describes Alexandria's ghosts, graveyards, legends, myths, and folklore as you tour the town and graveyards.

NOVEMBER

**Christmas Tree Lighting** is in Market Square, usually the Saturday after Thanksgiving. The ceremony, which includes choir singing, puppet shows, dance performances, and an appearance by Santa and his elves, begins at 7pm. The night the tree is lit, thousands of tiny lights adorning King Street trees also go on.

DECEMBER

**The Annual Scottish Christmas Walk** takes place on the first weekend in December.

Activities include kilted bagpipers, Highland dancers, a parade of Scottish clans (with horses and dogs), caroling, fashion shows, storytelling, booths (selling crafts, antiques, food, hot mulled punch, heather, fresh wreaths, and holly), and children's games. The event is organized by and benefits the non-profit Campagna Center, whose programs assist local families, children, and the community (www.campagnacenter.org/scottish walkweekend; ✆ **703/549-0111**).

**The Historic Alexandria Candlelight Tour** visits seasonally decorated historic Alexandria homes and an 18th-century tavern. Colonial dancing, string quartets, madrigal and opera singers, and refreshments are part of the celebration. Second weekend in December.

## What to See & Do

Colonial and post-Revolutionary buildings are Old Town Alexandria's main attractions. My favorites are the Carlyle House and Gadsby's Tavern Museum, but they're all worth a visit.

These sites are most easily accessible via the King Street Metro station, combined with a ride on the free King Street Trolley to the center of Old Town. The exceptions are the Alexandria Black History and Resource Center, whose closest Metro stop is the Braddock Street station, and Fort Ward, to which you should drive or take a taxi.

Old Town is also known for its fine shopping opportunities. Brand-name stores, charming boutiques, antiques shops, art galleries, and gift shops sell everything you might desire. Notable local favorite shops include **Bellacara,** 1000 King St. (www.bellacara.com; ✆ **703/299-9652**), for fragrant soaps and more than 50 brands of luxe skin- and haircare products; **Society Fair,** 277 S. Washington St. (www.societyfair.net; ✆ **703/683-3247**), Cathal Armstrong's (of Restaurant Eve, p. 252) venture, part bakery/market/butchery/wine bar/demo kitchen; **An American in Paris,** 1225 King St., Ste. 1 (www.anamerican inparisoldtown.com; ✆ **703/519-8234**), where one must knock on the door to enter and sort through the beautiful, one-of-a-kind cocktail dresses and evening gowns for sale; and **Red Barn Mercantile,** 1117 King St. (www.redbarn mercantile.com; ✆ **703/838-0355**), recognized in *Washington City Paper*'s 2016 annual "Best of" issue as the "best place to buy a gift," no matter the occasion or person, college graduate to toddler's birthday.

**Alexandria Black History Museum** ★    In 1939, African Americans in Alexandria staged a sit-in to protest the segregation of blacks from Alexandria's main library. The black community built its own public library, and it is this 1940s building that now serves as the Black History Resource Museum.

The Athenaeum in Alexandria.

The center exhibits historical objects, photographs, documents, and memorabilia relating to black citizens of Alexandria from the 18th century forward. In addition to the permanent collection, the museum presents rotating exhibits, genealogy workshops, book signings, and other activities. A half-hour may be enough time to spend at the center.

The museum is actually on the outskirts of Old Town. Once you've explored the museum, it makes sense to walk into Old Town, rather than taking the Metro or even a taxi. Have a staff person point you in the direction of Washington Street, east of the center; if you choose, you can turn right (or south) at Washington Street and walk 2 blocks or so to the **Lee-Fendall House** (p. 249) at Oronoco and Washington streets.

902 Wythe St. (at N. Alfred St.). www.alexblackhistory.org. ℂ **703/746-4356.** Admission $2. Tues–Sat 10am–4pm. Metro: Braddock Rd.; from the station, walk across the parking lot and bear right until you reach the corner of West and Wythe sts., where you'll proceed 5 blocks east along Wythe until you reach the center.

**The Athenaeum ★**  This grand building, with its Greek Revival architectural style, stands out among the narrow Old Town houses on the cobblestone street. Built in 1851, the Athenaeum has been many things: the Bank of the Old Dominion, where Robert E. Lee kept his money prior to the Civil War; a commissary for the Union Army during the Civil War; a church; a triage center where wounded Union soldiers were treated; and a medicine warehouse. Now the hall serves as an art gallery and performance space for the Northern Virginia Fine Arts Association. Pop by to admire the Athenaeum's imposing exterior, including the four soaring Doric columns and its interior hall: 24-foot-high ceilings, enormous windows, and whatever contemporary art is on display. This won't take you more than 20 minutes.

201 Prince St. (at S. Lee St.). www.nvfaa.org. ℂ **703/548-0035.** Free admission (donations accepted). Thurs–Fri and Sun noon–4pm; Sat 1–4pm. Closed major holidays.

# biking TO OLD TOWN ALEXANDRIA & MOUNT VERNON

One of the nicest ways to view the Washington skyline is from across the river while biking in Virginia. You'll have a breathtaking view of the Potomac and of Washington's grand landmarks: the Kennedy Center, Washington Monument, Lincoln Memorial, Jefferson Memorial, and National Cathedral off in one direction, and the Capitol off in the other. Rent a bike at one of Bike & Roll's locations or at Thompson Boat Center, across from the Kennedy Center and right on the bike path (p. 202). Hop on the pathway that runs along the Potomac River and head toward the memorials and the Arlington Memorial Bridge. In Washington, this is the Rock Creek Park Trail; when you cross Memorial Bridge (near the Lincoln Memorial) into Virginia, the name changes to the Mount Vernon Trail, which leads, not surprisingly, straight to Mount Vernon.

Of course, this mode of transportation is also a great way to see Old Town Alexandria and Mount Vernon. The trail carries you past Reagan National Airport via two pedestrian bridges that take you safely through the airport's roadway system. Continue on to Old Town, where you should lock up your bike, walk around, tour some of the historic properties listed in this chapter, and take in some refreshment from one of the many excellent restaurants before you proceed to Mount Vernon. The section from Memorial Bridge to Mount Vernon is about 19 miles in all.

**Carlyle House Historic Park** ★★ One of Virginia's most architecturally impressive 18th-century homes, Carlyle House also figured prominently in American history. A social and political center, the house was visited by the great men of the day, including George Washington. But its most important moment in history occurred in April 1755, when Major General Edward Braddock, commander-in-chief of His Majesty's forces in North America, met with five Colonial governors here and asked them to tax colonists to finance a campaign against the French and Indians. Colonial legislatures refused to comply, one of the first instances of serious friction between America and Britain.

When it was built, Carlyle House was a waterfront property with its own wharf. In 1753, Scottish merchant John Carlyle completed the mansion for his bride, Sarah Fairfax of Belvoir, a daughter of one of Virginia's most prominent families. It was designed in the style of a Scottish/English manor house and is lavishly furnished; Carlyle, a successful merchant, had the means to import the best furnishings and appointments available abroad for his new Alexandria home.

Tours are given on the hour and half-hour and take about 45 minutes; allow another 10 or 15 minutes if you plan to tour the tiered garden of brick walks and boxed parterres. Two of the original rooms, the large parlor and the dining room, have survived intact; the former, where Braddock met the governors, still retains its original fine woodwork, paneling, and pediments. The house is furnished in period pieces; however, only a few of Carlyle's possessions remain. In an upstairs room, an architecture exhibit depicts 18th-century construction methods.

121 N. Fairfax St. (btw. Cameron and King sts.). www.carlylehouse.org. ⓒ **703/549-2997.** Admission $5 adults, $3 children 5–12, free for children 4 and under. Tues–Sat 10am–4pm; Sun noon–4pm.

**Historic Christ Church** ★★ This sturdy red-brick Georgian-style church would be an important national landmark even if its two most distin-

| Planning Note |
| --- |
| Many Alexandria attractions are closed on Mondays. |

guished members had not been Washington and Lee. It has been in continuous use since 1773; the town of Alexandria grew up around this building—it was once known as the "Church in the Woods." Over the years, the church has undergone many changes, adding the bell tower, church bell, galleries, and organ by the early 1800s, and the "wineglass" pulpit in 1891. For the most part, the original structure remains, including the hand-blown glass in the windows.

Christ Church has had its historic moments. Washington and other early church members fomented revolution in the churchyard, and Robert E. Lee met here with Richmond representatives to discuss Lee's taking command of Virginia's military forces at the beginning of the Civil War. You can sit in the pew where George and Martha sat with her two Custis grandchildren, or in the Lee family pew. You might also want to walk through the graveyard and note how old the tombstones are, some dating from the mid- to late 1700s.

World dignitaries and U.S. presidents have visited the church over the years. One of the most memorable of these visits took place shortly after Pearl

Christ Church in Old Town Alexandria.

Harbor, when Franklin Delano Roosevelt attended services with Winston Churchill on the World Day of Prayer for Peace, January 1, 1942.

Of course, you're invited to attend a service (Sun at 8 and 10am and 5pm; Wed at 12:05pm). There's no admission charge, but donations are appreciated. A guide gives brief lectures to visitors. A gift shop is open Tuesday through Saturday 10am to 4pm, and Sunday 8:45am to noon. Twenty minutes should do it here. Be sure to check out the website before you visit, because it offers a wealth of information about the history of the church and town.

118 N. Washington St. (at Cameron St.). www.historicchristchurch.org. © **703/549-1450.** Donations appreciated. Mon–Sat 9am–4pm; Sun 2–4:30pm. Closed all federal holidays.

**Fort Ward Museum & Historic Site** ★ A short drive from Old Town is a 45-acre museum and park that transports you to Alexandria during the

Civil War. The action here centers, as it did in the early 1860s, on an actual Union fort that Lincoln ordered erected. It was part of a system of Civil War forts called the "Defenses of Washington." About 90% of the fort's earthwork walls are preserved, and the Northwest Bastion has been restored with six mounted guns (originally there were 36). A model of 19th-century military engineering, the fort was never attacked by Confederate forces. Self-guided tours begin at the Fort Ward ceremonial gate.

Visitors can explore the fort and replicas of the ceremonial entrance gate and an officer's hut. A museum of Civil War artifacts on the premises features changing exhibits that focus on subjects such as Union arms and equipment, medical care of the wounded, and local war history.

There are picnic areas with barbecue grills in the park surrounding the fort. Living-history presentations take place throughout the year. This is a good stop if you have young children, in which case you could spend an hour or two here (especially if you bring a picnic).

4301 W. Braddock Rd. (btw. Rte. 7 and N. Van Dorn St.). www.fortward.org. © **703/746-4848.** Free admission (donations welcome). Park daily 9am–sunset. Museum Tues–Sat 10am–5pm; Sun noon–5pm. Call for information regarding special holiday closings. From Old Town, follow King St. west, go right on Kenwood Ave., then left on W. Braddock Rd.; continue for a mile to the entrance on the right.

**Friendship Firehouse** ★    Alexandria's first firefighting organization, the Friendship Fire Company, was established in 1774. In the early days, the company met in taverns and kept its firefighting equipment in a member's barn. Its present Italianate-style brick building dates from 1855; it was erected after an earlier building was, ironically, destroyed by fire. Local tradition holds that George Washington was involved with the firehouse as a founding member, active firefighter, and purchaser of its first fire engine, although research does not confirm these stories. The museum displays an 1851 fire engine, old hoses, buckets, and other firefighting apparatus. This is a tiny place that you can easily visit in 20 minutes.

107 S. Alfred St. (btw. King and Prince sts.). www.alexandriava.gov/friendshipfirehouse. © **703/746-3891.** Admission $2. Sat–Sun 1–4pm.

**Gadsby's Tavern Museum** ★★    Alexandria commanded center stage in 18th-century America, and Gadsby's Tavern the spotlight. The tavern consisted of two buildings—one Georgian, one Federal, dating from around 1785 and 1792 respectively. Innkeeper John Gadsby combined them to create "a gentleman's tavern," which he operated from 1796 to 1808; it was considered one of the finest in the country. George Washington was a frequent dinner guest; he and Martha danced in the second-floor ballroom, and it was here that Washington celebrated his last birthday. The tavern also welcomed Thomas Jefferson, James Madison, and the Marquis de Lafayette (the French soldier and statesman who served in the American army under Washington during the Revolutionary War and remained close to Washington). It was the setting of lavish parties, theatrical performances, small circuses, government meetings, and concerts. Itinerant merchants used the tavern to display their wares, and traveling doctors treated a hapless clientele (these were rudimentary professions in the 18th century) on the premises.

The rooms have been restored to their 18th-century appearance. On the 30-minute tour, you'll get a good look at the Tap Room, a small dining room; the Assembly Room, the ballroom; typical bedrooms; and the underground icehouse, which was filled each winter from the icy river. Tours depart 15 minutes before and after the hour. Cap off the experience with a meal right next door, at the restored Colonial-style restaurant, **Gadsby's Tavern,** 138 N. Royal St., at Cameron Street (www.gadsbystavernrestaurant.com; ✆ **703/548-1288**).

134 N. Royal St. (at Cameron St.). www.gadsbystavern.org. ✆ **703/746-4242.** Admission $5 adults, $3 children 5–12, free for children 4 and under. Tours Apr–Oct Tues–Sat 10am–5pm, Sun–Mon 1–5pm; Nov–Mar Wed–Sat 11am–4pm, Sun 1–4pm. Closed most federal holidays.

## Lee-Fendall House Museum ★★

This handsome Greek Revival–style house is a veritable Lee family museum of furniture, heirlooms, and documents. "Light-Horse Harry" Lee never actually lived here, but he was a frequent visitor, as was his good friend George Washington. He did own the original lot, but sold it to Philip Richard Fendall (himself a Lee on his mother's side), who built the house in 1785.

Thirty-seven Lees occupied the house over a period of 118 years (1785–1903), and it was in this house that Harry wrote Alexandria's farewell address to George Washington, delivered when he passed through town on his way to assume the presidency. (Harry also wrote and delivered the famous funeral oration to Washington that contained the words, "First in war, first in peace, and first in the hearts of his countrymen.") During the Civil War, the house was seized and used as a Union hospital.

Thirty-minute guided tours interpret the 1850s era of the home and provide insight into Victorian family life. Much of the interior woodwork and glass is original. You may visit the Colonial garden, with its magnolia and chestnut trees, roses, and boxwood-lined paths, as part of your tour or on your own without a ticket.

614 Oronoco St. (at Washington St.). www.leefendallhouse.org. ✆ **703/548-1789.** Admission $5 adults, $3 children 5–17, free for children 4 and under. Wed–Sat 10am–4pm; Sun 1–4pm. Call ahead to make sure the museum is open, since it often closes for special events. Tours on the hour 10am–3pm. Closed Jan and Thanksgiving.

## The Lyceum ★

This Greek Revival building houses a museum depicting Alexandria's history from the 17th to the 20th century. It features changing exhibits and an ongoing series of lectures, concerts, and educational programs. The knowledgeable staff will be happy to answer questions.

The striking brick-and-stucco Lyceum also merits a visit. Built in 1839, it was designed in the Doric temple style to serve as a lecture, meeting, and concert hall. It was an important center of Alexandria's cultural life until the Civil War, when Union forces appropriated it for use as a hospital. After the war it became a private residence, and still later was subdivided for office space. In 1969, however, the city council's use of eminent domain prevented the Lyceum from being demolished in favor of a parking lot. Allow about 20 minutes here.

201 S. Washington St. (off Prince St.). www.alexandriahistory.org. © **703/746-4994.** Admission $2. Mon–Sat 10am–5pm; Sun 1–5pm. Closed Jan 1, Thanksgiving, and Dec 25.

## Old Presbyterian Meeting House ★

Presbyterian congregations have worshiped in Virginia since the Reverend Alexander Whittaker converted Pocahontas in Jamestown in 1614. The original version of this Presbyterian Meeting House was built in 1774. Although it wasn't George Washington's church, the Meeting House bell tolled continuously for 4 days after his death in December 1799, and memorial services were preached from the pulpit here by Presbyterian, Episcopal, and Methodist ministers. According to the Alexandria paper of the day, "The walking being bad to the Episcopal church, the funeral sermon of George Washington will be preached at the Presbyterian Meeting House." Two months later, on Washington's birthday, Alexandria citizens marched from Market Square to the church to pay their respects.

Many famous Alexandrians are buried in the church graveyard, including John and Sarah Carlyle; Dr. James Craik (the surgeon who treated—some say killed—Washington, dressed Lafayette's wounds at Brandywine, and ministered to the dying Braddock at Monongahela); and William Hunter, Jr., founder of the St. Andrew's Society of Scottish descendants, to whom bagpipers pay homage on the first Saturday of December. It's also the site of a Tomb of an Unknown Revolutionary War Soldier. Dr. James Muir, minister between 1789 and 1820, lies beneath the sanctuary in his gown and bands. The cemetery has a larger burial ground nearby that has been used since 1809.

When lightning struck and set afire most of the original Meeting House in 1835, parishioners rebuilt the church in 1837, incorporating as much as they could from the earlier structure. This is the church you see today. The present bell, said to be recast from the metal of the old one, was hung in a newly constructed belfry in 1843, and a new organ was installed in 1849. The Meeting House closed its doors in 1889 and for 60 years was used sporadically. But in 1949 it was reborn as a living Presbyterian U.S.A. church, and today the Old Meeting House looks much as it did following its first restoration. The original parsonage, or manse, is still intact. There's no guided tour. Allow 20 minutes.

323 S. Fairfax St. (btw. Duke and Wolfe sts.). www.opmh.org. © **703/549-6670.** Free admission, but you must obtain a key from the office to tour the church. Sun services 8:30 and 11am (only 10am in summer).

## Stabler-Leadbeater Apothecary Museum ★★

When its doors closed in 1933, this landmark drugstore was the second oldest in continuous operation in America. Run for five generations by the same Quaker family (beginning in 1792), the store counted Robert E. Lee (who purchased the paint for Arlington House here), George Mason, Henry Clay, John C. Calhoun, and George Washington among its famous patrons. Gothic Revival decorative elements and Victorian-style doors were added in the 1840s. Today the apothecary looks much as it did in Colonial times, its shelves lined with original handblown gold-leaf-labeled bottles (the most valuable collection of antique medicinal bottles in

**Original gold-leafed bottles in the Stabler-Leadbeater Apothecary Museum in Alexandria.**

the country), old scales stamped with the royal crown, patent medicines, and equipment for bloodletting. The clock on the rear wall, the porcelain-handled mahogany drawers, and two mortars and pestles all date from about 1790. Among the shop's documentary records is this 1802 order from Mount Vernon: "Mrs. Washington desires Mr. Stabler to send by the bearer a quart bottle of his best Castor Oil and the bill for it." The museum is open for guided tours only, which take place 15 minutes before and after the hour, and last 30 minutes.

105–107 S. Fairfax St. (near King St.). www. apothecarymuseum.org. ℂ **703/746-3852.** Admission $5 adults, $3 children 5–12, free for children under 5. Apr–Oct Tues–Sat 10am–5pm, Sun–Mon 1–5pm; Nov–Mar Wed–Sat 11am–4pm, Sun 1–4pm. Closed major holidays.

**Torpedo Factory** ★  This block-long, three-story building was built in 1918 as a torpedo shell-case factory but now accommodates some 82 artists' studios, where 165 professional artists and craftspeople create and sell their own works. Here you can see artists at work in their studios: from potters to painters, as well as those who create stained-glass windows and fiber art.

On permanent display are exhibits on Alexandria history provided by Alexandria Archaeology (www.alexandriaarchaeology.org, ℂ **703/746-4399**), which is headquartered here and engages in extensive city research. A volunteer or staff member is on hand to answer questions. Art lovers may end up browsing for an hour or two.

105 N. Union St. (btw. King and Cameron sts., on the waterfront). www.torpedofactory. org. ℂ **703/838-4565.** Free admission. Daily 10am–6pm (Thurs until 9pm). Archaeology exhibit area Tues–Fri 10am–3pm; Sat 10am–5pm; Sun 1–5pm. Closed Jan 1, Easter, July 4, Thanksgiving, and Dec 25.

## Where to Eat, Stay & Play

Old Town Alexandria is in the midst of a big redevelopment centered on its waterfront. The plan calls for new hotels, restaurants, shops, bars, and town houses; a rebuilt pier; and a 1½-mile riverwalk. Most of these attractions probably will not be up and running in 2017, but just in case, be sure to visit the waterfront while you're here, which is recommended in any case. Among the possible 2017 debuts are a Kimpton hotel, the Hotel Indigo, at Union and Duke sts., and Vola's Dockside Grill and Hi-Tide Lounge, at 7 King St. Otherwise, you can count on finding the restaurants, bars, and hotels, described below, at your service.

## WHERE TO EAT

A number of Alexandria restaurants are so well liked that Washingtonians drive over just to dine. The following are among the best to suit assorted budgets, tastes, and styles; all are easily accessible via the King Street Metro station, combined with a ride on the free King Street Trolley to the center of Old Town.

### Expensive

**Restaurant Eve** ★★★ NEW AMERICAN/ASIAN Named for the first child of owners Cathal (the chef) and Meshelle Armstrong, Eve is nationally recognized and locally beloved. Lately, the Irish chef has been incorporating Filipino tastes into his dishes, drawing from his wife's heritage. So, at dinner, look for the like of "Filipino Street BBQ" mixed in with entrees such Basque stew and veal sweetbreads on the nightly a la carte menu, and expect to see an Asian Tasting Menu. Chef Armstrong also prepares nightly five-course and seven-course tasting menus of seasonal offerings, like breast of squab with heirloom beets and sweet onions, reflective of his commitment to using the fresh meats and produce of local farmers. Don't forego dessert, like the warm shortcake with Virginia strawberries. And be sure to read over the wine and cocktails list, because sommelier and "liquid savant" Todd Thrasher gained such renown for his inventive concoctions—"Millions of Peaches" (peach vodka, champagne-vinegar-pickled peaches, and poached peaches), "Jose's Yin and Tonic" (made with house-made tonic)—that he opened a nearby speakeasy lounge, **PX**, located just above **Eamonn's A Dublin Chipper** (see below), where he dispenses more fun drinks and good times.

110 S. Pitt St. (near King St.). www.restauranteve.com. ☎ **703/706-0450.** Reservations recommended. Lunch main courses $19–$24; a la carte dinner main courses $36–$42; 5-course tasting menu $105; 7-course tasting menu $140; Asian tasting menu $65 (served family-style); lunch menu special (served at the bar weekdays 11:30am–3:30pm) $15 for any 2 items. Mon–Fri 11:30am–2pm; Mon–Sat 5:30–10pm (bar and lounge stays open later).

### Moderate

**Blackwall Hitch** ★ SEAFOOD/AMERICAN For a tasty meal that comes with a view, this is your place. The huge (seats 500), glass-enclosed restaurant and its two patios sit right on the waterfront, overlooking the Potomac River and the Torpedo Factory (see p. 251). Its interior holds two dining rooms, an oyster bar, a bar/lounge where live music plays Wednesday to Sunday evenings and at Sunday brunch, and the upstairs Crow's Nest bar, a perfect niche for boat- and people-watching. The decor leans toward a nautical theme; the menu, likewise, leans seaward, with choices that include an excellent lobster roll, fish and chips, and crab cakes, but with many plain old American offerings too, flatbreads to burgers. There's even a kids' menu of chicken tender, burger, and pasta fare, $5 to $7 each.

5 Cameron St. (on the waterfront). www.theblackwallhitch.com. ☎ **703/739-6090.** Reservations recommended. Main courses lunch and dinner $13–$35, Sun brunch $34.99 per adult, $14.99 per child 13 and under. Mon–Wed 11am–1am; Thurs–Sat 11am–2am; Sun 10am–1am.

**Inexpensive**

**Eamonn's A Dublin Chipper** ★ FISH & CHIPS   Fish and chips and a few sides (onion rings, coleslaw)—that's what we're talking here. But it's charming. Upstairs is **PX,** an exclusive lounge, where mixologist Todd Thrasher may be on hand to shake the drinks he's created. This is another in the strand of restaurant experiences that Cathal and Meshelle Armstrong are perpetrating on this side of the Potomac. The Chipper is named after their son Eamonn, **Restaurant Eve** (see above) for their firstborn daughter. The Armstrongs have a following, so expect a crowd.

728 King St. www.eamonnsdublinchipper.com. ℰ **703/299-8384.** Reservations not accepted. Main courses $6–$10. Mon–Wed 11:30am–10pm; Thurs 11:30am–11pm; Fri 11:30am–midnight; Sat noon–midnight; Sun noon–closing.

**La Madeleine** ★ FRENCH CAFE   It may be part of a self-service chain, but this place has its charms. Its French-country interior has a beamed ceiling, oak floors, a wood-burning stove, and maple hutches displaying crockery and pewter mugs. The range of affordable menu items here makes this a good choice for families with finicky eaters in tow.

La Madeleine opens early—at 7am Sunday, 6:30am every other day—so come for breakfast to feast on fresh-baked croissants, Danish, scones, muffins, and brioches, or a heartier bacon-and-eggs plate. Throughout the day, there are salads, sandwiches (including a traditional croque monsieur), and hot dishes ranging from quiche and pizza to rotisserie chicken with a Caesar salad. After 5pm, additional choices include pastas and specials such as beef tenders *en merlot* or herb-crusted pork tenderloin, both served with garlic mashed potatoes and green beans amandine. Conclude with a fruit tart, or chocolate, vanilla, and praline triple-layer cheesecake with graham-cracker crust. Wine and beer are served.

500 King St. (at S. Pitt St.). www.lamadeleine.com. ℰ **703/739-2854.** Reservations not accepted. Main courses breakfast $5–$9, lunch and dinner $5–$13. Sun 7am–10pm; Mon–Thurs 6:30am–10pm; Fri–Sat 6:30am–11pm.

## NIGHTLIFE

Old Town Alexandria's nightlife options center on the bar scene, which is nearly as varied as the one across the Potomac in the District. In fact, a number of popular, in-town restaurant-bars have outposts here, including **Pizzeria Paradiso** (p. 106), at 124 King St. (www.eatyourpizza.com; ℰ **703/837-1245**), whose cozy bar is situated behind a large glass fireplace and serves 14 drafts, American microbrews and Belgian beers, and hosts happy hour Monday through Thursday from 5 to 7pm. If you're in the mood for raucous karaoke, shuffleboard, and skeeball, make your way to **The Light Horse,** 715 King St. (www.thelighthorserestaurant.com; ℰ **703/549-0533**), where downstairs is a restaurant, but upstairs is where you want to be. And for cocktails, live jazz, and a view of the Potomac, snag a seat in the lounge of **Blackwall Hitch** Wednesday through Sunday evenings (see listing above for more information).

## WHERE TO STAY

With 4,200+ hotel guest rooms, Alexandria will have no trouble accommodating you should you decide to stay overnight. Hotels run the budget gamut, from **Comfort Inns** (www.comfortinn.com) at the low end to the posh **Lorien Hotel and Spa,** 1600 King St. (www.lorienhotelandspa.com; © **703/894-3434**) at the luxe end. As noted above, more hotels are expected to open in Old Town proper in late 2017 or in 2018. For now, only two properties lie in the heart of historic Old Town. The **Hotel Monaco Alexandria,** at 480 King St. (www.monaco-alexandria.com; © **800/368-5047** or 703/549-6080), is a luxury boutique property with 241 stylish rooms, a pool, a health club, and a fine restaurant. Rates vary by season and date, but expect to pay from $170 to $300 on weekends ($229–$370 weekdays) for a standard double room.

**Morrison House,** 116 S. Alfred St. (www.morrisonhouse.com; © **866/834-6628** or 703/838-8000), is also a standout, and even more so now, having undergone a multimillion-dollar renovation in 2016. Its 45 rooms are appointed with floor-to-ceiling windows; vibrant red, white, and blue hues; marble bathrooms; decorative fireplaces; and the like. Rates can start at $169 for the smallest room off-season on the weekend and at $329 for a standard room on a weekday in season.

# SELF-GUIDED WALKING TOURS

One of the greatest pleasures to be had in the nation's capital is walking. You round a corner and spy the Capitol standing proudly at the end of the avenue. You stroll a downtown street and chance to look up and bam, there it is: the tip of the Washington Monument. People brush past you on the sidewalk speaking a pastiche of languages. You decide to walk rather than take the Metro or a taxi back to your hotel and discover a gem of a museum. A limousine pulls up to the curb and discharges—who? A foreign ambassador? The president himself? A famous author or athlete or human rights activist?

Beautiful sights, historic landmarks, unpredictable encounters, and multicultural experiences await you everywhere in Washington. Follow any of these three self-guided walking tours and see for yourself.

## WALKING TOUR 1: STROLLING AROUND THE WHITE HOUSE

| | |
|---|---|
| START: | **White House Visitor Center, 1450 Pennsylvania Ave. NW (Metro: Federal Triangle or Metro Center).** |
| FINISH: | **The Penn Quarter (Metro: Federal Triangle or Metro Center).** |
| TIME: | **1½ hours to 2 hours (not including stops). It's about a 1.6-mile trek.** |
| BEST TIME: | **During the day. If you want to hit all of the museums, stroll on a Thursday or Friday.** |
| WORST TIME: | **After dark, as some streets can be deserted.** |

The White House is the centerpiece of a national park, President's Park, which includes not just the house itself but also its grounds, from the Ellipse to Pennsylvania Avenue to Lafayette Square; the U.S. Treasury Building on 15th Street; and the Eisenhower Executive Office Building on 17th Street. The individual histories of many of the surrounding buildings and sites are entwined with that of the White House. As you wend your way from landmark to landmark, you'll be mingling with White House administration staff, high-powered attorneys, diplomats, and ordinary office workers.

# Strolling Around the White House

**1** U.S. Treasury Building

**2** Pennsylvania Avenue

**3** Lafayette Square

**4** St. John's Episcopal Church, Lafayette Square

**5** Decatur House

**6** White House

**7** Renwick Gallery

**8** Eisenhower Executive Office Building

**9** Taylor Gourmet 🍴

**10** Octagon House

**11** Corcoran Gallery

**12** DAR Museum and Period Rooms

**13** Art Museum of the Americas

**14** Ellipse

But all of you are treading the same ground as early American heroes—like Stephen Decatur, whose house you'll see—and every president since George Washington (though the White House was not finished in time for him to live there).

This tour circumnavigates the White House grounds, with stops at historic sites and several noteworthy museums, as well. The White House Visitor Center (see "Midtown," in chapter 6) is a good place to begin and end (for one thing, it's got restrooms!). *Note:* Tours of the White House require advance reservations, as do tours of the U.S. Treasury Building. Go to www.treasury.gov/about/education/pages/tours.aspx to register for a Treasury Building tour; for White House tour info, see p. 168.

*Start: From the White House Visitor Center, stroll up 15th Street to your first stop, at 15th and F streets NW.*

---

## 1 U.S. Treasury Building

Hamilton! How strange and wondrous is it that in the year 2017 everybody is talking about Alexander Hamilton, who died in 1795? Well, by "everybody," we mean theatergoers: Lin-Manuel Miranda's brilliant musical *Hamilton* has brought the man and his times to life on Broadway (and to a theater near you, if you're lucky). On this tour, you must settle for Hamilton, the statue. It stands outside the south end of the U.S. Treasury Building, too close to the White House for security's comfort to allow stray tourists a better look, so you must resign yourself to gazing at him from a distance through the black iron fencing. Hamilton, who devised our modern financial system, was the first secretary of the Treasury, established by Congress in 1789. Once you've caught a glimpse of Hamilton's statue, turn your attention to the Treasury's headquarters, America's oldest office building, constructed between 1836 and 1869. Its most notable architectural feature is the colonnade you see running the length of the building: 30 columns, each 36 feet tall, carved out of a single piece of granite. In its lifetime, the building has served as a Civil War barracks, as a temporary home for President Andrew Johnson following the assassination of President Lincoln in 1865, and as the site of President Ulysses S. Grant's inaugural reception. Today the building houses offices for the U.S. treasurer, the secretary of the Treasury, its general counsel, and their staffs.

Continue north on 15th Street and turn left onto the Pennsylvania Avenue promenade, where you'll notice the statue of Albert Gallatin, the fourth Secretary of the Treasury, standing accessibly on the north side of the Treasury Building. Continue along:

## 2 Pennsylvania Avenue

Say hello to the president, who resides in that big white house beyond the black iron fencing. Security precautions put in place in 1995 keep this 2-block section of Pennsylvania Avenue closed to traffic. But that's a good thing. You may have to dodge bicyclists, roller skaters, joggers, and random Frisbees, but not cars. Ninety Princeton American elm trees line

A view of Pennsylvania Avenue and the White House from above.

the 84-foot-wide promenade, which offers plenty of great photo ops as you stroll past the White House. There are benches here, too, in case you'd like to sit and people-watch. L'Enfant's original idea for Pennsylvania Avenue was that it would connect the legislative branch (Congress) at one end of the avenue with the executive branch (the president's house) at the other end.

Turn your back on the White House and walk across the plaza to enter:

### 3 Lafayette Square

This 7-acre public park is known as a gathering spot for protesters. (In pleasant weather, when the White House keeps its doors and windows open, one can actually hear the protesters from inside the White House, as I discovered during a recent White House tour.) In its early days, the grounds held temporary shelters for the slaves building the White House, then open-air market stands, then tents for a military encampment. The park is named after the Marquis de Lafayette, a Frenchman who served under George Washington during the Revolutionary War. But it's General Andrew Jackson's statue that centers the park. Erected in 1853, this was America's first equestrian statue. It's said that sculptor Clark Mills trained a horse to maintain a reared-up pose so that Mills could study how the horse balanced its weight. Other park statues are dedicated to foreign soldiers who fought in the War for Independence, including Lafayette; Tadeusz Kościuszko, from Poland; Prussian Baron von Steuben; and Frenchman Comte de Rochambeau.

Walk through the park and cross H Street to reach 1525 H St. NW, the site of:

### 4 St. John's Episcopal Church on Lafayette Square

St. John's is known as "the Church of the Presidents" because every president since James Madison has attended at least one service here. If you tour the church, look for pew 54, eight rows from the front, which is the one traditionally reserved for the current president and first family. Other things to notice in this 1816 church, designed by Benjamin Henry Latrobe, are the steeple bell, which was cast by Paul Revere's son and has been in continuous use since its installation in 1822, and the beautiful stained-glass windows. And be careful not to overlook the Lincoln Pew at the very back of the church, where Lincoln would sit alone for evening services during the Civil War, slipping in after other congregants had arrived and slipping out before they left.

Directly across the street from St. John's is the Hay-Adams Hotel, which turns 89 this year (p. 65). Re-cross H Street to stand in front of 748 Jackson Place NW, the:

## 5 Decatur House

In addition to St. John's, Latrobe designed this Federal-style brick town house in 1818 for Commodore Stephen Decatur, a renowned naval hero in the War of 1812. Decatur and his wife, Susan, established themselves as gracious hosts in the 14 short months they lived here. In March 1820, two days after hosting a ball for President James Monroe's daughter, Marie, Decatur was killed in a gentleman's duel by his former mentor, James Barron. Barron blamed Decatur for his 5-year suspension from the Navy, following a court-martial in which Decatur had played an active role. Other distinguished occupants have included Henry Clay and Martin Van Buren, when each was serving as Secretary of State (Clay under Pres. John Quincy Adams, Van Buren under Pres. Andrew Jackson). Decatur House is the centerpiece of the David M. Rubenstein Center for White House History and is open for house tours on a limited basis. (Decatur House, which includes slave quarters, is a stop on the African American History itinerary; see p. 41 for more information.) The White House Historical Association's gift shop is at the entrance to Decatur House, at 1610 H St.

Walk back through Lafayette Square to return to the Pennsylvania Avenue plaza, where you'll have another chance to admire the:

## 6 White House

As grand as the White House is, it is at least one-fourth the size that Pierre L'Enfant had in mind when he planned a grand palace to house the President. George Washington and his commission had something else in mind, however, and dismissed L'Enfant, though they kept L'Enfant's site proposal. An Irishman named James Hoban designed the building, having entered his architectural draft in a contest held by George Washington, beating out 52 other entries. Although Washington picked the winner, he was the only president never to live in the White House, or "President's Palace," as it was called before whitewashing brought the name "White House" into use. Construction of the White House took 8 years, beginning in 1792, when its cornerstone was laid. Its facade is made of the same stone used to construct the Capitol. See p. 165 for in-depth information about the White House and tours.

Turn around and head toward the northwest corner of the plaza, at 17th Street, to reach the:

## 7 Renwick Gallery

Its esteemed neighbors are the White House and, right next door, the Blair-Lee House, where the White House sends overnighting foreign dignitaries. The Renwick (p. 164), nevertheless, holds its own. This distinguished redbrick-and-brownstone structure was the original location for the Corcoran Gallery of Art. James Renwick designed the building (if it reminds you of the Smithsonian Castle on the Mall, it's because Renwick designed that one, too), which opened in 1874. When the collection outgrew its quarters, the Corcoran moved to its current location in 1897 (see below). Decorative arts and American crafts are the focus of the Renwick, which since 1972 has operated as an annex of the Smithsonian American Art Museum, 8 blocks away in the Penn Quarter. By all means, head inside.

The U.S. Treasury Building.

Turn left on 17th Street, where you'll notice on your left the:

## 8 Eisenhower Executive Office Building

Old-timers still refer to this ornate building as the "OEOB," for "Old Executive Office Building"; as it sounds, the Eisenhower Executive Office Building houses the offices of people who work in or with the Executive Office of the President. Originally, the structure was called the State, War, and Navy Building; when its construction was completed in 1888, it was the largest office building in the world. During the Iran-Contra scandal of the Reagan presidency, the OEOB became famous as the site of document shredding by Colonel Oliver North and his secretary, Fawn Hall. Open to the public? Nope.

Cross 17th Street, then cross to the other side of Pennsylvania Avenue. See all the sandwich places? You can choose Potbelly's if you'd like, but I'd rather you try a local favorite, at 1750 Pennsylvania Ave. NW:

## 9 Taylor Gourmet 🍱

Italian hoagies, cheesesteaks, we're talking crusty bread filled with luscious sliced meats and cheeses and herbs, or grilled vegetables, if you're of that persuasion. Smaller, less expensive versions for children are also on the menu (www.taylorgourmet.com; ℭ 202/393-0800).

After you've satisfied your hunger, walk westward to 18th Street NW, turn left and stroll 3 blocks to New York Avenue, where you'll spy the unmistakable:

## 10 Octagon House

Lots of history in this old house. But first, before you enter, admire its unique shape. Count its sides and you'll discover that the Octagon is, in fact, a hexagon. Designed by Dr. William Thornton, first architect of the U.S. Capitol, this 1801 building apparently earned its name from interior features, though experts disagree about that. Enter the Octagon to view the round rooms; the central, oval-shaped staircase that curves gracefully to the third level; the hidden doors; and the triangular chambers. Built originally for the wealthy Tayloe family, the Octagon served as a temporary president's home for James and Dolley Madison after the British torched the White House in 1814. On February 17, 1815, President Madison sat at the circular table in the upstairs circular room and signed the Treaty of Ghent, establishing peace with Great Britain. The house has belonged to the American Institute of Architects since 1899. See p. 298 for more info about tours.

Cross New York Avenue and return to 17th Street, where you should turn right and walk to the Corcoran Gallery. You'll not be able to go inside.

## 11 Corcoran Gallery of Art

This gallery, which was the first art museum in Washington and one of the first in the country, has always had a penchant for playing the wild card. In 1851, gallery founder William Corcoran caused a stir when he displayed artist Hiram Powers' *The Greek Slave,* which was the first publicly exhibited, life-size American sculpture depicting a fully nude female figure. (Visit the American Art Museum [p 179], where an exhibit, "Measured Perfection: Hiram Powers' *Greek Slave,*" displays another version of that bare-naked lady, along with other artworks by Powers and an examination of his techniques, until Feb. 19, 2017.) *Note:* The Corcoran is now one entity in a tripartite arrangement with George Washington University and the National Gallery of Art; it will re-open to the public eventually, but not in 2017.

Walk to 17th Street and turn right, away from the White House. Follow it down to D Street and turn right, following the signs that lead to the entrance of the:

## 12 DAR Museum and Period Rooms

The National Headquarters of the Daughters of the American Revolution comprises three joined buildings that take up an entire block. The middle building, Memorial Continental Hall, is the one you'll enter. Dedicated to the heroes of the American Revolution, the building's cornerstone was laid in 1902 with the same trowel that George Washington used to lay the cornerstone for the Capitol. At the time, the front of the building faced the White House pasture, where presidential cattle grazed. At any rate, what you're here for is the DAR Museum, which rotates exhibits of items from its 33,000-object collection, and the 31 period rooms, representing decors from the past, as interpreted by different states. The museum's collections veer from folk art to decorative arts and include old rocking chairs, ceramics, needlework samplers, and lots of silver. Quilters from far and wide come to admire a large collection of quilts, many of which are kept in glass sleeves that you can pull out from a case for better viewing. Period rooms are viewable from the doorways, a velvet rope preventing your entry. Highlights include the New Jersey Room, which replicates an English Council chamber of the 17th century, with woodwork and furnishings created from the salvaged oak timbers of the British frigate *Augusta,* which sank during the Revolutionary War; an opulent Victorian Missouri parlor; and New Hampshire's "Children's Attic," filled with 19th-century toys, dolls, and children's furnishings. You can tour the museum and period rooms on your own, but you might consider taking a free docent-led tour if you're interested in American decorative arts.

Exit the DAR, turning left and continuing along D Street to 18th Street, where you'll turn left again and follow to 201 18th St. NW, the pretty, Spanish colonial–style building that houses the:

## 13 Art Museum of the Americas

Off the beaten path, but just slightly—across Constitution Avenue, the World War II Memorial is a short walk to the left, and the Vietnam Veterans Memorial a short walk to the right—the Art Museum of the Americas (AMA) showcases the works of contemporary Latin American and Caribbean artists. For example, a recent exhibit focused on the theme of mobility and migration, as interpreted by Spanish and Latin American artists living in New York City. You'll be on your own; a tour takes 30 minutes, tops. Not to miss: a stunning loggia whose tall beamed ceiling and wall of deep-blue tiles set in patterns modeled after Aztec and Mayan art constitute a work of art on its own. A series of French (and usually locked) doors leads to a terrace and the museum's garden, which separates the museum from the Organization of American States (OAS) headquarters that owns it. When you leave the museum, you may notice the nearby sculptures of José Artigus, "Father of the Independence of Uruguay," and a large representation of liberator Simón Bolívar on horseback.

From 18th Street, head back in the direction of the White House, turning right on C Street, which takes you past the AMA's garden and the OAS headquarters. Turn left on 17th Street and follow it to E Street. Then cross 17th Street and pick up the section of E Street that takes you between the South Lawn of the White House and the:

## 14 Ellipse

Did you know that it's possible to bring a blanket and some food and picnic on the Ellipse? It's true. That is, it's true in the nation's capital sense of the word, meaning that if a White House event requires increased security and the Secret Service tell you to skedaddle, you'd best skedaddle. Otherwise, though, feel free to stroll the grounds. The Ellipse continues to be the site for the National Christmas Tree Lighting Ceremony every December, and a spot near the Zero Milestone monument remains a favored place for shooting photos against the backdrop of the

White House. If you're ready to call it a day, keep walking a few more steps to return to 15th Street NW in the Penn Quarter, and its many options for an end-of-stroll repast.

## WALKING TOUR 2: **GEORGETOWN**

| | |
|---|---|
| START: | **Kafe Leopold's (DC Circulator bus; nearest Metro stop: Foggy Bottom).** |
| FINISH: | **Mount Zion United Methodist Church (DC Circulator bus; nearest Metro stop: Foggy Bottom).** |
| TIME: | **2½ to 3 hours (not including stops). The distance is about 3½ miles.** |
| BEST TIME: | **Weekday mornings are best to start out. If you want to attend a service at Mount Zion United Methodist Church, as well as do the house and museum tours, Sunday is your best day, and you should simply reverse the order of your stops, beginning at Mount Zion.** |
| WORST TIME: | **Saturday, when Georgetown's crazy social scene sometimes spills over into the back streets.** |

The Georgetown famous for its shops, restaurants, and bars is not the Georgetown you'll see on this walking tour. Instead, the circuit will take you along quiet streets lined with charming houses and stately trees that remind you of the town's age and history. The original George Town, comprising 60 acres and named for the king of England, was officially established in 1751. It assumed new importance in 1790 when President George Washington, with help from his Secretary of State, Thomas Jefferson, determined that America's new capital city would be located on a site nearby, on the Potomac River. Georgetown was incorporated into the District of Columbia in 1871.

Get your stroll off to a good start by stopping first for pastries or something more substantial at 3315 Cady's Alley NW, no. 213, the charming:

1 Kafe Leopold's 🍺

Through a passageway and down a flight of stairs from busy M Street NW lies a cluster of chi-chi shops and Kafe Leopold's (www.kafeleopolds.com; ℂ **202/965-6005**), a cute little Austrian coffeehouse that serves breakfast items until 4pm and assorted other delicious dishes all day. Onion tarts, veal schnitzel, tea sandwiches, endive salad, croque-monsieur sandwiches, apple strudel, smoked fish with caperberries, Viennese coffee, and champagne cocktails are all on the menu. Leopold's opens daily at 8am and stays open until at least 10pm.

Return now to M Street, turn left, and continue to 3350 M St. NW, where you'll find the:

2 Forrest-Marbury House

No one notices this nondescript building on the edge of Georgetown near Key Bridge. But the plaque on its pink-painted brick facade hints at reasons for giving the 1788 building a once-over. Most significant is the fact that on March 29, 1791, Revolutionary War hero Uriah Forrest hosted a dinner here for his old friend George Washington and landowners who were being asked to sell their land for the purpose of creating the federal

# Strolling Around Georgetown

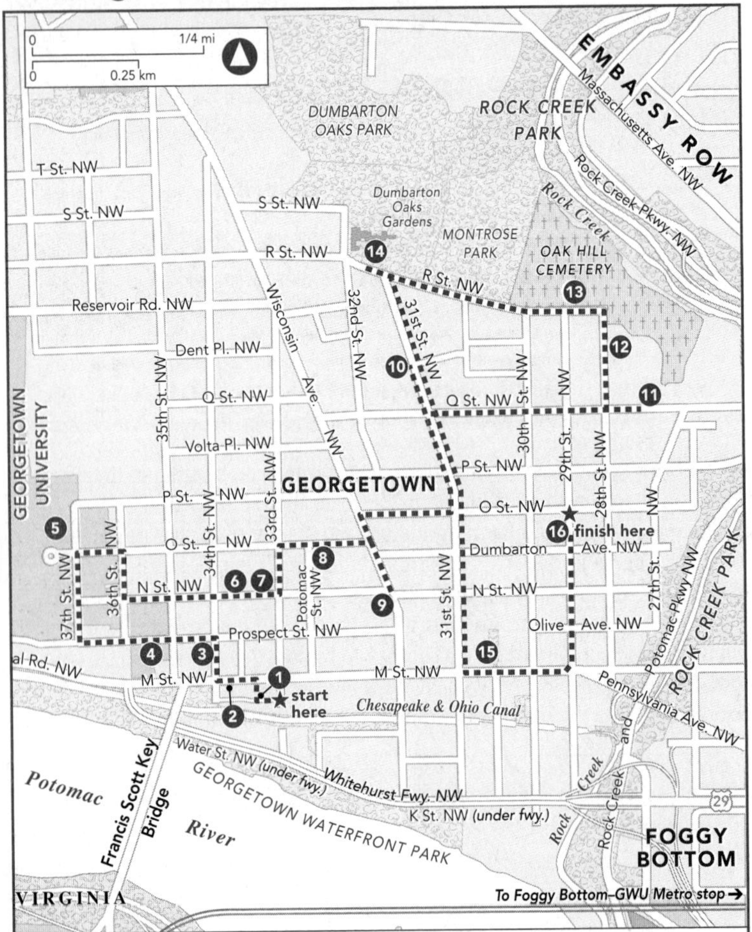

1. Kafe Leopold's ☕
2. Forrest-Marbury House
3. Halcyon House
4. Prospect House
5. Georgetown University
6. Cox's Row
7. 3307 N St.
8. St. John's Episcopal Church, Georgetown
9. Martin's Tavern ☕
10. Tudor Place
11. Dumbarton House
12. Evermay
13. Oak Hill Cemetery
14. Dumbarton Oaks and Garden
15. Old Stone House
16. Mount Zion United Methodist Church

A view of Georgetown from above.

city of Washington, District of Columbia. The meeting was a success, and America's capital was born. Forrest and his wife lived here until Federalist William Marbury bought the building in 1800. Marbury is the man whose landmark case, *Marbury v. Madison,* resulted in the recognition of the Supreme Court's power to rule on the constitutionality of laws passed by Congress and in the institutionalization of the fundamental right of judicial review. The building has served as the Ukrainian Embassy since December 31, 1992. The interior is not open to the public.

Walk to the corner of M and 34th streets, cross M Street, and walk up 34th Street one block to Prospect Street, where you'll cross to the other side of 34th Street to view 3400 Prospect St. NW, the:

## 3  Halcyon House

Benjamin Stoddert, a Revolutionary War cavalry officer and the first secretary of the Navy, built the smaller, original version of this house in 1789 and named it for a mythical bird said to be an omen of tranquil seas. (Stoddert was also a shipping merchant.) The Georgian mansion, like its neighbor Prospect House, is situated upon elevated land, the Potomac River viewable beyond. The river lapped right up to Stoddert's terraced garden—designed by Pierre Charles L'Enfant, no less—220 years ago.

Sometime after 1900, an eccentric named Albert Clemons, a nephew of Mark Twain, bought the property and proceeded to transform it, creating the four-story Palladian facade and a maze of apartments and hallways between the facade and Stoddert's original structure. Clemons is said to have filled the house with religious paraphernalia, and there are numerous stories about the house involving sightings of shadowy figures and sounds of screams and strange noises in the night. Owners of Halcyon House since Clemons's death in 1938 have included Georgetown University and a noted local sculptor, John Dreyfuss. In 2011, Japanese pharmaceutical moguls Dr. Sachiko Kuno and Dr. Ryuji Ueno purchased Halcyon House and Evermay (see p. 269).

Continue along Prospect Street to no. 3508, the site of:

## 4 Prospect House

This privately owned house was built in 1788 by James Maccubbin Lingan, a Revolutionary War hero and wealthy tobacco merchant. He is thought to have designed the house himself. Lingan sold the house in the 1790s to a prosperous banker named John Templeman, whose guests included President John Adams and the Marquis de Lafayette. In the late 1940s, James Forrestal, the secretary of defense under President Harry Truman, bought the house and offered it to his boss as a place for entertaining visiting heads of state, because the Trumans were living in temporary digs at Blair House while the White House was being renovated. The restored Georgian-style mansion is named for its view of the Potomac River. Note the gabled roof with dormer window and the sunray fanlight over the front door; at the rear of the property (not visible from the street) is an octagonal watchtower used by 18th-century ship owners for sightings of ships returning to port.

Keep heading west on Prospect Street until you reach 37th Street. Turn right and follow 37th Street to its intersection with O Street, where you'll see:

## 5 Georgetown University

Founded in 1789, Georgetown is Washington's oldest university and the nation's first Catholic university and first Jesuit-run university. Founder John Carroll, the first Catholic bishop in America and a cousin of a Maryland signer of the Declaration of Independence, opened the university to "students of every religious profession." His close friends included Benjamin Franklin and George Washington, who, along with the Marquis de Lafayette, addressed students from "Old North," which is the campus's oldest building. After the Civil War, students chose the school colors blue (the color used for Union uniforms) and gray (the color used for Confederate uniforms) to celebrate the end of the war and to honor slain students. The 104-acre campus is lovely, beginning with the stunning, spired, Romanesque-style stone building on display beyond the university's main entrance on 37th Street. That would be Healy Building, which is named for Patrick Healy, university president from 1873 to 1882 and the first African American to head a major, predominantly white university.

Turn right on O Street and walk 1 block to 36th Street, where you'll turn right again. Stroll past Holy Trinity Church, built in 1829, and continue to N Street, where you should turn left to view Holy Trinity's parish chapel (3519 N St.), the city's oldest standing church. Built in 1794, the chapel has been in continuous use ever since. Continue farther on N Street, strolling several blocks until you reach nos. 3327 to 3339, collectively known as:

## 6 Cox's Row

Built in 1817 and named for their owner and builder, John Cox, these five charming houses exemplify Federal-period architecture, with their dormer windows, decorative facades, and handsome doorways. Besides being a master builder, Cox was also Georgetown's first elected mayor, serving

22 years. He occupied the corner house at no. 3339 and housed the Marquis de Lafayette next door at no. 3337 when he came to town in 1824.

Follow N Street to the end of the block, where you'll see:

## 7 3307 N St. NW

John and Jacqueline Kennedy lived in this brick town house while Kennedy served as the U.S. senator from Massachusetts. The Kennedys purchased the house shortly after the birth of their daughter Caroline. Across the street at no. 3302 is a plaque on the side wall of the brick town house inscribed by members of the press in gratitude for kindnesses received there in the days before Kennedy's presidential inauguration. Another plaque honors Stephen Bloomer Balch (1747–1833), a Revolutionary War officer who once lived here.

Turn left on 33rd Street and walk 1 block north to O Street. Turn right on O Street and proceed to no. 3240, the site of:

## 8 St. John's Episcopal Church, Georgetown

Partially designed by Dr. William Thornton—first architect of the Capitol, who also designed the Octagon (see p. 164), and Tudor Place (see below)—the church was begun in 1796 and completed in 1804. Its foundation and walls, at least, are original. Its early congregants were the movers and shakers of their times: President Thomas Jefferson (who contributed $50 toward the building fund), Dolley Madison, Tudor Place's Thomas and Martha Peter, and Francis Scott Key. To tour the church, stop by the office, just around the corner on Potomac Street, weekdays between 10am and 4pm, or attend a service on Sunday at 9am or 11am. Visit www.stjohnsgeorgetown.org or call ✆ 202/338-1796 for more info.

Follow O Street to busy Wisconsin Avenue and turn right, walking south to reach this favorite Washington hangout. Too early for a break? Return here or to another choice restaurant later; you're never far from Wisconsin Avenue wherever you are in Georgetown.

## 9 Martin's Tavern 🍴

At 1264 Wisconsin Ave. NW (www.martinstavern.com; ✆ 202/333-7370), you'll find this American tavern, run by a string of Billy Martins, the first of whom opened the tavern in 1933. The original Billy's great-grandson is running the show today. So it's a bar, but also very much a restaurant (bring the children—everyone does), with glass-topped white tablecloths, paneled walls, wooden booths, and an all-American menu of burgers, crab cakes, Cobb salad, and pot roast. Martin's is famous as the place where John F. Kennedy proposed to Jacqueline Bouvier in 1953—look for booth no. 3. See p. 111.

Back outside, cross Wisconsin Avenue, follow it north to O Street, and turn right. Walk to 31st Street and turn left; follow it until you reach the entrance to the grand estate at 1644 31st St. NW:

## 10 Tudor Place

Yet another of the architectural gems designed by the first architect of the Capitol, Dr. William Thornton, Tudor Place crowns a hill in Georgetown,

**10**

**SELF-GUIDED WALKING TOURS** | Georgetown

set among beautiful gardens first plotted some 200 years ago. The 5½-acre estate belonged to Martha Washington's granddaughter, Martha Custis Peter, and her husband, Thomas Peter; Martha Custis purchased it in 1805 using an $8,000 legacy left to her by her step-grandfather, George Washington. Custis-Peter descendants lived here until 1983.

Tours of the house ($10) are docent-led only and reveal rooms decorated to reflect various periods of the Peter family tenancy. Exceptional architectural features include a clever floor-to-ceiling windowed wall, whose glass panes appear to curve in the domed portico (an optical illusion: It's the woodwork frame that curves, not the glass itself). On display throughout the first-floor rooms are more than 100 of George Washington's furnishings and other family items from Tudor Place's 8,000-piece collection. Docents reveal the rich history of the estate. From a sitting-room window in this summit location, Martha Custis Peter and Anna Maria Thornton (the architect's wife) watched the Capitol burn in 1814, during the War of 1812. The Peters hosted a reception for the Marquis de Lafayette in the drawing room in 1824. Friend and family relative Robert E. Lee spent his last night in Washington in one of the upstairs bedrooms.

Tours of the gardens ($3) are self-guided, with or without the use of an audio guide; a bowling green and boxwood ellipse are among the plum features. Tudor Place (www.tudorplace.org; ✆ **202/965-0400**) is open Tuesday to Saturday 10am to 4pm and Sunday noon to 4pm, with tours given every hour on the hour. *Note:* Tudor Place is closed for the entire month of January.

From 31st Street, retrace your steps as far back as Q Street, where you'll turn left and walk several blocks to reach 2715 Q St. NW:

## 11 Dumbarton House

This stately redbrick mansion (www.dumbartonhouse.org; ✆ **202/337-2288**), originally called Bellevue, was built between 1799 and 1805. In 1915, it was moved 100 yards to its current location to accommodate the placement of nearby Dumbarton Bridge over Rock Creek. The house exemplifies Federal-period architecture, which means that its rooms are almost exactly symmetrical on all floors and are centered by a large hall. Federal-period furnishings, decorative arts, and artwork fill the house; admire the dining room's late-18th-century sideboard, silver and ceramic pieces, and paintings by Charles Willson Peale. One of the original owners of Dumbarton House was Joseph Nourse, first register of the U.S. Treasury, who lived here with his family from 1805 to 1813. Dumbarton House is most famous as the place where Dolley Madison stopped for a cup of tea on August 24, 1814, while escaping the British, who had just set fire to the White House. It is open year-round Tuesday to Sunday from 11am to 3pm. Admission is $5, and tours are self-guided.

Exit Dumbarton House and turn right, retrace your steps along Q Street, and turn right on 28th Street. Climb the hill to reach 1623 28th St. NW, the estate of:

## 12 Evermay

This is a private residence, purchased in 2011 by Japanese pharmaceutical moguls Dr. Sachiko Kuno and Dr. Ryuji Ueno. And though much of the estate is obscured by brick ramparts and dense foliage, what's on view is impressive. As the plaque on the estate wall tells you, Evermay was built from 1792 to 1794 by Scottish real-estate speculator and merchant Samuel Davidson with the proceeds Davidson made from the sale of lands he owned around the city, including part of the present-day White House and Lafayette Square properties. By all accounts, Davidson was something of an eccentric misanthrope, guarding his privacy by placing menacing advertisements in the daily papers with such headlines as EVERMAY PROCLAIMS, TAKE CARE, ENTER NOT HERE, FOR PUNISHMENT IS NEAR.

Follow the brick sidewalk and iron fence that run alongside to:

## 13 Oak Hill Cemetery

Founded in 1850 by banker/philanthropist/art collector William Wilson Corcoran (founder of the former Corcoran Gallery of Art), Oak Hill is the final resting place for many of the people you've been reading about, within this chapter and in other chapters of this book. Corcoran is buried here, in a Doric temple of a mausoleum, along with the Peters of Tudor Place (see above) and the son of William Marbury of the Forrest-Marbury House (see p. 263). Corcoran purchased the property from George Corbin Washington, a great-nephew of President Washington. The cemetery consists of 25 beautifully landscaped acres adjacent to Rock Creek Park, with winding paths shaded by ancient oaks. Look for the Gothic-style stone Renwick Chapel, designed by James Renwick, architect of the Renwick Gallery (p. 164), the Smithsonian Castle (p. 155), and New York's St. Patrick's Cathedral. The Victorian landscaping, in the Romantic tradition of its era, strives for a natural look: Iron benches have a twig motif, and many of the graves are symbolically embellished with inverted torches, draped obelisks, angels, and broken columns. Even the gatehouse is worth noting; designed in 1850 by George de la Roche, it's a beautiful brick-and-sandstone Italianate structure.

Oak Hill Cemetery.

Want to go for a stroll here? Download a cemetery map (www.oakhill cemeterydc.org), or stop by the gatehouse (© 202/337-2835) to pick one up. The grounds and gatehouse are open weekdays from 9am to 4:30pm; the grounds are also open Saturday 11am to 4pm and on Sunday from 1 to 4pm.

Exit Oak Hill through the main entrance, and continue on the brick pathway to your right, strolling along R Street past Montrose Park until you reach the garden entrance to Dumbarton Oaks, on 31st Street. Or, if you'd prefer to visit the historic house and museum, continue around the corner to enter at 1703 32nd St. NW.

## 14  Dumbarton Oaks and Garden

In the mood for love? Head straight to the walled gardens, whose tiered park includes masses of roses, a Mexican tile–bordered pebble garden, a wisteria-covered arbor, cherry-tree groves, overlooks, and lots of romantic winding paths. The oldest part of Dumbarton Oaks mansion dates from 1801; since then the house has undergone considerable change, notably at the hands of a couple named Robert and Mildred Bliss, who purchased the property in 1920. As Robert was in the Foreign Service, the Blisses lived a nomadic life, amassing collections of Byzantine and Pre-Columbian art, books relating to these studies, and volumes on the history of landscape architecture. After purchasing Dumbarton Oaks, the Blisses inaugurated a grand re-landscaping of the grounds and remodeling of the mansion to accommodate their collections and the library, which now occupy the entire building. In 1940, the Blisses conveyed the house, gardens, and art collections to Harvard University, Robert's alma mater. In the summer of 1944, at the height of World War II, Dumbarton Oaks served as the location for a series of diplomatic meetings that would cement the principles later incorporated into the United Nations charter. The conferences took place in the Music Room, which you should visit to admire the immense 16th-century stone chimney piece, 18th-century parquet floor, and antique Spanish, French, and Italian furniture. (See p. 189 for more information about the museum and gardens.) Dumbarton Oaks Museum (www.doaks.org; © 202/339-6401) is open year-round Tuesday to Sunday 11:30am to 5:30pm, with free admission. The garden is open Tuesday to Sunday 2 to 6pm from March 15 to October 31, for an admission fee of $10; and Tuesday to Sunday 2 to 5pm from November 1 to March 14, with free admission.

From the intersection of R and 31st streets, follow 31st Street downhill all the way to M Street and turn left to find your next destination at 3051 M St. NW:

## 15  Old Stone House

Located on one of the busiest streets in Washington, the unobtrusive Old Stone House offers a quiet look back at life in early America, starting in 1765, when the Layman family built this home. Originally, the structure was simply one room made of thick stone walls, oak ceiling beams, and packed dirt floors. In 1800, a man named John Suter bought the building and used it as his clock-maker's shop. The grandfather clock you see on the second floor is the only original piece remaining in the house. Acquired by the National Park Service in the 1950s, the Old Stone House today shows small rooms furnished as they would have been in the late 18th century, during the period when Georgetown was a significant tobacco and shipping port. Park rangers provide information and sometimes demonstrate cooking in an open hearth, spinning, and making pomander balls. Adjacent to and behind the house is a terraced lawn and 18th-century English garden, a spot long frequented by Georgetown shop and office workers seeking a respite. Old Stone House (www.nps.gov/olst; © **202/426-6851**) is open daily 11am to 6pm; the garden is open daily dawn to dusk.

Turn left on M St. and walk 2 blocks to 29th Street, where you should turn left and walk about 3 blocks to:

## 16 Mount Zion United Methodist Church

Attend the 11am Sunday worship service here and you'll be among the city's oldest black congregation, established 201 years ago. By 1816, African Americans, both freed slaves and the enslaved, had already been living in Georgetown for decades. But blacks were not allowed to have their own church, so they worshipped at white churches, sitting in the balcony, apart from the white worshippers. In 1816, a man named Shadrack Nugent led 125 fellow black congregants to split from the nearby Montgomery Street Church (now Dumbarton United Methodist Church) and form their own congregation. The dissidents built a church, known as the "Little Ark," at 27th and P streets, and worshipped there

**Shops in Georgetown.**

until a fire destroyed the meeting house in 1880. (The congregation was all black, but the times still required a white man to be their pastor!) Meanwhile, a new and larger church was already under construction, on land purchased from a freed slave and prominent businessman named Alfred Pope, whose property adjoined the churches on 29th Street. The Mount Zion United Methodist Church held its first service in 1880, in the partially completed lecture hall, and dedicated the finished redbrick edifice you see today in 1884. The church proper actually lies on the second floor, whose high tin ceiling, beautiful stained-glass windows (called "comfort" windows for the sense of tranquility their pastel tints are said to imbue), and hand-carved pews are original features. A number of families in this 200-person congregation are descendants of the church's first founders, although only one or two congregants actually live in the neighborhood now. Mount Zion United Methodist Church welcomes all who are interested to attend its Sunday services, but otherwise is not open to the general public (www.mountzionumcdc.org; ✆ **202/234-0148**).

Now re-trace your steps to M Street. You're in the middle of Georgetown, surrounded by restaurants, shops, and bars. Go crazy! See chapters 5, 7, and 8 for recommendations.

**WALKING TOUR 3: DUPONT CIRCLE/ EMBASSY ROW**

| | |
|---|---|
| START: | **Dupont Circle (Metro to Dupont Circle).** |
| FINISH: | **Vice President's Residence/U.S. Naval Observatory (take the N2, N4, N6 busses back to either Dupont Circle or Farragut North).** |
| TIME: | **2 hours (not including stops). The distance is about 2 miles.** |
| BEST TIME: | **Any day is fine unless you want to tour the Brewmaster's Castle and/ or Anderson House, in which case you should see the descriptions for their public tour days and times, and plan accordingly.** |
| WORST TIME: | **Nighttime, as you won't be able to see the details on the houses.** |

This is a rather lengthy walk. It's worthwhile, I think, especially because you'll see nearly the whole world—or at least its embassies—on this route. (To see more, look for the national flags of other embassies located on side streets a few steps to the left or right.)

If you feel yourself tiring, you can catch the N2 Metrobus at a number of stops along this route and it will take you back to Dupont Circle. Some of the walk is uphill, which is why I'm suggesting this precaution. You can do the walk in reverse, taking the bus to your starting point as well, though the more interesting Gilded Age sites are closer to Dupont Circle, and I want you to see those while you're still fresh.

Embassies are not normally open to visitors. Some do organize art shows and concerts featuring homeland artists, and sometimes you'll see notices about them in the *Washington Post* and *Washington City Paper*. For ways to tap into embassy events, see "The Best of D.C.'s International Scene" box, p. 231.

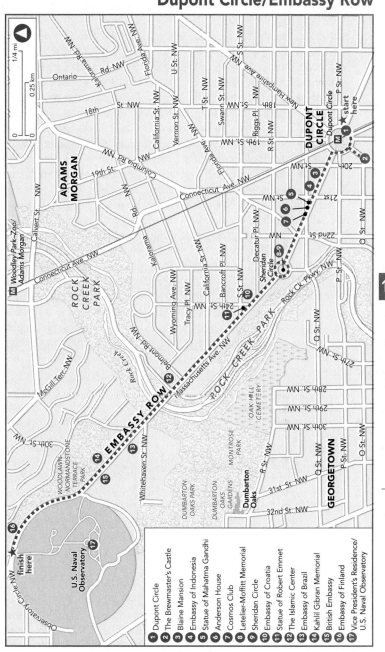

1. Dupont Circle
2. The Brewmaster's Castle
3. Blaine Mansion
4. Embassy of Indonesia
5. Statue of Mahatma Gandhi
6. Anderson House
7. Cosmos Club
8. Letelier-Moffitt Memorial
9. Sheridan Circle
10. Embassy of Croatia
11. Statue of Robert Emmet
12. The Islamic Center
13. Embassy of Brazil
14. Kahlil Gibran Memorial
15. British Embassy
16. Embassy of Finland
17. Vice President's Residence/ U.S. Naval Observatory

As for food, you won't find much of it as you wander along. Better to pick up a picnic at Teaism (p. 107) and stop in one of the garden areas along the way to nosh.

---

## 1 Dupont Circle

We'll start right in the center of the traffic circle so you can get a good look around. Dupont Circle is one of the most famous place names in D.C., at one and the same time a historic district, a traffic circle, and a progressive neighborhood that's been home, since the mid-'70s, to the city's GLBT community. In fact, every year on the Tuesday before Halloween, thousands of Washingtonians turn out to watch dozens of outrageously dressed drag queens sprint in high heels down 17th Street in the heart of the Dupont Circle neighborhood, participating in the High Heel Race, an event that's taken place annually since 1986.

Named for Civil War Naval hero Samuel Francis Du Pont, the circle is placed exactly where Washington's famed architect Charles Pierre L'Enfant envisioned it, though construction didn't begin until 1871, long after L'Enfant's death. For its center, Congress commissioned a small bronze statue of the Admiral, but the proud Du Pont family would have none of it. Without asking permission, they commissioned the two men behind the Lincoln Memorial—sculptor Daniel Chester French and architect Henry Bacon—to create the fountain you see in front of you. It replaced the bronze statue in 1921; on its shaft are allegorical figures representing the elements a sea captain needs to navigate and propel the boat forward. See if you can figure out which is "the stars," which is "the sea," and which is "the wind."

Cross Massachusetts Avenue to New Hampshire Avenue until you come to Sunderland Place, and see at 1307 New Hampshire Ave.:

## 2 The Brewmaster's Castle (the Christian Heurich House Museum)

Known in less polite circles as "burp castle," this is the house beer built. Christian Heurich was a highly successful brewer who, in the first half of the 20th century, was Washington, D.C.'s largest landowner and employer, after the federal government. He loved his work so much that he never retired, continuing to manage his brewery until his death at the age of 102 in 1945. That wasn't just a work ethic—the man had murals celebrating the joys of beer in his breakfast room and used as the slogan for his company, "Beer recommended for family use by Physicians in General." Yup, those were the days. You can see the interior on **tours** (Thurs–Sat 11:30am, 1pm, 2:30pm; $5 requested donation; www.heurichhouse.org; ⓒ **202/429-1894**).

And if you can tour it, do so—the house is notable not just for the colorful history of its owner but for its importance architecturally. Built between 1892 and 1894, it is likely the first domestic structure framed with steel and poured concrete, an effort to make it fireproof. (The

Daniel Chester French's marble fountain in the center of Dupont Circle.

salamander symbol, at the top of the tower, was used as a superstitious shield against fire.) Many consider this Romanesque-style, 31-room structure to be one of the most intact late-Victorian structures in the country. But I really like spotting the gargoyles.

Walk toward 20th Street, turn right and continue north 2 blocks to Massachusetts Avenue. Turn left and on the corner you'll find 2000 Massachusetts Ave., which is:

### 3 Blaine Mansion

The last standing mansion from the early days of Dupont Circle, this imposing brick and terracotta structure retains the name of its first owner: James G. Blaine. Had it not been for the Mugwumps—and don't you love it that we used to have political parties with such colorful names— he might well have become president instead of Grover Cleveland. As it was, charges of corruption involving illicit dealings with the railroads, ahem, derailed his campaign. This, despite the fact that Blaine had a longer and more distinguished career than most, having served as secretary of state twice, congressman and senator from Maine, and speaker of the House. The vertical sweep of the house surely impresses as much as the man, though to be honest, he barely lived here. Once the home was built, he decided it would be too costly to maintain and he leased it, first to Levi Leiter (an early co-owner of Marshall Field) and then to George Westinghouse. Yes, that Westinghouse. The latter bought it in 1901 and lived here until his death in 1914.

Continue in the same direction on Massachusetts Avenue to our first embassy at 2020 Massachusetts Ave.:

### 4 Embassy of Indonesia

The ornate structure occupied today by the Embassy of Indonesia is said to have cost $835,000 when it was built in 1903—the city's most expensive house at the time. Sadly, by the time the house was purchased by the

Indonesians in 1951, the family fortune was so depleted that they let it go for a mere $350,000. A reminder that housing bubbles have been around for quite some time.

The man who commissioned its construction, Thomas Walsh, came to the United States from Ireland in 1869 at the age of 19. He headed west, and in 1876 struck it rich not once but twice, finding what is widely thought to be one of the richest veins of gold in the world. Suddenly a modern-day Midas, he moved his family to Washington, figuring a grand 60-room mansion was the way to make a splash in society. And remembering his roots, he's said to have embedded a nugget of gold ore in the porch. You'll notice that this neo-Baroque mansion is unusually curvaceous. That's because it's meant to evoke the look of an ocean liner. A grand staircase in the home itself is a direct copy of one on the White Star ocean liner.

The fortune depleter, daughter Evalyn Walsh McLean, was notable for the tragic turn her life took. Despite the jaunty title of her autobiography, *Father Struck It Rich!,* not much else went right in her life. Her son was killed at the age of 9 in a car crash and her daughter overdosed as a young woman. Husband Edward Beale McLean, an heir to the *Post* fortune, turned out to be an alcoholic, and together they burned through some $100 million. A large chunk of it went to the purchase of the famed Hope Diamond. Those who believe the diamond is cursed claim that her misfortunes started with that purchase. She died nearly penniless at the age of 58. The diamond is now on display at the National Museum of Natural History (see p. 151). The ornate and blindingly white statue poised outside the embassy depicts Saraswati, the Hindu goddess of learning and wisdom. Since Indonesia is home to the world's largest Muslim population, the display of a Hindu figure is intended to express Indonesia's respect for religious freedom.

Keep walking in the same direction to a small triangular park where you'll find the:

5 Statue of Mahatma Gandhi

Striding purposefully, the man who led India to freedom from British rule in 1947 seems to be headed (aptly) for the **Embassy of India** (2107 Massachusetts Ave.), just across the adjacent side street. His walking stick, simple bowl, dress, and age in the sculpture suggest that this is a portrait of him on the famed protest march when he and a number of followers walked 200 miles to the Arabian Sea to collect salt (and evade the British tax on that condiment). A turning point in the non-violent fight for Indian freedom, it's an apt subject for this striking portrait.

Keep walking in the same direction to 2118 Massachusetts Ave., the:

6 Anderson House

Larz Anderson, an American diplomat, and his wife Isabel Weld Perkins, author and Red Cross volunteer, took advantage of their immense Boston wealth and built not just a home but a palace. Their intent? To create a space large enough to serve as a headquarters for the Society of the Cincinnati, of which Larz was a member (and to which they bequeathed the home upon their death). Guided tours to this museum of the gilded age and clubhouse are available (see full write-up on p. 181). The membership of the society, founded in 1783, is composed of male descendants of officers in George Washington's Continental Army.

The building itself—sporting a cavernous two-story ballroom, a dining room seating 50, grand staircase, massive wall murals, acres of marble, and 23-karat gold trim—is palatial.

Head across the street to 2121 Massachusetts Ave., the:

## 7 Cosmos Club

A prestigious private social club, Cosmos Club was founded in 1878 as a gathering place for scientists and public policy intellectuals. The National Geographic Society spun off from the Cosmos 10 years later. The Cosmos Club's first meeting was held in the home of John Wesley Powell, the soldier and explorer who first navigated the Colorado River through the Grand Canyon in a dory. Since then, 3 presidents, 2 vice presidents, a dozen Supreme Court justices, 36 Nobel Prize winners, 61 Pulitzer Prize winners, and 55 recipients of the Presidential Medal of Freedom have numbered among its ranks. But none of them were women until 1998, when the Washington, D.C., Human Rights Office ruled that the club's men-only policy was discriminatory and illegal.

The club is the latest occupant of a French-inspired chateau built in 1901 with the railroad wealth of Richard and Mary Scott Townsend. His fortune came from the Erie Line; hers from the Pennsylvania Railroad (no joke). They hired the famed New York architectural firm of Carrère and Hastings, which created the New York Public Library, to build a chateau designed to resemble the Petit Trianon—the royal hideaway at Versailles. Somewhat superstitious, the couple had the structure built around an older one. Apparently, a gypsy had once predicted that Mrs. Townsend would die "under a new roof." Despite these precautions, Mrs. Townsend did eventually pass away (darn!).

As you head toward Sheridan Square, look for the Romanian Chancery and the Embassy of Ireland (2234 Massachusetts Ave. NW). In front of these two is the:

## 8 Letelier/Moffitt Memorial

On September 21, 1976, Orlando Letelier, the former foreign minister of ousted Chilean President Salvador Allende offered his colleague Ronni Karpen Moffitt a ride home. A car bomb killed them both. This small cylindrical monument honors their memory. Thousands showed up later that week for a hastily organized protest funeral march. Eventually, five men were prosecuted for the crime. One, who led police to the others, was given just 2 years of prison time before being taken into the witness protection program. For years, rumors circulated that the American government was also in some way involved.

## 9 Sheridan Circle

The Civil War officer mounted on his muscular horse is General Philip H. Sheridan, commander of the Union cavalry and the Army of the Shenandoah. His horse Rienzi, who carried him through 85 battles and skirmishes, became almost as famous during the war as "the steed that saved the day."

Sculpted by Gutzon Borglum, who carved the presidential faces on South Dakota's Mount Rushmore, the statue depicts Sheridan rallying his men at the Battle of Cedar Creek in northern Virginia on October 19, 1864. Sheridan was 15 miles north in the town of Winchester when a Confederate force under General Jubal A. Early surprised and drove back his army. Racing to the battle site on stout-hearted Rienzi, Sheridan led his men in a victorious counterattack.

Sheridan's wife is said to have chosen the site for the statue, which is flanked by two hidden pools. His son, Second Lieutenant Philip H. Sheridan, Jr., served as a model for the statue. He was present at the unveiling in 1908, as was President Theodore Roosevelt. I suggest crossing (carefully) into the circle to get a close-up look.

Carefully cross the Circle again, back to Massachusetts Avenue and continue going north-west to 2343 Massachusetts Ave., the:

## 10 Embassy of Croatia

Outside the building the muscular figure of St. Jerome the Priest (A.D. 341–420) sits hunched over a book, his head in his hand. Jerome, the

**A statue of Union General Philip Sheridan.**

Today, about 75 embassies, chanceries, or ambassadorial residences are located on or near the 2-mile stretch of Massachusetts Avenue between Dupont Circle and Wisconsin Avenue NW. As a result, it was dubbed Embassy Row.

A word on those distinctions: An *embassy* is the official office or residence of the ambassador. Some ambassadors live and work in the embassy; others maintain separate residences, commuting to their job like the rest of us. A *chancery* is the embassy's office; this is where you might apply for a visitor's visa. It could be located within the embassy or not. Some countries also provide separate offices for special missions, such as the military attaché's office. In all, more than 180 countries maintain a diplomatic presence in Washington.

pedestal of the statue informs us, was "the greatest Doctor of the Church." This is a reference to his work in translating the Bible from Hebrew into Latin, a version called the Vulgate because it was in the language of the common people of the day. Historically, it is considered the most important vernacular edition of the Bible. At times in his younger years, Jerome's religious faith declined; he became involved in numerous theological disputes, and he spent several years in the desert leading an ascetical life while fighting temptations. I get the feeling this glum statue is commemorating those troubled times. The statue initially sat on the grounds of the Franciscan Abbey near Catholic University; it was moved here when the nation of Croatia was created at the breakup of Yugoslavia.

Continue walking to the 2400 block of Massachusetts Avenue where, in a triangular park, you'll see the:

## 11 Statue of Robert Emmet

Although somewhat obscured by foliage, the Irish revolutionary stands in a pose that he reportedly struck in Dublin in 1803 when a British court sentenced him to death by hanging. He appears to be gazing toward the Embassy of Ireland 2 blocks away. Born in 1778, Emmet led a failed uprising in Dublin on July 23, 1803. The statue was presented to the Smithsonian Institution in 1917 as a gift to the American public from a group of American citizens of Irish ancestry. It was moved to its present site in 1966, marking the 50th anniversary of Irish independence.

Note the numerous embassies en route to the next stop, including the **Embassy of Japan** (2520 Massachusetts Ave.), set back behind the cobblestone courtyard. The 1932 Georgian revival–style structure suggests the Far East with a subtle "rising sun" above the balcony over the door.

On the right is the **Embassy of Turkey** (2525 Massachusetts Ave.). The statue in front is of Mustafa Kemal Ataturk, the founder of modern Turkey.

Just before the bridge, head to 2551 Massachusetts Ave.:

## 12 The Islamic Center

The 160-foot tall white limestone minaret, soaring above Embassy Row, makes the Islamic Center impossible to miss. From it, a loudspeaker intones the call to prayer five times daily. Built in 1949, the center does not line up directly with the street; instead it faces Mecca. On Friday afternoons, throngs of the faithful pour into the mosque for prayer services, many of them embassy employees attired in their native dress. At times, prayer rugs are spread in the courtyard or even on the sidewalk outside the iron railing fence. This is when Embassy Row takes on its most dramatic multicultural look.

Visitors are welcome inside (daily 10am–5pm), so don't be shy about stepping through the open gates. But be sure to remove your shoes before entering the mosque itself; leave them in one of the slots provided on the entrance wall. Men should dress neatly; no shorts. Women are not allowed to wear sleeveless clothes or short dresses and must cover their hair. The interior, filled with colorful Arabic art, is well worth these preliminaries. Persian rugs drape the floor, overlapping one another; 7,000 blue tiles cover the lower walls in mosaic patterns; eight ornate pillars soar overhead, ringing a huge copper chandelier. The carved pulpit is inlaid with ivory, and stained-glass windows add more color.

Cross the bridge. Take a look down: 75 feet below is Rock Creek Parkway as well as the 1,700-acre Rock Creek Park (see p. 196). At the other end of the bridge, walk on and take the time to look at the embassies you'll be passing until you get to 3000 Massachusetts Ave., the:

## 13 Embassy of Brazil

This stately, palace-like building next to the big, black, boxlike building (the chancery) is the ambassador's residence. The older building, derived from an Italian Renaissance palazzo, was designed in 1931 by John Russell Pope, a leader of the city's early-20th-century neoclassicist movement. The Jefferson Memorial, National Gallery of Art, and National Archives are among Pope's other local works.

Keep walking in the same direction and look to the right side to find the:

## 14 Kahlil Gibran Memorial

An elaborate 2-acre garden, eight-sided star fountain, circular walkway, shaded benches, and bronze bust celebrate the life and achievements of the Lebanese-American philosopher. Dedicated on May 24, 1991, it is a gift "to the people of the United States" from the Kahlil Gibran Centennial Foundation. Born in 1883 in a village near the Biblical Cedars of Lebanon, Gibran arrived in Boston as a child. Building a successful career as an artist and author, he published widely quoted books in English and Arabic. He died in New York City in 1931. Excerpts from his writings are etched into the memorial's circular wall, among them: "We live only to discover beauty. All else is a form of waiting." If you need to rest your feet, this lovely garden is the perfect place to do so.

Continue your stroll to 3100 Massachusetts Ave., the:

## 15 British Embassy

Out in front and instantly recognizable in a familiar pose, **Sir Winston Churchill** stands in bronze. One foot rests on embassy property, thus British soil; the other is planted on American soil. Anglo-American unity is the symbolism, but the placement also reflects Churchill's heritage as the child of a British father and American mother. And, of course, his right hand is raised in the iconic familiar V for Victory sign he displayed in World War II. His other hand often sports a small bouquet of fresh flowers, left by admirers. The English-Speaking Union of the United States commissioned the statue, which was erected in 1966. The statue stands on a granite plinth; beneath it are blended soils from Blenheim Palace, his birthplace; from the rose garden at Chartwell, his home; and from his mother's home in Brooklyn, NY. Turn your back on Churchill for a moment and look directly across the street to see a smiling Nelson Mandela gazing back at you, his arm raised in a clenched fist. Churchill and Mandela appear to be communicating. Mandela stands in front of the South African Embassy, which erected this statue in 2013.

The U-shaped, redbrick structure rising behind the World War II prime minister is the main chancery, built in 1931. Sir Edwin Lutyens, one of Great Britain's leading architects of the day, designed both it and the ambassador's residence, located out of sight behind the chancery. The American Institute of Architects describes the pair as a "triumph," noting that Lutyens rejected the prevailing passion for neoclassical structures and instead created a colonial American design. Others suggest it looks like an 18th-century English country house. Whatever, it makes an impressive show. Too bad the concrete box on the right, an office building dedicated by Queen Elizabeth II in 1957, failed to match the architectural standard Lutyens set. The round glass structure, another unfortunately bland modern addition, is for conferences.

Cross Massachusetts Ave. at the stoplight and step from the crosswalk onto the grassy path straight ahead of you to find a steep, heavily wooded slope that drops into a slender canyon. It is Rock Creek Trail, and if you wish you could take a little nature detour. It's amazing how quickly, within 60 seconds really, you leave the hubbub of the

---

### Wise Words

An embassy in Washington, D.C., is different from embassies in most other capitals, where people visit them only if they have to; that is, to get a visa or to conduct official business. In Washington, D.C., embassies are expected to be much more. They need to be able to open windows on the life and culture of the countries they represent, not only for the select few, but for all Washingtonians and visitors to the capital who want to know. Many do, because Americans are curious by nature.
—Jukka Valtasaari, Finnish ambassador, 1988–1996 and 2001–2005

city and find yourself in nature. Okay, enough greenery. Continue walking to 3301 Massachusetts Ave., the dramatic:

## 16 Embassy of Finland

An abstract metal-and-glass front forms a green wall of climbing plants on a bronze, gridlike trellis. Within, huge windows in the rear look out onto a thickly forested slope, as if—to quote architectural historian William Morgan—"The Finns have brought a bit of the woods to Washington." Completed in 1994, the embassy was designed to display the life and culture of Finland. The embassy is open for tours one afternoon a month, 2 to 4pm, and you must register in advance.

From the Finnish Embassy, look across the street to the green slope behind the tall iron fence. That white Victorian-style house partially visible atop the hill is the:

## 17 Vice President's Residence/U.S. Naval Observatory

Number One Observatory Circle is the official residence of the U.S. vice president. The wooded estate surrounding the residence is the site of the U.S. Naval Observatory; the large white dome holding its 12-inch refracting telescope is easily seen on the right. Built in 1893, the veep's house initially was assigned to the observatory's superintendent. But in 1923 the chief of naval operations took a liking to it, booted out the superintendent, and made the house his home. In 1974, Congress evicted the Navy and transformed it into the vice president's residence.

Up to that time, vice presidents occupied their own homes, as Supreme Court judges, Cabinet members, and senators still do. But providing full security apparatus for the private homes of each new vice president became expensive. Nelson Rockefeller, vice president in the Gerald Ford administration, was the first potential resident, but he used the house only for entertaining. So Vice President Walter Mondale became the first official occupant,

The telescope at the U.S. Naval Observatory.

followed by the elder Bush, Quayle, Gore, and Cheney. If you see a big tent on the front lawn, it usually means the vice president is hosting a gala reception.

The observatory moved from Foggy Bottom to its present location in 1910. At the time, the hilltop site was rural countryside. One of the oldest scientific agencies in the country, the U.S. Naval Observatory was established in 1830. Its primary mission was to oversee the Navy's chronometers, charts, and other navigational equipment. Today it remains the preeminent authority on precise time. Scientists take observations of the sun, moon, planets, and selected stars; determine the precise time; and publish astronomical data needed for accurate navigation.

# PLANNING YOUR TRIP

A s with any trip, a little preparation is essential. This chapter provides a variety of planning tools, including information on getting to D.C., tips on transportation within the city, and additional on-the-ground resources.

## GETTING THERE

### By Plane

Three airports serve the Washington, D.C., area. General information follows that should help you determine which airport is your best bet.

**Ronald Reagan Washington National Airport (DCA)** lies 4 miles south of D.C., across the Potomac River in Virginia, about a 10-minute trip by car in non-rush-hour traffic, and 15 to 20 minutes by Metro anytime. Its proximity to the District and its direct access to the Metro rail system are reasons why you might want to fly into National. The Metropolitan Washington Airports Authority oversees both National and Dulles airports. Visit the website **www.fly-reagan.com** for airport information, or call ✆ **703/417-8000.** For Metro information, go online at **www.wmata.com.**

**Washington Dulles International Airport (IAD)** is 26 miles outside the capital, in Chantilly, Virginia, a 35- to 45-minute ride to downtown in non-rush-hour traffic. Of the three airports, Dulles handles more daily international flights, with about 35 airlines flying nonstop to 126 destinations, including 47 foreign cities. The airport is not as convenient to the heart of Washington as National, but it's more convenient than BWI, thanks to an uncongested airport access road that travels half the distance toward Washington. The airport's website is **www.flydulles.com** and its information line is ✆ **703/572-2700.**

Last but not least is **Baltimore–Washington International Thurgood Marshall Airport (BWI),** which is located about 45 minutes from downtown, a few miles outside of Baltimore. One factor especially has always recommended BWI to travelers: the major presence of **Southwest Airlines.** Its service comprises two-thirds of the airport's business, and it often offers real bargains. (Southwest also serves Dulles and National airports, but in a much smaller capacity.) Currently, BWI is in the midst of expanding its international flight options, and building the infrastructure to support that. In May 2015, BWI inaugurated the services of the low-fare international airline, WOW, which flies to Iceland, with easy connections to European destinations. BWI offers the greatest number of daily nonstop flights, 296, its 16 airlines flying to 67 domestic destinations and 12 international destinations. Call ☎ **410/859-7111** for airport information, or point your browser to **www.bwi-airport.com.**

## GETTING INTO TOWN FROM THE AIRPORT

Each of the three airports offers similar options for getting into the city. All three airports could really use better signage, especially because their ground transportation desks always seem to be located quite a distance from the gate at which you arrive. Keep trudging, and follow baggage claim signs, because ground transportation operations are always situated near baggage carousels.

**TAXI SERVICE**    For a trip to downtown D.C., you can expect a taxi to cost close to $15 for the 10- to 20-minute ride from National Airport, $60 to $68 for the 35- to 45-minute ride from Dulles Airport, and about $90 for the 45-minute ride from BWI.

**SUPERSHUTTLE**    These vans offer shared-ride, door-to-door service between the airport and your destination, whether in the District or in a suburban location. You make a reservation by phone or online (www.supershuttle.com; ☎ **800/258-3826**) and then proceed to the SuperShuttle desk or computerized kiosk in your airport to check in. The only drawback to this service is the roundabout way the driver must follow, as he or she drops off or picks up other passengers en route. If you arrive after the SuperShuttle desk has closed, you can summon a van by calling customer service at the above number or using the computerized kiosk on-site. The 24-hour service bases its fares on zip code, so to reach downtown, expect to pay about $14, plus $10 for each additional person, from National; $29, plus $10 per additional person, from Dulles; and $37, plus $12 per additional person, from BWI. SuperShuttle also tacks on a $1 to $2 fuel charge in certain vicinities, Maryland being one.

### Public Transportation Options by Airport
### FROM RONALD REAGAN WASHINGTON NATIONAL AIRPORT

If you are not too encumbered with luggage, you should take **Metrorail** into the city. Metro's Yellow and Blue Lines stop at the airport and connect via an enclosed walkway to level two, the concourse level of the main terminal, adjacent to terminals B and C. If yours is one of the airlines that still uses the "old" terminal A (Sun Country, Southwest, Air Canada, Frontier), you'll have a longer walk to reach the Metro station. Signs pointing the way can be confusing, so ask an airport employee if you're headed in the right direction; or, better yet, head out to the curb and hop a shuttle bus to the station, but be sure to ask the driver to let you know when you've reached the enclosed bridge that leads to the Metro (it may not be obvious, and drivers don't always announce the stops). **Metrobuses** also serve the area, should you be going somewhere off the Metro route. But Metrorail is fastest, a 15- to 20-minute non-rush-hour ride to downtown. If you haven't purchased a SmarTrip fare card online in advance (see box on SmarTrip cards, p. 291), you can do so at the Metro station. The base fare is $1.75, and goes up from there depending on when (fares increase during rush hours) and where you're going.

If you're renting a car from an on-site **car rental agency**—**Alamo** (www.alamo.com), **Avis** (www.avis.com), **Budget** (www.budget.com), **Enterprise** (www.enterprise.com), **Hertz** (www.hertz.com), or **National** (www.national-car.com)—go to level two, the concourse level, follow the pedestrian walkway to the parking garage, find garage A, and descend one flight. You can also take the complimentary airport shuttle (look for the sign posted at the curb outside the terminal) to parking garage A. If you've rented from off-premises agencies **Dollar** (www.dollar.com) or **Advantage** (www.advantage.com), head outside, and catch the shuttle bus.

To get downtown by car, follow the signs out of the airport for the George Washington Parkway, headed north toward Washington. Stay on the parkway until you see signs for I-395 north to Washington. Take the I-395 north exit, which takes you across the 14th Street Bridge. Stay in the left lane crossing the bridge and follow the signs for Route 1, which will put you on 14th Street NW. (You'll see the Washington Monument off to your left.) Ask your hotel for directions from 14th Street and Constitution Avenue NW. Or take the more scenic route, always staying to the left on the GW Parkway as you follow the signs for Memorial Bridge. You'll be driving alongside the Potomac River, with the Capitol and memorials in view across the river; then, as you cross over Memorial Bridge, you're greeted by the Lincoln Memorial. Stay left coming over the bridge, swoop around to the left of the Memorial, take a left on 23rd Street NW, a right on Constitution Avenue, and then, if you want to be in the heart of downtown, left again on 15th Street NW (the Washington Monument will be to your right).

**FROM WASHINGTON DULLES INTERNATIONAL AIRPORT**  Metrorail trains do not connect directly with Dulles Airport yet, so you must first catch the **Washington Flyer Silver Line Express Bus** (www.washfly.com; ℰ **888/927-4359**) to reach the closest Metro station, the Silver Line's Wiehle Ave./Reston East depot. Find the counter at Arrivals Door #4 in the main terminal or, if you're in the baggage claim area, go up the ramp at the sign for Door #4, to purchase the $5 ticket for the bus. Buses to the Wiehle Ave./Reston East Metro station run daily, every 15 minutes; the trip takes about 10 minutes. Once you arrive at the Metro station, you can purchase a Metro SmarTrip fare card to board a Silver Line train bound for Largo Town Center, which heads into D.C.

It may be more convenient to take the **Metrobus** (no. 5A) that runs between Dulles (buses depart from curb 2E, outside the Ground Transportation area) and the L'Enfant Plaza Metro station, located across from the National Mall and the Smithsonian museums, and downhill from nearby Capitol Hill. The bus departs every 30 to 40 minutes weekdays, hourly on weekends. It costs $7 (you must use a SmarTrip card—see box, p. 291—or have exact change) and takes 45 minutes to an hour.

If you're renting a car at Dulles, head down the ramp near the baggage-claim area and walk outside to the curb for your rental car's shuttle-bus stop. The buses come every 5 minutes or so en route to nearby rental lots. Almost all the major companies are represented (see above for their websites).

To reach downtown Washington from Dulles by car, exit the airport and stay on the Dulles Access Road, which leads right into I-66 east. Follow I-66 east, which takes you across the Theodore Roosevelt Memorial Bridge; be sure to stay in the center lane as you cross the bridge, and this will put you on Constitution Avenue (Rte. 29). Ask your hotel for directions from this point.

## FROM BALTIMORE–WASHINGTON INTERNATIONAL AIRPORT
Washington's Metro service runs an Express Metro Bus ("B30") between its Metrorail Green Line Greenbelt station and BWI Airport. The airport has two bus stops on its lower level, one in the International Concourse, the other in Concourse A/B. Look for PUBLIC TRANSIT signs to find the bus, which operates daily, departs every 40 minutes, takes about 30 minutes to reach the station, and costs $7. At the Greenbelt Metro station, you purchase a Metro farecard and board a Metro train bound for Branch Avenue, which will take you into the city. Depending on where you want to go, you can either stay on the Green Line or get off at the Fort Totten station to transfer to a Red Line train, whose stops include Union Station and various downtown locations.

You also have the choice of taking either an **Amtrak** (www.amtrak.com; ✆ **800/872-7245**) or the Penn line of the **Maryland Rural Commuter** train, or MARC (http://mta.maryland.gov/marc-train; ✆ **866/743-3682**), into the city. Both trains travel between the BWI Railway Station and Washington's Union Station, about a 30- to 45-minute ride. Both Amtrak's service (starting at $15 per person, one-way, depending on time and train type) and MARC's service ($7 per person, one-way) are daily. A courtesy shuttle runs every 12 minutes or so between the airport and the train station; stop at the desk near the baggage-claim area to check for the next departure time of both the shuttle bus and the train. Trains depart about once per hour.

BWI operates a large off-site car rental facility. From the ground transportation area, board a shuttle bus to the lot.

Here's how you reach Washington: Look for signs for I-195 and follow the highway west until you see signs for Washington and the Baltimore–Washington Parkway (I-295); head south on I-295. Get off when you see the signs for Rte. 50/New York Avenue, which leads into the District, via New York Avenue NE. Ask your hotel for specific directions from there.

## By Car

More than one-third of visitors to Washington arrive by plane, and if that's you, don't consider renting a car. The traffic in the city and throughout the region is abysmal, parking spaces are hard to find, garage and lot charges are exorbitant, and hotel overnight rates are even worse. Furthermore, Washington is amazingly easy to traverse on foot. Our public transportation and taxi systems are accessible and comprehensive, as well.

But if you are like most visitors, you're planning on driving here. No matter which road you take, there's a good chance you will have to navigate some portion of the **Capital Beltway** (I-495 and I-95) to gain entry to D.C. The Beltway girds the city, its approximately 64-mile route passing through Maryland and Virginia, with some 50 interchanges or exits leading off from it. The Beltway is nearly always congested, but especially during weekday morning and evening rush hours (roughly 5:30–9:30am and 3–7pm). Drivers can get a little crazy, weaving in and out of traffic.

The District is 240 miles from New York City, 40 miles from Baltimore, 700 miles from Chicago, 500 miles from Boston, and about 630 miles from Atlanta.

## By Train

**Amtrak** (www.amtrak.com; ✆ **800/USA-RAIL** [872-7245]) offers daily service to Washington from New York, Boston, and Chicago. Amtrak also travels daily between Washington and points south, including Raleigh, Charlotte, Atlanta, cities in Florida, and New Orleans. Amtrak's **Acela Express** trains offer the quickest service along the "Northeast Corridor," linking Boston, New York, Philadelphia, and Washington, D.C. The trains travel as fast as 150 mph, making the trip between New York and Washington in times that range from less than 3 hours to 3 hours and 45 minutes, depending on the number of stops in the schedule. Likewise, Acela Express's Boston–Washington trip takes anywhere from 6½ hours to more than 8 hours, depending on station stops.

Amtrak runs fewer Acela trains on weekends and honors passenger discounts, such as those for seniors and AAA members, only on weekend Acela travel.

Amtrak offers a smorgasbord of good-deal rail passes and discounted fares; although not all are based on advance purchase, you may have more discount options by reserving early. Tickets for up to two children ages 2 to 15 cost half the price of the lowest available adult fare when the children are accompanied by a fare-paying adult. For more information, go to **www.amtrak.com.** *Note:* Most Amtrak travel requires a reservation, which means that every traveler is guaranteed, but not assigned, a seat.

Amtrak trains arrive at historic **Union Station** (see p. 128 for an in-depth description), 50 Massachusetts Ave. NE (www.unionstationdc.com; ✆ **202/ 371-9441**), a short walk from the Capitol, near several hotels, and a short cab or Metro ride from downtown. Union Station is D.C.'s transportation hub, with its own Metrorail station, Metrobus and DC Circulator bus stops, taxi stands, bikeshare and bike rental locations, rental car facilities, tour bus centers, intracity bus travel operations, and connection to D.C. Streetcar service.

## By Bus

Bus travel is now in vogue, thanks to the rise of fabulously priced, comfortable, clean, and fast bus services. Quite a number of buses travel between Washington, D.C., and New York City, and a growing number travel between D.C. and cities scattered up and down the East Coast.

Check out one of these fleets: **BoltBus** (www.boltbus.com; ✆ **877/265-8287**) travels multiple times a day between D.C.'s Union Station and NYC for $1 to $44 each way. **Megabus** (www.megabus.com; ✆ **877/462-6342**) travels between Washington, D.C.'s Union Station and NYC (also many times a day) for as little as $1 and as much as $46, one-way (most fares run in the $13 to $25 range); and travels between D.C. and 19 other locations, including Boston, Toronto, and Knoxville, Tennessee, for similarly low fares. **Vamoose Bus** (www.vamoosebus.com; ✆ **212/695-6766**) travels between Rosslyn, Virginia's stop near the Rosslyn Metro station and Bethesda, Maryland's stop near the Bethesda Metro station, and locations near NYC's Penn Station, for $20 to $60 each way, accruing one point for every dollar you've paid for your ticket. Collect 120 points and you ride one-way for free.

**Greyhound** (www.greyhound.com; ✆ **800/231-2222**), the company behind BoltBus, travels all over the country for rates as cheap as BoltBus and other operations; its bus depot is also at Union Station.

# GETTING AROUND

Washington is one of the easiest U.S. cities to navigate, thanks to its manageable size and easy-to-understand layout. I wish I could boast as well about the city's comprehensive public transportation system of trains and buses. Ours is the second-busiest rail transit network and the sixth-largest bus network in the country. It used to be swell, but 40 years of increased usage and inadequate maintenance and repairs put the system into crisis mode in 2016, a situation that in 2017 you may have to reckon with (see "By Public Transportation," below, for more details).

Here's what I recommend as you plan your trip: Choose lodging close to where you want to be, whether that is the center of the city, near the offices where you're doing business, or in a favorite neighborhood, and then consider all of the transportation options at your service. Options: that's what this chapter is all about. In addition, I recommend the website **www.godcgo.com,** an initiative of the D.C. government's Department of Transportation that covers and updates information about traversing the city, from every angle, with links to *Washington Post* articles reporting on the latest traffic and transit news. You might just find yourself shunning transportation anyway, for the pleasure of walking or bike-riding your way around the compact and beautiful capital.

# City Layout

Washington's appearance today pays homage to the 1791 vision of French engineer Pierre Charles L'Enfant, who created the capital's grand design of sweeping avenues intersected by spacious circles, directed that the Capitol and the White House be placed on prominent hilltops at either end of a wide stretch of avenue, and superimposed this overall plan upon a traditional street grid. The city's quadrants, grand avenues named after states, alphabetically ordered streets crossed by numerically ordered streets, and parks integrated with urban features are all ideas that started with L'Enfant. President George Washington, who had hired L'Enfant, was forced to dismiss the temperamental genius after L'Enfant apparently offended quite a number of people. But Washington recognized the brilliance of the city plan and hired surveyors Benjamin Banneker and Andrew Ellicott, who had worked with L'Enfant, to continue to implement L'Enfant's design. (For further background, see chapter 2.)

The U.S. Capitol marks the center of the city, which is divided into **northwest (NW), northeast (NE), southwest (SW),** and **southeast (SE) quadrants.** Most, but not all, areas of interest to tourists are in the northwest. The boundary demarcations are often seamless; for instance, you are in the northwest quadrant when you visit the National Museum of Natural History, but by crossing the National Mall to the other side to visit the Sackler Gallery, you put yourself in the southwest quadrant. Pay attention to the quadrant's geographic suffix; as you'll notice when you look on a map, some addresses appear in multiple quadrants (for instance, the corner of G and 7th sts. appears in all four).

**MAIN ARTERIES & STREETS**   From the Capitol, North Capitol Street and South Capitol Street run north and south, respectively. East Capitol Street divides the city north and south. The area west of the Capitol is not a street at all, but the National Mall, which is bounded on the north by Constitution Avenue and on the south by Independence Avenue.

The primary artery of Washington is **Pennsylvania Avenue,** which is the scene of parades, inaugurations, and other splashy events. Pennsylvania runs northwest in a direct line between the Capitol and the White House—if it weren't for the Treasury Building, the president would have a clear view of the Capitol—before continuing on a northwest angle to Georgetown, where it becomes M Street.

**Constitution Avenue,** paralleled to the south most of the way by Independence Avenue, runs east-west, flanking the Capitol and the Mall. Washington's longest avenue, **Massachusetts Avenue,** runs parallel to Pennsylvania (a few avenues north). Along the way, you'll find Union Station and then Dupont Circle, which is central to the area known as Embassy Row. Farther out are the Naval Observatory (the vice president's residence is on the premises), Washington National Cathedral, American University, and, eventually, Maryland.

**Connecticut Avenue,** which runs more directly north (the other avenues run southeast to northwest), starts at Lafayette Square, intersects Dupont Circle, and eventually takes you to the National Zoo, on to the charming residential neighborhood known as Cleveland Park, and into Chevy Chase, Maryland, where you can pick up the Beltway to head out of town. Connecticut Avenue, with its chic-to-funky array of shops and clusters of top-dollar to good-value restaurants, is an interesting street to stroll.

**Wisconsin Avenue** originates in Georgetown; its intersection with M Street forms Georgetown's hub. Wisconsin Avenue basically parallels Connecticut Avenue; one of the few irritating things about the city's transportation system is that the Metro does not connect these two major arteries in the heart of the city. (Buses do, and, of course, you can always walk or take a taxi from one avenue to the other; read about the supplemental bus system, the DC Circulator, on p. 296.) Metrorail's first stop on Wisconsin Avenue is in Tenleytown, a residential area. Follow the avenue north and you land in the affluent Maryland cities of Chevy Chase and Bethesda.

**FINDING AN ADDRESS**   If you understand the city's layout, it's easy to find your way around. As you read this, have a map handy.

Each of the four corners of the District of Columbia is exactly the same distance from the Capitol dome. The White House and most government buildings and important monuments are west of the Capitol (in the northwest and southwest quadrants), as are major hotels and tourist facilities.

Numbered streets run north-south, beginning on either side of the Capitol with 1st Street. Lettered streets run east-west and are named alphabetically, beginning with A Street. (Don't look for J, X, Y, or Z streets, however—they

---

### Be Smart: Buy a SmarTrip Card

If you are planning on using D.C.'s Metro system while you're here, do yourself a favor and order a **SmarTrip** card online at www.wmata.com in advance of your trip, so you'll have it with you when you arrive in D.C. SmarTrip is the name for Metro's permanent, rechargeable card that pays your way in the subway system, on Metro and DC Circulator buses, and on other area transit systems, like the DASH buses in Old Town Alexandria, Virginia. Fast and easy to use, you just touch the card to the target on a faregate inside a Metro station, or farebox inside a Metrobus. You can also purchase SmarTrip cards at vending machines in any Metro station; and at

WMATA headquarters (weekdays only), 600 5th St. NW; its sales office at Metro Center (weekdays only), 12th and F streets NW; or at one of many retail stores, such as Giant or Safeway grocery stores; by purchasing the card ahead of time you'll avoid the hassle at the Metro station, where first-time use of the vending machines can be confusing. The cost of a SmarTrip card is $2. You can add value and special value passes as needed online and at the SmarTrip Card Fare Vending/Passes machines in every Metro station, or even on a Metrobus, using the farebox. For more info, contact Metro (www.wmata.com; ✆ 888/762-7874).

don't exist.) After W Street, street names of two syllables continue in alphabetical order, followed by street names of three syllables; the more syllables in a name, the farther the street is from the Capitol.

Avenues, named for U.S. states, run at angles across the grid pattern and often intersect at traffic circles. For example, New Hampshire, Connecticut, and Massachusetts avenues intersect at Dupont Circle.

With this in mind, you can easily find an address. On lettered streets, the address tells you exactly where to go. For instance, 1776 K St. NW is between 17th and 18th streets (the first two digits of 1776 tell you that) in the northwest quadrant (NW). *Note:* I Street is often written as "Eye" Street to prevent confusion with 1st Street.

To find an address on numbered streets, you'll probably have to use your fingers. For instance, 623 8th St. SE is between F and G streets (the sixth and seventh letters of the alphabet; the first digit of 623 tells you that) in the southeast quadrant (SE). *One thing to remember:* You count B as the second letter of the alphabet even though B Street North and B Street South are now Constitution and Independence avenues, respectively, but because there's no J Street, K becomes the 10th letter, L the 11th, and so on.

## By Public Transportation
### METRORAIL

In 2017, at the age of 41, D.C.'s **Metrorail** system is undergoing major surgery, repair, and reconstruction to "eliminate maintenance backlogs and restore infrastructure to good health," and improve safety and service reliability. The SafeTrack Plan, as the operation is called, was initiated in mid-2016 following the January 2015 death of a passenger from smoke inhalation due to a fire on the track, and an ongoing series of alarming malfunctions. Metro delays and accidents had become the everyday norm. SafeTrack is attempting to accomplish "three years' worth of work accelerated into one year."

You should expect delays and possible cancellation of service on segments of different lines throughout the long period of repair and maintenance. Check Metro's website for the latest updates or do as locals do: Sign up for Metro alerts (www. metroalerts.info) to receive timely announcements of Metrorail and Metrobus service delays, disruptions, schedule changes, advisories, and enhancements.

If you do ride Metrorail, try to avoid traveling during rush hour (Mon–Fri 5–9:30am and 3–7pm), since delays can be frequent, lines at fare machines

---

**Metro Etiquette 101**

To avoid risking the ire of commuters, be sure to follow these guidelines: Stand to the right on the escalator so that people in a hurry can get past you on the left. And when you reach the train level, don't puddle at the bottom of the escalator, blocking the path of those coming behind you; move down the platform. Eating, drinking, and smoking are strictly prohibited on the Metro and in stations.

Metrorail doesn't go to Georgetown, and although Metro buses do (nos. 31, 32, 36, 38B, D1, D2, D3, D5, D6, and G2), the public transportation I'd recommend is that provided by the **DC Circulator bus** (p. 296), which travels two Georgetown routes: one that runs between the Rosslyn, Virginia, and Dupont Circle Metro stations, stopping at designated points in Georgetown along the way, and a second one that runs between Georgetown and Union Station. The buses come by every 10 minutes; the Rosslyn-Georgetown-Dupont Circle route operates from 7am to midnight Sunday through Thursday, 7am to 2am Friday and Saturday; the Georgetown-Union Station route operates from 7am to 9pm daily. One-way fares cost $1.

long, trains overcrowded, and Washingtonians at their rudest. You can expect to get a seat during off-peak hours (weekdays 9:30am–3pm, weeknights after 7pm, and weekends). All cars are air-conditioned.

Metrorail's base system of 91 stations and 117 miles of track includes locations at or near almost every sightseeing attraction; it also extends to suburban Maryland and northern Virginia. There are six lines in operation—**Red, Blue, Orange, Yellow, Green,** and the new **Silver** line. The Silver Line for now has five stops that snake off the Orange line in Northern Virginia; future stops will lead eventually to Washington Dulles Airport. The lines connect at several central points, making transfers relatively easy. All but Yellow, Green, and Silver Line trains stop at Metro Center; all except Red and Silver Line trains stop at L'Enfant Plaza; all but Blue, Orange, and Silver Line trains stop at Gallery Place–Chinatown. See the map inside the back cover of this book.

Metro stations are indicated by discreet brown columns bearing the station's name and topped by the letter M. Below the M is a colored stripe or stripes indicating the line or lines that stop there. To reach the train platform of a Metro station, you need a computerized **SmarTrip** card (see box p. 291). SmarTrip Card Fare Vending, Add Value, and Exitfare Vending machines are located inside the vestibule areas of the Metro stations. The blue SmarTrip Card Fare Vending machines sell SmarTrip cards for $10 ($2 for the card and $8 in trip value), add value up to $300, and add special value passes to your SmarTrip card; the machines accept debit and credit cards, and bills up to $20, with change up to $10 returned in coins. The black Fare Vending machines are strictly for adding value to your current SmarTrip card; again, the machines accept cash only, up to $20, with change up to $10 returned in coins. Some Metro stations also have blue Express SmarTrip Card Dispenser machines, which sell individual SmarTrip cards for $10 ($2 for the purchase, plus $8 in fare value).

Metrorail fares are calculated on distance traveled and time of day. Base fare during **non-peak hours** (Mon–Fri 9:30am–3pm and 7pm–midnight; all day Saturday until midnight; and all day Sunday) ranges from a **minimum of $1.75** to a **maximum of $3.60.** During **peak hours** (Mon–Fri 5–9:30am and 3–7pm; Fri and Sat midnight–3am), the fare would range from a **minimum of $2.15** to a **maximum of $5.90.**

For best value, consider buying a $14.50 **1-Day** or a $36 **7-Day short trip** pass for travel on Metrorail. You can buy these online, adding the value to the SmarTrip card you're purchasing, or at the machines in the stations. See Metro's website for details.

Up to two children ages 4 and under can ride free with a paying passenger. Seniors (65 and older) and travelers with disabilities (with valid proof) ride Metrorail and Metrobus for a reduced fare.

To get to the train platforms, you enter the station through the faregates, touching your SmarTrip card to the SmarTrip logo–marked target on top of the regular faregates or on the inside of the wide faregates. When you exit a station, you simply touch your card again to the SmarTrip logo-marked target on the faregate at your destination. If you arrive at a destination and the exit faregate tells you that you need to add value to your SmarTrip card to exit, use the brown Exitfare machines near the faregate to add the necessary amount—cash only.

Most Metro stations have more than one exit. To save yourself time and confusion, try to figure out ahead of time which exit gets you closer to where you're going. In this book, I include the appropriate exit for every venue.

## Getting to the Atlas District

The long-awaited DC Streetcar is up and running, transporting people between Union Station and to points along H Street NE in the hopping, nightlife-rich neighborhood known as the Atlas District. The distance between Union Station and the heart of the Atlas District is less than 1 mile; the entire Union Station-to-Benning Road streetcar segment is 2.4 miles. All you have to do is ride Metro to Union Station, and transfer to the streetcar from there. Here's the deal, though: When you arrive at the Union Station Metro stop, you have to make your way up through the station to the bus deck level of the parking garage, then walk and walk and walk the marked pathway that leads to the streetcar stop on H St. Dimly lit during the day, the garage is downright creepy at night. That's one drawback. Second,

from Union Station, you're actually not that far, only a couple of blocks, from the start of the Atlas District; personally, I think it makes more sense to just walk the distance. Third, SmarTrip cards don't work on the streetcar, an inconvenience. (At press time, fares had yet to be decided, so rides were free. In 2017, you can expect to buy a ticket from a kiosk posted at each stop.) And finally, even more inconvenient is the fact that just as streetcar service was launched in 2016, with weekend hours running until 2am, Metrorail was curtailing its weekend hours, stopping trains at midnight. In other words, unless Metro has reinstated its 'til-3am weekend service, the vaunted late-night transportation option for partyers in the Atlas District is a no-go. Taxi! For more information, go to www.dcstreetcar.com.

Metrorail opens at 5am weekdays and 7am Saturday and Sunday, operating until midnight nightly. By the time you read this, it's possible that Metro may have restored weekend hours to stay open until 3am Friday and Saturday, its normal schedule prior to the implementation of the SafeTrack improvement program in June 2016. Bottom line: Visit www.wmata.com for the most up-to-date information on Metro routes and schedules.

## METROBUS

The Transit Authority's bus system is a comprehensive operation that encompasses 1,500 buses traveling 325 routes, making about 12,000 stops, operating within a 1,500-square-mile area that includes major arteries in D.C. and the Virginia and Maryland suburbs. The system is gradually phasing in new, sleekly designed, red and silver buses that run on a combination of diesel and electric hybrid fuel.

The Transit Authority is also working to improve placement of bus stop signs. For now, look for red, white, and blue signs that tell you which buses stop at that location. Eventually, signage should tell you the routes and schedules for the buses that stop there. In the meantime, the Transit Authority has inaugurated electronic NEXT BUS signs at some bus stops that post real-time arrival information and alerts. You can also use your smartphone to find out when the next bus is due to arrive by accessing the website, www.wmata.com, clicking on busETA, and entering the relevant intersection, bus route # or bus stop code.

Base fare in the District, using a SmarTrip card, is $1.75, or $4 for the faster express buses, which make fewer stops. There may be additional charges for travel into the Maryland and Virginia suburbs. Bus drivers are not equipped to make change, so if you have not purchased a SmarTrip card (see box, p. 291) or a pass, be sure to carry exact change.

If you'll be in Washington for a while and plan to use the buses a lot, buy a 1-week pass ($17.50), which must be loaded onto a SmarTrip card (see box, p. 291).

Most buses operate daily around-the-clock. Service is quite frequent on weekdays, especially during peak hours, and less frequent on weekends and late at night.

Up to two children 4 and under ride free with a paying passenger on Metrobus, and there are reduced fares for seniors (© **202/637-7000**) and travelers with disabilities (© **202/962-1245** or 962-1100; see "Disabled Travelers," p. 302, for transit information). If you leave something on a bus, on a train, or in a station, call Lost and Found Monday through Friday 9am to 5pm at © **202/962-1195.**

## By Car

If you must drive, be aware that traffic is always thick during the week, parking spaces hard to find, and parking lots ruinously expensive. You can expect to pay overnight rates of $25 to $50 at hotels, hourly rates starting at $8 at

## DC Circulator

Meet D.C.'s fantastic supplemental bus system. It's efficient, inexpensive, and convenient, traveling six circumscribed routes in the city. These red-and-gray buses travel:

- The **Southeast D.C. route** between the Potomac Avenue Metro Station and points in Anacostia, via Barracks Row (weekdays 6am–7pm Oct–Mar, weekdays 6am–9pm and Sat 7am–9pm Apr–Sept).

- The **East-West route** between upper Georgetown and Union Station (7am–9pm daily, with a special service added between upper Georgetown and the intersection of 14th and K sts. NW, from 9pm–midnight Sun–Thurs, 9pm–2am Fri–Sat).

- **A second Georgetown route** that travels between the Rosslyn Metro station in Virginia and the Dupont Circle Metro station in the District, via Georgetown (Sun–Thurs 7am–midnight, Fri–Sat 7am–2am).

- The **Union Station–to–Washington Navy Yard track** (located near Nationals Park, the service operates 6am–7pm weekdays Oct–March, 6am–9pm weekdays and 7am–9pm Sat Apr–Sept, with extended hours on Nationals game days).

- The route between the **Woodley Park–Zoo** Metro station and the **McPherson Square** Metro station (7am–midnight Sun–Thurs; 7am–3:30am Fri–Sat), via Adams Morgan and the U&14th Street Corridors.

- The **National Mall** route, which loops the National Mall from Union Station and stops at 14 other sites en route (Winter: weekdays 7am–7pm, weekends 9am–7pm; Summer: weekdays 7am–8pm, weekends 9am–8pm).

Buses stop at designated points on their routes (look for the distinctive red-and-gold sign, often topping a regular Metro bus stop sign) every 10 minutes. The fare at all times is $1, and you can order passes online at www.commuter-direct.com, or pay upon boarding with the exact fare or the use of a SmarTrip Metro card. For easy and fast transportation in the busiest parts of town, you can't beat it. Go to www.dccirculator.com or call ☏ **202/962-1423.**

downtown parking lots and garages, and flat rates starting at $20 in the most popular parts of town, such as Georgetown and Penn Quarter. If you're hoping to snag a parking space on the street, you may or may not be happy to know that the D.C. government makes it as easy as possible for you to pay for that spot: Although the city still has many traditional parking meters that take coins, all 17,000 on-street metered spaces now allow you to use your cell-phone to pay for parking. Sign up online at www.parkmobile.com, or download the app, to register your license plate number and credit card or debit card number. Once you arrive in D.C. and park on a street that requires payment for parking, you simply call the phone number marked on the meter or nearby kiosk, or use the app, and follow the prompts to enter the location ID marked on the meter and the amount of time you're paying for. Some kiosks allow you to use cash or a credit card to pay for parking time, in which case you print a receipt and place it against the windshield.

D.C.'s traffic circles can be confusing to navigate. The law states that traffic already in the circle has the right of way, but you can't always depend on drivers to obey that law. You also need to be aware of rush-hour rules: Sections of certain streets in Washington become **one-way** during rush hour: Rock Creek Parkway, Canal Road, and 17th Street NW are three examples. Other streets change the direction of some of their traffic lanes during rush hour. Connecticut Avenue NW is the main one: In the morning, traffic in four of its six lanes travels south to downtown, and in late afternoon/early evening, downtown traffic in four of its six lanes heads north; between the hours of 9am and 3:30pm, traffic in both directions keeps to the normally correct side of the yellow line. Lit-up traffic signs alert you to what's going on, but pay attention. Unless a sign is posted prohibiting it, a right-on-red law is in effect.

*FYI:* If you don't drive to D.C. but need a car while you're here, you can rent one at the airport or at Union Station, as noted earlier in this chapter, or you can turn to a car-sharing service. **Zipcar** (www.zipcar.com; ℰ **866/494-7227**), **Car2Go** (www.car2go.com; ℰ **877/488-4224**), and **Enterprise Car-Share** (www.enterprisecarshare.com; ℰ **855/383-1212**) all operate in D.C.

## By Taxi, Uber, Lyft, or Split

The D.C. taxicab system charges passengers according to time- and distance-based meters. Fares may increase, but at press time, fares began at $3.25, plus $2.16 per each additional mile, $1 per additional passenger, and 50¢ per piece of luggage that the driver places in the trunk. Other charges might apply (for instance, if you telephone for a cab, rather than hail one in the street, it'll cost you $2.). *Note:* The big news about D.C. taxis is that they accept credit cards.

Try **Diamond Cab Company** (ℰ **202/387-4011**) or **Yellow Cab** (www.dcyellowcab.com; ℰ **202/544-1212**). You can download the free DC Taxi app from the website www.dctaxi.com, and order your transportation using your smartphone, a la Uber.

Or you can download the app for **Uber** (www.uber.com), **Lyft** (www.lyft.com), or **Split** (www.split.us), all of which operate in the District.

## By Bike

Thanks to a robust bike-share program (**Capital BikeShare,** www.capitalbikeshare.com, ℰ **877/430-2453,** is the nation's largest, with more than 3,000 bikes and 350 bike stations), Washington, D.C., is increasingly a city where locals themselves get around by bike. The flat terrain of the National Mall and many neighborhoods make the city conducive to two wheels. Sixty-nine miles of marked bike lanes throughout D.C., and bike paths through Rock Creek Park, the C&O Canal in Georgetown, along the waterfront via the Anacostia Riverwalk Trail, and around the National Mall encourage the practice, too. Interested? Visit the www.godcgo.com website and click on the "Bicycling" link under "Ways to Get Around" to download a map that shows bike lanes and Capital BikeShare stations, which are all over. The Capital BikeShare program might be a better option economically for members who use the bikes for short commutes, but be sure to consider that option, along with traditional bike-rental companies (p. 301), which are also plentiful.

# GUIDED TOURS

D.C. offers a slew of guided tours, from themed jaunts that take you to sites at which famous scandals occurred to Segway tours of Capitol Hill. Beyond the ones in this chapter are additional tour services found on the **Cultural Tourism D.C.** website, **www.culturaltourismdc.org** (go to "Our Programs" to view a list of self-guided neighborhood heritage walking trails). If you're here in September, be sure to check out Cultural Tourism D.C.'s Walkingtown D.C. offering of free tours throughout the city over the course of 10 days.

## On Foot

**DC by Foot:** These tours are ostensibly free, but you are highly encouraged to pay at the end of the tour whatever you think the experience was worth. DC by Foot (www.freetoursbyfoot.com/washington-dc-tours; ✆ **202/370-1830**) guides like to spin humor with history as they shepherd participants around the sites, narrating all the way. History is the emphasis on the popular National Mall tour, but other offerings cover such topics as spies and scandals or Lincoln's assassination; the outfit has expanded to include food, bike, bus, and photography tours, too. Unlike other guided tours, DC by Foot operates year-round, although on a restricted schedule during the winter.

  **Washington Walks:** Excellent guides and dynamite in-depth tours of neighborhoods off the National Mall make Washington Walks (www.washington walks.com; ✆ **202/484-1565**) a long-time favorite of travelers. The "Get Local Saturdays" series of tours is especially popular, traveling to a different locale weekly and revealing surprising facts. Public walks take place April through October; private and group tours are year-round. Tours are $20 per person.

  **DC Metro Food Tours:** DC Metro (www.dcmetrofoodtours.com; ✆ **202/851-2268**) conducts participants on 3½-hour-long gastronomic adventures within a particular neighborhood, serving side dishes of historical and cultural references. For example, a Georgetown tour might include a walk along the C&O Canal; a sampling of in-house-made pasta at a decades-old restaurant; tales of the neighborhood's famous residents, like President and Jacqueline Kennedy; finishing with dessert at one of the city's best bakeries. Inquire about pub crawls, which include stops at three to six bars. Rates vary from about $30 to $65 per person.

  **The Guild of Professional Tour Guides of Washington, D.C.:** Would you like your tour tailored to your interest in women's history or architecture? The Guild (www.washingtondctourguides.com; ✆ **202/966-4935**), which is a membership organization for licensed, professional tour guides and companies, offers a slew of set tours (click on "Find a Tour"), but also operates a guide-for-hire service on its website (click on "Search," then choose "Use HireGuides4DC form"). You simply enter your dates, interests, and other details, and individual guides respond to your query. You choose from among the responders, but the price is always the same: $40 per hour for a minimum of 4 hours. These guides are the best of the best, with many members doubling as docents at places like the Capitol Visitor Center.

**Spies of Washington Walking Tours** (www.spiesofwashingtontour.com; ✆ 703/569-1875) offers four walking tours that focus on espionage-related sites in Georgetown and around the White House, Pennsylvania Avenue, Capitol Hill, and the Russian Embassy areas. Carol Bessette, a retired Air Force intelligence officer, conducts the tours, which cost $15 per person.

**Segway Tours** (http://dc.citysegwaytours.com; ✆ 877/734-8687) offers 2- and 3-hour tours year-round daily. Though technically they aren't "on foot," Segways are self-propelling scooters that operate based on "dynamic stabilization" technology, which uses your body movements. The 2-hour tours cost $65 per person; the 3-hour tours cost $75 per person. The cost includes training. Ages 16 and up.

## By Bus

The three major companies that offer narrated bus tours of the city all operate out of Union Station: **Big Bus Tours** (www.bigbustours.com; ✆ 877/332-8689), **City Sights DC** (www.citysightsdc.com; ✆ 202/650-5444), and **Old Town Trolley** (www.trolleytours.com/washington-dc/; ✆ 202/682-0079). I think Old Town Trolley tours provide the best interpretive narration. Old Town Trolley is also the only service authorized by Arlington National Cemetery to provide narrated tours throughout the cemetery (see p. 192). That being said, some prefer Big Bus and City Sights because they are double-decker buses (which can be a fun point of view; and they have air-conditioned interiors, which the trolleys do not).

Bus tours depart from Columbus Circle, Union Station's front plaza, right through the Main Hall doors. You can buy tickets ahead of time online, at some hotels, or in the station. At least one bus tour, City Sights, provides scheduled free shuttle service between select hotels and Union Station, so be sure to inquire about that. All three of the bus tours provide hop on and off service and all three offer a night tour, which I recommend.

While each tour offers different routes and variations, the basic framework essentially follows that of Old Town Trolley's model which is a fixed-price, on-off narrated service as you travel in three loops around the city, with a transfer point at the Lincoln Memorial (to go on to Arlington Cemetery), and a second transfer point near Ford's Theatre (to get to Georgetown and to Washington National Cathedral). In the case of Old Town, the vehicles are trolleys, not buses; although enclosed and heated in winter, the trolleys in summer open their windows, meaning that most of the trolleys are not air-conditioned. Trolleys operate daytime tours daily from 9am to 5:30pm. You can buy tickets online in advance and at a discount ($35.10 for adults, $26.10 for children 4 to 12, free for children 3 and under) and use those e-tickets to board at any of the stops. The full narrated tour takes 2 hours (if you don't get off and tour the sites, obviously), and trolleys come by every 30 minutes or so. Check the website for info about "Monuments by Moonlight" and other tours.

## By Boat

Potomac cruises offer sweeping vistas of the monuments and memorials, Georgetown, the Kennedy Center, and other Washington sights. Read the information below carefully, because not all boat cruises offer guided tours. Some of the following boats leave from the Washington waterfront and some from Old Town Alexandria. The Washington waterfront is under development in 2017, so be sure to check boarding and parking information carefully online if you're booking a cruise that leaves from a D.C. dock.

**Spirit of Washington Cruises,** Pier 4 at 6th and Water streets SW (www. spiritcruises.com/washington-dc; ⓒ **866/302-2469;** Metro: Waterfront), offers a variety of trips daily, including evening dinner, lunch, and brunch cruises, as well as a half-day excursion to Mount Vernon and back. Lunch and dinner cruises include DJ entertainment. The *Spirit of Washington* is a luxury, climate-controlled harbor cruise ship with carpeted decks, three bars, and huge panoramic windows designed for sightseeing.

**Dandy Restaurant Cruises** (www.dandydinnerboat.com; ⓒ **703/683-6076**) operates *Nina's Dandy,* a climate-controlled, glassed-in floating restaurant that runs year-round. You board the vessel in Old Town Alexandria, at the Prince Street pier, between Duke and King streets. Trips range from a 2½-hour weekday lunch cruise to a 3-hour Saturday dinner cruise.

*Odyssey* (www.odysseycruises.com; ⓒ **866/306-2469**) was designed specifically to glide under the bridges that cross the Potomac. The boat looks like a glass bullet, its wraparound, see-through walls and ceiling allowing for great views. You board the *Odyssey* at the Gangplank Marina, on Washington's waterfront at 6th and Water streets SW (Metro: Waterfront). Cruises available include lunch, Sunday brunch, and dinner excursions, with live entertainment provided during each cruise.

From April through October, the **Potomac Riverboat Company** ★ (www. potomacriverboatco.com; ⓒ **877/511-2628** or 703/684-0580) offers several 90-minute round-trip, narrated tours aboard sightseeing vessels that take you past Washington landmarks or along Old Town Alexandria's waterfront; certain cruises also travel to Mount Vernon, where you hop off and re-board after you've toured the estate. You board the boats at the pier behind the Torpedo Factory in Old Town Alexandria at the foot of King Street, or, for the Washington monuments and memorials tour, at Georgetown's Washington Harbour. A concession stand sells light refreshments onboard. From late March through October, the company also operates water taxis that travel between Old Town Alexandria and the National Mall, docking not far from the FDR and Lincoln memorials; and, in baseball season, between Old Town Alexandria and Nationals Park.

The **Capitol River Cruise's** *Nightingales* (www.capitolrivercruises.com; ⓒ **800/405-5511** or 301/460-7447) are historic 65-foot steel riverboats that can accommodate 90 people. The *Nightingales'* narrated jaunts depart Georgetown's Washington Harbour every hour on the hour, from 11am to 7pm, April through October (with a 9pm outing offered in summer months only). The 45-minute narrated tour travels past the monuments and memorials to National Airport and back. Bring a picnic or eat from the snack bar. To get here, take the Metro to Foggy Bottom and then walk into Georgetown, following Pennsylvania Avenue, which becomes M Street. Turn left on 31st Street NW and follow to the Washington Harbour complex on the water.

Old Town Trolley also operates **DC Ducks** (www.dcducks.com; © **202/832-9800**), which feature unique land and water tours of Washington aboard the *DUKW,* an amphibious army vehicle (boat with wheels) from World War II that accommodates 30 passengers. Ninety-minute guided tours aboard the open-air canopied craft include a land portion taking in major sights—the Capitol, Lincoln Memorial, Washington Monument, White House, and Smithsonian museums—and a 30-minute Potomac cruise. Passengers board just outside the main entrance to Union Station. Hours vary, but departures April through October are usually 10am to 4pm, every hour on the hour.

## By Bike

**Bike and Roll DC ★★** (www.bikeandrolldc.com; © **202/842-2453**) offers a more active way to see Washington, from March to December. The company has designed several different biking tours, including the popular Capital Sites Ride, which takes you past museums, memorials, the White House, the Capitol, and the Supreme Court. The ride takes 3 hours, covers 7 to 8 miles, and costs $40 per adult, $30 per child 12 and under. Bike the Sites provides a comfortable mountain bicycle fitted to your size, a bike helmet, a water bottle, a light snack, and two guides to lead the ride. Tours depart from a location near the National Mall, at 955 L'Enfant Plaza SW, North Building Suite 905 (Metro: L'Enfant Plaza), and guides impart historical and anecdotal information as you go. Tours also depart from the steps of the National Museum of American History, on the Mall. Other Bike and Roll locations rent bikes: at Old Town Alexandria (© **703/548-7655**), and at Union Station (© **202/962-0206**). Rates vary depending on the bike you choose but always include helmet, bike, lock, and pump; there's a 2-hour minimum.

# [FastFACTS] WASHINGTON, D.C.

**Area Codes** Within the District of Columbia, the area code is 202. In Northern Virginia it's 703, and in D.C.'s Maryland suburbs, the area code is 301. You must use the area code when dialing a phone number, whether it's a local 202, 703, or 301 phone number.

**Business Hours** Most museums are open daily 10:30am to 5:30pm; some, including several of the Smithsonians, stay open later in spring and summer. Most banks are open from 9am to 5pm weekdays, with some open Saturdays as well, for abbreviated hours. Stores typically open between 9 and 10am and close between 8 and 9pm from Monday to Saturday.

**Customs** For customs info, consult the U.S. Customs website, www.cbp.gov.

**Disabled Travelers**
Although Washington, D.C., is one of the most accessible cities in the world for travelers with disabilities, it is not perfect—especially when it comes to historic buildings, as well as some restaurants and shops. Theaters, museums, and government buildings are generally well equipped. Still, for least hassle call ahead to places you hope to visit to find out specific accessibility features. In the case of restaurants and bars, I'm afraid you'll have to work to pin them down—no one wants to discourage a potential customer. Several sources might help. Destination: D.C.'s website offers some helpful, though hardly comprehensive, information, http://washington.org/DC-information/washington-dc-disability-information, including links to the **Washington Metropolitan Transit Authority,** which publishes accessibility information on its website, www.wmata.com.

**Doctors** Most hotels are prepared for medical emergencies and work with local doctors who are able to see ill or injured hotel guests. Also see "Hospitals," below.

**Drinking Laws** The legal age for purchase and consumption of alcoholic beverages is 21; proof of age is required and often requested at bars, nightclubs, and restaurants, so

it's always a good idea to bring ID when you go out. Do not carry open containers of alcohol in your car or any public area that isn't zoned for alcohol consumption. The police can fine you on the spot. Don't even think about driving while intoxicated.

Liquor stores are closed on Sunday but many other types of stores often sell beer and wine, even on Sunday. Bars and nightclubs serve liquor until 2am Sunday through Thursday and until 3am Friday and Saturday.

**Electricity** Like Canada, the United States uses 110–120 volts AC (60 cycles), compared to 220–240 volts AC (50 cycles) in most of Europe, Australia, and New Zealand. Downward converters that change 220–240 volts to 110–120 volts are difficult to find in the United States, so bring one with you.

**Embassies & Consulates** All embassies are located here in the nation's capital. To find yours, you can call directory information in Washington, D.C. (✆ **202/555-1212**) or check www.embassy.org/embassies.

**Emergencies** Call ✆ **911** for police, fire, and medical emergencies. This is a toll-free call.

If you encounter serious problems, contact the **Travelers Aid Society International** (www.travelersaid.org; ✆ **202/546-1127**), a nationwide, nonprofit, social-service organization

geared to helping travelers in difficult straits, from reuniting families separated while traveling to providing food and/or shelter to people stranded without cash. Travelers Aid operates help desks at Washington Dulles International Airport, Ronald Reagan Washington National Airport, and Union Station. At Baltimore–Washington International Thurgood Marshall Airport, a volunteer agency called **Pathfinders (✆ 410/859-7826)** mans the customer service desks throughout the airport.

**Family Travel** Field trips during the school year and family vacations during the summer keep Washington, D.C., crawling with kids all year long. More than any other city, perhaps, Washington is crammed with historic buildings, arts and science museums, parks, and recreational sites to interest young and old alike. The fact that so many attractions are free is a boon to the family budget.

Look for boxes on family-friendly hotels, restaurants, and attractions in their appropriate chapters.

**GLBT Travelers** The nation's capital is most welcoming to the gay and lesbian community. In fact, as of March 9, 2010, same-sex couples can now legally marry each other in the nation's capital. Even if you're not planning to get married here, you should know that D.C.'s GLBT population is one of the largest in the country, with 10% of

| WHAT THINGS COST IN WASHINGTON, D.C. | U.S.$ |
| --- | --- |
| Taxi from National Airport to downtown | 15.00 |
| Double room, moderate | 250.00 |
| Double room, inexpensive | 150.00 |
| Three-course dinner for one without wine, moderate | 50.00 |
| Glass of wine | 10.00 |
| Cup of coffee | 2.50 |
| 1 gallon regular unleaded gas | 2.40 |
| Admission to most museums | Free |
| 1-day Metrorail pass | 14.50 |

residents identifying themselves as such. The capital's annual, week-long Capital Pride celebration is held in June, complete with a street fair and a parade.

Dupont Circle is the unofficial headquarters for gay life, site of the annual 17th Street High Heel Drag Race on the Tuesday preceding Halloween, and home to long-established gay bars and dance clubs (see chapter 8), but the whole city is pretty much GLBT-friendly.

**Hospitals** If you don't require immediate ambulance transportation but still need emergency-room treatment, call one of the following hospitals (and be sure to get directions): Children's Hospital National Medical Center, 111 Michigan Ave. NW (☎ **202/476-5000**); George Washington University Hospital, 900 23rd St. NW, at Washington Circle (☎ **202/715-4000**); Medstar Georgetown University Hospital, 3800 Reservoir Rd. NW (☎ **202/444-2000**); or Howard University

Hospital, 2041 Georgia Ave. NW (☎ **202/865-6100**).

**Internet & Wi-Fi** More and more hotels, resorts, airports, cafes, and retailers are offering free Wi-Fi. Likewise, all three D.C. airports offer complimentary Wi-Fi. All of the D.C. hotels listed in chapter 4 offer Internet access, and nearly all offer it for free.

**Legal Aid** While driving, if you are pulled over for a minor infraction (such as speeding), never attempt to pay the fine directly to a police officer; this could be construed as attempted bribery, a much more serious crime. Pay fines by mail or directly into the hands of the clerk of the court. If accused of a more serious offense, say and do nothing before consulting a lawyer. In the U.S., the burden is on the state to prove a person's guilt beyond a reasonable doubt, and everyone has the right to remain silent, whether he or she is suspected of a crime or is actually arrested. Once arrested, a person can make one telephone call to a party of

his or her choice. The international visitor should call his or her embassy or consulate.

**Mail** At press time, domestic postage rates were 34¢ for a postcard and 47¢ for a letter. For international mail, a first-class letter of up to 1 ounce costs $1.15; a first-class postcard costs the same as a letter.

**Mobile Phones** AT&T, Verizon, Sprint, Nextel, and T-Mobile are among the cellphone networks operating in Washington, D.C., so there's a good chance you'll have full and excellent coverage anywhere in the city.

International visitors should check their **GSM (Global System for Mobile Communications) wireless network** to see where GSM phones and text messaging work in the U.S.

You can **rent** a phone before you leave home from **InTouch USA** (www.intouchusa.us; ☎ **800/872-7626** in the U.S., or 703/222-7161 outside the U.S.).

You can purchase a pay-as-you-go phone from all sorts of places, from

Amazon.com to any Verizon Wireless store. In D.C., Verizon has a store at Union Station (📞 **202/682-9475**) and another at 1314 F St. NW (📞 **202/624-0072**), to name just two convenient locations.

**Money & Costs**   If you are traveling to Washington, D.C., from outside the United States, you should consult a currency exchange website such as http://www.xe.com/currencyconverter to check up-to-the-minute exchange rates before your departure.

Anyone who travels to the nation's capital expecting bargains is in for a rude awakening, especially when it comes to lodging. Less expensive than New York and London, Washington, D.C.'s daily hotel rate nevertheless reflects the city's popularity as a top destination among U.S. travelers, averaging $252 (according to most recent statistics). D.C.'s restaurant scene is rather more egalitarian: heavy on the fine, top-dollar establishments, where you can easily spend $100 per person, but with plenty of excellent bistros and small restaurants offering great eats at lower prices. When it comes to attractions, though, the nation's capital has the rest of the world beat, because most of its museums and tourist sites offer free admission.

In Washington, D.C., ATMs are ubiquitous, in locations ranging from the National Gallery of Art's gift shop to Union Station to grocery stores.

***Note:*** Many banks impose a fee every time you use a card at another bank's ATM, and that fee is often higher for international transactions (up to $5 or more) than for domestic ones (where they're rarely more than $2).

In addition to debit cards, credit cards are the most widely used form of payment in the United States. Beware of hidden credit card fees while traveling internationally. Check with your credit or debit card issuer to see what fees, if any, will be charged for overseas transactions. Fees can amount to 3% or more of the purchase price.

**Newspapers & Magazines**   Washington's preeminent newspaper is the *Washington Post,* available online and sold in bookstores, train and subway stations, drugstores, and sidewalk kiosks all over town. These are also the places to buy other newspapers, such as the *New York Times,* and *Washingtonian* magazine, the city's popular monthly full of penetrating features, restaurant reviews, and nightlife calendars. The websites of these publications are: www.washingtonpost.com, www.nytimes.com, and www.washingtonian.com.

Also be sure to pick up a copy of *Washington City Paper,* a weekly publication available free all over the city, at CVS drugstores, movie theaters, you name it, but also online at www.washingtoncitypaper.com.

**Police**   The number of different police agencies in Washington is quite staggering. They include the city's own Metropolitan Police Department, the National Park Service police, the U.S. Capitol police, the Secret Service, the FBI, and the Metro Transit police. The only thing you need to know is: In an emergency, dial 📞 **911.**

**Safety**   In the years following the September 11, 2001, terrorist attack on the Pentagon, the federal and D.C. governments, along with agencies such as the National Park Service, have continued to work together to increase security, not just at airports but also around the city, including at tourist attractions, and in the subway. The most noticeable and, honestly, most irksome aspect of increased security at tourist attractions can be summed up in three little words: **waiting in line.** Although visitors have always had to queue to enter the Capitol, the Supreme Court, and other federal buildings, now it can take more time to get through because of more intense scrutiny when you finally reach the door.

Besides lines, you will notice the intense amount of security in place around the White House and the Capitol, as well as a profusion of vehicle barriers.

Just because so many police are around, you shouldn't let your guard down. Washington, like any urban area, has a criminal element, so it's important to stay alert and take normal safety precautions. See "The Neighborhoods in Brief" in chapter 3 to get a better idea of where you might feel most comfortable.

Avoid deserted areas, especially at night, and don't go into public parks at night unless there's a concert or a similar occasion attracting a crowd.

Avoid carrying valuables with you on the street, and don't display expensive cameras or electronic equipment. If you're using a map, consult it inconspicuously—or better yet, try to study it before you leave your room. In general the more you look like a tourist, the more likely someone will try to take advantage of you. If you're walking, pay attention to who is near you as you walk. If you're attending a convention or event where you wear a name tag, remove it before venturing outside. Hold on to your purse, and place your wallet in an inside pocket. In theaters, restaurants, and other public places, keep your possessions in sight. Also remember that hotels are open to the public, and in a large hotel, security may not be able to screen everyone entering. Always lock your room door.

**Senior Travel**   Members of **AARP** (www.aarp.org; *C* **888/687-2277**) get discounts on hotels, airfares, and car rentals. Anyone over 50 can join.

With or without AARP membership, seniors often find that discounts are available to them at hotels, so be sure to inquire when you book your reservation.

Venues in Washington that grant discounts to seniors include the Metro; certain theaters, such as the Shakespeare Theatre; and those few museums, such as the Phillips Collection, that charge for entry. Each place has its own eligibility rules, including designated "senior" ages: The Shakespeare Theatre's is 60 and over, the Phillips Collection's is 62 and over, and the Metro discounts seniors 65 and over.

**Smoking**   The District is smoke free, meaning that the city bans smoking in restaurants, bars, and other public buildings. Smoking is permitted outdoors, unless otherwise noted.

**Taxes**   The United States has no value-added tax (VAT) or other indirect tax at the national level. The sales tax on merchandise is 5.75% in the District, 6% in Maryland, and 6% in northern Virginia. Restaurant tax is 10% in the District, 6% in Maryland, and varied in Virginia, depending on the city and county. Hotel tax is 14.5% in the District, from 5% to 8% in Maryland, and an average of 6% in Virginia.

**Telephones**   Most long-distance and international calls can be dialed directly from any phone. **To make calls within the United States and to Canada,** dial 1 followed by the area code and the seven-digit number. **For other international calls,** dial 011 followed by

the country code, the city code, and the number you are calling.

Calls to area codes **800, 888, 877,** and **866** are toll free. However, calls to area codes **700** and **900** (chat lines, bulletin boards, "dating" services, and so on) can be expensive—charges of 95¢ to $3 or more per minute. Some numbers have minimum charges that can run $15 or more.

For **directory assistance** ("Information"), dial **411** for local numbers and national numbers in the U.S. and Canada. For dedicated long-distance information, dial 1 then the appropriate area code, plus 555-1212.

**Time**   The continental United States is divided into **four time zones:** Eastern Standard Time (EST)—this is Washington, D.C.'s time zone—Central Standard Time (CST), Mountain Standard Time (MST), and Pacific Standard Time (PST). Alaska and Hawaii have their own zones. For example, when it's 9am in Los Angeles (PST), it's noon in Washington, D.C. (EST), 5pm in London (GMT), and 2am the next day in Sydney.

**Daylight saving time** is in effect from 2am on the second Sunday in March to 2am on the first Sunday in November. Daylight saving time moves the clock 1 hour ahead of standard time, so come that first Sunday in November, the clock is turned back one hour.

**Tipping**   In hotels, tip **bellhops** at least $1 per bag ($2–$3 if you have a lot of luggage) and tip the

**chamber staff** $1 to $2 per day (more if you've left a big mess). Tip the **doorman** or **concierge** only if he or she has provided you with some specific service (for example, calling a cab for you or obtaining difficult-to-get theater tickets). Tip the **valet-parking attendant** $1 every time you get your car.

In restaurants, bars, and nightclubs, tip **service staff** and **bartenders** 15% to 20% of the check, tip **checkroom attendants** $1 per garment, and tip **valet-parking attendants** $1 per vehicle.

As for other service personnel, tip **cab drivers** 15% of the fare; tip **skycaps** at airports at least $1 per bag ($2–$3 if you have a lot of luggage); and tip **hairdressers** and **barbers** 15% to 20%.

**Toilets**   You won't find public toilets or "restrooms" on the streets of D.C., but they can be found in hotel lobbies, bars, restaurants, museums, and service stations, and at many sightseeing attractions. Starbucks and fast-food restaurants abound in D.C., and these might be your most reliable option. Restaurants and bars in resorts or heavily visited areas may reserve their restrooms for patrons.

**Visas**   The U.S. State Department has a Visa Waiver Program (VWP) allowing citizens of the following countries to enter the United States without a visa for stays of up to 90 days: Andorra, Australia, Austria, Belgium, Brunei, Chile, Czech Republic, Denmark, Estonia, Finland, France, Germany, Greece, Hungary, Iceland, Ireland, Italy, Japan, Latvia, Liechtenstein, Lithuania, Luxembourg, Malta, Monaco, the Netherlands, New Zealand, Norway, Portugal, San Marino, Singapore, Slovakia, Slovenia, South Korea, Spain, Sweden, Switzerland, Taiwan, and the United Kingdom. (**Note:** This list was accurate at press time; for the most up-to-date list of countries in the VWP, consult https://travel.state.gov/content/visas/en/visit/visa-waiver-program.html.) Even though a visa isn't necessary, in an effort to help U.S. officials check travelers against terror watch lists before they arrive at U.S. borders, visitors from VWP countries must register online through the Electronic System for Travel Authorization (ESTA) before boarding a plane or a boat to the U.S. Travelers must complete an electronic application providing basic personal and travel eligibility information. Authorizations will be valid for up to 2 years or until the traveler's passport expires, whichever comes first. Currently, there is one $14 fee for the online application. Existing ESTA registrations remain valid through their expiration dates. **Note:** As of April 1, 2016, travelers from VWP countries must have an e-Passport to be eligible to enter the U.S. without a visa. E-Passports contain computer chips capable of storing biometric information, such as the required digital photograph of the holder.

Furthermore, the State Department states that "Under the Visa Waiver Program Improvement and Terrorist Travel Prevention Act of 2015, travelers in the following categories are no longer eligible to travel or be admitted to the United States under the Visa Waiver Program (VWP):

Nationals of VWP countries who have traveled to or been present in Iran, Iraq, Sudan, or Syria after March 1, 2011 (with limited exceptions for travel for diplomatic or military purposes in the service of a VWP country), and Nationals of VWP countries who are also nationals of Iran, Iraq, Sudan, or Syria.

These individuals will still be able to apply for a visa using the regular appointment process at a U.S. Embassy or Consulate."

Canadian citizens may enter the United States without visas, but will need to show passports and proof of residence.

Citizens of all other countries must have (1) a valid passport that expires at least 6 months later than the scheduled end of their visit to the U.S., and (2) a tourist visa.

For more information about U.S. visas, go to **www.travel.state.gov** and click on "Visas."

**Visitor Information Destination D.C.** is the official tourism and convention corporation for Washington, D.C., www.washington.org. Call ⓒ **202/789-7000** to speak directly to a staff "visitor services specialist" and get answers to your specific questions about the city. Destination D.C.'s website is a good source for the latest travel information, including upcoming exhibits at the museums and anticipated closings of tourist attractions. The website is also a source for maps, which you can download and print.

Once you've arrived, you're welcome to stop by Destination D.C.'s fourth floor offices at 901 7th Street NW (Metro: Gallery Place–Chinatown, H St. exit), to pick up the visitors guide and maps. Office hours are Monday to Friday 8:30am to 5pm.

**National Park Service** information kiosks are located inside or near the Jefferson, Lincoln, FDR, Vietnam Veterans, Korean War, and World War II memorials, and at the Washington Monument (www.nps.gov/nama for National Mall and Memorial Parks sites; ☏ **202/426-6841** or 619-7222).

The **White House Visitor Center,** on the first floor of the Herbert Hoover Building, Department of Commerce, 1450 Pennsylvania Ave. NW (btw. 14th and 15th sts.; ☏ **202/208-1631,** or 202/456-7041 for recorded information), is open daily (except for New Year's Day, Christmas Day, and Thanksgiving) from 7:30am to 4pm.

The **Smithsonian Information Center,** in the Castle, 1000 Jefferson Dr. SW (www.si.edu; ☏ **202/633-1000,** or TTY [text telephone] 633-5285), is open every day but Christmas from 8:30am to 5:30pm; knowledgeable staff answer questions and dispense maps and brochures.

Visit the D.C. government's website, **www.dc.gov,** and that of the nonprofit organization Cultural Tourism DC, **www.culturaltourismdc.org,** for more information about the city. The latter site in particular provides helpful and interesting background knowledge of D.C.'s historic and cultural landmarks, especially in neighborhoods or parts of neighborhoods not usually visited by tourists.

# Index

See also Accommodations and Restaurant indexes, below.

## General Index

### A

AARP, 305
Accommodations, 53–83. *See also* Accommodations Index
    Adams Morgan, 66–70
    alternative, 55–56
    best, 9
    on or near Capitol Hill, 56–60
    Capitol Riverfront, 61–62
    Dupont Circle, 71–75
    for extended stays in the heart of the city, 67
    family-friendly, 64
    Foggy Bottom/West End, 75–78
    Georgetown, 79–81
    getting the best deal, 53–55
    jazz at, 74
    Midtown, 65–66
    new hotels, 82
    Old Town Alexandria, 254
    online and app discounts, 55
    outside the city, 56
    Penn Quarter, 62–65
    price categories, 56
    rates, 54
    sales tax, 55
    U & 14th Street Corridors, 70
    Woodley Park, 81–83
Acela Express, 288
Adams Morgan
    accommodations, 66–70
    in brief, 46–47
    restaurants, 104
    shopping, 206
Addison/Ripley Fine Art, 208
Addresses, finding, 291
African American Civil War Memorial and Museum, 17, 44, 185
African-American Family Day at the National Zoo, 24
African-Americans
    African American Civil War Memorial and Museum, 185
    Alexandria Black History Museum (Old Town Alexandria), 244
    Black History Month, 23
    Frederick Douglass National Historic Site (Cedar Hill), 41, 44, 190
    in history of Washington, D.C., 17–18
    National Museum of African American History and Culture, 146–148
AirBnB, 56
Airports and air travel, 284–287
AKA White House District, 67
Albert Einstein Memorial, 184

Albert Einstein Planetarium (National Air and Space Museum), 141
Alexandria Black History Museum, 244–245
Alexandria Colonial Tours, 243
Alexandria Convention and Visitors Association, 243
Alexandria Convention and Visitors Association's Visitors Center at Ramsay House, 242
Alexandria Festival of the Arts, 243
Alexandria Tours, 243
A Mano, 212–213
America!, 215
America by Air exhibit (National Air and Space Museum), 140
American Art Museum, Smithsonian American, 179–180
The American Presidency: A Glorious Burden (National Museum of American History), 150
American Stories (National Museum of American History), 149
Amtrak, 287, 288
Anacostia
    in brief, 47
    museums in, 190
Anacostia Community Museum, 190
Anacostia Riverwalk Trail, 202
An American in Paris (Old Town Alexandria), 244
Anderson House, 181, 276–277
Andrés, José, 96
The Annual Scottish Christmas Walk (Old Town Alexandria), 244
Antiques, 207–208
Apartment rentals, 67
*The Apotheosis of Washington*, 118
Appalachian Spring, 213
Apple Store, 210–211
Area codes, 301
Arena Stage, 219–220
Arlington County (Virginia), 191–195
Arlington House, The Robert E. Lee Memorial, 193
Arlington National Cemetery (Virginia), 192–194
*Armed Freedom*, 118
Art Museum of the Americas, 163, 262
Art museums and galleries
    Art Museum of the Americas, 163, 262
    The Athenaeum (Old Town Alexandria), 245
    commercial art galleries, 208–209
    Corcoran Gallery of Art, 261
    Dumbarton Oaks, 189–190
    Freer Gallery of Art, 134
    Hirshhorn Museum and Sculpture Garden, 135
    Kreeger Museum, 190–191

National Gallery of Art, 31, 143–145
    National Museum of African Art, 148–149
    National Museum of Women in the Arts, 177
    Phillips Collection, 34, 182–183
    Renwick Gallery of the Smithsonian American Art Museum, 164–165
    Sackler Gallery, 154–155
    Smithsonian American Art Museum and National Portrait Gallery, 179–180
Arts and Industries Building, 130–131
*The Asthmatic Escaped II, 1992* (Damien), 135
The Athenaeum (Old Town Alexandria), 245
Atlas District
    in brief, 47
    getting to, 294
    restaurants, 85–88
Attractions, 115–204
    best ways to see them like a local, 7–8
    calling ahead or checking online, 122
    Capitol Hill, 115–130
    Dupont Circle, 180–183
    Foggy Bottom, 183–184
    Georgetown, 189–191
    for kids, 200, 201
    Northern Virginia, 191–195
    Old Town Alexandria, 244–251
    parks, 195–199
    Penn Quarter, 169–180
    U & 14th Street Corridors, 184–185
    Upper Northwest D.C. (Glover Park, Woodley Park and Cleveland Park), 185–189
Avenue Jack, 211

### B

Bakery cafes, 112
Baltimore-Washington International Thurgood Marshall Airport (BWI), 284–285, 287
Barmy Wines & Liquors, 217
Barracks Row
    in brief, 47
    restaurants, 88–93
Bars, 224–228
Bartholdi, Frédéric Auguste, 156
Bartholdi Park, 156
Baseball, 233
Basketball, 233
Beauty products, 209
Behind the Badge (National Postal Museum), 126
Bellacara (Old Town Alexandria), 244
Belmont, Alva, 40
Belmont-Paul Women's Equality National Monument, 39, 127
Ben's Chili Bowl, 19
Benton, Thomas Hart, 135
Berlin Wall exhibit, 178

313

## Accommodations

## Restaurants

# Map List

# Photo Credits

Published by
**FROMMER MEDIA LLC**

ISBN 978-1-62887-282-8 (paper), 978-1-62887-283-5 (e-book)

Editorial Director: Pauline Frommer
Developmental Editor: Michael Kelly
Production Editor: Lynn Northrup
Cartographer: Roberta Stockwell
Photo Editor: Meghan Lamb
Indexer: Maro Riofrancos

For information on our other products or services, see www.frommers.com.

Frommer Media LLC also publishes its books in a variety of electronic formats. Some content that appears in print may not be available in electronic formats.

Manufactured in the United States of America

5 4 3 2 1

## ABOUT THE AUTHOR

In her 30 years of writing about Washington, D.C., for many publications, **Elise Hartman Ford** has explored every angle of the city, from the top of the Washington Monument to the bottom of the legendary mint julep served at the Willard Hotel's Round Robin bar. Her work has appeared in the *Washington Post, Washingtonian* magazine, *National Parks* magazine, the travel website Home & Abroad, and countless other national, regional, trade, and online publications. Ford is the author of several other guidebooks in addition to this one, and is currently the primary Washington, D.C., author for the new travel website, Bindu Itineraries (www.bindumedia.com).

## ABOUT THE FROMMER'S TRAVEL GUIDES

For most of the past 50 years, Frommer's has been the leading series of travel guides in North America, accounting for as many as 24 percent of all guidebooks sold. I think I know why.

Though we hope our books are entertaining, we nevertheless deal with travel in a serious fashion. Our guidebooks have never looked on such journeys as a mere recreation, but as a far more important human function, a time of learning and introspection, an essential part of a civilized life. We stress the culture, lifestyle, history, and beliefs of the destinations we cover, and urge our readers to seek out people and new ideas as the chief rewards of travel.

We have never shied from controversy. We have, from the beginning, encouraged our authors to be intensely judgmental, critical—both pro and con—in their comments, and wholly independent. Our only clients are our readers, and we have triggered the ire of countless prominent sorts, from a tourist newspaper we called "practically worthless" (it unsuccessfully sued us) to the many rip-offs we've condemned.

And because we believe that travel should be available to everyone regardless of their incomes, we have always been cost-conscious at every level of expenditure. Though we have broadened our recommendations beyond the budget category, we insist that every lodging we include be sensibly priced. We use every form of media to assist our readers, and are particularly proud of our feisty daily website, the award-winning Frommers.com.

I have high hopes for the future of Frommer's. May these guidebooks, in all the years ahead, continue to reflect the joy of travel and the freedom that travel represents. May they always pursue a cost-conscious path, so that people of all incomes can enjoy the rewards of travel. And may they create, for both the traveler and the persons among whom we travel, a community of friends, where all human beings live in harmony and peace.

Arthur Frommer